BARRON'S

MCAS
MATH

Massachusetts Comprehensive
Assessment System

Donna Helene Guarino, M. Ed.
Mathematics Teacher
Lincoln Sudbury Regional High School
Sudbury, MA

Debra Sima Bieler, Ed. M.
Mathematics Teacher
Lincoln Sudbury Regional High School
Sudbury, MA

BARRON'S

All inquiries should be addressed to:
Barron's Educational Series, Inc.
250 Wireless Boulevard
Hauppauge, New York 11788
www.barronseduc.com

ISBN-13: 978-0-7641-3484-5
ISBN-10: 0-7641-3484-1

Library of Congress Catalog Card No. 2006042849

Library of Congress Cataloging-in-Publication Data
Guarino, Donna
    MCAS—mathematics / by Donna Guarino, Debra Bieler.
       p. cm.
    Includes index.
    ISBN-13: 978-0-7641-3484-5
    ISBN-10: 0-7641-3484-1
      1. Mathematics—Examinations, questions, etc. 2. Mathematical ability—Testing. 3.
    Massachusetts Comprehensive Assessment System—Study guides. 4. Educational tests and meas-
    urements—Massachusetts—Study guides.   I. Bieler, Debra.   II. Title.

    QA43.G83 2006
    510.76—dc22   2006042849

PRINTED IN THE UNITED STATES OF AMERICA

9 8 7 6 5 4 3 2 1

Contents

Chapter 1.   **Introduction / 1**

Chapter 2.   **Review Test / 5**

Chapter 3.   **Test-Taking Strategies / 33**

Chapter 4.   **Number Sense and Operations / 47**

Types of Numbers / 47   Ratios, Proportions, and Percents / 71

Properties of Real Numbers / 50   Estimation / 79

Simplifying / 59   Problems Involving Money / 89

Chapter 5.   **Patterns, Relations, and Algebra / 95**

Algebraic Expressions / 95   Inequalities and Absolute Value / 147

Factoring Polynomials / 100   Systems of Linear Equations / 153

Linear Equations / 106   Patterns / 160

Quadratic Equations / 116   Vertex Edge Graphs / 168

Linear Functions / 119   Everyday Problems and Applications / 171

Other Functions / 141

Chapter 6.   **Geometry and Measurement / 177**

Points, Lines, Segments, Rays, and Planes / 177   Coordinate Geometry / 224

Angles and Lines / 180   Transformations / 237

Angles in Triangles and Circles / 190   Perimeter and Area / 247

Triangles / 198   Similar and Congruent Polygons / 273

Polygons / 211   Surface Area and Volume / 282

Quadrilaterals / 218   Three-Dimensional Figures / 305

Chapter 7.   **Data Analysis, Statistics, and Probability / 317**

Statistics / 317   Probability / 356

Displaying Data / 329

Chapter 8.   **MCAS Practice Tests / 375**

Practice Test 1, Session A / 377   Practice Test 2, Session A / 405

Practice Test 1, Session B / 389   Practice Test 2, Session B / 419

Index / 433

Preface

The learning standards in the Massachusetts *Mathematics Curriculum Framework* (2000) are the basis for the MCAS exam. As experienced full-time public high school teachers in Massachusetts, we have become very familiar with the *Framework* and believe it to be rich and comprehensive. If a student is able to solve a majority of the MCAS problems in the five content strands (1. Number Sense and Operations, 2. Patterns, Relations, and Algebra, 3. Geometry, 4. Measurement, and 5. Data Analysis, Statistics, and Probability), then that student has learned a considerable amount of math by the end of tenth grade. Our belief in the quality of the *Framework* and our desire to help the students of Massachusetts obtain an enhanced understanding and appreciation for mathematics motivated us to write this book.

We would like to thank our family and friends for their support and patience throughout this endeavor. We would also like to thank Kathleen Ganteaume, our editor at Barron's, for her hard work on this project. We are grateful for our close-knit, fun, and spirited department members at Lincoln-Sudbury Regional High School. Their individual talents and creativity never cease to inspire us. A very special thanks also to Alex Isakov, Kevin Liu, and Brian Smith for their keen editing skills.

Donna Guarino and Debra Bieler

Chapter 1 | **Introduction**

▰▰▰▰▰▰▰▰▰▰▰▰▰▰▰▰▰▰▰▰▰▰▰▰▰▰▰▰▰▰▰▰▰▰▰

Welcome

Congratulations on taking your first step to a successful grade 10 MCAS math test. The MCAS, the Massachusetts Comprehensive Assessment System, is an exam designed to test your ability to answer questions on what you have learned in 9th and 10th grade mathematics.

The Frameworks

The content of the mathematics on the MCAS exam is based on the *Massachusetts Curriculum Frameworks (2000)*. The frameworks divide the subject areas into five categories:

1. Number Sense and Operations
2. Patterns, Relations, and Algebra
3. Geometry
4. Measurement
5. Data Analysis, Statistics, and Probability

Content of the measurement questions often intertwine with geometry. We have combined geometry and measurement as one chapter. Each of the other subject areas has its own chapter.

The Test

There are two mathematics sections on the MCAS that are administered in the spring over a two-day period. The first day's test includes approximately 14 multiple-choice, 4 short-answer, and 3 open-response questions. The second day's test includes approximately 18 multiple-choice and 3 open-response questions. The multiple-choice questions are followed by answer choices A, B, C, or D. There will only be one correct answer choice.

The Scoring

Each multiple-choice question is marked either right or wrong, with a score of 0 or 1. You are not penalized for guessing so you should always fill in an answer for a multiple-choice question.

The short-answer questions do not have answers provided. These answers are graded either right or wrong, with a score of 0 or 1 on the scoring rubric. On the open-response questions, there are several parts to the questions, and you are graded on your answer and the quality of your explanation. The graders follow a rubric where the highest a student can score on the open-response is a 4 and the lowest is a 0. If you know part of an open-response question, and not all of it, write down what you know. Be sure to explain your reasoning to the best of your ability, show all work, and label all answers! Examples of all three types of problems are used throughout this text. Further discussion about the scoring rubric of open-response questions can be found in Chapter 3.

Your final grade will be given a ranking that falls into one of the following four categories: Advanced, Proficient, Needs Improvement, or Failing. If the test seems difficult while you are taking it, remember that the Department of Education does not have a formula for converting your raw score into these four categories until after the tests are administered. In other words, if a lot of people are struggling with the same questions as you, this will be to your advantage. Even better, if you know a little bit more than a lot of people, you could end up in the Advanced or Proficient categories!

Graduation Requirement

Passing the MCAS is a graduation requirement for public schools in the state of Massachusetts. It is important that you do the best that you can on this test and be well-rested on the days that you are taking the test. The more time that you spend studying now, the more confident you will be and the better your chances of success later.

Scholarships

Students who perform well on this test currently have the potential to receive scholarship money to state universities. This is additional motivation to study for the MCAS.

The Reference Sheet

The MCAS test comes with a math formula sheet that you may use as a reference throughout the exam. This is convenient because you won't have to memorize many of the geometry formulas that you will need for this test! We have included a copy of it with the practice tests in the back of the book, and we discuss the formulas in Chapter 6.

Calculator Usage

On the first day of testing, you will not be permitted to use a calculator for any question. On the second day, you may use a calculator. You should have either a graphing or a standard scientific calculator. If you forget to bring your own calculator, your school will provide one. It is a good idea to bring your own however, so that you are familiar with its functioning and capabilities. You should assume that all practice problems in this book are meant to be done without a calculator. If a problem is designed to be used with a calculator we have included the calculator symbol to indicate that you may use a calculator for that problem.

How To Use This Book

1. Take the Review Test in Chapter 2 to determine what areas of mathematics you need to work on. The Review Test covers the basic topics from each section of the book. If you get a problem wrong, you will know where your areas of weakness lie. You should divide the Review Test into sections and complete it over the course of several days. It is not intended to be taken in a single seating.

2. Read Chapter 3.

3. Read the sections in Chapters 4–7 that correspond to the incorrect problems on your Review Test. Then do the practice problems for those sections. If you got the problems correct on an entire section of the Review Test, you may wish to skip the reading of the section and go straight to the practice problems. The headings of the questions on the Review Test match the order of the contents in each chapter. **It is important that you still do the practice problems** even if you got the review questions correct. The practice problems are asked in the format of the MCAS (multiple-choice, short-answer, open-response), while the review questions are not. Additionally, the practice problems are comprehensive and address the variations of problem types, whereas the Review Test is merely an overview intended to identify your areas of weakness.

4. Take the practice tests in Chapter 8.

5. All practice problems have solutions in this book, so check your answers!

6. Occasionally there is a star ★ marked on a question in this book. This star means that the question is particularly challenging and, although not common, problems of this level of difficulty occasionally appear on the MCAS. They are worth practicing once you have mastered the easier problems.

About This Book

The problems in this book have been created to mimic actual MCAS questions asked on previous exams as far back as 1999. We have included at least one of each problem type from past years in either our examples, practice problems, or sample tests. The more familiar you are with MCAS-like questions, the smoother your test-taking experience will be.

This book contains material that has been released to the public by the Massachusetts Department of Education. The Massachusetts Department of Education has not endorsed the contents of this book.

Chapter 2 | Review Test

Number Sense and Operations

Types of Numbers

1. What numbers form the set of natural numbers?
2. What numbers form the set of integers?
3. Is –4 a whole number?
4. Is a fraction a real number?
5. Is $\sqrt{81}$ a rational number?
6. Is $\frac{-3}{5}$ a rational number?

Properties of Real Numbers

1. What is the smallest prime number?
2. List all the positive factors of 36.
3. List the first three multiples of 6.
4. What is the reciprocal of 4?
5. What is $|8-10|$?
6. What is -2^4?
7. What is $(-2)^6$?
8. What is $(4 \cdot 3)^2$?
9. What is $(4+3)^2$?
10. Evaluate the expression: $\frac{x+2y}{3x}$ for $x=-5$, and $y=10$.
11. Which property of addition is demonstrated by the equation: $4+6=6+4$?
12. Which property of addition is demonstrated by the equation: $4+(6+3)=(4+6)+3$?
13. What property of multiplication is demonstrated by the equation: $(a \cdot b) \cdot c = a \cdot (b \cdot c)$?
14. What property is demonstrated by the equation: $3(2x+6)=6x+18$?
15. What number is the additive identity?
16. What number is the multiplicative identity?
17. What is the additive inverse of the number 32?
18. What is the multiplicative inverse of the number $-\frac{7}{11}$?

36 = 9x4
36 = 6x6
36 = 1x36
36 = 2x18
36 = 3x12

Simplifying

1. Simplify: $\sqrt{180}$

2. Simplify: $\sqrt[3]{64}$

3. Simplify: $3x^6 \cdot 5x^2$

4. Simplify: $\left(6a^5 b\right)^2$

5. Simplify: $\dfrac{15x^4 y^9}{18x^6 y}$

6. Simplify: $\left(13ab^{16}\right)^0$

7. Rewrite without negative exponents: $\dfrac{n^{-6}}{n^2}$.

8. Simplify: $\left(\dfrac{9x}{5y^3}\right)^2$

9. Simplify: $9(3-1) - 6 \div 3 + 7 \cdot 2$

10. For what value of x is the equation $8^7 \cdot x = 8^9$ true?

11. What is the value of the expression: $5\left|7-12\right| + 13$?

12. Simplify: $\left(-1\right)^{21}\left(23\right)$

13. Simplify: $\dfrac{32 - 20(3-4)}{12 - 2^3}$

14. Simplify: $2^{13} \cdot 5^{13}$

15. Simplify the expression: $23x - 4(x-5)$

Ratios, Proportions, Percents

1. Reduce the ratio: 24 : 36.
2. If the ratio of x to 3 is equal to 5 to 8, find x.

3. Solve the proportion $\dfrac{a}{w} = \dfrac{b}{c}$ for w in terms of a, b, and c.
4. What is 35% of 80?
5. Increase the number 70 by 30%.
6. If the price of a house, p, increases by 5% each year for six years, what is its price at the end of the sixth year, in terms of p?

Estimation

1. Between which two integers does $\sqrt{61}$ fall on the real number line?

2. Approximate $\left(107 \cdot 4.96\right) + \left(2013 \div 12\right)$ to the nearest hundred.

3. Approximate to the nearest inch, the length of an edge of a cube whose volume is 128 in³.

Problems, Involving Money

1. A decorative ribbon costs $2.75 per yard. How much would 12 feet of it cost?
2. A truck rental costs $20.00 for the day, plus $0.35 for each mile driven. How much would the rental cost for two days and 240 miles?
3. A math tutor earns $42.00 for a 45-minute session with a student. What is that tutor's hourly wage?
4. After a discount of 15%, the savings on a pair of sneakers was $5.10. What was the original price of the sneakers?

Patterns, Relations, and Algebra

Algebraic Expressions

1. Expand and simplify $(2x+5)^2$.

2. Simplify $(3x+5)-(7x-2)$ completely.

3. Simplify the expression below by combining like terms.

$$3a^2b - 5ab + 7ba^2 + 14ba - 11ab^2$$

4. What is the degree of the polynomial: $4x^5 + 5x^6 - 3x^2 + 2$?

5. Multiply $\quad 2(x+1)(x^2 - x + 1), \quad$ then

simplify by combining like terms.

Factoring Polynomials

Factor the expressions in Questions 1–4 completely.

1. $x^2 - 16$
2. $x^2 - 8x + 12$
3. $3x^2 + 5x - 2$
4. $3a^3 + 6a^2$
5. The area of a rectangle in square feet is $x^2 + 7x - 30$. The expression for the length of the rectangle is $x + 10$ feet. What is the expression for the number of feet in the width of the rectangle?

Linear Equations

1. Solve for x in the linear equation: $4(x+10) + 3x = 26$
2. Set up an equation to solve the given word problem: "*Thirty less than one fourth of a number is 18.*"

3. Solve the following equation for x: $0.3(4x+6) = 0.15(2x+18)$
4. A school is planning to increase its staffing by 10 employees each year, to keep up with an increasing enrollment. If there are currently 75 employees currently working at the school, write an equation to find the number of employees, E, at the school after n years.

Quadratic Equations

1. What are the solutions to the equation: $0 = x^2 - 5x - 14$?

2. Find all values of x that satisfy the equation: $0 = 2x^2 + x - 15$.

Linear Functions

Use the graph below to answer Questions 1 and 2.

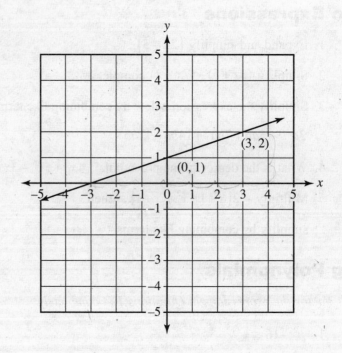

1. Write the equation of the line above in slope-intercept form.
2. What is the x-intercept of the above line?

3. Does the point $(6, -3)$ lie on the line $y = \dfrac{2}{3}x - 8$?

4. What is the y-intercept of the line $2x + 4y = 8$?
5. A linear relationship is shown in the table below. What is the value of a?

x	−3	0	1	2	3
y	a	5	1	−3	−7

6. A phone company charges a fixed rate of $25 per month plus an additional charge of $0.10 per minute used. Write an equation that computes the cost per month, C, in terms of m, total minutes used.

Other Functions

1. Which of the following equations matches the graph below?

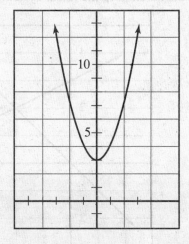

A. $f(x) = (x + 3)^2$

B. $f(x) = (x - 3)^2$

C. $f(x) = x^2 + 3$

D. $f(x) = x^2 - 3$

2. Which function will have a greater y value when x is equal to 10:
   $f(x) = 3^x$ or $f(x) = 3^{-x}$?

Inequalities and Absolute Value

1. Solve for x: $3x + 8 \le 5x + 18$.

2. Graph the solution set for the compound linear inequality: $x < 8$ and $x \ge 3$.

3. Graph the solution set for the compound linear inequality: $x > 8$ or $x \le 3$.

4. Solve for x: $3|x - 6| = 12$

5. Graph the solution set for the absolute value inequality: $|x + 4| < 5$.

6. Graph the solution set for the absolute value inequality: $|x + 4| \ge 5$.

Systems of Linear Equations

1. Solve the system for x and y.

   $2x + 3y = 9$

   $y - 2x = 19$

2. If $y = x - 9$ and $4y - 2x = y + 3$, solve for x and y.

3. What is the solution to the linear system graphed below?

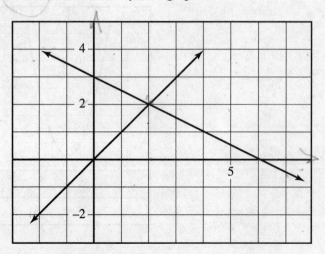

4. A school teacher purchased one piece of candy for each of her 100 students. Each student received either a chocolate, which cost $0.35 a piece, or a hard candy which cost $0.15 a piece. If she spent a total of $23.40 on her students before tax, how many of each type of candy did she buy?

Patterns

1. Find the 7th term in the sequence: 10, 6, 2, –2, . . .
2. Find the 10th term in the quadratic sequence: –1, 1, 4, 8, 13, 19, . . .
3. Find the fifth term in the geometric sequence: 4, 20, 100, . . .
4. Find an equation for a_n in terms of n, using the table below.

n	–2	–1	0	1	2	3	n
a_n	5	2	1	2	5	10	?

5. What is the next term in the Fibonacci Sequence: 1, 1, 2, 3, 5, 8, . . .
6. What is the next term in the sequence: 4, 1, 5, 2, 6, 3, 7, . . .

Vertex Edge Graphs

1. A paper delivery boy must travel down each street in the route shown below. Additionally, he must start and end on the point R. Is it possible for him to travel down every street exactly once?

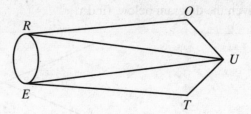

Everyday Problems and Applications

1. In physics, the kinetic energy of an object is found using the formula,

$$K = \frac{1}{2}mv^2$$

where K is the kinetic energy measured in Joules, m is the mass of the object measured in kilograms, and v is the velocity of the object measured in meters per second.

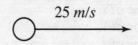

If an object has 450 Joules of kinetic energy and is moving at a constant speed of 25 meters per second, find the object's mass to the nearest tenth?

2. Ray traveled 330 miles in 5 hours and 30 minutes. What was his average speed in miles per hour?

Geometry and Measurement

Points, Lines, Segments, Rays, and Planes

1. Name the ray shown below.

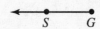

2. If C is the midpoint of $\overline{AB}$, find x.

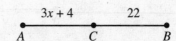

Angles and Lines

1. If ∠B is an acute angle, and ∠B = $(2x + 6)°$, what are the restrictions on x?
2. How many degrees are in a right angle?
3. If ∠1 is supplementary to ∠2, and ∠1 is 140°, find the measure of ∠2.
4. What is the sum of two complementary angles?
5. Given the diagram below, find x.

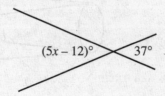

$(5x - 12)°$ 37°

Use the diagram to answer Questions 6–8.

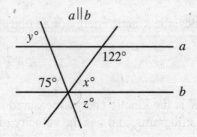

$a\|b$

$y°$

122°

a

75° $x°$

b

$z°$

6. Find the value of x.
7. Find the value of y.
8. Find the value of z.

9. $\overline{HK}$ bisects angle ∠DHG in the diagram below.

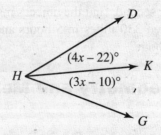

D

$(4x - 22)°$ K

H

$(3x - 10)°$

G

Find the value of x.

10. $\overline{LJ}$ is perpendicular to $\overline{NK}$. If ∠LJK = $3x - 12$, find the value of x.

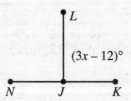

L

$(3x - 12)°$

N   J   K

Angles in Triangles and Circles

1. Find the value of x in the figure below.

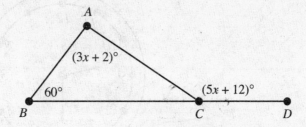

2. The angles in a triangle are in a ratio of $3 : 4 : 5$. Classify the triangle as acute, obtuse, or right.

3. $\overline{DJ}$ is a diameter of circle E. What is the measure of $\angle K$?

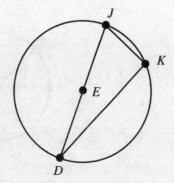

4. In the diagram below, if $\overline{OP} \parallel \overline{MN}$, $m\angle LPO = 60°$ and $m\angle M = 25°$, find the measure of $m\angle L$.

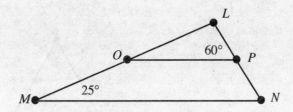

5. If the measure of $\overset{\frown}{RT} = 90°$, and the measure of $\overset{\frown}{ST} = 160°$, find $m\angle T$.

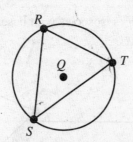

6. What is the measure of the obtuse angle formed by the minute and the hour hands of a clock at 9:30?

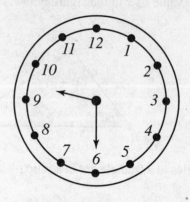

7. Circle with center C is shown below. If the measure of $\angle ACD = 52°$, find the measure of $\overset{\frown}{DB}$.

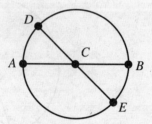

Triangles

1. Arrange the angles of $\triangle ABC$ in order from least to greatest. (Figure not drawn to scale.)

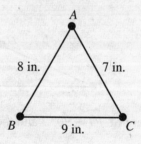

2. Triangle DEF is isosceles with base $\overline{EF}$. If $m\angle D = 44°$, find the measure of $\angle F$.

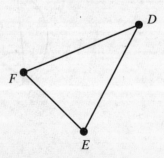

3. All three sides of $\triangle GHI$ are integers. If $GH = 21$ units and $HI = 3$ units, what are the smallest and the largest possible lengths of $\overline{GI}$?

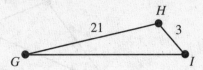

4. The sides of a triangle are 6 inches, 8 inches, and 11 inches. Classify the triangle as acute, obtuse, or right.

5. What is the perimeter of isosceles triangle $\triangle ABC$ below with altitude $\overline{AN}$ of 15 units, and base $\overline{BC}$ of 16 units?

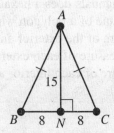

6. If $SR = 6\sqrt{2}$ units in the diagram below, what is the length of $\overline{QT}$?

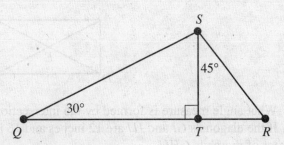

Use the diagram below for Questions 7–8.

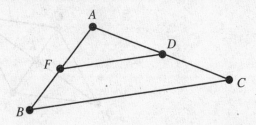

7. If F and D are the midpoints of the sides of $\triangle ABC$ and $BC = 11$ centimeters, find FD.

8. If F and D are the midpoints of the sides of $\triangle ABC$, and $\angle B = 48°$, find $m\angle AFD$.

9. If *BD* is the median to side $\overline{AC}$ in $\triangle ABC$, find the value of *x*.

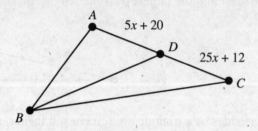

Polygons

1. How many diagonals does a hexagon have?
2. What is the name of a polygon whose interior angles add up to 1,440°?
3. What is the sum of the exterior angles of a pentagon?
4. What is the measure of each exterior angle of a regular octagon?
5. What is measure of each interior angle of a regular nonagon?

Quadrilaterals

1. What is the name for a regular quadrilateral?
2. If *DE* = 8 cm, what is the sum of the diagonals of rectangle *ABCD* below?

3. What angle measure is formed by the intersection of the diagonals of a rhombus?
4. If the diagonals *GI* and *HJ* are 12 inches and 16 inches, respectively, find the perimeter of rhombus *GHIJ*.

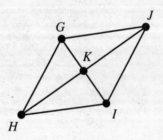

Coordinate Geometry

Use the points A(–2, 3) and B(6, 8) for Questions 1–3.

1. Find the midpoint of $\overline{AB}$.

2. Find the length of $\overline{AB}$.

3. Find the slope of $\overline{AB}$.

4. If the point $M(3, 5)$ is the midpoint of $\overline{CD}$ and the coordinates of point D are $(9, 8)$, find the coordinates of point C.

5. Which point below is **not** collinear with the other three?

$$(1, 4) \ (0, 2) \ (-1, -2) \ (-2, -5)$$

6. What is the most specific name for the quadrilateral with vertices:

$$(-5, 1) \ (-2, 5) \ (3, 5) \ (0, 1)$$

7. What is the most specific name for the quadrilateral with vertices:

$$(-5, 1) \ (-2, 5) \ (3, 5) \ (6, 1)$$

8. What is the most specific name for the quadrilateral with vertices:

$$(-5, 1) \ (-3, 4) \ (3, 0) \ (1, -3)$$

Transformations

1. Suppose that $\triangle ABC$ is translated 2 units to the right and 3 units up. What are the coordinates of the image of point A?

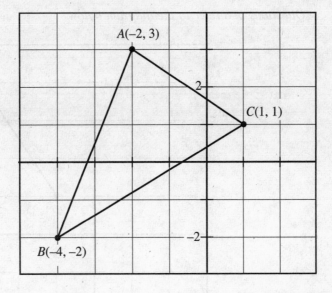

2. If △*FGE* is rotated 180° clockwise about the origin, find the coordinates of the image of point *F*.

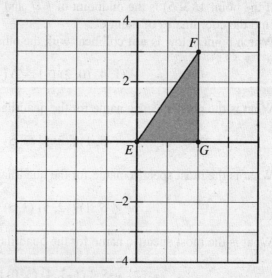

3. If the point (*a, b*) is reflected over the *y*-axis, what are the coordinates of the image point?

4. If the point (*a, b*) is reflected over the *x*-axis, what are the coordinates of the image point?

5. If the point (*a, b*) is reflected over the line *y* = *x*, what are the coordinates of the image point?

Questions 6–8 refer to the diagram below.

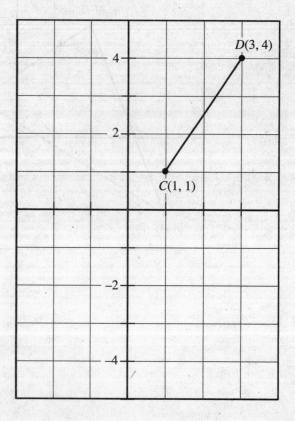

6. If segment $\overline{CD}$ is reflected over the y-axis, what are the coordinates of the image point C'?

7. If segment $\overline{CD}$ is reflected over the x-axis, what are the coordinates of the image point D'?

8. If segment $\overline{CD}$ is reflected over the line $y = x$, what are the coordinates of the image point D'?

Perimeters and Areas

1. The area of a rectangle is 288 units^2. If its sides have lengths that are consecutive even integers, find the length of the longer side.
2. The area of a triangle is 42 in.^{2}. If the height of the triangle is 6 inches, find the length of the base.
3. What is the circumference of a circle with a radius of 5 feet?
4. What is the area of a circle with a radius of 5 feet?

Use circle C below for Questions 5–7.

12 × 12 = 144 × 3.14

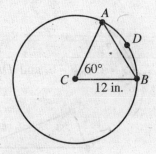

5. What is the arc length of $\overline{ADB}$?
6. What is the area of the sector ACB?
7. What is the area of the segment ADB?
8. What is the height of an equilateral triangle with area $49\sqrt{3}$ square units?
9. Find the area of a square with a perimeter of 10 inches.

Use the isosceles trapezoid shown below for Questions 10 and 11.

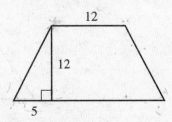

10. What is the perimeter of the isosceles trapezoid?
11. What is the area of the isosceles trapezoid?

Similar and Congruent Polygons

Use the diagram below for Questions 1 and 2.

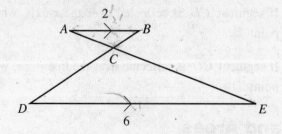

1. What is the ratio of perimeters of ΔABC to ΔEDC?
2. What is the ratio of areas of ΔABC to ΔEDC?
3. Find the value of x.

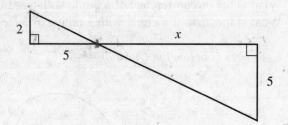

4. If $\overline{DE} \parallel \overline{BC}$, $\overline{AD} = 4$, $\overline{DB} = 6$, and $\overline{DE} = 6$, find the length of $\overline{CB}$.

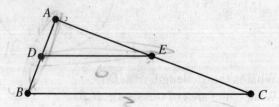

5. $\overline{EB}$ and $\overline{DC}$ have lengths of 3 inches and 9 inches, respectively. If AB = 4 inches, find BC.

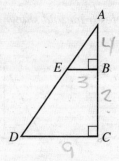

Use the diagram below for Questions 6 and 7.

ΔABC ~ ΔDEF

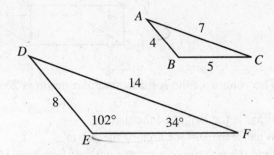

6. Find *EF*.
7. Find *m∠A*.

Surface Area and Volume

1. What is the volume of the rectangular pyramid below, with base dimensions of 7 cm by 6 cm and height of 12 cm?

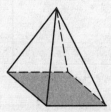

2. What is the volume of a cone with base area of 25π cm^2 and height of 10 cm?

Use the figure below for Questions 3 and 4.

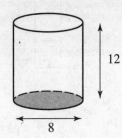

The cylindrical glass shown has a height of 12 units and a base diameter of 8 units.

3. Find the lateral surface area of the glass.
4. Find the volume of the cylindrical glass.

Use the figure below for Questions 5 and 6.

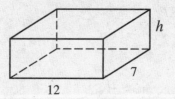

The volume of the solid rectangular prism is 252 in.³.

5. What is the height of the prism?
6. What is the surface area of the prism?
7. Find the volume of a sphere with surface area 144π in.².

Three–Dimensional Figures

1. What solid is formed by folding the net below along the solid lines?

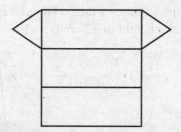

2. Which of the nets below CANNOT be folded along the solid lines to form a cube?

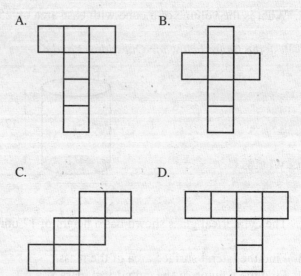

A.

B.

C.

D.

Data Analysis, Statistics, and Probability

Statistics

1. What is the median of the numbers: 13, 16, 4, 18, 20, 12?
2. What is the mode of the numbers: 34, 78, 56, 45, 34, 86, 45, 34?
3. What is the mean of the numbers: 13, 16, 4, 18, 20, 12?
4. If the average of five numbers is 30, what would a sixth number have to be to raise the average to a 32?
5. What is the range of the numbers: 56, 83, 923, 100, 467, 47, 87?
6. A video store rented 36 DVDs on Wednesday, 51 on Thursday, 72 on Friday, and 77 on Saturday. What was the average number of DVDs rented per day from Wednesday to Saturday?
7. Lisa was raising money for a charity, and asked people at work for a donation in one of five suggested amounts. According to the table below, what was the average dollar contribution per person who donated?

Donation	Number of People
$ 5	23
$10	30
$20	14
$50	5
$100	2

Displaying Data

Use the box and whisker plot to answer Questions 1 and 2.

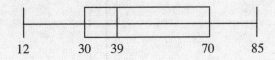

1. What is the range of the data?
2. What is the median of the data?

Use the bar graph to answer Questions 3 and 4.

The bar graph below shows the number of breakfasts served during one week at a restaurant called Ed's Place.

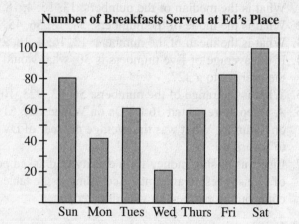

Number of Breakfasts Served at Ed's Place

3. By what percent did the number of breakfasts served decrease from Tuesday to Wednesday?
4. What fraction of the total weekly breakfasts for the week shown was served on Monday?
5. Complete the stem and leaf plot for the numbers in the table below.

98	93	85	83	78
62	87	54	75	88

```
9 |
8 |
7 |
6 |
5 |
```

6. Complete the line plot for the number of each letter grade, given the data in the table.

{Key: A = 90–100 ; B = 80–89 ; C = 70–79, . . .}

98	93	85	83	78
62	87	54	75	88

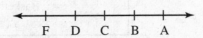

F   D   C   B   A

7. What is the best whole number approximation for the *y*-intercept of the line of best fit for the scatterplot below?

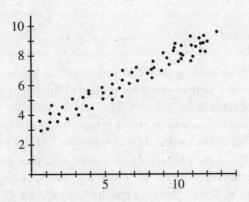

Use the pie chart for Questions 8 and 9.

Forty-eight college students were asked what their favorite high school math subject was. Their responses are shown in the pie chart below.

Favorite Math Subject

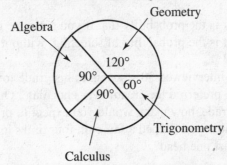

8. What percent of the students said that Trigonometry was their favorite high school math subject?

9. How many students said that Calculus was their favorite high school math subject?

Use the Venn Diagram below to answer Questions 10–12.

Students Playing Certain Sports

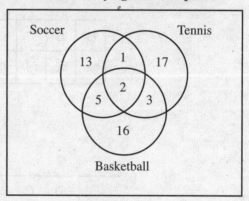

10. How many students play soccer only?
11. How many students play all three sports?
12. How many students play both tennis and basketball?

Probability

1. In how many orders can you rank five books from best to worst?
2. List the sample space for groups of three using the people: Jaclyn, Tony, Meg, Shanna, and Charlie.
3. What is the probability of tossing a fair die and it landing on a number less than four?
4. What is the probability of tossing a fair die twice, and it landing on a 1 both times?
5. What is the probability of tossing two dice and having their sum be 7?
6. Vernon is rolling a fair die in a game he is playing. The sides of the die are numbered 1 to 6. Four times in a row he has rolled a 4. What is the probability that he will roll a 4 on his fifth roll?

Use the information below for Questions 7 and 8.

A bag of gum balls contains:
5 red, 3 yellow, 2 blue, and 4 green

7. What is the probability that if you pick one gumball out of the bag, you get a green?
8. What is the probability of selecting, without replacement, first one red, and then one blue?
9. Sam interviewed 30 students in his grade for a statistics project and found that 12 of them preferred ice cream over chocolate. Out of the total number of 480 students in his grade, how many would you expect to prefer chocolate over ice cream?
10. Suppose you flipped a fair coin four times in a row. What is the probability of tossing at least one head?

11. A certain carnival game of throwing darts awards a prize to anyone who can hit the board shown below on either of the shaded 8 inch by 8 inch squares in the corners. What is the probability that if a dart lands on the board, it lands on either one of the two shaded regions?

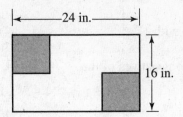

12. Kelly is going out for the evening. In her wardrobe, she has narrowed her choices down to 6 different blouses, 3 different pairs of jeans, and 4 different pairs of shoes. How many outfits can she make by combining one of each of these items?

Use the spinner below to answer Questions 13 and 14.

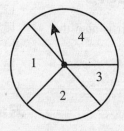

13. Using the apparent divisions, what is the probability that if you spin the spinner once, it lands on a 2?

14. If you spin the spinner 60 times, how many times would you expect to land on the 4?

Solutions to Review Test
Solutions to Number Sense

Types of Numbers

1. Counting numbers that begin with 1.
   $\{1, 2, 3, \ldots\}$
2. Whole numbers, zero, and the negatives of the set of whole numbers:
   $\{\ldots -3, -2, -1, 0, 1, 2, 3, \ldots\}$
3. No.
4. Yes. A fraction is a rational number, and rational numbers are a subset of the reals.
5. Yes. It is rational.
6. Yes.

Properties of Real Numbers

1. The smallest prime number is 2. It is also the only even prime.
2. $\{1, 2, 3, 4, 6, 9, 12, 18, 36\}$
3. $\{6, 12, 18\}$
4. $\dfrac{1}{4}$
5. 2
6. -16
7. 64
8. 144
9. 49
10. -1
11. Commutative property of addition
12. Associative property of addition
13. Associative property of multiplication
14. Distributive property
15. 0
16. 1
17. -32
18. $-\dfrac{11}{7}$

Simplifying

1. $6\sqrt{5}$
2. 4
3. $15x^8$
4. $36a^{10}b^2$

5. $\dfrac{5y^8}{6x^2}$
6. 1
7. $\dfrac{1}{n^8}$
8. $\dfrac{81x^2}{25y^6}$
9. 30
10. 8^2
11. 38
12. -23
13. 13
14. 10^{13}
15. $19x + 20$

Ratios, Proportions, Percents

1. $2 : 3$
2. $\dfrac{15}{8}$
3. $\dfrac{ac}{b}$
4. 28
5. 91
6. $(1.05)^6 \, p$

Estimation

1. 7 and 8
2. 700
3. 5 in.

Problems Involving Money

1. $11.00
2. $124.00
3. $56.00
4. $34.00

Solutions to Patterns, Relations, and Algebra

Algebraic Expressions

1. $4x^2 + 20x + 25$
2. $-4x + 7$
3. $10a^2b + 9ab - 11ab^2$
4. six
5. $2x^3 + 2$

Factoring Polynomials

1. $(x+4)(x-4)$
2. $(x-6)(x-2)$
3. $(3x-1)(x+2)$
4. $3a^2(a+2)$
5. $x-3$

Linear Equations

1. $x = -2$
2. $\frac{1}{4}x - 30 = 18$
3. $x = 1$
4. $E = 75 + 10n$

Quadratic Equations

1. $x = 7, -2$
2. $x = \frac{5}{2}, -3$

Linear Functions

1. $y = \frac{1}{3}x + 1$
2. $(-3, 0)$

3. No.
4. $(0, 2)$
5. $a = 17$
6. $C = 25 + 0.10m$

Other Functions

1. C
2. $f(x) = 3^x$

Inequalities and Absolute Value

1. $x \geq -5$
2.
3.
4. $x = 10, 2$
5.
6.

Systems of Linear Equations

1. $x = -6$ and $y = 7$
2. $x = 30$ and $y = 21$
3. $x = 2, y = 2$
4. 42 chocolates and 58 hard candies

Patterns

1. -14
2. 53
3. 2,500
4. $a_n = n^2 + 1$
5. 13
6. 4

Vertex Edge Graphs

1. Yes. Example: R-O-U-R-E-U-T-E-R

Everyday Problems and Applications

1. 1.4 kg
2. 60 miles per hour

Solutions to Geometry and Measurement

Points, Lines, Segments, Rays, and Planes

1. $\overrightarrow{GS}$

2. $x = 6$

Angles and Lines

1. $-3 < x < 42$
2. $90°$
3. $40°$
4. $90°$
5. $\dfrac{49}{5}$
6. $58°$
7. $75°$
8. $75°$
9. $x = 12$
10. $x = 34$

Angles in Triangles and Circles

1. $x = 25$
2. Acute
3. $90°$
4. $95°$
5. $55°$
6. $105°$
7. $128°$

Triangles

1. $\angle B$, $\angle C$, $\angle A$
2. $68°$
3. Smallest = 19 units
   Largest = 23 units

4. Obtuse
5. 50 units
6. $6\sqrt{3}$ units
7. 5.5 cm
8. $48°$
9. $x = \dfrac{2}{5}$

Polygons

1. 9
2. Decagon
3. $360°$
4. $45°$
5. $140°$

Quadrilaterals

1. Square
2. 32 cm
3. $90°$
4. 40 inches

Coordinate Geometry

1. $\left(2, \dfrac{11}{2}\right)$

2. $\sqrt{89}$

3. $\dfrac{5}{8}$

4. $(-3, 2)$
5. $(0, 2)$
6. Rhombus
7. Isosceles trapezoid
8. Rectangle

Transformations

1. $A'(0, 6)$
2. $F'(-2, -3)$
3. $(-a, b)$
4. $(a, -b)$
5. (b, a)
6. $C'(-1, 1)$
7. $D'(3, -4)$
8. $D'(4, 3)$

Perimeters and Areas

1. 18 units
2. 14 inches
3. 10π feet
4. 25π square feet
5. 4π inches
6. 24π in.^{2}
7. $24\pi - 36\sqrt{3}$ in.^{2}
8. $7\sqrt{3}$ units
9. $\dfrac{25}{4}$ in.^{2}
10. 60 units
11. 204 units^2

Similar and Congruent Polygons

1. $\dfrac{1}{3}$
2. $\dfrac{1}{9}$
3. $x = \dfrac{25}{2}$
4. 15 units
5. 8 inches
6. 10 units
7. $44°$

Surface Area and Volume

1. 168 cm^3
2. $\dfrac{250\pi}{3}$ cm^3
3. 96π units^2
4. 192π units^3
5. 3 inches
6. 282 in.^{2}
7. 288π in.^{3}

Three–Dimensional Figures

1. Triangular prism
2. D

Solutions to Data Analysis, Statistics, and Probability

Statistics

1. 14.5
2. 34
3. 13.833
4. 42
5. 876
6. 59
7. Approximately $15.47

Displaying Data

1. 73
2. 39
3. $66.\overline{66} \approx 66.67\%$
4. $\dfrac{1}{11}$

5.

9	3 8
8	3 5 7 8
7	5 8
6	2
5	4

6.
```
                    X
                    X
          X    X    X
     X    X    X    X    X
   ←—|————|————|————|————|——→
     F    D    C    B    A
```

7. $(0, \underline{3})$
8. $16.\overline{66}\% \approx 16.67\%$
9. 12
10. 13
11. 2
12. 5

Probability

1. 120
2. JTM JTS JTC
   JMS JMC
   JSC

   TMS TMC
   TSC

   MSC

3. $\dfrac{1}{2}$

4. $\dfrac{1}{36}$

5. $\dfrac{1}{6}$

6. $\dfrac{1}{6}$

7. $\dfrac{2}{7}$

8. $\dfrac{5}{91}$

9. 288

10. $1 - P(0) = 1 - \dfrac{1}{16} = \dfrac{15}{16}$

11. $\dfrac{1}{3}$

12. 72

13. $\dfrac{1}{4}$

14. 20

Chapter 3 | **Test-Taking Strategies**

There are several key test-taking strategies for you to remember while solving problems on the MCAS. We will thoroughly cover these strategies in the Solutions to Practice sections, so be on the lookout for the bold lettered advice!

Using Your Answer Choices

On the multiple-choice questions of the test, do not forget that you have the answers in front of you. This should greatly impact how you solve the problem.

Consider Practice Question #2 from Properties of Real Numbers in Chapter 4:

When 90 is divided by a number, x, the quotient is 12 with a remainder of 6. What is the value of x?

A. 6
B. 7
C. 8
D. 9

Use your answer choices to help you solve this problem. Working backwards, try multiplying each answer choice by 12 and adding 6, until you get 90 as your answer. For example, to test answer choice D, you would multiply 9 by 12, and see if this is 6 away from 90. If it is, then this would be the answer. In general, your process will look like: $(x) \cdot 12 + 6 = 90$. Testing your answer choices would look like:

A. $(6) \cdot 12 + 6 = 78$

B. $(7) \cdot 12 + 6 = 90 \checkmark$

C. $(8) \cdot 12 + 6 = 102$

D. $(9) \cdot 12 + 6 = 114$

Next, consider Practice Question #16 from Perimeter and Area Chapter 6:

The sides of a square are expanded to form a rectangle with side lengths that are 3 inches and 5 inches longer than those of the original square. If the new rectangle's area is 168 in.^{2}, what was the area of the original square?

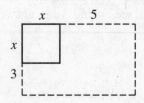

A. 15 in.^{2}
B. 64 in.^{2}
C. 81 in.^{2}
D. 96 in.^{2}

Let's do this problem using the answer choices. You will need the geometry formulas for computing the area of both a square and a rectangle.

Square: $area = side^2$ Rectangle: $area = base \cdot height$

Work backwards! Your answer choices list the original area of the square. Find out what the length of each square's side would be to get that area. To do this, take the square root of the area.

~~A.~~ $\sqrt{15}$ Ignore. Not a perfect square.

B. $\sqrt{64} = 8$

C. $\sqrt{81} = 9$

~~D.~~ $\sqrt{96}$ Ignore. Not a perfect square.

Now answer choices B and C are all you have to consider. Find expressions for the base and height of the new rectangle by adding 5 to one side and 3 to the other. You are looking for a rectangle that has an area of 168 in.^{2}.

~~B.~~ $base = 8 + 5 = 13$; $height = 8 + 3 = 11$; $area = 13 \cdot 11 = 143$ in.^{2}

C. $base = 9 + 5 = 14$; $height = 9 + 3 = 12$; $area = 14 \cdot 12 = 168$ in.^{2}

The correct answer is choice C.

Consider if this same problem were NOT a multiple-choice question. The process for solving would have involved you setting up a quadratic equation and solving as follows:

$$(x+5)(x+3) = 168 \rightarrow x^2 + 8x + 15 = 168 \rightarrow x^2 + 8x - 153 = 0 \rightarrow (x+17)(x-9) = 0 \rightarrow$$
$$x = 9 \text{ and } x = -17$$

Since x represents a length, it cannot equal a negative number, making 9 the original length for the side of the square. Using the geometry formula for finding the area of a square: $area = side^2$, you get an answer of 81 in.^{2}.

As you can see, using your answer choices is simpler than solving a quadratic equation!

Next, consider Practice Question #1 from Patterns in Chapter 5:

n	−1	0	1	2	3	4
a_n	2	1	2	5	10	17

If the pattern in the table continues, which of the following expressions represents a_n?

A. $2n^2$

B. $2n^2 + 1$

C. $3n - 1$

D. $n^2 + 1$

This question would be far more complicated if the answer choices were not included. Your job is to find the expression for a_n that works for all the numbers in the table. Look at the last pair of values in the table, when $n = 4$, $a_n = 17$. These values don't work in the formula given in answer choice A. Notice: A̶. $a_n = 2n^2 = 2(4)^2 = 32$. Because $32 \neq 17$, you can eliminate this answer choice. You can also eliminate answer choice B because it is one more than choice A, so it equals 33 and not 17. Likewise, eliminate answer choice C: C̶. $a_n = 3n - 1 = 3(4) - 1 = 11$. This leaves you with answer choice D. You should verify its formula: D. $a_n = n^2 + 1 = 4^2 + 1 = 17.\checkmark$

A quick glance at the other numbers in the table should clarify that squaring them and adding one yields the value of a_n.

Process of Elimination

If you are not sure of the right answer to a multiple-choice question, see if you can eliminate wrong answer choices.

Consider Practice Question #4 from Linear Functions in Chapter 5:

Mr. Klein asked his students to report the number of hours they spent studying for the final exam. He then plotted the results on the scatterplot below.

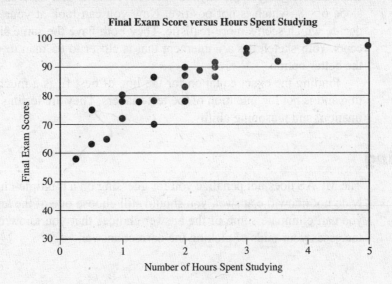

Final Exam Score versus Hours Spent Studying

Which of the following equations correctly approximates the line of best fit?

A. $y = -8x + 40$
B. $y = -8x + 65$
C. $y = 8x + 40$
D. $y = 8x + 65$

This question is asking you to imagine that there is a line passing through, and is as close to, as many of the points on the graph as possible, and to find the equation of that line. First, make an approximate sketch of the line of best fit.

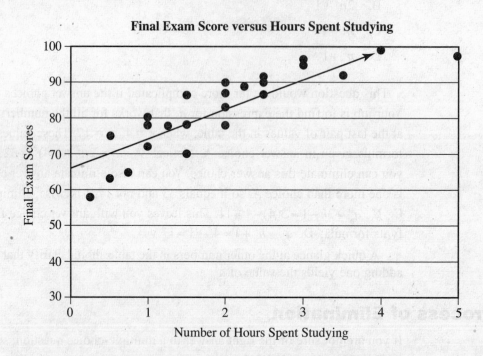

Final Exam Score versus Hours Spent Studying

Now, look at your answer choices and see if any of them can be eliminated. The slope of the line is clearly positive. As the number of hours spent studying increases, so do the exam scores. Therefore, answer choices A and B can be crossed off. They both have a slope of –8, which is not positive. Now you can look at your remaining two options to decide which seems more realistic. They both have the same slope, but different y intercepts. Your sketch has a y intercept that is closer to 65 than to 40, so answer choice D is the better option.

Finding the exact equation for the line of best fit is a much more complicated question and is not the intention of the test-makers. They are testing your elimination, approximation, and reasoning ability.

Guessing

The MCAS does not penalize you for guessing on a multiple-choice question. If you really do not know the answer, you should still choose one of the answer choices. Sometimes you can eliminate some of the answer choices that you know do not make sense, which increases your odds of picking the correct answer.

Choosing Your Own Numbers

Sometimes it is to your advantage to make up a number of your own to help you solve a problem.

Consider Practice Question #3 from Ratios, Proportions, and Percents in Chapter 4:

An item is on sale for 50% off of its original price. What percent increase is needed to return the sale item back to its original price?

A. 25%
B. 50%
C. 75%
D. 100%

Although you are not given a price for the item in this question, it is beneficial for you to make up a price and preferably a price that is easy to work with, like $100. If the item's original cost had been $100 and is on sale for 50% off, the new price is $50. In order to increase the item to its original price, it will need to increase by $50, which is the price that it is presently at. The percent increase is 100%.

Using $100 as a starting point for this problem makes the question more concrete.

Rounding and Approximating

When answer choices on multiple-choice questions are very far apart in value, it will not hurt you to round or approximate, particularly on the noncalculator portion of the MCAS.

Consider Practice Question #6 from Estimation in Chapter 4:

The value of $\dfrac{62.87 \cdot 309}{6.13}$ is closest to

A. 30
B. 300
C. 3,000
D. 30,000

Round and simplify: $\dfrac{60 \cdot 300}{6} = 10 \cdot 300 = 3,000.$

For more discussion on rounding, please refer to Estimation in Chapter 4.

Using Your Calculator

Remember to take advantage of your calculator on the calculator portion of the MCAS!

Be familiar with the buttons and operations you are using, such as finding square roots, changing between decimals and fractions, using parentheses, and so on.

Consider Practice Question #11 from Surface Area and Volume in Chapter 6:

The total surface area of a cube is 84 square inches. Which of the following measures is closest to the length of its edge?

A. 1.5 in.
B. 3.7 in.
C. 4.6 in.
D. 9.1 in.

The formula for the surface area of a cube is $SA = 6e^2$ where e is the length of an edge. Substitute 84 in. for the surface area and solve for e: $84 = 6e^2 \rightarrow 14 = e^2$. Use the square root button on your calculator to find the square root of 14: $e = \sqrt{14} \approx 3.7$ in.

When you use the calculator buttons, you may need to insert some extra parentheses into the problem. Such is the case in Practice Question #4 from Estimation in Chapter 4:

The following expression represents the amount of money in Doug's saving's account.

$$3{,}000\left(1 + \frac{0.03}{2}\right)^4$$

Which of the following is closest to the amount of money in Doug's saving's account?

    A. $3,180
    B. $3,200
    C. $3,220
    D. $3,240

This should be typed into your calculator as follows: $3000\left(1 + \left(.03 \div 2\right)\right)^{\wedge}4 = 3184.09$. So the correct answer would be A.

You should familiarize yourself with the buttons on your calculator, and practice using it on the calculator questions in this book.

Open-Response Questions Are Not "All or Nothing"!

The open-response questions are graded on a rubric from 0 to 4, where 4 is the highest score and 0 is the lowest. There are multiple parts to these questions; therefore, it is possible to get partial credit. In other words, if you know something **write it down**!

Show all of your work on these questions. You are being graded not only on the accuracy of your mathematics but also on the steps that you take to get to the answer and your explanation.

Label your answer with units. For example, if the question is talking about area, and lengths are measured in centimeters, your answer should say cm².

Scoring Rubric for Open-Response Student Solutions

Below is a sample rubric for scoring a student response to a question involving Linear Functions, in Chapter 5.

4 points

The student demonstrates an **excellent** understanding of the concepts involved in solving an everyday problem that can be modeled with linear functions. The student is able to write a linear equation to model the problem, solve the equation correctly, and accurately graph the linear function.

3 points

The student demonstrates **sufficient** understanding of the concepts involved in solving an everyday problem that can be modeled with linear functions. The student is able to write a linear equation to model the problem, solve a linear equation, and graph a line, but some aspect of the response (relatively minor) is flawed.

2 points

The student demonstrates a **fair** understanding of the concepts involved in solving an everyday problem that can be modeled with linear functions. Some parts of the response are done correctly, while others are not.

1 point

The student demonstrates only a **minimal** understanding of the concepts involved in solving an everyday problem that can be modeled with linear functions.

0 points

The student demonstrates **insufficient** understanding of the concepts involved in solving an everyday problem involving linear functions to receive any points.

The following pages show five hypothetical student responses, receiving 4–0 points, to Practice Question #11 from Linear Functions Chapter. It is as follows:

11. For lunch, Shannon usually buys pasta salad and an iced tea from either of two delicatessens near her office building. The prices for the two different delis are shown below.

Joan and Ed's Deli	Carmine's Delicatessen
pasta salad . . . . $0.45 per oz.	pasta salad. . . . $0.50 per ounce
iced tea . . . . . . $1.45 a bottle	iced tea. . . . . . . $1.00 a bottle

   a. How many ounces of pasta salad can Shannon buy at Joan and Ed's, together with a bottle of iced tea, for $4.60? Show or explain how you found your answer.
   b. Write an equation that shows C, the cost in dollars of Shannon's lunch at Carmine's Delicatessen, if she buys a bottle of iced tea and n ounces of pasta salad. Use your equation to determine how much money it would cost Shannon to purchase 8 ounces of pasta salad, along with an iced tea. Show or explain how you found your answer.

c. Graph the equation you wrote in part b on the grid below, using the horizontal axis for the number of ounces of pasta salad and using the vertical axis for the cost. Show or explain how you found your answer.

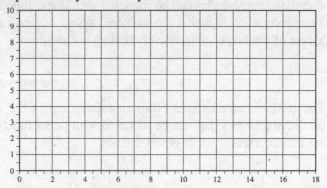

d. What is the maximum number of ounces of pasta salad Shannon can buy, provided she always buys an iced tea, so that her complete lunch is less expensive at Carmine's than it is at Joan and Ed's? Show or explain how you found your answer.

Student A: 4 points

(All equations are correct. All solutions are accurate. All explanations make sense.)

a. First, I set up an equation for the cost of a lunch at Joan & Ed's, where J is the cost, in dollars, of the lunch, and n is the number of ounces of pasta salad:

$$J = 1.45 + 0.45n$$

Then, I substituted $4.60 in for J and solved for n:

$$4.60 = 1.45 + 0.45n$$
$$3.15 = 0.45n$$
$$7 = n$$

Answer = 7 ounces

b. The equation for the cost, C, of a lunch of iced tea and n ounces of pasta salad at Carmine's, is:

$$C = 1.00 + 0.50n$$

I substituted 8 in for n and evaluated C:

$$C = 1.00 + 0.50(8)$$
$$C = 1.00 + 4.00$$
$$C = 5.00$$

Answer = $5.00

c. I used the fact that a line is an equation of the form: $y = mx + b$, where m is the slope and b is the y-intercept. Here, C represents y and n represents x. First, I plotted the y-intercept, which was 1.00. Then, I used the fact that $slope = \dfrac{rise}{run}$, so a slope of 0.5, or 1/2 meant that I would advance up one unit and to the right two units, to get my next point. Continuing this, I plotted a few points and graphed the line.

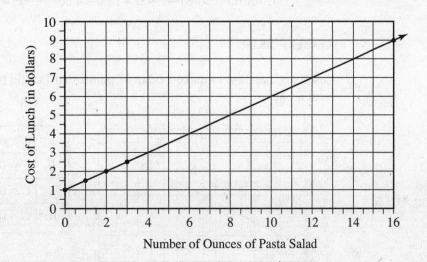

d. The cost for lunch at Joan and Ed's is: $J = 1.45 + 0.45n$. I set up an inequality making the cost for lunch at Carmine's be less than the cost at Joan and Ed's, and solved for n:

$$1.00 + 0.50n < 1.45 + 0.45n \longrightarrow 0.05n < 0.45 \longrightarrow n < 9$$

It is less expensive at Carmines when Shannon buys less than 9 ounces of pasta salad.

Answer = less than 9 oz

Student B: 3 points

(All equations are correct. Error in solving the equation in part a. All other parts are accurate.)

a. Set up an equation for the cost of a lunch at Joan & Ed's, where J is the cost, in dollars, of the lunch, and n is the number of ounces of pasta salad:

$$J = 1.45 + 0.45n$$

Replace J with \$4.60 and solve for n:

$$4.60 = 1.45 + 0.45n$$
$$6.05 = 0.45n$$
$$n \approx 13.5$$

Answer = 13.5 oz

b. The equation for the dollar cost, C, of a lunch of iced tea and n ounces of pasta salad at Carmine's, is

$$C = 1.00 + 0.50n$$

I substituted 8 in for n and evaluated C:

$$C = 1.00 + .50(8) \longrightarrow C = 1.00 + 4.00 \longrightarrow C = 5.00$$

Answer = $5.00

c. I used my equation to make a table of points that I could then plot and connect to form a line.

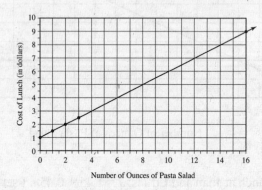

Number of Ounces of Pasta Salad

n	$C = 0.5(n) + 1.00$	C
0	$C = 0.5(0) + 1.00$	1.00
2	$C = 0.5(2) + 1.00$	2.00
16	$C = 0.5(16) + 1.00$	9.00

d. The cost for lunch at Joan and Ed's is: $J = 1.45 + 0.45n$. I set up an inequality making the cost for lunch at Carmine's be less than the cost at Joan and Ed's, and solved for n:

$$1.00 + .50n < 1.45 + 0.45n \longrightarrow 0.05n < 0.45 \longrightarrow n < 9$$

It is less expensive at Carmines when Shannon buys less than 9 ounces of pasta salad.

Answer = less than 9 oz

Student C: 2 points

(Parts a and b are correct. In part c, the constant slope for the iced tea at the beginning is wrong. In part d, the student fails to flip the inequality when dividing by a negative.)

a. First, subtract $1.45 for the iced tea, and Shannon has $4.60 − 1.45 = 3.15 left for the pasta salad. Next, divide by the price per ounce of pasta salad to get the number of ounces of pasta salad: $3.15 ÷ 0.45 = 7$ ounces.

Answer: 7 ounces

b. The equation for the dollar cost, C, of a lunch of iced tea and n ounces of pasta salad at Carmine's, is:

$$C = 1.00 + 0.50n$$

I substituted 8 in for n and evaluated C:

$$C = 1.00 + 0.50(8)$$
$$C = 1.00 + 4.00$$
$$C = 5.00$$

Answer = $5.00

c. Since the iced tea always costs $1.00, I made that line horizontal. Then, the number of ounces of pasta salad makes the line slant up $0.50 for each 1 oz of pasta salad.

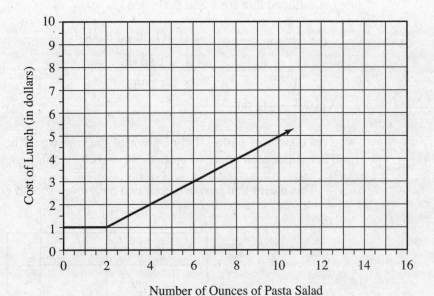

d. The cost for lunch at Joan and Ed's is: $J = 1.45 + 0.45n$. I let the equation for lunch at Carmine's be less than Joan and Ed's and solved for n.

$$1.45 + 0.45n > 1.00 + 0.50n$$
$$-0.05n > -0.45$$
$$n > 9$$

It is less expensive at Carmines when Shannon buys more than 9 ounces of pasta salad.

Answer = more than 9 oz

Student D: 1 point

(Correct steps and execution in part a only. Wrong equation in part b. The graph in part c shows an incorrect execution of slope = 0.5. A wrong answer with no work on part d.)

    a. Subtract $1.45 and divide by $0.45 to get the number of ounces:

$$(4.60 - 1.45) / 0.45 = 7 \text{ ounces}$$

    Answer: 7 oz

    b. The equation for the dollar cost, C, of a lunch of iced tea and n ounces of pasta salad at Carmine's, is:

$$C = (1.00 + 0.50)n$$

I substituted 8 in for n and evaluated C:

$$C = (1.00 + .50) \cdot 8$$
$$C = 1.50 \cdot 8$$
$$C = 12.00$$

Answer = $12.00

    c. Zero ounces of pasta salad means that the cost would be $1.00 for the iced tea. Then, since each ounce of pasta salad costs 0.50, this makes the slope of the graph $\frac{1}{2}$. This means that between each two points you should go up 2 units and over 1.

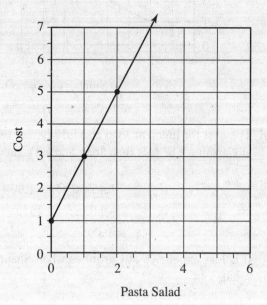

    d. 8 ounces.

Student E: 0 points

(Wrong or no equations. No correct answers. Few or no explanations. Part d left blank.)

X. $\dfrac{\$4.60}{.45} = 10.2$

Answer = 10.2 oz

X. $C = n - 1 / 0.45$

$8 - 1.00 = 7.00$

$7.00 \div 0.45 \approx \$15.56$

Answer = \$15.56

X. Zero ounces of pasta salad means that the cost would be \$1.00 for the iced tea. Then, since each ounce of pasta salad costs 0.50, this makes the slope of the graph

$\dfrac{1}{2}$. This means that between each two points you should go up 2 units and over 1.

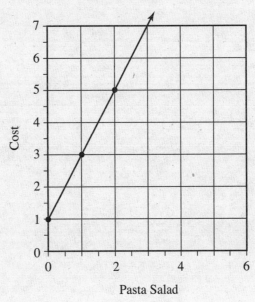

Pasta Salad

Remember the Key Ingredients for Full Credit on Open-Response Questions!

- *Correct model for the situation.*
- *100% accurate solution with steps shown.*
- *Coherent response to accompany the steps and thought processes.*

Take Your Time

Each of the two math sections is designed to last 60 minutes. However, you will not be asked to hand in the test if you are still working on it when the 60 minutes are over. So remember, don't rush, read the questions carefully, and check your answers. You have as much time as you need!

Be Prepared

The more you know about the MCAS going into the test, the easier and more successful your test-taking experience will be. For example, use the reference sheet when you take the practice tests so that you know what formulas need to be memorized and what formulas are given. The more you practice, the more comfortable and confident you will feel!

Chapter 4 | Number Sense and Operations

Types of Numbers

The MCAS uses the terms for the types of numbers in the **real number** system and even asks questions that require you to categorize the number. It is important to memorize these definitions.

- **Real numbers** are any numbers that can be located on a number line. They include negative numbers, positive numbers, zero, fractions, decimals that terminate, repeating decimals, and decimals that never end and have no repeating pattern. Repeating decimals, such as 1.3333333 . . . can be written as $1.\overline{3}$.

- **Natural numbers** are the set of counting numbers that begin with the number "1."

$$\{1, 2, 3, 4, 5, 6, \ldots\}$$

- **Whole numbers** include the set of natural numbers and the number "0."

$$\{0, 1, 2, 3, 4, 5, 6, \ldots\}$$

- **Integers** include the set of whole numbers and their negatives.

$$\{\ldots -3, \ -2, \ -1, \ 0, \ 1, \ 2, \ 3, \ldots\}$$

- **Perfect Squares** are numbers that result from multiplying a whole number by itself.

$$\{0, 1, 4, 9, 16, 25, \ldots\}$$

The square root of 9 is 3 and is written as $\sqrt{9} = 3$ because $3^2 = 3 \cdot 3 = 9$.

- **Rational numbers** can be expressed as a ratio of two integers. In other words, they can be written as fractions. $0, \ -6, \ 3, \ \frac{2}{5}, \ -\frac{1}{3}, \ 0.25, 0.\overline{2}, \ \sqrt{25}$ are all examples of rational numbers.

0 can be expressed as $\frac{0}{5}$, -6 as $-\frac{12}{2}$, 3 as $\frac{12}{4}$, 0.25 as $\frac{1}{4}$, $0.\overline{2}$ as $\frac{2}{9}$, and $\sqrt{25}$ as $\frac{5}{1}$. Terminating decimals (decimals that end) and repeating decimals (decimals that repeat forever such as $0.\overline{2}$) are rational.

- **Irrational numbers** are numbers that cannot be expressed as a ratio of two integers. In other words, they cannot be expressed as fractions. $\sqrt{3}$ and π are examples of irrational numbers. In decimal form, irrational numbers do not terminate (do not end) and there is not a repeating pattern. You can distinguish a square root as being irrational if the number underneath the radical sign is not a perfect square.

The Real Number System

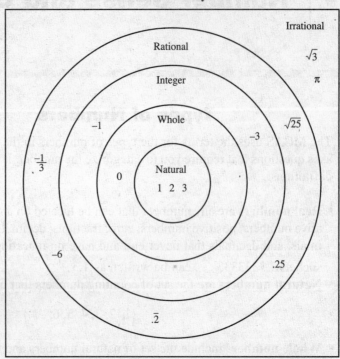

> ** Remember: A decimal that is both nonrepeating and nonterminating is irrational.
> The square root of a number that is not a perfect square is irrational.*

Examples: Types of Numbers

Example 1. How many numbers in the following list of numbers are irrational?

$$\sqrt{16},\ -\frac{4}{2},\ \sqrt{17},\ 1.6,\ 0.\overline{45},\ \pi,\ 0,\ 3,\ \sqrt{2}$$

A. 1
B. 2
C. 3
D. 4

Solution:
There are three that are irrational. Going through the list:

$\sqrt{16} = 4$ is rational. It can be expressed as the quotient of two integers, such as $\frac{4}{1}$. It is also an integer, a whole number, and a natural number.

$-\frac{4}{2} = -2$ is rational. It is also an integer.

$\sqrt{17}$ is irrational. It cannot be expressed as a quotient of two integers because 17 is not a perfect square. If you changed it into a decimal, it would be nonterminating and nonrepeating.

1.6　　　　　is rational because it is a terminating decimal and can therefore be written as the quotient of two integers, such as $\frac{16}{10}$.

$0.\overline{45}$　　　is rational because it is a repeating decimal and can therefore be written as the quotient of two integers, such as $\frac{5}{11}$.

π　　　　　　is irrational. As a decimal, it is approximately 3.141592654 . . . and is non-terminating and nonrepeating. π cannot be written as a quotient of two integers.

0 and 3　　are rational. They are both integers and whole numbers.

$\sqrt{2}$　　　　is irrational. 2 is not a perfect square. The decimal is approximately 1.41421 . . . and does not terminate or repeat.

Answer: C

Practice: Types of Numbers

1. Which of the following is irrational?
   A. 3π
   B. $0.\overline{34}$
   C. 0.9
   D. $\frac{1}{4}$

2. Which of the following is rational but not an integer?
   A. $\sqrt{13}$
   B. $\frac{10}{5}$
   C. $\frac{1}{9}$
   D. 12

Solutions to Practice: Types of Numbers

1. Repeating decimals can be expressed as fractions, $0.\overline{34} = \frac{34}{99}$, so $0.\overline{34}$ is rational. Terminating decimals can be expressed as fractions, $0.9 = \frac{9}{10}$, which is rational. $\frac{1}{4}$ is already in fractional form, so it is clearly rational. 3π cannot be expressed as a fraction or a repeating or terminating decimal. It is irrational.

   Answer: A

2. $\sqrt{13}$ is irrational. $\frac{10}{5} = 2$, which is an integer. 12 is also an integer. $\frac{1}{9}$ is rational but is not an integer.

Answer: C

Properties of Real Numbers

The following vocabulary may be used to describe real numbers and operations performed on real numbers:

- **Even** numbers are integers that you can divide by 2 without a remainder.

$$\{\ldots -6, \ -4, \ -2, \ 0, \ 2, \ 4, \ 6, \ldots\}$$

- **Odd** numbers are integers that when you divide them by 2, there is a remainder.

$$\{\ldots -5, \ -3, \ -1, \ 1, \ 3, \ 5, \ 7, \ldots\}$$

Even + Even = Even 2 + 4 = 6	Odd − Even = Odd 7 − 4 = 3
Even + Odd = Odd 3 + 4 = 7	Odd − Odd = Even 7 − 5 = 2
Odd + Odd = Even 3 + 5 = 8	Odd · Odd = Odd 3 · 5 = 15
Even − Even = Even 6 − 4 = 2	Even · Even = Even 2 · 4 = 8
Even − Odd = Odd 6 − 5 = 1	Even · Odd = Even 2 · 3 = 6

You do not need to memorize the above table because you can pick numbers to remind yourself of these properties without much effort.

- A **prime** number is a natural number that is only divisible (without a remainder) by the integers 1 and the number itself. 2 is the smallest prime number and the only even prime number.

$$\{2, 3, 5, 7, 11, 13, \ldots\}$$

> * *Remember: 0 and 1 are not prime numbers.*
> *2 is the smallest prime number.*
> *2 is the only even prime number.*

- The **factors** of an integer are the divisors (without a remainder) of the number. The factors of 24 are 1, 2, 3, 4, 6, 8, 12, 24. When listing the factors, you can pair them according to pairs that multiply to the number itself. For example, $1 \cdot 24 = 24$, $2 \cdot 12 = 24$, $3 \cdot 8 = 24$, $6 \cdot 4 = 24$.

- The **multiples** of an integer can be divided (without a remainder) by the integer itself. When you list the multiples of an integer, begin with the integer itself. Listing the multiples of an integer is like counting by the number. The multiples of 7 are 7, 14, 21, 28, 35, 42, ...

- The **reciprocal** of a number is the result when 1 is divided by the number. If the number is expressed as a ratio (or fraction), you can flip the fraction to find the reciprocal. The reciprocal of $\frac{2}{3}$ is $\frac{3}{2}$. The reciprocal of -4 is $-\frac{1}{4}$. The reciprocal of 1 is 1. The sign of the number does not change when you find the reciprocal.

- The **absolute value** of a number is the positive integral distance between the number and 0. The symbol used for the absolute value is two vertical lines outside the number: $\left| -3 \right| = 3$. The absolute value of a negative number is positive and the absolute value of a positive number is positive. $\left| 3 \right| = 3$. Be careful when simplifying within absolute value symbols. Do operations on the inside first. For example, $\left| -6 + 4 \right| = \left| -2 \right| = 2$. (Don't turn the -6 into a $+6$.)

- **Exponents** are used as a shorthand for repeated multiplication. Instead of writing $2 \cdot 2 \cdot 2 \cdot 2 \cdot 2$, you can write 2^5. Two is called the base, and five is the exponent or power. $(-1)(-1)(-1) = (-1)^3 = -1$. $(-1)(-1)(-1)(-1) = (-1)^4 = 1$. A negative number raised to an odd exponent will be negative because there will be an odd number of negative numbers being multiplied. A negative number raised to an even exponent will be positive because there will be an even number of negative numbers being multiplied.

- **Variables** are used in place of an unknown quantity. The variable is usually assigned a letter such as x, y, a, or b. Variables operate the same way numbers do. For example, just like $3 + 3 = 2 \cdot 3$, $x + x = 2 \cdot x$, which is written as $2x$.

- A **negative** number is a number that is less than zero. A **positive** number is a number greater than zero. Zero is neither positive nor negative. When multiplying negative and positive numbers together, follow the rules:

$$negative \cdot negative = positive$$
$$positive \cdot positive = positive$$
$$negative \cdot positive = negative$$

Properties of Equality

- The **commutative** properties of addition and multiplication say that the order in which you add or multiply two numbers does not change the sum or product. For example:

$$3 + 4 = 4 + 3 \qquad 3 \cdot 4 = 4 \cdot 3$$

- The **associative** properties of addition and multiplication say that the way you group three or more numbers when adding or multiplying does not change the sum or product. For example:

$$(3+4)+2 = 3+(4+2) \qquad (2\cdot 3)\cdot 4 = 2\cdot(3\cdot 4)$$

or   or

$$7+2 = 3+6 = 9 \qquad 6\cdot 4 = 2\cdot 12 = 24$$

- The **distributive** property says that when a term is multiplied by a number of terms in parentheses, each term in those parentheses should be multiplied by the leading term outside the parentheses. For example:

$$3(x+2y-1) = 3x+6y-3$$

Identities

- The **additive identity** is the number 0. This means that 0 can be added to any number without changing that number's value.

$$5+0 = 5$$

- The **multiplicative identity** is the number 1. This means that 1 can be multiplied by any number without changing that number's value.

$$5\cdot 1 = 5$$

Inverses

- The **additive inverse** of a number is that same number, but with the opposite sign. The sum of any number and its additive inverse is 0. The additive inverse of 6 is –6.

$$-6+6 = 0$$

- The **multiplicative inverse** of a number is the reciprocal of that number. The product of any number and its multiplicative inverse is 1. The multiplicative inverse of 6 is $\frac{1}{6}$.

$$6\cdot \frac{1}{6} = 1$$

Property	Statement	Example
Commutative property of addition	$x + y = y + x$	$3 + 4 = 4 + 3$
Commutative property of multiplication	$x \cdot y = y \cdot x$	$3 \cdot 4 = 4 \cdot 3$
Associative property of addition	$(x + y) + z = x + (y + z)$	$(3 + 4) + 2 = 3 + (4 + 2)$
Associative property of multiplication	$(x \cdot y) \cdot z = x \cdot (y \cdot z)$	$(2 \cdot 3) \cdot 4 = 2 \cdot (3 \cdot 4)$
Distributive property	$x(y + z - a) = xy + xz - xa$	$3(x + 2y - 1) = 3x + 6y - 3$
Additive identity	$x + 0 = x$	$5 + 0 = 5$
Multiplicative identity	$x \cdot 1 = x$	$5 \cdot 1 = 5$
Additive inverse	$x + (-x) = 0$	$6 + (-6) = 0$
Multiplicative inverse	$x \cdot \left(\dfrac{1}{x}\right) = 1$	$6 \cdot \left(\dfrac{1}{6}\right) = 1$

Examples: Properties of Real Numbers

Example 1. Rick wants to solve the equation $\dfrac{1}{3}x = 5$. Which property of real numbers best describes the operation that Rick must use to solve for x?

    A. Distributive property
    B. Additive inverse
    C. Associative property of addition
    D. Multiplicative inverse

Solution

To solve this equation, Rick would want to isolate the variable, x. This means, he would want x to be alone on one side of the equation. In other words, Rick would have to do something to the $\dfrac{1}{3}x$ so that it would become $1x$, or just x. Since $\dfrac{1}{3}x$ is an operation of multiplication, Rick would need to multiply $\dfrac{1}{3}$ by its multiplicative inverse, which is 3. Once he multiplies one side of the equation by 3, he must multiply the other side by 3 in order to balance the equation.

Answer: D

Example 2. If the distributive property is used to simplify the expression below, what is the result?

$$a(b+c)-d(e-f)$$

- A. $ab+ac-de+df$
- B. $ab+ac-de-df$
- C. $ab+c-de-f$
- D. $ab+c-de+f$

Solution

The distributive property says that each term in the first parentheses should be multiplied by a and each term in the second parentheses should be multiplied by $-d$. Be careful to pay attention to the signs of the numbers that you are multiplying. $a(b+c)-d(e-f)=ab+ac-de+df$.

Answer: A

Example 3. Let x and y be real numbers with $0 < x < y < 1$.

Which of the following is not necessarily true?

- A. $y^2 > x^2$
- B. $x-y<0$
- C. $x+y>1$
- D. $y-x>0$

Solution

A. Not the answer because y is greater than x so y^2 must be greater than x^2, which makes choice A true. **Choose your own numbers** to convince yourself that this is true. Suppose $x=\dfrac{1}{3}$ and $y=\dfrac{1}{2}$, then $\left(\dfrac{1}{2}\right)^2=\dfrac{1}{4}$ and $\left(\dfrac{1}{3}\right)^2=\dfrac{1}{9}$ and $\dfrac{1}{4}>\dfrac{1}{9}$.

   You can also use decimal examples. Suppose $x = 0.1$ and $y = 0.5$, then $(0.1)^2 = 0.01$ and $(0.5)^2 = 0.25$ and $0.25 > 0.01$.

B. Not the answer because $x < y$, so $x - y$ must be less than zero, so choice B is true.

C. Correct answer because $x + y > 1$ is not necessarily true.

   For example, if $x=\dfrac{1}{5}$ and $y=\dfrac{1}{4}$, $\dfrac{1}{5}+\dfrac{1}{4}=\dfrac{4}{20}+\dfrac{5}{20}=\dfrac{9}{20}<1$.

D. Not the answer because $y > x$, so $y - x$ must be greater than zero. This makes choice D true.

Answer: C

Example 4. Beth simplified the expression $1 \cdot a^2$ to a^2. Which of the following properties of real numbers did Beth use?

    A. Commutative property of multiplication
    B. Multiplicative identity
    C. Associative property of addition
    D. Additive identity

Solution

    Beth used the multiplicative identity, which says that when you multiply a number by 1, the result is the number itself. So, when you multiply a^2 by 1, the result is a^2.

    Answer: B

Practice: Properties of Real Numbers

1. The distributive property is used to simplify the expression below.

$$5xy\left(3a + b\right) + 2$$

    Which of the following is the result?

    A. $15xya + b + 2$
    B. $3a + 5xyb + 2$
    C. $15xya + 5xyb + 10xy$
    D. $15xya + 5xyb + 2$

2. When 90 is divided by a number, x, the quotient is 12 with a remainder of 6. What is the value of x?

    A. 6
    B. 7
    C. 8
    D. 9

3. Let a and b represent real numbers with $a > 0$ and $b > 0$. Which of the following statements is not true?
    A. $ab > 0$
    B. $ab < 0$
    C. $a + b > 0$
    D. $\dfrac{a}{b} > 0$

4. Each of the statements below is true for particular values of real numbers
   $a, b, c, d, e,$ and f.
   $a, b, c, d, e,$ and f are distinct nonnegative numbers and $c \neq 1$.

$$a \cdot b = 0 \text{ and } a \neq 0$$

$$c^d = c$$

$$\frac{1}{2} \cdot d \cdot e = f$$

   a. What is the numerical value of b? Explain your reasoning.

   b. What is the numerical value of d? Explain your reasoning.

   c. If $f = 3$, what is the numerical value of e? Explain your reasoning.

5. Hayden multiplied both sides of the equation below by $\frac{1}{3}$.

$$3x = 7$$

   Which other operation would have achieved the same result?

   A. Dividing by 3 on both sides of the equation
   B. Adding 3 on both sides of the equation
   C. Subtracting 3 on both sides of the equation

   D. Dividing by $\frac{1}{3}$ on both sides of the equation

6. The temperature outside increases from $-3°$ Fahrenheit to $8°$ Fahrenheit. Which of the following expressions represents the number of degrees that the temperature increased?

   A. $\left| 8 - 3 \right|$
   B. $\left| 3 - 8 \right|$
   C. $\left| 8 - (-3) \right|$
   D. $(8 - 3)^2$

7. The acceptable pH range for the water in swimming pools is 7.2 to 7.8. The pH should satisfy the following inequality:

$$\left| pH - 7.5 \right| \leq 0.3$$

   Which pH level does not satisfy the inequality?

   A. 7.2
   B. 7.3
   C. 7.5
   D. 7.9

8. Adam is monitoring the outside temperature in degrees Fahrenheit each morning for his science project. On Monday, he noted that the temperature had increased 4 degrees from Sunday. On Tuesday it had increased 2 more degrees. On Wednesday it had decreased 8 degrees, and on Thursday it had decreased 1 more degree and measured in at 26 degrees Fahrenheit. What was the original temperature on Sunday?

Use the expression below to answer Question 9.

$$5x - 2(3x - 7)$$

9. Which could be the first step in simplifying the expression above?
   A. $5x - 6x + 7$
   B. $5x - 6x - 14$
   C. $5x - 6x - 7$
   D. $5x - 6x + 14$

Solutions to Practice: Properties of Real Numbers

1. Multiply each term in the parentheses by $5xy$, then add 2 at the end.

$$5xy(3a + b) + 2 = 15xya + 5xyb + 2$$

Answer: D

2. **Use your answer choices** to help you solve this problem. Even if you forgot that the word quotient means your answer after you divide a number, you should be able to get that from reading the question. Try multiplying $12 \cdot 6 = 72$, which is not 6 away from 90. Try the next answer choice: $12 \cdot 7 = 84$, which is 6 away from 90 so the correct answer choice is B.

Answer: B

3. The statements $a > 0$ and $b > 0$ simply mean that both a and b are positive. **Choose your own numbers**, any two positive numbers, such as 3 and 2, and test the answer choices. You are looking for a false statement.
   A. Not the answer. Because $3 \cdot 2 = 6$ and $6 > 0$, answer choice A is true. In general, two positive numbers have a positive product.
   B. Correct answer. Because 6 is not less than 0, answer choice B is false. In general, it is impossible to multiply two positive real numbers and end up with a negative number.
   C. Not the answer. Because $3 + 2 = 5$ and $5 > 0$, answer choice C is true. In general, two positive numbers have a positive sum.
   D. Not the answer. Because $\dfrac{3}{2} > 0$, answer choice D is true. Two positive numbers have a positive quotient.

Answer: B

4. a. Since $a \neq 0$, but the product $a \cdot b = 0$, b must equal 0.

   Answer: 0

   b. Distinct means that all the numbers are different from each other. Nonnegative numbers are positive numbers or the number zero. The condition $c \neq 1$ is given in the problem, and since all the values are distinct and $b = 0$, $c \neq 0$. Any number raised to the first power is equal to itself. The statement $c^d = c$ would make $d = 1$. Try plugging in a positive value for c to check this result. Suppose $c = 2$ $\rightarrow 2^d = 2 \rightarrow 2^1 = 2$.

   Answer: 1

   c. Since $d = 1$, $\frac{1}{2} \cdot 1 \cdot e = 3 \rightarrow \frac{1}{2} e = 3$. e must be 6 because half of 6 is 3.

   Answer: $e = 6$

5. The correct answer choice is A. Dividing by 3 on both sides of the equation and multiplying by $\frac{1}{3}$ achieve the same result, and both result in $1x$. Dividing by $\frac{1}{3}$ is the same as multiplying by 3, which would have resulted in $9x$. This would've been incorrect.

   Answer: A

6. You can think of the increase in temperature as the sum of the increase from –3 to 0 and from 0 to 8. $3 + 8 = 11$. This also can be calculated as $8 - (-3)$ or as it is written with the absolute value symbol in choice C.

   Answer: C

7. **Use your answer choices** and plug in the values to find the one that does not satisfy the inequality. Choice D does not work because $|7.9 - 7.5| = |0.4| = 0.4$, which is not less than or equal to 0.3.

   Answer: D

8. Work your way backwards on this problem. Thursday's $26° + 1 =$ Wednesday's $27°$. Wednesday's $27° + 8 =$ Tuesday's $35°$. Tuesday's $35° - 2 =$ Monday's $33°$. Monday's $33° - 4 =$ Sunday's. Another way of solving this is algebraically. Call the temperature on Sunday, x. On Monday, it has increased $4°$, so in terms of x, Monday's temperature is $x + 4$. Tuesday's is $x + 6$, Wednesday's is $x - 2$, and Thursday's is $x - 3$. Since Thursday ends up being $x - 3$ and you know that the temperature on Thursday is $26°$, you can set up an equation and solve: $x - 3 = 26 \rightarrow x = 29$.

   Answer: $29°$

9. Use the distributive property to get rid of the parentheses. Don't forget that you are multiplying by a negative number, so the $-2 \cdot -7$ will give you $+14$. $5x - 2(3x - 7) = 5x - 6x + 14$. Although simplifying the remaining expression by combining like terms would leave you with $-x + 14$, you can see by the answer choices that you do not have to go that far.

Answer: D

Simplifying

Roots

- The square root symbol, $\sqrt{}$, is also called a **radical sign.** It is the inverse operation of squaring a number. The **square root** of a number is the number that you could multiply by itself (squared) to get the number inside the radical. For example, $\sqrt{9} = 3$ because

$$\sqrt{9} = \sqrt{3 \cdot 3} = \sqrt{(3)^2} = 3$$

Another way of writing $\sqrt{9}$ is $9^{\frac{1}{2}}$. The number 9 is called a **perfect square** because there is a whole number, namely 3, that can be squared to get 9.

Simplifying Square Roots

- In general, each pair of factors inside a radical sign is equal to one of the factors outside. (Consider the preceding example.) If a number is not a perfect square, you may express it as a product of its prime factors, and pull out the pairs. For example:

$$\sqrt{12} = \sqrt{2 \cdot 2 \cdot 3} = 2\sqrt{3}$$

To simplify the square roots of larger numbers that are not perfect squares, consider rewriting them as the product of two numbers, one of them being the highest perfect square possible. Then bring the perfect square out of the square root in simplified form.

$$\sqrt{72} = \sqrt{36 \cdot 2} = 6\sqrt{2}$$

If you are simplifying a radical where there is a number being multiplied in front, you must multiply whatever factor you pull out with the number that is there. For example:

$$3\sqrt{50} = 3\sqrt{25 \cdot 2} = 5 \cdot 3\sqrt{2} = 15\sqrt{2}$$

In the real number system, zero is the smallest number for which you can take the square root. Because $0 \cdot 0 = 0$, it follows that $\sqrt{0} = 0$. It is also true that $\sqrt{1} = 1$. You cannot take the square root of a negative number. If you reverse the operation, there is no real number that you can square and wind up with a negative number. You should be very familiar with the following perfect squares so that you can use them in your work without the use of your calculator:

0, 1, 4, 9, 16, 25, 36, 49, 64, 81, 100, 121, 144, 169, 196, and 225

Other Roots

- The **cube root** of a number is the number that you would multiply by itself (cubed) three times to get the number that is being cube rooted. $\sqrt[3]{8} = 2$ because $2 \cdot 2 \cdot 2 = 8$. Another way of writing $\sqrt[3]{8}$ is $8^{\frac{1}{3}}$. The number 8 is a **perfect cube** because there is a whole number that can be cubed to get that number. To simplify a cube root that is not a perfect cube, rewrite the number as a product of two numbers, one of them being the highest perfect cube possible. Then bring the perfect cube out of the root in simplified form. $\sqrt[3]{128} = \sqrt[3]{64 \cdot 2} = 4\sqrt[3]{2}$. Unlike a square root, you can take the cube root of a negative number. $\sqrt[3]{-8} = -2$ because $(-2)(-2)(-2) = -8$. When you cube a negative number, the result is negative. You should be very familiar with the following perfect cubes so that you can use them in your work without the use of your calculator:

$$0, 1, 8, 27, 64, 125, \text{ and } 216$$

- You can take the **fourth root** of a number, **fifth root,** and so on. The processes for doing so are the same as the ones described earlier.

Simplifying Exponents

Multiplication

- When you multiply two numbers with the same base, you add the exponents, and the base remains the same. For example, $x^3 \cdot x^2 = x^5$. This makes sense because $x^3 \cdot x^2 = x^1 \cdot x^1 \cdot x^1 \cdot x^1 \cdot x^1 = x^5$. Another example is $2x^2 \cdot 4x^5 = 8x^7$.

  Rule: $x^a \cdot x^b = x^{(a+b)}$

Raising to a Power

- Because raising to a power is equivalent to multiplying a term by itself several times, we can think of these problems as repeated multiplication problems. Look at what happens when you square the quantity x^3: $\left(x^3\right)^2 = x^3 \cdot x^3 = x^{(3+3)} = x^6$. In general, when raising to a power, you multiply the exponents. Another example is $\left(2x^4\right)^3 = 8x^{12}$.

  Rule: $\left(x^a\right)^b = x^{ab}$

Distributive Property

- The distributive property applies to the exponent over multiplication (not addition). The powers must be the same! Sometimes, it is convenient to simplify by multiplying the bases. For example:

$$3^2 \cdot 2^2 = \left(3 \cdot 2\right)^2 = 6^2 = 36$$

Rule: $x^a \cdot y^a = \left(xy\right)^a$

---

* *Remember*: $3^2 + 2^2 = 13$ *AND NOT* $3^2 + 2^2 \neq \left(3 + 2\right)^2 = 25$

Division

- Now look at dividing terms with the same base.

$$\frac{x^5}{x^2} = \frac{x \cdot x \cdot x \cdot x \cdot x}{x \cdot x} = \frac{x \cdot x \cdot x \cdot \cancel{x} \cdot \cancel{x}}{\cancel{x} \cdot \cancel{x}} = \frac{x^3}{1} = x^3$$

Crossing out the common factors in the numerator and denominator leaves you with three factors of x in the numerator. In general, when dividing terms with the same base, simply subtract the power of the denominator from the power of the numerator. For example:

$$\frac{2^{10}}{2^3} = 2^7, \quad \frac{2^3}{2^{10}} = 2^{-7} = \frac{1}{2^7}, \quad \frac{x^7}{x^3} = x^4$$

Rule: $\dfrac{x^a}{x^b} = x^{(a-b)}$, $x \neq 0$

Negative Exponents

- If the power of the denominator is greater than the power of the numerator, you are left with a negative exponent. Notice that $\dfrac{x^2}{x^3} = x^{(2-3)} = x^{-1}$. Writing out the individual factors will show you that $x^{-1} = \dfrac{1}{x}$:

$$\frac{x^2}{x^3} = \frac{\cancel{x} \cdot \cancel{x}}{x \cdot \cancel{x} \cdot \cancel{x}} = \frac{1}{x}$$

In general, negative exponents in the numerator are positive exponents in the denominator. A negative exponent can be rewritten as 1 divided by the number without the negative exponent (just make it positive). For example:

$$3^{-2} = \frac{1}{3^2} \text{ and } \frac{1}{4^{-3}} = \frac{1}{\frac{1}{4^3}} = 4^3$$

Rule: $x^{-n} = \dfrac{1}{x^n}$, $x \neq 0$.

Distributive Property

• The distributive property applies to the exponent over division. For example:

$$\left(\frac{2x}{y}\right)^3 = \frac{8x^3}{y^3}$$

Rule: $\left(\dfrac{x}{y}\right)^a = \dfrac{x^a}{y^a}$ $(y \neq 0)$.

---

* *Remember: Any number to the 0 power is equal to 1:* $3^0 = 1$.
        Any number to the first power is equal to the number itself: $3^1 = 3$.

* *Remember: You cannot divide a number by 0.*
        A number divided by 0 is considered undefined.

Order of Operations

When simplifying an expression with more than one operation, you must follow the proper order of operations. The order is as follows:

1. First simplify all expressions that are grouped within **p**arentheses or brackets or absolute value.
2. Next, simplify **e**xponents and roots.
3. Next, calculate **m**ultiplication and **d**ivision in order from left to right.
4. Finally, calculate **a**ddition and **s**ubtraction in order from left to right.

Some people remember this order with the acronym **PEMDAS** (parentheses, exponents, multiplication and division, addition and subtraction). Remember that multiplication and division and then addition and subtraction are calculated in order from left to right. Consider the following example

Simplify the expression: $1 - 4\left(-5 + 2 \cdot 2\right)^2 + 4 \div 2$

P   *Simplify parentheses first, multiplication before addition:*

$1 - 4\left(-5 + \underline{2 \cdot 2}\right)^2 + 4 \div 2$

$1 - 4\left(-5 + 4\right)^2 + 4 \div 2$

$1 - 4\left(-1\right)^2 + 4 \div 2$

E   *Simplify exponents:*

$1 - 4\underline{\left(-1\right)^2} + 4 \div 2$

$1 - 4 \cdot 1 + 4 \div 2$

MD   *Calculate multiplication, then division—multiplication first because it comes first when reading from left to right:*

$$1 - \underline{4 \bullet 1} + \underline{4 \div 2}$$
$$1 - 4 + 2$$

AS   *Calculate subtraction, then addition—subtraction first because it comes first when reading from left to right:*

$$-3 + 2 = -1$$

Examples: Simplifying

Example 1. What is the simplified form of the expression $\sqrt{245}$?

   A. $7\sqrt{5}$
   B. $14\sqrt{5}$
   C. $24\sqrt{5}$
   D. $49\sqrt{5}$

Solution

Rewrite 245 as the product of two numbers, one of them being the highest perfect square possible: $\sqrt{245} = \sqrt{49 \cdot 5}$. Pull the $\sqrt{49}$ out of the square root as 7. $\sqrt{245} = 7\sqrt{5}$.

Answer: A

Example 2. For what value of x is the equation below true?

$$7^2 \cdot x = 7^{10}$$

Solution

If the bases are the same, the rules of exponents say that when you are multiplying, you add the exponents. To make this equation work, x must be $7^8 \rightarrow 7^2 \cdot 7^8 = 7^{10}$.

Answer: 7^8

Example 3. What is the value of the expression below?

$$8(9 - 5) - 3(2 + 4 - (7 - 6))$$

   A. 4
   B. 14
   C. 17
   D. 145

Solution

This is an order of operations problem. Start with the innermost parentheses $(7 - 6) = 1$ so $8(9 - 5) - 3(2 + 4 - (7 - 6)) = 8(9 - 5) - 3(2 + 4 - 1)$. Next, perform the operations in the other two parentheses, $9 - 5 = 4$ and since addition and subtraction is calculated left to right, $2 + 4 = 6$ and then $6 - 1 = 5$. So now you are left with $8(4) - 3(5)$. Multiplication comes before subtraction so multiplying left to right $8 \cdot 4 = 32$ and $3 \cdot 5 = 15$. Finally, $32 - 15 = 17$.

Answer: C

Example 4. What is the value of the expression $4|3 - 6| - 15$?
    A. -27
    B. -3
    C. 21
    D. 51

Solution

This is an order of operations problem. The absolute value symbol should be treated like parentheses and calculated first. $|3 - 6| = |-3| = 3 \rightarrow 4 \cdot 3 - 15$. Next, multiply: $4 \cdot 3 = 12$. Finally, $12 - 15 = -3$.

Answer: B

Example 5. Simplify $\left(3x^2 y^4\right)\left(5xy^2\right)$.

Solution

$$\left(3x^2 y^4\right)\left(5xy^2\right)$$

$$= 3 \cdot 5 \cdot x^2 \cdot x^1 \cdot y^4 \cdot y^2 \qquad$$ *Rearrange so that constants are together on the left-hand side, and terms with the same base are grouped together so that you can simplify exponents.*

$$= 15x^3 y^6 \qquad$$ *Multiply the constants together, and multiply variables with the same base by adding their exponents.*

Answer: $15x^3y^6$

Example 6. Rewrite $4x^3 y^{-5}$ with no negative exponents.

    A. $\dfrac{4x^3}{y^5}$

    B. $\dfrac{4}{x^3 y^5}$

    C. $\dfrac{1}{4x^3 y^5}$

    D. $-4x^3 y^5$

Solution

Only y is raised to a negative power, so only y goes into the denominator. $4x^3 y^{-5} = \dfrac{4x^3}{y^5}$.

Answer: A

Example 7. Simplify $\left(5a^3b^7\right)^2$ using properties of exponents.

    A. $10a^6b^{14}$

    B. $10a^5b^9$

    C. $25a^5b^9$

    D. $25a^6b^{14}$

Solution

Raise each factor in the parentheses to the second power. Multiply the exponents if there are any. $\left(5a^3b^7\right)^2 = 5^2 \cdot a^6 \cdot b^{14} = 25a^6b^{14}$.

Answer: D

Example 8. Evaluate the expression $4x - 5y^3 + 9$ for $x = -3$ and $y = 2$.

Solution

Plug-in the values for x and y. It will often help to use parentheses when you do your substitutions.

$$= 4(-3) - 5(2)^3 + 9 = -12 - 5(8) + 9$$
$$= -12 - 40 + 9 = -52 + 9 = -43$$

Answer: –43

Practice: Simplifying

1. Which one of the following statements is false?

    A. $\sqrt[3]{50} > \sqrt{4}$

    B. $\sqrt{16} < \sqrt[3]{210}$

    C. $10^{\frac{1}{3}} < \sqrt{8}$

    D. $\sqrt[3]{120} > \sqrt{25}$

2. What is the solution to the equation $\sqrt{x} = 14$?

3. $2^3 \cdot 3^3$ is the same as

    A. 5^3

    B. 5^6

    C. 6^3

    D. 6^6

4. Which equation is false for all positive values of x?

    A. $x^3 = -x(x^2)$

    B. $\sqrt{x^4} = x^2$

    C. $x^2 = x \cdot x$

    D. $\sqrt{x^2} = x$

5. Which statement is NOT true?

    A. $3^3 < 47 < 4^3$

    B. $3(5^2) < 100 < 2(7^2)$

    C. $-1^2 < \left(\dfrac{1}{2}\right)^3 < (-1)^2$

    D. $5^3 < 130 < 12^2$

6. What is the value of the expression below?

$$8^2 + 3^3$$

    A. 25
    B. 83
    C. 91
    D. 108

7. What is the value of the expression below?

$$-1\left(4^2 - 4\right)$$

    A. -12
    B. -4
    C. -1
    D. 0

8. What is the value of the expression below?

$$(-1)^9 \left(3 \cdot 2^4\right)$$

    A. $-1,296$
    B. -48
    C. 48
    D. 1,296

9. A cube has a volume of 125 cubic centimeters. What is the length, in centimeters, of each edge of the cube?

10. What is the value of the expression below?

$$\left(3^2 - 2^2\right)\left(5^2 - 4^2\right)$$

A. 1
B. 4
C. 36
D. 45

11. What is the value of the expression below?

$$3\left(2^5 - 1\right)$$

A. 27
B. 28
C. 93

What is the value of the expression below?

below.

A. −14
B. 2
C. 4
D. 6

14. Evaluate $\dfrac{5(2x - 4y) - 2(3x + 4y)}{x + 7y}$ for $x = 3$ and $y = -1$.

15. Carol wants to evaluate the expression below using the order of operations.

$$3 + 18 \div 6 \cdot 2 \div \left(-3 + 4\right) + 1$$

Which of the following represents the correct value for this expression?

A. 8
B. 10
C. 13
D. 15

16. What is the value of the expression shown below?

$$|4 - 7 \cdot 2| - 5$$

A. 1
B. 5
C. 10
D. 17

17. What is the value of the expression below?

$$5 - 6|4 - 7|$$

A. −13
B. −3
C. 2
D. 13

18. A rational expression is shown below.

$$\frac{x^4 - x^2}{4}$$

What is the value of the expression when $x = 3$?

A. 12
B. 14
C. 16
D. 18

19. Suppose that a new operation is defined for all real numbers.
The rule for the new operation is given below.

$$a \,\square\, b = a^b + ab$$

For example: $2 \,\square\, 4 = 2^4 + 2 \cdot 4 = 16 + 8 = 24$

a. What is the value of $5 \,\square\, 3$? Show your work.

b. What is the value of $16 \,\square\, \dfrac{1}{2}$? Show your work.

c. If c is a real number, prove that $c \,\square\, 0 = 1$. Show your work.

Solutions to Practice: Simplifying

1. ~~A.~~ True because $\sqrt{4} = 2$, which is equal to $\sqrt[3]{8}$. Since $\sqrt[3]{50} > \sqrt[3]{8}$ then $\sqrt[3]{50} > \sqrt{4}$.
   ~~B.~~ True, because $\sqrt{16}$ is equal to 4, which is the same as $\sqrt[3]{64}$. The $\sqrt[3]{210}$ is greater than $\sqrt[3]{64}$ so the inequality is true.
   ~~C.~~ True, but these two values are much closer in value than those of choices A and B. $8^{\frac{1}{3}}$ is 2, so $10^{\frac{1}{3}}$ is still very close to 2. $\sqrt{8}$ is almost $\sqrt{9}$, which is 3. So, $10^{\frac{1}{3}}$ is closer to 2, and $\sqrt{8}$ is closer to 3.
   D. False, this is the correct answer. $\sqrt[3]{120}$ is less than $\sqrt[3]{125}$, which equals 5. Therefore, $\sqrt[3]{120}$ cannot be greater than $\sqrt{25}$, which equals 5.

   Answer: D

2. This question is asking: the square root of what number is 14? The answer is 196. To find the answer, calculate 14^2.

   Answer: B

3. The following rule of exponents applies to this question: $x^a \cdot y^a = (xy)^a$. Since the exponents are both 3, you can multiply the bases and keep the exponent the same: $2^3 \cdot 3^3 = (2 \cdot 3)^3 = 6^3$.

   Answer: C

4. A. False, this is the correct answer. $-x(x^2) = -x^3$ not x^3.
   ~~B.~~ True because $\sqrt{x^4} = x^2$ is true because $x^2 \cdot x^2 = x^4$.
   ~~C.~~ True because $x^2 = x \cdot x$ is true because of the rules of exponents.
   ~~D.~~ True because $\sqrt{x^2} = x$ is true because $x^1 \cdot x^1 = x^2$.

   Answer: A

5. ~~A.~~ True because $27 < 47 < 64$.
   B. False, this is the correct answer. Even though $100 > 75$, it is not less than 98.
   ~~C.~~ True. In choice C, it is important to understand the difference between -1^2 and $(-1)^2$. Using the order of operations on -1^2, you calculate the exponent first and then multiply that value by the negative. The value of -1^2 is -1. $(-1)^2$, however, is squaring the entire parentheses. This means $(-1)(-1) = 1$. Choice C is true because $-1 < \frac{1}{8} < 1$.
   ~~D.~~ True because $125 < 130 < 144$.

   Answer: B

6. $8^2 + 3^3 = 64 + 27 = 91$

Answer: C

7. Using the order of operations, $-1(4^2 - 4) = -1(16 - 4) = -1(12) = -12$.

Answer: A

8. $(-1)^9(3 \cdot 2^4) = (-1)(3 \cdot 16) = (-1)(48) = -48$

Answer: B

9. The volume of a cube is the length of the edge of the cube, cubed. Since the volume of the cube is 125 cubic centimeters, to find the edge, calculate the cube root of 125. $\sqrt[3]{125} = 5$.

Answer: 5 cm

10. $(3^2 - 2^2)(5^2 - 4^2) = (9 - 4)(25 - 16) = 5 \cdot 9 = 45$

Answer: D

11. $3(2^5 - 1) = 3(32 - 1) = 3 \cdot 31 = 93$

Answer: C

12. $\dfrac{2^4 - 2^3}{2^2} = \dfrac{16 - 8}{4} = \dfrac{8}{4} = 2$

Answer: A

13. $\dfrac{16 - 2(3 - 7)}{12 - 2^3} = \dfrac{16 - 2(-4)}{12 - 8} = \dfrac{16 + 8}{4} = \dfrac{24}{4} = 6$

Answer: D

14. $\dfrac{5(2(3) - 4(-1)) - 2(3(3) + 4(-1))}{(3) + 7(-1)} = \dfrac{5(6 + 4) - 2(9 - 4)}{3 - 7} = \dfrac{5(10) - 2(5)}{-4} = \dfrac{50 - 10}{-4} =$

$\dfrac{40}{-4} = -10$

Answer: -10

15. $3 + 18 \div 6 \cdot 2 \div (-3 + 4) + 1 = 3 + 18 \div 6 \cdot 2 \div 1 + 1 = 3 + 3 \cdot 2 \div 1 + 1 =$

$3 + 3 \cdot 2 \div 1 + 1 = 3 + 6 \div 1 + 1 = 3 + 6 + 1 = 10$

Answer: B

16. $|4 - 7 \cdot 2| - 5 = |4 - 14| - 5 = |-10| - 5 = 10 - 5 = 5$

    Answer: B

17. $5 - 6|4 - 7| = 5 - 6|-3| = 5 - 6 \cdot 3 = 5 - 18 = -13$

    Answer: A

18. $\dfrac{3^4 - 3^2}{4} = \dfrac{81 - 9}{4} = \dfrac{72}{4} = 18$

    Answer: D

19. a. $5 \,\square\, 3 = 5^3 + 5 \cdot 3 = 125 + 15 = 140$

    Answer: 140

    b. Recall that raising a number to the one half power is the same as taking the square root.

    $$16 \,\square\, \frac{1}{2} = 16^{\frac{1}{2}} + 16 \cdot \frac{1}{2} = \sqrt{16} + 8 = 4 + 8 = 12$$

    Answer: 12

    c. Recall that any number raised to the power of zero is equal to 1.
    $c \,\square\, 0 = c^0 + c \cdot 0 = 1 + 0 = 1$

    Answer: 1

Ratios, Proportions, and Percents

Ratios

- A **ratio** is a comparison of two quantities in the form of a fraction. The ratio can be written in any of the following forms: $\dfrac{a}{b}$, $a:b$, a to b. A ratio should be reduced. For example, if there are 10 boys and 15 girls in a room, you can say that the ratio of boys to girls is $\dfrac{10}{15} = \dfrac{2}{3}$. You could also say that the ratio of boys to total people in the room is $\dfrac{10}{25} = \dfrac{2}{5}$.

Proportions

- A **proportion** is an equation in which two ratios are set equal to each other. For example, if $\frac{2}{5}$ is equivalent to the ratio of 6 to a number, you can set up the following proportion:

$$\frac{2}{5} = \frac{6}{x}$$

Since the numerator of 2 is multiplied by 3 to get the numerator of 6, you can do the same to the denominator. Multiply 5 by 3 to get 15.

$$\frac{2}{5} = \frac{2(3)}{5(3)} = \frac{6}{15}$$

To check that ratios are equivalent, they must reduce to the same fraction. $\frac{6}{15}$ reduces to $\frac{2}{5}$.

- Another method of solving proportions is **cross multiplying**. This is useful in more complicated proportions for which you cannot find the common multiplier. The bottom right number multiplies with the top left number and the top right number multiplies with the bottom left. The products are set equal to each other as follows:

$$\frac{2}{5} = \frac{7}{x} \longrightarrow \quad \frac{2}{5} = \frac{7}{x}$$

$$2x = 35$$
$$x = 17.5$$

Percents

- **Percents** are a fraction "out of 100." For example, 30% means $\frac{30}{100}$. If asked to find a percent of a number, you can change the percent to a fraction or decimal and multiply it by the number. For example, 12% of $50 = \frac{12}{100} \cdot 50 = 6$ or $0.12 \cdot 50 = 6$.

  You can also find the percent of a number by setting up a proportion. Consider each side of the proportion as a ratio of *part to whole*. For example, to answer the question, "what is 30% of 50?" set up the proportion: $\frac{30}{100} = \frac{x}{50}$. Solving, $x = 15$.

- To convert a **fraction** to a **percent**, multiply the fraction by 100. For example, converting $\frac{1}{5}$ to a percent looks like: $\frac{1}{5} \cdot 100 = 20\%$.

Percent Increase and Decrease

- Suppose you wanted to decrease a number x by 25%. You could either calculate 25% of x and then subtract that from the original value, or you can just take 75% of the original value. They will result in the same number because $1x - 0.25x = 0.75x$. Likewise, to increase a number x by 25%, you can just compute 125% of the original value because $1x + 0.25x = 1.25x$.

A common error in dealing with percents is the misconception that you can decrease a number by a certain percent and then increase by the same percent to return to the original number. For example, suppose you begin with the number 100. If you subtract 20% from 100, which equals 20, your result is 80. Now add 20% of 80, which equals 16, to 80 and you end up with 96, not 100! This happens because 20% of 80 is less than 20% of 100.

• Suppose you wanted to repeatedly decrease a number by 25%, perhaps over a certain period of time, let's say 5 years. A shortcut approach is to multiply your number by 0.75 (a 25% decrease) for a total of five times. Your solution will look like:

$$0.75 \cdot 0.75 \cdot 0.75 \cdot 0.75 \cdot 0.75(x) = 0.75^5(x)$$

Examples: Ratios, Proportions, and Percents

Example 1. Oren collected data about the types of sports that juniors and seniors at his high school play after school. The following table shows the data that he collected.

Type of Sport	Number of Juniors	Number of Seniors
Basketball	301	136
Soccer	203	167
Tennis	68	121
Total	**572**	**424**

Based on the data in the table, which of the following is closest to the percent of juniors and seniors combined who play tennis?

A. 19%
B. 29%
C. 37%
D. 44%

Solution

There are a total of $68 + 121 = 189$ juniors and seniors playing tennis out of a total of $572 + 424 = 996$ juniors and seniors in the school. As a percent this is $\frac{189}{996} \cdot 100\%$. With a little bit of rounding and simplifying, you could rewrite this expression as $\frac{190}{1000} \cdot 100 = \frac{190}{10} = 19\%$.

Answer: A

Example 2. A computer is purchased for $3,000. Its value decreases each year according to the following schedule:

- The computer's value decreases by 35% in the first year.
- After the first year, its value decreases by 20% each year.

   a. What is the value of the computer at the end of one year? Explain or show how you found your answer.

   b. During which year will the computer's value decrease to less than half its original price? Explain or show how you found your answer.

   c. Suppose the value of another computer, which also costs $3,000, decreases at the rate of 25% each year. Which computer would have the greater value 3 years after it was purchased? Explain or show how you found your answer.

Solution:

   a. 35% of 3,000 is calculated by multiplying $0.35 \cdot 3,000 = 1,050$. The computer's value decreased in the first year by $1,050 so that its value at the end of the year was $1,950. You could also have answered this question by computing $0.65 \cdot 3,000 = \$1,950$.

   Answer: $1,950

   b. Compute the amount of decrease for the second year: $0.20 \cdot 1,950 = 390$. Its value at the end of the second year is $1,950 - \$390 = \$1,560$. Repeating the process for the third year, decrease the computer's value by $0.20 \cdot 1,560 = \$312$. The computer's value at the end of the third year is $1,248. Once the price is below $1,500, it is less than half the original price so this occurs during the third year.

     You could also have answered this question by computing $0.8 \cdot \$1,950 = \$1,560$ for the second year, and $0.8 \cdot \$1,560 = \$1,248$ for the third year.

   Answer: Third year

   c. We know from part b that the first computer has a value of $1,248 at the end of the third year. Now let's calculate the second computer:

$$0.25 \cdot 3,000 = 750 \rightarrow 3000 - 750 = 2,250.$$

At the end of the first year, the value is $2,250. For the second year, compute:

$$0.25 \cdot 2,250 = 562.50 \rightarrow 2250 - 562.50 = 1,687.50.$$

At the end of year two, the value is $1,687.50. Year three, compute:

$$0.25 \cdot 1,687.50 = 421.88 \rightarrow 1,687.50 - 421.88 = 1,265.62.$$

At the end of the third year the value of the second computer is $1,265.62, which is greater than the other computer. You could also have found this value by computing:

$$0.75^3 \cdot \$3,000 = \$1,265.62.$$

   Answer: Second computer

Example 3. Michele made 32 cups of fruit salad for a party. She mixed bananas and strawberries into the salad in a ratio of 5 : 3. Michele tasted the fruit salad and found that the banana taste was too strong so she added 4 cups of strawberries. What was the new ratio of bananas to strawberries?

    A. 5 : 3
    B. 5 : 5
    C. 5 : 4
    D. 5 : 6

Solution

The ratio of bananas to total fruit is $\dfrac{5}{8}$. Since there are 32 cups of fruit salad, to find the number of cups of bananas, set up the proportion: $\dfrac{5}{8} = \dfrac{x}{32}$ and cross multiply. $\dfrac{5}{8} = \dfrac{x}{32} \rightarrow 8x = 160 \rightarrow x = 20$. Originally, there were 20 cups of bananas and 12 cups of strawberries. Now, 4 more cups of strawberries have been added and the new ratio of bananas to strawberries is $\dfrac{20}{16} = \dfrac{5}{4}$.

Answer: C

Example 4. Tania took a test that had a total of 250 questions. There were 100 multiple-choice questions and 150 true-false questions.

a. There was a total of 200 points on the test. Each question was worth the same amount. What is the value of each question? Show or explain how you obtained your answer.

b. Suppose that 60% is the cutoff point for passing the test. What is the minimum number of questions a person can get right and still pass the test? Show or explain how you obtained your answer.

c. If Tania answers all of the multiple-choice questions correctly, what is the minimum percent of true-false questions that Tania must answer correctly in order to receive a score of 80% on the test? Show or explain how you obtained your answer.

Solution

a. $\dfrac{200\, pts}{250\, questions} = \dfrac{4}{5}\dfrac{pts}{question} = 0.8\dfrac{pts}{question}$

Each question is worth 0.8 of a point since $200 \div 250 = 0.8$.

Answer: 0.8

b. 60% of 250 questions $0.60 \cdot 250 = 150$. The minimum number of questions a person can get right is 150 questions.

Answer: 150

c. To receive a score of 80%, the minimum number of questions a person should get right is $0.80 \cdot 250 = 200$. Since Tania answered all of the multiple-choice questions correctly, she has already answered 100 questions. This means she has 100 questions left from the true-false questions that she must answer correctly in order to receive an 80%. Since there are 150 true-false questions, Tania must answer a minimum of $\frac{100}{150} = \frac{2}{3} \cdot 100 = 66\frac{2}{3}\%$ of the questions. Rounding up that would be approximately 67% of the questions.

Answer: 67%

Practice: Ratios, Proportions, and Percents

1. Kate jogs 9 miles in 2 hours. At this rate, how long will it take Kate to jog 6 miles?
    A. 1 hour

    B. $1\frac{1}{4}$ hours

    C. $1\frac{1}{3}$ hours

    D. $1\frac{2}{3}$ hours

2. Based on the graph, which is the best estimate of the percent of students choosing onion as their favorite pizza topping?

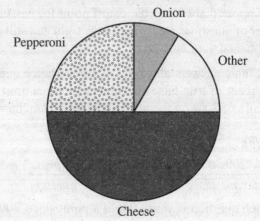

Student's Choices for Pizza Toppings

    A. 8%
    B. 16%
    C. 32%
    D. 64%

3. An item is on sale for 50% off of its original price. What percent increase is needed return the sale item back to its original price?
   A. 25%
   B. 50%
   C. 75%
   D. 100%

4. Adam paid $24,000 for his new car.

   a. Adam's father predicts that the car's value will decrease by approximately $2,200 per year. If he is correct, how many years after the date of purchase will the car be less than half the value of the original price? Show or explain how you obtained your answer.

   b. Adam's sister predicts that the value of the car will decrease by 12% each year. If she is correct, what will the car's value be after one year of purchase?

   c. Suppose Adam's sister is correct and the value of the car does depreciate (decrease in value) by 12% each year. At the end of how many years from the date of purchase will its value first be half its original cost? Show or explain how you obtained your answer.

5. David noticed that many of the students at his school had freckles on their faces. He randomly chose 20 students in his school and found that 6 had freckles. If David's sample is representative, which of the following is closest to the number of the 1,900 students at David's school who have freckles?
   A. 30
   B. 500
   C. 570
   D. 600

6. A recent mall survey showed that approximately 55% of the people surveyed prefer chocolate ice cream over vanilla. If 358 people were surveyed, which number best represents the number of people who responded to preferring chocolate.
   A. 100
   B. 150
   C. 200
   D. 250

Solutions to Practice: Ratios, Proportions, and Percents

1. If Kate jogs 9 miles in 2 hours, set up a proportion to find out how many hours it will take her to jog 6 miles.

$$\frac{9 \text{ mi}}{2 \text{ hr}} = \frac{6 \text{ mi}}{x \text{ hr}}$$

Cross multiply to solve for x: $9x = 12 \rightarrow x = \frac{4}{3} = 1\frac{1}{3}$ hours.

Answer: C

2. If you divide the circle into 4 equal parts, each part would be equivalent to 25% of the circle. For example, 25% of the students chose pepperoni as their favorite topping. The section shaded for onion looks like approximately a third of one of those 25% quadrants, so the best approximation is 8%.

   Answer: A

3. **Choose your own number** to solve this problem. Suppose an item's original cost had been $100. If it is on sale for 50% off, the new price is $50. In order to increase the item to its original price, it will need to increase by $50, which is the price that it is presently at. The percent increase is 100%.

   Answer: D

4. a. At the end of the first year, the value of the car is $24,000 - 2,200 = \$21,800$.
   At the end of the second year, the value of the car is $21,800 - 2,200 = \$19,600$.
   At the end of the third year, the value of the car is $19,600 - 2,200 = \$17,400$.
   At the end of the fourth year, the value of the car is $17,400 - 2,200 = \$15,200$.
   At the end of the fifth year, the value of the car is $15,200 - 2,200 = \$13,000$.
   At the end of the sixth year, the value of the car is $13,000 - 2,200 = \$10,800$.
   Once the value of the car is less than $12,000, it is less than half its original value. This occurs during the sixth year. You can also set up an algebraic equation to solve this problem: $24,000 - 2,200x = 12,000$, where x represents the number of years until the value will be equal to $12,000. If you solve this equation for x, you will get an answer of approximately 5.5 years.

   Answer: 6 years

   b. Instead of finding 12% of $24,000 and then subtracting it, you can go straight to finding 88% of $24,000 to find this answer: $0.88 \cdot 24,000 = \$21,120$.

   Answer: $21,120

   c. At the end of the first year, the value of the car is $0.88 \cdot 24,000 = \$21,120$.
   At the end of the second year, the value of the car is $0.88 \cdot 21,120 = \$18,585.60$.
   At the end of the third year, the value of the car is $0.88 \cdot 18,585.60 = \$16,355.32$.
   At the end of the fourth year, the value of the car is $0.88 \cdot 16,355.32 = \$14,392.68$.
   At the end of the fifth year, the value of the car is $.88 \cdot 14,392.68 = \$12,665.55$.
   At the end of the sixth year, the value of the car is $.88 \cdot 12,665.55 = \$11,145.68$.
   Once the value of the car is less than $12,000, it is less than half its original value. This occurs during the sixth year. You could also arrive at this value by finding the value of n for which: $0.88^n \cdot (\$24,000) < \$12,000$.

   Answer: 6 years

5. David found that $\dfrac{6}{20}$ kids have freckles, which is equivalent to $\dfrac{3}{10} = 0.3$ or 30%.
   30% of 1,900 students is $0.3 \cdot 1,900 = 570$.

   Answer: C

6. The answer choice must be a little bit more than half of 358 people. Half of 358 is 179. The closest answer choice above that is 200, answer choice C. The exact answer is $0.55 \cdot 358 = 197$.

Answer: C

Estimation

The MCAS requires you to estimate or approximate values of all different types, often without your calculator. These questions test your basic number sense and reasoning ability. Sometimes you will be asked to interpret data off a chart or graph.

Approximating Square Roots

- Without a calculator, you should be able to approximate the value of a square root. To do this, ask yourself, "What are the two closest perfect squares that the number is between, and which is it closer to?" For example, to approximate $\sqrt{40}$ you know that it is between $\sqrt{36}$ and $\sqrt{49}$, which are the numbers 6 and 7. Since 40 is closer to 36, $\sqrt{40}$ is closer to 6 than 7. It is a good idea to memorize the following approximations:

$$\sqrt{2} \approx 1.4 \quad \sqrt{3} \approx 1.7 \quad \sqrt{5} \approx 2.2$$

Rounding Numbers to Calculate

- If a question asks you to approximate an answer, it is important to look at the answer choices. If the difference between the numbers in the answer choices is great, rounding becomes very helpful! Take, for example, the following problem.

  Without a calculator approximate $(103 \div 11) + (4105 \cdot 3.98)$.

  A. 600
  B. 6,000
  C. 16,000
  D. 60,000

It is clear that a little rounding won't hurt. Change the problem to the following: $(100 \div 10) + (4000 \cdot 4) = 10 + 16,000 = 16,010$ or answer choice C. It would have been tedious, and unnecessary, to calculate this exact answer by hand!

Approximating with Higher Powers

- If a question asks you to approximate an answer raised to a power, it is important to look at your answers. For example, suppose you were asked to approximate $3(12)^4$. A very rough approximation would be: $3 \cdot 10^4 = 3 \cdot 10,000 = 30,000$. You know that 30,000 is an underestimate because 10 is less than 12. If the answer choices are A. 60, B. 600, C. 6,000, or D. 60,000, it is clear that D must be the answer because it is the only choice greater than 30,000.

Examples: Estimation

Example 1. The expression below was used to approximate a time in hours.

$$\sqrt{6^2 + 7^2}$$

Which of the following is closest to the approximate time in hours?

A. 9.2 hours
B. 10 hours
C. 10.5 hours
D. 11.2 hours

Solution

$\sqrt{6^2 + 7^2} = \sqrt{36 + 49} = \sqrt{85}$. Because $\sqrt{85}$ is a little bit greater than $\sqrt{81}$, which equals 9, the best answer choice is A. Ten hours is too large because that would be $\sqrt{100}$. This eliminates the other answer choices.

Answer: A

Example 2. Which of the following numbers is closest to the value of the expression below?

$$\left(703 \div 9\right) + \left(2105 \cdot 2.98\right)$$

A. 63
B. 630
C. 6,300
D. 63,000

Solution

The answer choices are so far apart from each other that rounding here will not hurt! $\left(700 \div 10\right) + \left(2,000 \cdot 3\right) = 70 + 6,000 = 6,070$. The closest choice is C.

Answer: C

Example 3. A cube has a volume of 68 in.^{3}. Which of the following is closest to the length of the edge of the cube?

A. 3
B. 4
C. 5
D. 6

Solution

The volume of a cube is the length of the edge, raised to the third power. This formula is on the MCAS reference sheet. Since the volume of the cube is 68 cubic inches, to find the edge, look for a number that, when cubed, gives you something close to 68. **Using your answer choices,** $4^3 = 64$, which is very close to 68. The best answer is choice B, since 3^3 is only 27 and 5^3 is 125, which is too large.

Answer: B

Example 4. For which of the following values of c and d is the following inequality true?

$$c < \sqrt{23} < d$$

A. $c = 3.5$ and $d = 4.0$
B. $c = 4.0$ and $d = 4.5$
C. $c = 4.5$ and $d = 5.0$
D. $c = 5.0$ and $d = 5.5$

Solution

You know that $\sqrt{23}$ is greater than $\sqrt{16}$, which is equal to 4. This eliminates answer choice A. You also know $\sqrt{23}$ is less than $\sqrt{25}$, which is equal to 5. This eliminates answer choice D. Since $\sqrt{23}$ is closer to $\sqrt{25}$ than $\sqrt{16}$, $\sqrt{23}$ must have a value closer to 5. Therefore, answer choice C is correct.

Answer: C

Example 5. Which is closest to $2 \cdot 11^4$?
A. 30
B. 300
C. 3,000
D. 30,000

Solution

Again, the answer choices are so far apart that rounding won't hurt here! $2 \cdot 10^4 = 2 \cdot 10,000 = 20,000$. The closest answer choice is D. Even though the actual answer is 29,282, you can still find the correct answer choice by rounding.

Answer: D

Practice: Estimation

1. Between which of the following two integers does $5\sqrt{17}$ lie on the number line?
   A. 18 and 19
   B. 19 and 20
   C. 20 and 21
   D. 21 and 22

2. $3\sqrt{10}$ is between
   A. 7 and 9
   B. 9 and 11
   C. 11 and 12
   D. 12 and 14

3. Which of the following is closest to the value of $\dfrac{10 - \sqrt{14}}{3}$?

    A. 1.04
    B. 2.09
    C. 6.26
    D. 12.57

4. The following expression represents the amount of money in Doug's saving's account.

$$3{,}000\left(1 + \frac{0.03}{2}\right)^{4}$$

Which of the following is closest to the amount of money in Doug's saving's account?

    A. $3,180
    B. $3,200
    C. $3,220
    D. $3,240

5. Diagonal $\overline{AC}$ of regular hexagon $ABCDEF$ is shown in the figure below. (A regular polygon has all sides congruent. See the section titled Polygons in Chapter 6 for more information.) The length of each side of the hexagon is 4 units.

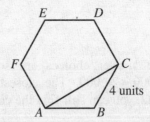

In a regular hexagon, the ratio of the length of a side to the length of a diagonal is shown below.

$$1 : \sqrt{3}$$

   a. Based on the ratio above, the length of diagonal $\overline{AC}$ is $4\sqrt{3}$ units. Using your calculator, approximate $4\sqrt{3}$ to the nearest tenth of a unit. Show or explain how you got your answer.

   b. Show or explain how an approximation of $4\sqrt{3}$, to the nearest tenth of a unit, can be made without the use of a calculator.

   c. Using your answer from part a, approximate the perimeter of $\triangle ABC$ to the nearest tenth of a unit. Show or explain how you got your answer.

   d. Is the exact perimeter of $\triangle ABC$ greater than, less than, or equal to your approximation in part c? Explain your reasoning.

6. The value of $\dfrac{62.87 \cdot 309}{6.13}$ is closest to

   A. 30
   B. 300
   C. 3,000
   D. 30,000

7. An ice cream store surveyed 300 customers. Each customer voted for his or her favorite of three flavors: chocolate, vanilla, and mint. The bar graph shows the results.

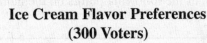

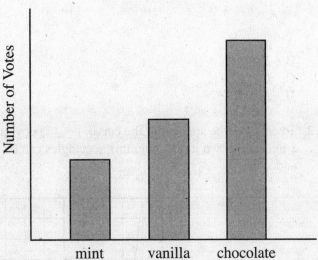

Based on the data in the graph, which of the following is the best estimate of the number of customers who voted for vanilla ice cream?

   A. 20
   B. 30
   C. 90
   D. 150

8. Which of the following is closest to $\sqrt{72}$?
   A. 7.9
   B. 8.5
   C. 8.8
   D. 9.2

9. A square has an area of 90 square centimeters. Which of the following measures is closest to the length of one its sides?
   A. 8.9 cm
   B. 9.1 cm
   C. 9.5 cm
   D. 9.7 cm

10. Which of the following numbers is closest to the value of the expression below?

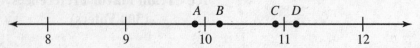

$$6.2\left(\frac{3.7 \cdot 2{,}101}{1{,}009}\right)$$

    A. 5
    B. 50
    C. 500
    D. 5,000

11. Which of the following points on the number line is closest to $\sqrt{125}$?

    A. *A*
    B. *B*
    C. *C*
    D. *D*

★ 12. To estimate the area under the curve $y = x^2$ between $x = 0$ and $x = 4$ bounded by the x-axis (as shown in the diagram), rectangles can be drawn within the region and then added up.

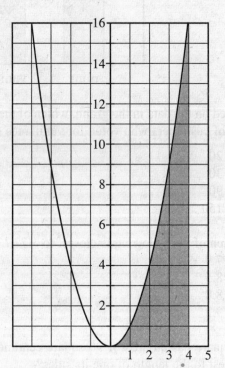

a. Melanie drew three rectangles I, II, and III as shown in the diagram below and added up their areas. What is the approximate area under the curve that Melanie should have calculated? Show or explain how you got your answer.

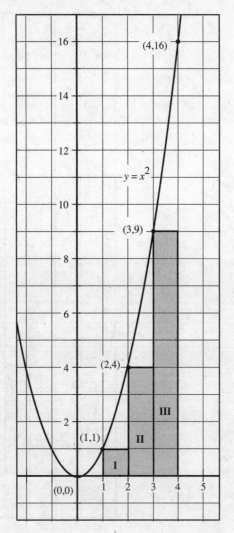

b. Susan drew four rectangles I, II, III, and IV as shown in the diagram below and added up their areas. What is the approximate area under the curve that Susan should have calculated? Show or explain how you got your answer.

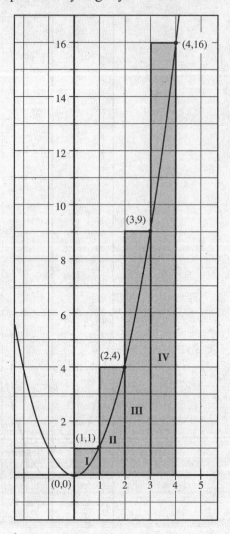

c. Explain the difference between Melanie and Susan's approximations. Based on the diagrams, why should Melanie and Susan have expected such results before calculating?

d. Describe a strategy that Melanie and Susan could use to approximate the area under the curve more precisely. In other words, how can they find an answer that is even closer to the exact area?

Solutions to Practice: Estimation

1. $\sqrt{17}$ is only a little bit greater than $\sqrt{16}$, which is equal to 4. Since $5 \cdot 4 = 20$, $5\sqrt{17}$ should be between 20 and 21.

Answer: C

2. $\sqrt{10}$ is only a little bit greater than $\sqrt{9}$, which is equal to 3. Since $3 \cdot 3 = 9$, $3\sqrt{10}$ should be between 9 and 11.

Answer: B

3. A slight underestimate of this problem would be to change the $\sqrt{14}$ to $\sqrt{16}$.

$\dfrac{10 - \sqrt{14}}{3} \approx \dfrac{10 - \sqrt{16}}{3} = \dfrac{10 - 4}{3} = \dfrac{6}{3} = 2$. The answer should be a little more than 2.

Answer: B

4. This is a calculator question, so you can punch the expression into your calculator to find the answer. It is an important test-taking strategy that you be familiar with the options on your **calculator and how to use them**. Be sure to use parentheses when necessary. The answer is $3,184, which is closest to answer choice A.

Answer: A

5. a. The calculator says 6.9282032 . . . . Since you are supposed to approximate to the nearest tenth, the questionable digit is the 9. Does it stay as a 9 or round up? So, should the answer be 6.9 or 7.0? The digit to the right of the 9 determines the answer. If it is a 5 or higher you round up and if it is a 4 or lower you keep it the same. Because it is a 2, you keep it the same. The answer is 6.9.

Answer: 6.9

b. $\sqrt{3}$ is approximately 1.7 and $1.7 \cdot 4 = 6.8$.

Answer: 6.8

c. $4 + 4 + 6.9 = 14.9$

Answer: 14.9

d. The exact perimeter is greater because in part a, we rounded down to find the diagonal approximation of 6.9.

Answer: greater

6. Round and simplify: $\dfrac{60 \cdot 300}{6} = 10 \cdot 300 = 3,000$.

Answer: C

7. Divide the mint graph into two equal squares, the vanilla into 3 squares, and the chocolate into 5. This is a total of 10 squares. If each square represents 30 people, this means 90 people voted for vanilla.

Answer: C

8. $\sqrt{72} = \sqrt{36 \cdot 2} = 6\sqrt{2}$. $\sqrt{2}$ is approximately 1.4 and $6 \cdot 1.4 = 8.4$.
The best answer choice is B.

Answer: B

9. The area of a square is the length of its side, squared. This means that the length of a side is the square root of its area. This will be discussed more in Chapter 6.

$$area = side^2 \xrightarrow{\;\;or\;\;} side = \sqrt{area}$$

The side of the square is $\sqrt{90}$. This is between $\sqrt{81} < \sqrt{90} < \sqrt{100}$ so $9 < \sqrt{90} < 10$. This eliminates answer choice A. Since 90 is roughly in the middle of both 81 and 100, and not significantly closer to either one, your answer will be roughly in the middle of 9 and 10, making answer choice C your best estimate.

Answer: C

10. Round and simplify: $6\left(\dfrac{4 \cdot 2{,}000}{1{,}000}\right) = 6(4 \cdot 2) = 6 \cdot 8 = 48$

Answer: B

11. $\sqrt{125}$ is a little bit greater than $\sqrt{121}$, which equals 11. The only possible answer that is greater than 11 is D.

Answer: D

12. a. Rectangle I has a base of length 1 and a height of 1 as well. The height is the y-coordinate of the point (1, 1). The area of Rectangle I is $1 \cdot 1 = 1$ unit^2. Rectangle II has a base of length 1 and a height of 4. The height is the y-coordinate of the point (2, 4). The area of Rectangle II is $1 \cdot 4 = 4$ unit^2. Rectangle III has a base of length 1 and a height of 9. The height is the y-coordinate of the point (3, 9). The area of Rectangle III is $1 \cdot 9 = 9$ unit^2. The sum of these three rectangles is $1 + 4 + 9 = 14$ unit^2.

Answer: 14 unit^2

b. Rectangle I has a base of length 1 and a height of 1 as well. The height is the y-coordinate of the point (1, 1). The area of Rectangle I is $1 \cdot 1 = 1$ unit^2. Rectangle II has a base of length 1 and a height of 4. The height is the y-coordinate of the point (2, 4). The area of Rectangle II is $1 \cdot 4 = 4$ unit^2. Rectangle III has a base of length 1 and a height of 9. The height is the y-coordinate of the point (3, 9). The area of Rectangle III is $1 \cdot 9 = 9$ unit^2. Rectangle IV has a base of length 1 and a height of 16. The height is the y-coordinate of the point (4, 16). The area of Rectangle IV is $1 \cdot 16 = 16$ unit^2. The sum of these four rectangles is $1 + 4 + 9 + 16 = 30$ unit^2.

Answer: 30 unit^2

c. Melanie's approximation is less than Susan's. This is to be expected because looking at the diagrams you should expect Melanie's to be an underestimate and Susan's to be an overestimate. Melanie's rectangles are all drawn underneath the curve and Susan's are drawn so that they stick out above the curve. Also Melanie only computed the areas of three rectangles; Susan computed the areas of four.

d. They could draw more rectangles that have a smaller base on the x-axis. This would improve the accuracy. Another option is to average their answers.

Problems Involving Money

The MCAS often asks questions using calculations that involve the use of money. It is important to pay attention to any conversions that have to be made in these problems.

Consider the following example:

If a person is paid $5 for every 30 minutes of work, how much will the person get paid for 10 hours of work?

Underline the key numbers and units in the problem:

If a person is paid <u>$5</u> for every <u>30 minutes</u> of work, how much will the person get paid for <u>10 hours</u> of work?

In this question, you are given information in minutes and then asked a question in hours. You must recognize that $5 for 30 minutes means $10 for 60 minutes, which is 1 hour. Solving, you get: $10 · 10 = $100 for 10 hours.

Next look at the following conversion question:

Alex went to the hardware store to buy <u>60 feet</u> of a garden hose. The hose costs <u>$1.50 per yard</u>. How much money does Alex need to buy the hose?

In order to answer this question, you must first convert the 60 feet to yards (3 feet = 1 yard). $60 \div 3 = 20$, so there are 20 yards in 60 feet. Since the hose costs $1.50 per yard, that means the hose costs $20 \cdot \$1.50 = \$30.00$.

An interesting money question is one that involves a fixed cost plus an additional charge. For example, a phone company might charge $25 a month plus $0.10 for every minute that the phone is used for the month. Or, a rental car might cost $150 for the week and $0.05 for every mile over 200 miles driven. The $25 and the $150 are the fixed costs. This relationship can be expressed with a linear equation. You can often solve these questions by setting up equations or tables.

Let's look at the phone company question:

A phone company charges $25 a month plus $0.10 for every minute that the phone is used for the month. How much will it cost Kevin if he talks on the phone for a total of 3 hours and 32 minutes for the month?

Convert 3 hours to 180 minutes and determine Kevin's total time: $180 + 32 = 212$ minutes. This means that the additional charge beyond the fixed cost is $\$0.10 \cdot 212 = \$21.20$. Add $21.20 to the fixed cost of $25 and the total charge for the month is $46.20.

A linear equation can also be set up where c represents cost in dollars and m represents the number of minutes used: $c = 25 + 0.10m$. Replace m with the number of minutes used to find the cost. Writing this equation is also helpful for an additional question such as:

Suppose Kevin's phone bill is $51, how many minutes did he talk on the phone?

Plug 51 into the equation for c and solve for m: $51 = 25 + 0.10m \rightarrow 26 = 0.10m \rightarrow m = 260$.

Kevin spoke 260 minutes, which is the equivalent of 4 hours and 20 minutes. Without an equation, you could go through the same process. First subtract the fixed cost from 51, then divide the result by 0.10.

For further work on fixed-cost equations see the section titled Linear Functions in Chapter 5. These are just some examples of the many types of word problems that involve money. Before you solve these problems, read them carefully, then make any necessary conversions and proceed. Don't be intimidated by word problems. They usually involve calculations that are logical, real-world examples. You can do it!

Examples: Problems Involving Money

Example 1. Bob gets paid $24.50 per hour for mowing lawns. If he is able to mow one lawn in approximately 45 minutes, which of the following is closest to the amount that he is being paid to mow one lawn.

A. $12
B. $16
C. $18
D. $22

Solution

Round Bob's hourly wage to $24. This means that he gets paid $6 for 15 minutes of work and $18 for 45 minutes of work.

Answer: C

Example 2. A bicycle shop has bicycles available for rent. The rental charge includes a $25 initial fee plus $6 for each day that the bike is rented.

a. What is the cost of renting a bike for 2 days? Show or explain how you obtained your answer.

b. What is the cost of renting a bike for 14 days? Show or explain how you obtained your answer.

c. Bill and his friend plan to rent one bike for 14 days and to share the cost equally. How much will each of them save by renting the bike together for the 14 days rather than renting the bike for 7 days each?

Solution

a. The fixed cost is $25.00 plus an additional $6.00 for each day. For 2 days, this yields the following equation: $25 + (6 \cdot 2) = 25 + 12 = \$37$.

Answer: $37

b. Similar to part a, for 14 days this gives us the following equation: $25 + (6 \cdot 14) = 25 + 84 = \$109$.

Answer: \$109

c. If they had each rented the bike for 7 days, they would have each paid $25 + (7 \cdot 6) = 25 + 42 = \$67$. Instead, they will split the \$109 (from part b), so each person will pay \$54.50. Each person saves $67 - 54.5 = \$12.50$.

Answer: \$12.50

Practice: Problems Involving Money

1. Elana charges \$7.50 an hour when she babysits. Which of the following is closest to the number of hours Elana will have to babysit if she is saving to buy a \$145 CD player?
   A. 5 hours
   B. 10 hours
   C. 15 hours
   D. 20 hours

2. Zach's motorcycle averages about 46 miles per gallon of gasoline. If gas prices range from \$2.20 to \$2.40 a gallon, which of the following is closest to the amount of money Zach would spend on gas for an 1,800 mile road trip this summer?
   A. \$80
   B. \$90
   C. \$100
   D. \$110

3. Charlie plans to spend \$5 at the candy store. The items he will buy are listed below.

   - 3 king size lollipops at \$0.35 each
   - 2 chocolate bars at \$0.65 each
   - $\frac{1}{2}$ pound of gummy bears at \$4.10 per pound
   - as many gum balls as possible at \$.05 each

   If Charlie cannot spend more than his \$5, how many gum balls can he buy?
   A. 12
   B. 14
   C. 16
   D. 18

4. Juanita's cell phone plan charges $50 a month for the first 300 minutes and $0.40 a minute for each additional minute over the first 300 minutes that she talks on the phone. If Juanita's phone bill is $110 for the month, how many total minutes did Juanita talk on the phone?

   A. 300
   B. 360
   C. 400
   D. 450

5. Tickets to an IMAX movie cost $8.00 per ticket for general admission and $5.50 per ticket for groups of 12 or more. Two groups of people, each with a different number of people, each pay $88.00. How many people were in each group?

Solutions to Practice: Problems Involving Money

1. If Elana charges $7.50 an hour, then in 2 hours she makes $15. In 20 hours she will make $150, which is close to the desired $145 CD player.

   Answer: D

2. Zach will use $\dfrac{1,800}{46} \approx 39$ gallons of gas on his trip. At the least, the cost will be $39 \cdot 2.20 = \$85.80$, and at most the cost will be $39 \cdot 2.40 = \$93.60$. Both of these amounts are closest to answer choice B.

   Answer: B

3. The total cost of the lollipops is $3 \cdot 0.35 = \$1.05$.
   The total cost of the chocolate bars is $2 \cdot 0.65 = \$1.30$.
   The total cost of the gummy bears is $\dfrac{1}{2} \cdot 4.10 = \$2.05$.
   The sum of the above items is $1.05 + 1.30 + 2.05 = \$4.40$. Since Charlie has $5 to spend, he has $0.60 left to spend on gum balls at $0.05 each: $60 \div 5 = 12$.

   Answer: A

4. Subtract the fixed cost of $50 from $110 to find out her charge for additional minutes. She was charged $110 - \$50 = \$60$ in additional minutes. Since each additional minute costs $0.40, compute the number of minutes she used by dividing: $\$60 \div \$0.40 = 150$ minutes. Add this to the first 300 minutes she used, for a total of $300 + 150 = 450$ minutes. Because this is an example of a fixed-rate problem, you can also set up a linear equation: $c = 50 + 0.40m$, where c represents cost and m represents minutes over 300. Since you know that the cost is $110, plug that into the equation for c. $110 = 50 + 0.40m \rightarrow 60 = 0.40m \rightarrow m = 150$. There are 150 additional minutes over the 300, so Juanita's total minutes were $300 + 150 = 450$ minutes.

   Answer: D

5. The general admission is $8 for groups that are less than 12 people. If a group of 11 people attended the movies, it would cost $11 \cdot 8 = \$88$. However, dividing 88 by 5.5, you can find the other answer. If a group of 16 people attended the movies at the reduced rate of $5.50, the cost would also be $16 \cdot 5.50 = \$88$.

Answer: 11 and 16

| Chapter 5 | **Patterns, Relations, and Algebra** |

Algebraic Expressions

- In algebra, a variable is a letter used in place of an unknown number. A number in front of a variable is called a coefficient. The operation between a coefficient and a variable is multiplication. You can add the same variables together using their coefficients, as shown below. Write $1x$ as x. You do not need to write the coefficient of 1.

$$x + x = 2x \qquad 3y + y + 7y = 11y \qquad 2w - 5w = -3w$$

> * *Remember: You can write a coefficient that is a fraction, such as* $\frac{1}{2}$*, as either* $\frac{1}{2}y$ *or* $\frac{y}{2}$.

- A **term** can be a product or quotient of variables and coefficients, or just a number. A number with no variables is called a **constant**. Some examples of terms are shown in the following table.

Constant terms	Variable Terms
5	$2a$
−24	$-30xy$
12.456	$2.5x^2$
$\dfrac{9}{11}$	$\dfrac{9c}{7ab^3}$

- An **expression** contains one or more terms. Terms are separated by addition or subtraction. For example, the expression $4x - 5y^3 + 9$ is made up of three terms, two variables, and one constant. Expressions can be evaluated only if values for those variables are given.
- **Evaluating** an expression means plugging in given values for the variables and simplifying using order of operations. For example, to evaluate the expression $4x - 5y^3 + 9$ for $x = 3$ and $y = -2$, you get $4(3) - 5(-2)^3 + 9 = 12 + 40 + 9 = 61$.
- In an expression, **like terms** have the same variables, each raised to the same power. To simplify an expression, combine like terms by adding or subtracting their coefficients. Here are some examples of simplifying expressions by combining like terms.

$$x^2 + 3x^2 \xrightarrow{\text{simplifies to}} 4x^2 \qquad$$ *The variables and powers are the same, so just add the coefficients.*

$2xy^2 + 3y^2x \xrightarrow{\text{simplifies to}} 5xy^2$ *The order of multiplication of the variables do not matter.*

$x^2 + 3x \xrightarrow{\text{does not simplify}} x^2 + 3x$ *You cannot simplify any further since x and x^2 are raised to different powers.*

- In algebra, an expression of the form $a_1x^n + a_2x^{n-1} + a_3x^{n-2} + \cdots + a_n$ is called a **polynomial**.
  Think of the suffix *nomial* as meaning *term*.

  $4x^3$ *is a* **monomial**. *It is made up of one term.*

  $3x^5 + 2x^3$ *is a* **binomial**. *It is made up of two terms.*

  $7x^2 - 8x + 5$ *is a* **trinomial**. *It is made up of three terms.*

- Polynomials are usually ordered by decreasing powers of *x*. A **linear expression** has 1 as its highest power of *x*. A **quadratic expression** has 2 as its highest power of *x*. A **cubic expression** has 3 as its highest power of *x*. The highest power of *x* is called the **degree** of the polynomial.

  $7x^2 - 8x + 5$ *is a* **quadratic expression**. *Its highest power of x is 2.*

  $5x^4 + 3x^2 - x + 6$ *is a* **fourth degree** *polynomial, because the highest power of x is 4.*

- You can perform operations with polynomials by using properties of exponents and combining like terms. Be especially careful when **squaring binomials**. The quantity $(a+b)^2$ is NOT equal to $a^2 + b^2$. Think of the entire group as being multiplied by itself. It will help you to write it twice: $(a+b)^2 = (a+b)(a+b)$. Distribute each term in the first group through each term in the second as shown in the numbered steps below.

$$(a+b)^2 = (a+b)(a+b) = a^2 + ab + ba + b^2$$

Combine the like terms *ab* and *ba* to get 2*ab*. You get $(a+b)^2 = a^2 + 2ab + b^2$. Similarly, $(a-b)^2 = a^2 - 2ab + b^2$.

---

* *Memory Tip: Think of the word FOIL when multiplying two binomials together. This stands for First Outer Inner Last and may help you pair terms together.*

$(\boldsymbol{a} + b)(\boldsymbol{a} + b)$	$(\boldsymbol{a} + b)(a + \boldsymbol{b})$	$(a + \boldsymbol{b})(\boldsymbol{a} + b)$	$(a + \boldsymbol{b})(a + \boldsymbol{b})$
First	*Outer*	*Inner*	*Last*

* *Remember: ab and ba are like terms because of the commutative property of multiplication.*

Examples: Algebraic Expressions

Example 1. Simplify $(3x - 7) - (4x - 3)$.

Solution

$3x - 7 - 1(4x - 3)$	*The first set of parentheses is not necessary. Replace the negative sign in the front of the second group with a –1.*
$3x - 7 - 4x + 3$	*Distribute the –1 through the second parentheses. The signs will change.*
$\underline{3x - 4x} + \underline{3 - 7}$	*Group together the like terms before you combine.*
$-x - 4$	*Combine like terms and you are done!*

Answer: $-x - 4$

Example 2. Expand and simplify the expression $(6 + x)^2$.

Solution

$(6 + x)(6 + x)$	*Write the binomial twice.*
$36 + 6x + 6x + x^2$	*Distribute the first group through the second, one term at a time.*
$x^2 + 12x + 36$	*Combine like terms. Order by decreasing power of x.*

Answer: $x^2 + 12x + 36$

Example 3. Multiply $-3(2x + 3)(x^3 + 4x - 7)$.

Solution

$-3\left[(2x + 3)(x^3 + 4x - 7)\right]$	*Group together only two factors at a time.*
$-3\left[2x^4 + 8x^2 - 14x + 3x^3 + 12x - 21\right]$	*Distribute the 2x first, and then the 3.*
$-3\left[2x^4 + 3x^3 + 8x^2 - 2x - 21\right]$	*Reorder by decreasing power of x.*
	Combine like terms.
$-6x^4 - 9x^3 - 24x^2 + 6x + 63$	*Distribute the –3 through the remaining group.*

Answer: $-6x^4 - 9x^3 - 24x^2 + 6x + 63$

Practice: Algebraic Expressions

1. The expression $5x^2 - 3x - 7 - x(6x + 2)$ is equivalent to
   A. $5x^2 - 9x - 5$
   B. $-x^2 - 5x - 7$
   C. $x^2 - 9x - 7$
   D. $11x^2 - 5x - 7$

2. Which of the following demonstrates the distributive property?
   A. $-6xz + 6xz - 2yz = 2yz$
   B. $2xy + (3xy + 5xz) = (2xy + 3xy) + 5xz$
   C. $7xz + 4xy + 11xz = 7xz + 11xz + 4xy$
   D. $3xy - 6xz = 3x(y - 2z)$

3. The junior class is planning to sell printed banners with the name of the school's football team on them for the homecoming game. Their cost for production is $2.25 per banner and $0.50 for each printing. Which of the following expressions represents their profit, in dollars, for selling n banners, if they plan to sell each for $4.00 at the game?
   A. $4.00 - (2.25 + 0.50)n$
   B. $4.00n - (2.25 + 0.50)$
   C. $4.00 - 2.25 - 0.50n$
   D. $(4.00 - 2.25 - 0.50)n$

4. What is the missing term in the quadratic expression below?
$$(3x - 4)(2x + 5) = 6x^2 + \underline{\quad} - 20$$

5. When a and b are real numbers, which of the following equations is **always** true?
   A. $a - b = b - a$
   B. $(a + b)^2 = a^2 + b^2$
   C. $-(a - b) = -a - b$
   D. $(a + b)^2 = a^2 + 2ab + b^2$

6. Which of the following expressions is equivalent to the one shown below?
$$(x - 4)(2x + 7)$$
   A. $2x^2 - 28$
   B. $2x^2 - x - 28$
   C. $2x^2 + x - 28$
   D. $2x^2 + x - 11$

7. Which of the following expressions is equivalent to the one shown below?
$$(d^5 + 4d^3 - 8d) - (d^5 + d - 1)$$
   A. $2d^5 + 4d^3 - 9d - 1$
   B. $4d^6 - 9d^2 - 1$
   C. $4d^3 - 9d + 1$
   D. $4d^3 - 7d + 1$

8. In the figure below, rectangle *ABCD* contains six smaller rectangles with dimensions shown.

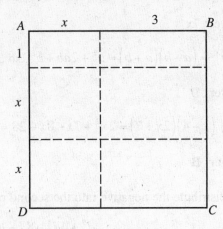

Which of the following represents the area of rectangle *ABCD*?

A. $3x + 4$

B. $2\left[\left(2x+1\right)+\left(x+3\right)\right]$

C. $\left(2x+1\right)\left(x+3\right)$

D. $3x \cdot 2x$

Solutions to Practice: Algebraic Expressions

1. Distribute the $-x$ through the parentheses. Remember that when multiplying terms with the same base, you add the exponents.

$$5x^2 - 3x - 7 - x(6x+2) = 5x^2 - 3x - 7 - 6x^2 - 2x.$$

Next, combine by adding the like terms together.

$$\underline{5x^2} \; \underline{\underline{-3x}} \; -7 \; \underline{-6x^2} \; \underline{\underline{-2x}} = -x^2 - 5x - 7.$$

Answer: B

2. **Eliminate incorrect answer choices**. Looking through the answer choices, answer A demonstrates the addition of like terms and is actually an incorrect statement, as $-2yz \neq 2yz$. Answer choice B demonstrates the associative property of addition. Answer choice C demonstrates the commutative property. Only answer choice D demonstrates the distributive property: $3xy - 6xz = 3x(y - 2z)$.

Answer: D

3. Compute the profit on each banner using the formula: *profit = income − expenses*. In this problem, each banner yields a profit of \$4.00 − (\$2.25 +\$0.50). Distributing the negative sign, you get 4.00 − 2.25 − 0.50. Since they will be making this profit on a single banner, multiplying this result by *n* will give you their total profit on *n* banners.

Answer: D

4. Multiplying the expression by distributing first the $3x$ and then the -4 you get: $(3x-4)(2x+5) = 6x^2 + 15x - 8x - 20 = 6x^2 + 7x - 20$. The missing term is $7x$.

   Answer: 7x

5. $(a+b)^2 = (a+b)(a+b) = a^2 + 2ab + b^2$, so answer D is correct.

   Answer: D

6. FOIL: $(x-4)(2x+7) = 2x^2 + 7x - 8x - 28 = 2x^2 - x - 28$

   Answer: B

7. First distribute the negative into the second parentheses:

   $$d^5 + 4d^3 - 8d - d^5 - d + 1$$

   Next, combine like terms:

   $$4d^3 - 9d + 1$$

   Answer: C

8. The area of the rectangle is the length of $\overline{AD}$ times the length of $\overline{AB}$. $AD = 2x+1$ and $AB = x+3$. When they are multiplied, the area is $(2x+1)(x+3)$.

   Answer: C

Factoring Polynomials

- **Factoring** is a process in which you rewrite an expression as the product of two or more factors. There are different techniques for factoring, depending on the expression you are given.

Greatest Common Factor

- Look for a greatest common factor in all the terms, and pull it out in front of the parentheses. Here are two examples.

  $4 + 24x = 4(1 + 6x)$ *The greatest common factor is 4.*

  $3x^3 + 6xy - 12x^2 y^2 z = 3x(x^2 + 2y - 4xy^2 z)$ *The greatest common factor is 3x.*

Difference of Two Squares

- If you have a binomial where each term is a perfect square and one is subtracted from the other, you can factor it as $a^2 - b^2 = (a+b)(a-b)$. A few examples are on the next page.

$$x^2 - 9 = (x + 3)(x - 3)$$
$$1 - 25a^2 = (1 - 5a)(1 + 5a)$$
$$4y^6 - 9x^2 = (2y^3 + 3x)(2y^3 - 3x)$$

Trinomials of the form $ax^2 + bx + c$

- In general, factoring a trinomial means to rewrite it as the product of two binomials. For example, consider the expression below.

Expanded		*Factored*
$x^2 + 7x - 30$	$\longleftrightarrow$	$(x + 10)(x - 3)$

Notice how the middle term of $7x$ is created. When expanded, the middle term is a combination of the outer terms in the parentheses and the inner terms. This fact will be helpful when you need to experiment to find the correct factors.

$$(x + 10)(x - 3) = x^2 \underline{-3x + 10x} - 30 = x^2 + 7x - 30$$

$$+10x$$
$$-3x$$

Factoring takes practice! First arrange the trinomial in decreasing powers of x. Some tricks and simple steps are detailed next.

Expressions of the form $x^2 + bx + c$

- In these expressions, the trinomial has a leading coefficient of $a = 1$. If the second sign in the trinomial is a + sign, or c is positive, the pair of parentheses will have the same sign inside.

$$(+)(+) \text{ or } (-)(-)$$

Check the sign of the middle term, b, of the trinomial. If it is positive, both signs in the parentheses are +, and if b is negative, both signs in the parentheses are −. Next, look for two numbers that, when **multiplied together**, give you the value of c and, when **added together**, give you the value of b.

Consider the two cases of the trinomial $x^2 \pm 13x + 30$. Think of two factors of 30 that **add up** to 13. They are 10 and 3.

$x^2 + 13x \boxed{+} 30 = (x + 10)(x + 3)$ *Both positive. The middle term is +13x.*

$x^2 - 13x \boxed{+} 30 = (x - 10)(x - 3)$ *Both negative. The middle term is −13x.*

- If the second sign in the trinomial is a − sign, the two numbers in the parentheses will have different signs. Check the sign of the middle term, b, in the trinomial to determine whether the larger number is positive or negative. If b is negative, you will put the $-$ in front of your larger number, and if b is positive, you will put the $+$ in front of your larger number. You will be looking for two numbers that, when multiplied together, give you the value of c and, when subtracted, give you the value of b.

Here you are looking for factors of 30 that **differ** by 7. They are 10 and 3.

$$x^2 - 7x \boxed{-} 30 = \quad (x-10)(x+3) \qquad \text{With the larger number negative, the middle term is } -7x.$$

$$x^2 + 7x \boxed{-} 30 = \quad (x+10)(x-3) \qquad \text{With the larger number positive, the middle term is } +7x.$$

- **Expressions of the form $ax^2 + bx + c$**

If you have a trinomial of the form $ax^2 + bx + c$, where a is a number other than 1, you may have to repeatedly check the middle term until you get the one you want. For example, suppose your trinomial is $2x^2 - 17x - 30$. In order to make the first term $2x^2$, you will need $2x$ and x to lead the parentheses $(2x\ )(x\ )$. Next, list the factors of 30. Following the guidelines from the last example, you are still looking for the difference of the factors to be 17, but the 2 has the effect of doubling one of the factors.

1	30
2	15
3	10
5	6

$\longrightarrow$

1	30
2	15
③	10•2
5	6

Position the negative sign so that you have $-17x$ when combining the inner and outer terms. Factoring, you get $(2x + 3)(x - 10) = x^2 \underline{-20x + 3x} - 30 \ = \ x^2 - 17x - 30$.

$+3x$

$-20x$

- You can also use a grid to help factor. Create a multiplication table with the first term in the upper left box and the last term in the lower right. Try different constants in the row and column headers, so that the remaining two boxes combine to make your middle term. Your factors are then your row and column headers.

$2x^2 - 17x - 30$

•	$2x$	
x	$2x^2$	
		-30

$\longrightarrow$

•	$2x$	$+3$
x	$2x^2$	$3x$
-10	$-20x$	-30

Answer: $(2x+3)(x-10)$

Examples: Factoring Polynomials

Example 1. Which one of the following is a factor of the expression $2x^2 - x - 3$?
A. $x - 2$
B. $x - 3$
C. $2x - 3$
D. $2x + 3$

Solution

The trinomial $2x^2 - x - 3$ has a negative c term, which means that one factor is positive and the other is negative. Try creating a multiplication table with two factors that multiply to –3. Be sure to position the factors so that the x terms add up to the middle term $-x$.

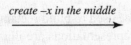

•	2x	
x	2x²	
		-3

create –x in the middle →

•	2x	-3
x	2x²	-3x
+1	+2x	-3

Check your answer by expanding the product: $(2x - 3)(x + 1) = 2x^2 - x - 3$. Therefore, one of the factors is $(2x - 3)$, and answer choice C is correct.

Answer: C

Practice: Factoring Polynomials

1. The area of a rectangle in square feet is represented by the expression $x^2 - 3x - 10$. The expression for the width of the rectangle is $x - 5$ feet. What is the expression for the number of feet in the length of the rectangle?
   A. $x - 5$
   B. $x - 2$
   C. $x + 5$
   D. $x + 2$

2. Which of the following is one of the factors of the expression $16 - 9x^2$?
   A. $(4 + 3x)$
   B. $(2 + 9x)$
   C. $(4 - 9x)$
   D. $(8 - 3x)$

Use the figure below to answer Question 3.

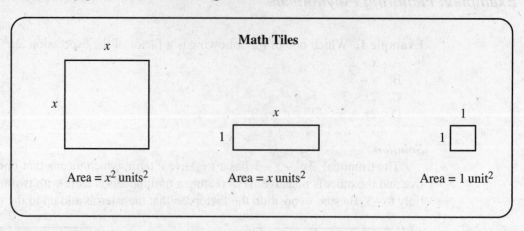

Math Tiles

Area = x^2 units^2 Area = x units^2 Area = 1 unit^2

3. Math tiles can be used to build rectangular arrays that represent quadratic expressions. Two different representations are illustrated below.

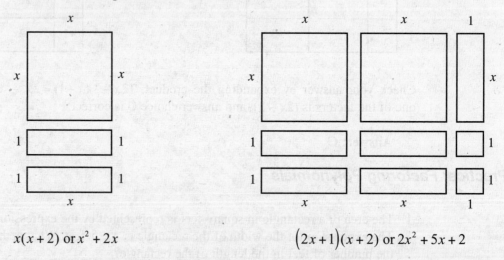

$x(x+2)$ or $x^2 + 2x$ $(2x+1)(x+2)$ or $2x^2 + 5x + 2$

a. Build a rectangular array, if possible, for each of the following expressions using the three different math tiles.

$$2x^2 + 2x \qquad 2x^2 + 3x + 1 \qquad 3x^2 + 4x + 1$$

b. How can you determine if a rectangular array can be built for an expression using the math tiles?

4. Which of the following is a factor of the polynomial below?
$36x^4 - 18x^3 - 12x^2$

A. $6x^2$
B. $6x^3$
C. $6x^4$
D. $6x^5$

5. Which of the following is one of the factors of the expression below?
   $9x^2 - 16$
   A. $9x - 4$
   B. $3x - 1$
   C. $3x + 5$
   D. $3x - 4$

Solutions to Practice: Factoring Polynomials

1. The area of a rectangle is equal to its length times its width. The formula is $A = lw$. This problem gives you an expression for its area and its width. Substituting these into the equation, you get: $x^2 - 3x - 10 = (x - 5) \cdot l$. The length is just the other factor of the area expression. Factoring fully, you get $x^2 - 3x - 10 = (x - 5)(x + 2)$ so the factor $x + 2$ is the width of the rectangle. You can also **use your answer choices** to solve this problem. You know that the last term must multiply to –10 and since you are already given x–5 as a factor, the only way you can get –10 is by multiplying –5 by +2. This only leaves answer choice D as an option. You can check this by FOILing.

Answer: D

2. The expression $16 - 9x^2$ is the difference of two perfect squares, as $(4)^2 = 16$ and $(3x)^2 = 9x^2$. The difference of two squares factors as $a^2 - b^2 = (a + b)(a - b)$, so the correct factorization of the expression is $(4 + 3x)(4 - 3x)$. Answer choice A is correct.

Answer: A

3. a. Creating an array with math tiles means arranging the tiles you have into a large rectangle. A single math tile is a rectangle with side of either length x or 1. There are three types of tiles, but only two different dimensions, or lengths of sides. x is the length of the longer side, and 1 is the length of the shorter. Each individual block is named by its area, found by multiplying its base and height together. Here are the three building blocks:

$$x^2 = x \cdot x = \boxed{}\, x \qquad x = x \cdot 1 = \boxed{}\, 1 \qquad 1 = 1 \cdot 1 = \boxed{}\, 1$$

As an example, if your expression has a $3x^2$ term in it, you must use three of the x^2 tiles. Likewise, $2x$ means that you must use two of the x tiles. Creating rectangular arrays that represent the expressions given to you in the problem, you get:

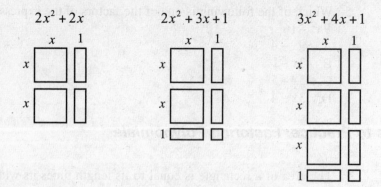

b. Looking at the row and column lengths, you see that the dimensions of the rectangular arrays are the factorizations of the expressions. For example:

$$2x^2 + 2x = 2x(x+1) \quad 2x^2 + 3x + 1 = (2x+1)(x+1) \quad 3x^2 + 4x + 1 = (3x+1)(x+1)$$

This means that in order to build a rectangular array, the expression must be factorable.

4. From your answer choices, it is clear that 6 is part of the correct answer! It is a factor of 36, 18, and 12. Next, look for the lowest exponent in the polynomial to determine the greatest common factor. In this case, it is x^2. So, $6x^2$ is a factor of the polynomial. Although it is not the greatest common factor, $6x$ is also a factor. It was not an answer choice, so the only correct choice is A.

Answer: A

5. The expression in this question is a difference of squares and can be factored as $(3x+4)(3x-4)$.

Answer: D

Linear Equations

• An **equation** is an algebraic sentence containing two or more terms separated by an equal sign. It denotes equal quantities on the left- and right-hand sides of the equal sign. You can perform identical mathematical operations to both sides, and the results will remain equal. Here are examples of some operations that produce equal quantities for all real numbers k, if $A = B$.

$kA = kB$	*You can multiply both sides by the same number.*
$k + A = k + B$	*You can add the same number to both sides.*
$A - k = B - k$	*You can subtract the same number from both sides.*
$A^2 = B^2$	*The squares of both sides will be equal.*
$\dfrac{A}{k} = \dfrac{B}{k} \; ; k \neq 0$	*You can divide both sides by any number other than zero.*
	*A fraction with zero in the denominator is **undefined**.*

- You can also add and subtract terms from both sides, to move them from one side of the equal sign to the other. For example, if $2x + 3y = 5y - 7x$, then

$$2x + 3y = 5y - 7x$$
$$\underline{+7x \qquad = \qquad +7x} \quad \textit{Add 7x to both sides to move all x terms to the left.}$$
$$9x + 3y = 5y$$
$$\underline{-3y = -3y} \qquad \textit{Subtract 3y from both sides to move all y terms to the right.}$$
$$9x = 2y$$

- **Solving** an equation means finding the value of the variable in the problem. You achieve this by isolating it on one side of an equation, with a coefficient of 1. If an equation has more than one variable in it, then you can only solve for a single variable **in terms of** the other variables in the equation. In the example above, you can only solve for x or y, in terms of the other. If $9x = 2y$,

Solving for x in terms of y

$$\frac{9x}{9} = \frac{2y}{9} \to x = \frac{2y}{9}$$

Solving for y in terms of x

$$\frac{9x}{2} = \frac{2y}{2} \to \frac{9x}{2} = y$$

- A **linear equation** is an equation that contains one variable, and the highest power of that variable is 1. In a linear equation, you can solve for the variable by performing identical operations to both sides until the variable is isolated. There is only one solution for x. Here is an example of a linear equation. It will be solved for you in the example section.

$$3x + 5 = 17 - 2(6x - 4x)$$

Word Problems

- When creating an equation from a word problem, here are some general guidelines for translating an English sentence into an algebraic sentence:

First decide what quantity should be x in the problem!

three more than x $\longrightarrow 3 + x$ *or* $x + 3$

three less than x $\longrightarrow x - 3$

x less 3 $\longrightarrow x - 3$

twice x $\longrightarrow 2x$

the opposite of x $\longrightarrow -x$

is $\longrightarrow =$

the sum of x and y $\longrightarrow x + y$ *or* $y + x$

the difference of x and y $\longrightarrow x - y$

the product of x and y $\longrightarrow xy$ *or* yx

the quotient of x and y $\longrightarrow \dfrac{x}{y}$

Examples: Linear Equations

Example 1. Solve for x in the equation: $3x + 5 = 17 - 2(6x - 4x)$.

Solution

This is a linear equation. Isolate the variable by combining like terms and performing the same operation to both sides.

$3x + 5 = 17 - 12x + 8x$ *Distribute the −2 to remove the parentheses.*

$3x + 5 = 17 \underline{- 12x + 8x}$ *Combine like terms on the same side.*

$3x + 5 = 17 - 4x$

$\underline{+ 4x \quad = \quad + 4x}$ *Add 4x to both sides to bring all x terms to the left.*

$7x + 5 = 17$

$\underline{-5 = -5}$ *Subtract 5 from both sides to get the x term by itself.*

$\dfrac{7x}{7} = \dfrac{12}{7}$ *Divide both sides by 7 to solve for 1x.*

$x = \dfrac{12}{7}$

Answer: $x = \dfrac{12}{7}$

Example 2. On a local commuter train, $\dfrac{1}{4}$ of the passengers got off at the first stop and 20 people got on. A total of 110 passengers were then on the train. Write an equation that can be solved for the number of passengers that were on the train before the first stop. Let x represent the number of passengers originally on the train. Solve your equation for x.

Solution

Let x represent the number of passengers originally on the train. After $\dfrac{1}{4}$ of the passengers got off, you are left with $x - \dfrac{1}{4}x = \dfrac{3}{4}x$ passengers. After twenty people get on the train, this value changes to $\dfrac{3}{4}x + 20$. This leaves 110 passengers on the train, so set the expression equal to 110 for your final equation $\dfrac{3}{4}x + 20 = 110$. Solving this equation, you get:

$$\frac{3}{4}x + 20 = 110$$

$$-20 = -20 \qquad \text{\textit{Subtract 20 from both sides.}}$$

$$\frac{3}{4}x = 90$$

$$\frac{4}{3} \cdot \frac{3}{4}x = 90 \cdot \frac{4}{3} \qquad \text{\textit{Multiply both sides by the reciprocal of }} \frac{3}{4}.$$

$$x = \frac{360}{3}$$

$$x = 120 \qquad \text{\textit{Simplify the resulting fraction.}}$$

Answer: $x = 120$

Practice: Linear Equations

1. If $5 + 4(3x - 2) = 29$, then $3x - 2$ equals
   A. 2
   B. 4
   C. 6
   D. 8

2. Solve the following equation for x.

$$0.25(x + 4) = 0.5x - 28$$

3. A pump company has 84 employees. It plans to increase its work force by 4 employees each month until it triples in size. Which of the following equations will help you to determine the number of months, m, for the company to triple in size?
   A. $84 + 4 = 3m$
   B. $3(84) = 4m$
   C. $(84 + 4)3 = m$
   D. $84 + 4m = 3(84)$

4. Reiko has a part-time job selling hats. She is paid $50.00 per week, plus $3.00 for each hat she sells.

   a. Reiko sold 24 hats in one week. What was her total weekly pay? Show your work or explain how you obtained your answer.

   b. One week Reiko was paid a total of $158.00. How many hats did she sell that week? Show your work or explain how you obtained your answer.

   c. Write an equation that represents the relationship between Reiko's weekly pay, P, and the number of hats, H, sold in one week.

   d. During her 8-week summer break, Reiko hopes to earn **at least** $1,000.00. What is the average number of hats Reiko must sell each week in order to earn at least $1,000.00? Show your work or explain how you obtained your answer.

5. The step squad at Janis Hill High is raising money to participate in a competition. They plan to sell tee-shirts with the school's name on them. The cost of each tee-shirt is $3.25, and the print cost for each is $0.85. If the club plans to sell each tee-shirt for $8.50, what is the fewest number of tee-shirts the club must sell to make a $400 profit?

A. 48
B. 77
C. 91
D. 98

6. Frank is planning on setting up a stand called Frank's Dogs, and selling hot dogs off a cart in front of Fenway Park. His fixed monthly expenses will be $800. Each hot dog will cost about $0.50 to make, and he will sell them for $3.25 each. He estimates that he can sell 1,000 hot dogs per month.

a. What would be Frank's monthly profit or loss on selling hot dogs? Explain or show how you found your answer.

b. What price per hot dog would Frank have to charge to break even (neither a profit nor a loss)? Explain or show how you found your answer.

c. Frank needs a formula to help him calculate his monthly profit or loss. Using the variables listed below, write a formula that will determine his monthly profit or loss.

- Fixed monthly expenses, F
- Cost to make each hot dog, c
- Selling price of each hot dog, p
- Number of hot dogs sold per month, n
- Monthly profit or loss, M

7. Mrs. Kelly is selling theater tickets for a community play that will run two performances, one on Saturday evening and one Sunday afternoon matinee. There are 150 seats in the theater. The Saturday evening tickets will cost $7.50 each, and the Sunday matinee $4.50 each. Mrs. Kelly's total expenses for producing the play are $1,500.00.

a. Suppose Mrs. Kelly sold 130 tickets on Saturday evening, and 64 tickets for the Sunday matinee. Based on this information, did she make enough money to cover her expenses for producing the play? Show your work or explain how you obtained your answer.

b. Write an equation that represents the amount of money Mrs. Kelly needs to collect from the sale of e Saturday evening tickets and m Sunday matinee tickets to pay for her total expenses.

c. What is the **minimum** number of Saturday evening tickets that she could sell and still break even by the end of the day on Sunday? Show your work or explain how you obtained your answer.

8. Solve the following equation for x:

   $2x + 5 = 6x + 21$

9. Which sequence of steps will NOT solve the equation $\frac{1}{4}x + 2 = 8$ for x?

   A. Subtract 2 from both sides, then multiply both sides of the equation by 4.

   B. Subtract 2 from both sides of the equation, then divide both sides by $\frac{1}{4}$.

   C. Divide both sides of the equation by $\frac{1}{4}$, then subtract 8 from both sides.

   D. Multiply both sides of the equation by 4, then subtract 2 from both sides.

10. Solve the following equation for x:

    $2(x + 2) + 2(2x + 3) = 8(x + 1)$

11. Which of the equations is TRUE for ALL values that could replace x?

    A. $5(x - 2) = 5x - 10$

    B. $\frac{7}{x} = \frac{x}{7}$

    C. $8(x - 3) = 8x - 3$

    D. $10 - x = x - 10$

12. Which of the following sentences does the equation $5x - 3 = x + 11$ correctly represent?

    A. 3 less than 5 times a number is 11.

    B. 3 more than 5 times a number is 11 more than the number.

    C. 5 times 3 less than a number is 11 more than the number.

    D. 3 less then 5 times a number is 11 more than the number.

13. Which equation represents the following statement:

    6 less than 4 times a number is 3 more than the number.

    A. $6 - 4x = 3 + x$

    B. $4x - 6 = 3 + x$

    C. $4x - 6 = 3x$

    D. $6 - 4x = 3x$

14. The price of the least expensive car on sale was $\frac{1}{3}$ the price of the most expensive car. Together, the two cars cost $80,000. Which equation represents the situation?

    A. $x - \frac{1}{3}x = 80,000$

    B. $\frac{3}{4}x = 80,000$

    C. $\frac{1}{4}x = 80,000$

    D. $x + \frac{1}{3}x = 80,000$

Solutions to Practice: Linear Equations

1. Notice that you do not need to solve for x. Instead, you need to solve for the expression $3x - 2$. This is the quantity inside the parentheses, so just isolate the parentheses. First, subtract five from both sides: $5 + 4(3x - 2) = 29 \longrightarrow 4(3x - 2) = 24$. Next, divide both sides by 4: $4(3x - 2) = 24 \longrightarrow (3x - 2) = 6$. So the answer is C.

   Answer: C

2. Since this is a noncalculator question, you may not want to work with decimals. To eliminate the decimals from the problem, you can multiply both sides of the equation by 100. (Choose 100 because the digit furthest to the right of the decimal point is in the hundredth's place.) Multiplying by 100, you get

$$0.25(x + 4) = 0.5x - 28 \longrightarrow 25(x + 4) = 50x - 2,800$$

   Next distribute the 25 to get rid of the parentheses: $25x + 100 = 50x - 2,800$.

   Subtract $50x$ and 100 from both sides to get the x term alone: $-25x = -2,900$.

   Finally, divide by –25 and simplify to solve for x: $x = \dfrac{-2,900}{-25} = 116$.

   Answer: $x = 116$

3. Tripling the size of the company's current work force gives you $3 \cdot 84$ employees, so the equation must equal this number. Therefore, you can **eliminate answer choices** A and C. Adding 4 employees each month would mean that in the first month you would have $84 + 4$ employees, the second month you would have $84 + 4(2)$ employees, the third would be $84 + 4(3)$ employees, and so on. Answer choice B is not correct because it does not take into account the original 84 employees in the company. The correct equation is $84 + 4m = 3(84)$.

   Answer: D

4. a. Reiko gets paid $50.00 each week, even if she sells no hats. In addition, she makes $3.00 per hat. Because she sold 24 hats, she would get an additional $24(\$3.00) = \$72.00$. Totaling up her pay, she earned $50.00 + $72.00 = $122.00.

   Answer: $122.00

b. First subtract her base pay of $50.00 from her weekly pay of $158.00. This will leave you with the money she earned from the sale of hats alone. $158.00 − $50.00 = $108.00. Next, divide this amount by $3.00 to determine how many hats she sold. $108 ÷ $3 = 36 hats.

Answer: 36 hats

c. Her base pay of $50 is not affected by the number of hats she sells, so it is not multiplied by H. Therefore, the equation used to compute her pay is $P = 50 + 3H$.

Answer: $P = 50 + 3H$

d. She is working for eight weeks, so she will receive a salary of $50 • 8 = $400 for the 8 weeks. To find the number of hats she must sell in total for the 8 weeks, replace P with 1,000 in the equation $P = 400 + 3H$. Then solve for H.

$$1000 = 400 + 3H \longrightarrow 600 = 3H \longrightarrow H = 200 \text{ hats}$$

Read the question carefully! It asks for the average number of hats she must sell each week. Divide 200 by 8 to get an average of 25 hats per week.

Answer: 25 hats per week

5. Use the formula *Profit = Income − Expenses*. Here, the expenses per tee-shirt are $3.25 + $0.85 = $4.10. If the club sells x tee-shirts, their total expense would be $4.10x. If they sell each tee-shirt for $8.50, they would take in $8.50x. Set the profit equal to $400 and solve for x: $400 = 8.50x − 4.10x \longrightarrow 400 = 4.4x \longrightarrow x \approx 90.9$ tee-shirts. Round this number to the nearest whole number for an answer of 91 tee-shirts.

Answer: C

6. a. The amount of money Frank earns or loses each month is equal to the money he brings in from the sale of the hot dogs, minus his expenses. Frank's expenses to operate the stand are $800 regardless of the number of hot dogs he sells. In addition, it costs him $0.50 to make each hot dog, so making n hot dogs would cost him $0.50n. Frank's profit or loss would be *Profit or Loss = Income − Expenses*.
Profit or Loss = $3.25n −($800.00 + $0.50n) = $3.25n −$800.00 − $0.50n.
If he sells about 1,000 hot dogs, this would come out to $3.25(1000) − $800.00 − $0.50(1000) = $1950.00.
Because this number is positive, it is considered a profit.

Answer: $1,950.00

b. *Breaking even* means that Frank's profit or loss is $0.00. Setting the equation in part a equal to zero gives you $0.00 = $3.25n − $800.00 − $0.50n. Assuming that he is still selling 1,000 hot dogs per month, as stated in part a, change n to 1,000. You want to figure out what price he would need to charge per hot dog to break even, so change 3.25 to a variable, such as p. Remove the dollar signs for convenience when solving.
$0 = p(1,000) − 800 − 0.50(1,000)$
$0 = 1,000p − 1,300 \longrightarrow 1,300 = 1,000p \longrightarrow 1.3 = p$
Changing back to dollars and cents, the price per hot dog would be $1.30.

Answer: $1.30

c. Use the variables listed: cost to make each hot dog = c, selling price per hot dog = p, number of hot dogs sold in one month = n, monthly profit or loss = M, fixed expenses = F. Three possible formulas that will determine Frank's monthly profit or loss are

$$M = np - (F + nc) \qquad M = np - nc - F \qquad M = n(p - c) - F$$

Answers may vary. See above.

7. a. $7.5 \cdot 130 + 4.5 \cdot 64 = 975 + 288 = \$1,263$, which is less than $\$1,500$ so Mrs. Kelly did not make enough money to cover her expenses.

Answer: No

b. $7.5e + 4.5m = 1,500$

c. If all of the tickets are sold on Sunday, Sunday's earnings would be $4.5 \cdot 150 = \$675$. This leaves $1,500 - 675 = \$825$ that would need to have been earned on Saturday to break even. $7.5e = 825 \rightarrow e = 110$. If 110 tickets were sold on Saturday and 150 tickets on Sunday, then Mrs. Kelly will break even.

Answer: 110

8. Subtract $2x$ on both sides of the equation so that you are left with the equation $5 = 4x + 21$. Next, subtract 21 on both sides, so that you are left with $-16 = 4x$. Divide both sides by 4. $x = -4$ is your final answer.

Answer: $x = -4$

9. Answer choice D is the only one that doesn't work. If you multiply the equation by 4, it will read as follows: $x + 8 = 32$. The next step in solving for x would be subtracting 8 from both sides of the equation. Choice D says to subtract 2, not 8. Note that multiplying by 4 and dividing by $\frac{1}{4}$ mean the same thing.

Answer: D

10. Start by using the distributive property:
$$2(x + 2) + 2(2x + 3) = 8(x + 1) \rightarrow 2x + 4 + 4x + 6 = 8x + 8.$$
Next, combine like terms on the same side of the equation; $6x + 10 = 8x + 8$. Subtract $6x$ on both sides, $10 = 2x + 8$, and subtract 8 on both sides, $2 = 2x$. Divide by 2, $x = 1$.

Answer: $x = 1$

11. A. True. This is the distributive property and is true for all values of x.

~~B.~~ False. This is not true for all values of x. For example, suppose $x = 1$.

$$\frac{7}{1} \neq \frac{1}{7}$$

~~C.~~ False. This is not true for all values of x. For example, suppose $x = 0$.

$$8(0 - 3) \neq 8(0) - 3$$
$$-24 \neq -3$$

~~D.~~ False. This is not true for all values of x. For example, suppose $x = 1$.

$$10 - 1 \neq 1 - 10$$
$$9 \neq -9$$

Answer: A

12. ~~A.~~ These words are close to the equation but are missing the x being added to the 11. Answer choice A would translate to the symbolic equation $5x - 3 = 11$.

~~B.~~ The equation should read "3 <u>less</u> than 5 times a number" not "3 more" because 3 is being subtracted from $5x$.

~~C.~~ 5 times 3 less than a number means $5(x - 3) = 5x - 15$, which does not equal $5x - 3$.

D. This is the correct answer.

Answer: D

13. ~~A.~~ The equation in answer choice A would read: "6 minus 4 times a number is 3 more than the number." The statement in the question translates to $4x - 6$, not $6 - 4x$.

B. This is correct.

~~C.~~ $3x$ is 3 times a number not 3 more than a number.

~~D.~~ This has the 6 and the $4x$ in the wrong order and $3x$ instead of $3 + x$.

Answer: B

14. Call the price of the most expensive car, x. The price of the least expensive car is $\frac{1}{3}x$. Together, $x + \frac{1}{3}x = 80,000$.

Answer: D

Quadratic Equations

- A **quadratic equation** is an equation that contains one variable, and the highest power of that variable is 2. There are at most two solutions for that variable, lets call it x. To solve this type of equation, first set the equation equal to zero by moving all terms to the same side. Next, arrange the terms by decreasing power of x.

$$ax^2 + bx + c = 0$$ *Arrange all terms on one side in decreasing power of x. The equation must have one side equal to 0.*

You then have a choice when solving. You can either factor the trinomial and set each factor equal to zero to solve for x, or you may use the quadratic formula which is shown below.

$$x = \frac{-b \pm \sqrt{b^2 - 4(a)(c)}}{2a}$$ *Quadratic formula*

Any quadratic solution on the noncalculator section of the MCAS is almost always factorable. Factoring is usually quicker than using the quadratic formula; however, this formula will be particularly useful to you if you routinely experience difficulty factoring. You should use whichever method is more comfortable and gives you fewer errors.

Examples: Quadratic Equations

Example 1.
Solve for x.

$$3x^2 - 8x - 5 = 2x^2 + 4x + 40$$

Solution
First Method
There are two ways to solve a quadratic equation. The first method shown is factoring.

$3x^2 - 8x - 5 = 2x^2 + 4x + 40$ *Subtract $2x^2$ from both sides.*

$x^2 - 8x - 5 = 4x + 40$ *Subtract $4x$ from both sides.*

$x^2 - 12x - 5 = 40$ *Subtract 40 from both sides so equation equals 0.*

$x^2 - 12x - 45 = 0$ *Factor.*

$(x - 15) \cdot (x + 3) = 0$ *Set each factor equal to zero and solve for x.*

$x - 15 = 0 \quad x + 3 = 0$
$x = 15 \qquad x = -3$

Answer: $x = 15$ and $x = -3$

Second Method
If you are unable to factor the equation, or it is **prime** and does not factor, you will have to use the quadratic formula. You will still need to rearrange the equation so that it is in the form $ax^2 + bx + c = 0$. Let's pick up at that step and continue.

$x^2 - 12x - 45 = 0$ *The equation must be set equal to zero.*

Using the quadratic formula, $a = 1$, $b = -12$, $c = -45$.

$$x = \frac{-b \pm \sqrt{b^2 - 4(a)(c)}}{2a} = \frac{12 \pm \sqrt{(-12)^2 - 4(1)(-45)}}{2(1)} = \frac{12 \pm \sqrt{144 + 180}}{2} = \frac{12 \pm \sqrt{324}}{2} = \frac{12 \pm 18}{2}$$

So $x = $
$$\frac{12 + 18}{2} = \frac{30}{2} = 15$$
$$\frac{12 - 18}{2} = \frac{-6}{2} = -3$$

Answer: $x = 15$ and $x = -3$

Practice: Quadratic Equations

1. Solve the following equation for x.

   $3x^2 - 11x + 6 = 0$

2. Find **all** the values of x that satisfy the following equation.

   $2x^2 + 5x - 12 = 0$

3. What are the solutions to the equation below?

   $x^2 - 6x - 16 = 0$?

4. Solve the quadratic equation shown below.

   $x^2 - 3x + 2 = 0$

   What is the sum of the two solutions?
   A. -4
   B. -3
   C. 3
   D. 4

5. Rebecca solved a quadratic equation and found the solutions to be -7 and $\frac{4}{3}$. Which of the following is equivalent to the quadratic equation that Rebecca solved?
   A. $(x + 7)(4x - 3) = 0$
   B. $(x + 7)(3x - 4) = 0$
   C. $(x - 7)(4x + 3) = 0$
   D. $(x - 7)(3x + 4) = 0$

6. What are the solutions to the equation below?

$$2x^2 - 3x - 27 = 0$$

A. 9, –3
B. 2, 3
C. 4.5, –3
D. 9.5, 3

Solutions to Practice: Quadratic Equations

1. You can either factor the expression or use the quadratic formula. First, by factoring, you get: $3x^2 - 11x + 6 = 0 \longrightarrow (3x - 2)(x - 3) = 0$.

   Setting each factor equal to zero, you get $3x - 2 = 0$ and $x - 3 = 0$.

   Solving for x gives you: $x = \dfrac{2}{3}$ and $x = 3$.

   Using the quadratic formula, you get the same answers. Let $a = 3, b = -11, c = 6$. Then

$$x = \frac{-b \pm \sqrt{b^2 - 4(a)(c)}}{2a} = \frac{11 \pm \sqrt{(-11)^2 - 4(3)(6)}}{2(3)} = \frac{11 \pm \sqrt{121 - 72}}{6} = \frac{11 \pm \sqrt{49}}{6} = \frac{11 \pm 7}{6}$$

$$\text{So } x = \begin{cases} \dfrac{11+7}{6} = \dfrac{18}{6} = 3 \\ \dfrac{11-7}{6} = \dfrac{4}{6} = \dfrac{2}{3} \end{cases}$$

   Answer: $x = \dfrac{2}{3}$ and $x = 3$

2. You can either factor the expression or use the quadratic formula. First, factoring, you get: $2x^2 + 5x - 12 = 0 \longrightarrow (2x - 3)(x + 4) = 0$.

   Setting each factor equal to zero, you get $2x - 3 = 0$ and $x + 4 = 0$.

   Solving for x gives you: $x = \dfrac{3}{2}$ and $x = -4$.

   Using the quadratic formula, you get the same answers. $a = 2, b = 5, c = -12$. Then,

$$x = \frac{-b \pm \sqrt{b^2 - 4(a)(c)}}{2a} = \frac{-5 \pm \sqrt{(5)^2 - 4(2)(-12)}}{2(2)} = \frac{-5 \pm \sqrt{121}}{4} = \frac{-5 \pm 11}{4}$$

$$\text{So } x = \begin{cases} \dfrac{-5+11}{4} = \dfrac{6}{4} = \dfrac{3}{2} \\ \dfrac{-5-11}{4} = \dfrac{-16}{4} = -4 \end{cases}$$

   Answer: $x = \dfrac{3}{2}$ and $x = -4$

3. You can factor the quadratic and then set each parentheses equal to 0:

$$(x-8)(x+2)=0$$

$x-8=0$ and $x+2=0$

$x=8 \qquad x=-2$

Answer: $x=8$ and $x=-2$

4. You can factor the quadratic and then set each parentheses equal to 0:

$$(x-2)(x-1)=0$$

$x-2=0$ and $x-1=0$

$x=2 \qquad x=1$

The sum of these solutions is 3.

Answer: C

5. **Use your answer choices.** Which one would give you Rebecca's solutions if you set the parentheses equal to 0 and solved? The correct answer is choice B. Do not be tempted by choice A, which would give you solutions -7 and $\frac{3}{4}$.

Answer: B

6. You can factor the quadratic and then set each parentheses equal to 0:

$$(2x-9)(x+3)=0$$

$2x-9=0$ and $x+3=0$

$x=\dfrac{9}{2} \qquad x=-3$

Answer: C

Linear Functions

- A **relation** is any rule or correspondence between two quantities, usually x and y. This rule may be expressed as a formula, such as $y=x^2$, a graph, or a list of ordered pairs, such as $\{(0, 2), (1, 3), (2, 4)\}$. When you are dealing with ordered pairs, the first coordinate is x and the second is y. In short, a relation is some relationship between two variables. Some examples of relations are shown below.

    a. $x^2+y^2=9$ 	 b. $y=2x-5$ 	 c. $\{(4, 2), (4, -2), (9, 3), (9, -3)\}$

    d. 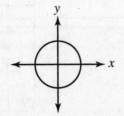	 	 e.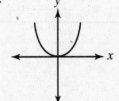

- A **function** is a special type of relation, in which each input for x has at most one output for y. Examples a, c, and d above are NOT functions, since in each you can find a single value of x for which there is more than one corresponding value of y. Graphically, if you drew a vertical line, and it crosses your graph more than once in any location, the relation is not a function. Observe below:

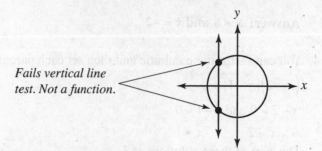

Fails vertical line test. Not a function.

More specifically, a function is a series of operations, or a rule, performed on some algebraic input to generate an output. For example, pretend that whenever you give a number to Fred, he doubles it and then takes away five. You can call Fred's process the function f and then say $f(x) = 2x - 5$. If you give Fred the number a, then he returns $2a - 5$. So what if you gave him the number 3? You would write this as

$$f(3) = 2(3) - 5$$
$$f(3) = 6 - 5$$
$$f(3) = 1$$

- The notation $f(3) = 1$ means that when you evaluate the function for $x = 3$ you get an answer of 1. The input into the function is called the **independent variable**, and the outcome is called the **dependent variable**. The outcome's value is dependent on the particular rule of the function. When graphing functions on a coordinate plane, the input is the x value, and the outcome is the y value.

- A function of the form $f(x) = mx + b$ is called a **linear function**, because all the (x, y) pairs that make the sentence true fall on a straight line. The highest power of a variable in a linear function is one. Let's look at the function $f(x) = 2x - 5$ used earlier. To graph this, we can generate a table of values, where $y = 2x - 5$. You can randomly select the x values, but be sure to use the function to compute the corresponding y values.

x	$y = 2x - 5$	y
-1	$y = 2(-1) - 5$	-7
0	$y = 2(0) - 5$	-5
3	$y = 2(3) - 5$	1
4	$y = 2(4) - 5$	3
5	$y = 2(5) - 5$	5

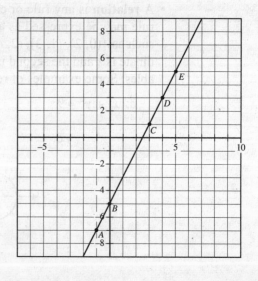

* *Remember: The x-axis is horizontal, and the y-axis is vertical. The points shown on page 120 are A(–1, –7), B(0, –5), C(3, 1); D(4, 3), and E(5, 5).*

- The formula for finding the **slope of a line** given two points is: $m = \dfrac{y_2 - y_1}{x_2 - x_1}$.

This is an algebraic formula for the statement that $slope = \dfrac{rise}{run} = \dfrac{change\ in\ y}{change\ in\ x}$.

When looking at a line from left to right, a positive slope goes up, a negative slope goes down, a zero slope is horizontal, and an undefined (or no slope) is vertical.

positive slope

negative slope

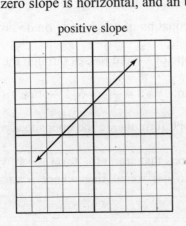
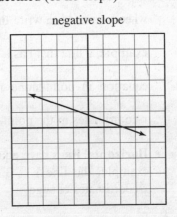

zero slope

undefined (no slope)

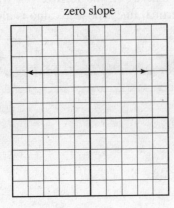
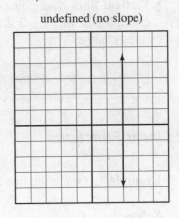

- The **slope-intercept form** for the equation of a line is $y = mx + b$, where m is the slope and b is the y-intercept. Take any linear equation, such as $2x + 5y = 10$, and solve for y in terms of x, and the equation will now be in slope-intercept form. This form is helpful to use when graphing.

$2x + 5y = 10$	*Original linear equation*
$5y = -2x + 10$	*Subtract 2x from both sides.*
$y = -\dfrac{2}{5}x + 2$	*Solve for y in terms of x.*
$m = -\dfrac{2}{5},\ b = 2$	*The slope is the coefficient of x, and the y-intercept is the constant.*

To graph a line once it is in slope-intercept form, first plot the y-intercept of the line. This is where the line crosses the y-axis, and its coordinates are $(0, b)$. Next, use the y-intercept as a starting point, and advance to another point on the line using its slope. The slope should be considered a ratio of rise over run. The numerator of the fraction tells you how many units to move in a vertical direction. If the numerator is positive, you move upward, and if it is negative, you move downward. The denominator of the fraction tells you how many units to move in a horizontal direction. If the denominator is positive you move to the right, and if it is negative, you move to the left.

- The **point-slope form** for the equation of a line is: $(y - y_1) = m(x - x_1)$, where m is the slope and (x_1, y_1) is any point that you know is on that line. This form is helpful to use when you need to write the equation of a line and you do not know the y-intercept. For example, a line that has a slope of $\frac{2}{3}$ and passes through the point $(5, -8)$ will have the equation in point-slope form: $y + 8 = \frac{2}{3}(x - 5)$. Notice that the sign of the x- and y-coordinates in the point-slope formula are the opposite sign of the point itself.

- **Horizontal lines** have equations that are in the form $y = k$, where k is any constant. For example, the line $y = 3$ is a horizontal line whose y value is always 3, while the x-coordinates change.

- **Vertical lines** have equations that are in the form $x = k$ where k is any constant. For example, the line $x = 2$ is a vertical line whose x value is always 2, while the y-coordinates change.

> ** Note: Vertical lines are not functions. Horizontal lines are functions.*

Examples: Linear Functions

Example 1. Graph the line $3x + 2y = 8$.

Solution

First solve for y to put the equation in slope-intercept form.

$$3x + 2y = 8$$
$$2y = -3x + 8$$
$$y = -\frac{3}{2}x + 4$$

The y-intercept of the line is 4 and the slope is $\frac{-3}{2}$. To graph, first plot the point $(0, 4)$. From there, move down three units and to the right two units to plot your second point. Connect the points to form your line.

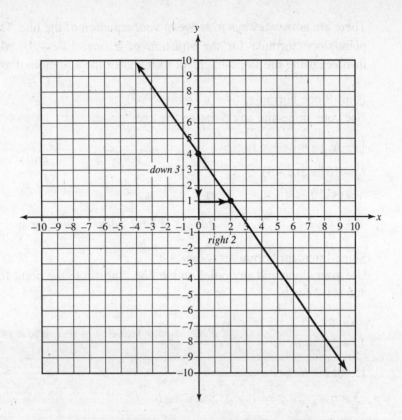

Example 2. The table below indicates a relationship between *x* and *y*.

x	y
2	7
4	11
6	15
8	19
10	23

Write an equation for *y* in terms of *x*.

Solution

For each constant change in *x*, there is a corresponding constant change in *y*. Here, as *x* goes up by two units, *y* increases by four. This indicates a linear relationship between *x* and *y*. First, find the slope choosing any pair of points. Your choice will not change the value of the slope. The slope between any two points on a line is the same.

(2, 7) and (6, 15)   *Choose two points.*

$$m = \frac{y_2 - y_1}{x_2 - x_1} = \frac{15 - 7}{6 - 2} = \frac{8}{4} = 2$$ *Compute the slope using the formula.*

There are now two ways to arrive at your equation of the line. The first involves using the point-slope formula for the equation of a line: $(y - y_1) = m(x - x_1)$, and the second involves using the slope-intercept formula for the equation of a line:

<u>Point-Slope Formula:</u> $(y - y_1) = m(x - x_1)$
Use your slope and any point on the line.

$(y - y_1) = m(x - x_1)$
$(y - 15) = 2(x - 6)$ *Plug in your value of m = 2, and a point such as (6, 15).*

$y - 15 = 2x - 12$ *Distribute the 2.*

$y = 2x + 3$ *Add 15 to both sides to solve for y.*

<u>Slope-Intercept Formula:</u> $y = mx + b$
Use your slope and any point on the line. Substitute the point for x and y in the equation and solve for b.

$y = mx + b$
$15 = 2(6) + b$ *Plug in your value of m = 2, and a point such as (6, 15).*

$15 = 12 + b$

$3 = b$ *Solve for b.*

Rewrite the equation for any point (x, y): $y = 2x + 3$

Answer: $y = 2x + 3$

Practice: Linear Functions

1. What is the y-intercept of the line defined by $y = 3x - 6$?
   A. $(0, -6)$
   B. $(0, 3)$
   C. $(0, 6)$
   D. $(0, 2)$

Use the table below to answer Question 2.

x	−4	0	1	2	3
y	a	−2	1	4	7

2. A linear relationship between x and y is shown in the above table. What is the value of a?
   A. $a = -3$
   B. $a = -5$
   C. $a = -12$
   D. $a = -14$

Use the table below to answer Question 3.

x	1	3	5	9	11
y	2	12	22	42	52

3. Which equation shows the relationship between x and y in the table above?
   A. $y = 5x + 3$
   B. $y = 5x - 3$
   C. $y = -5x + 3$
   D. $y = -5x - 3$

4. Mr. Klein asked his students to report the number of hours they spent studying for the final exam. He then plotted the results on the scatterplot below.

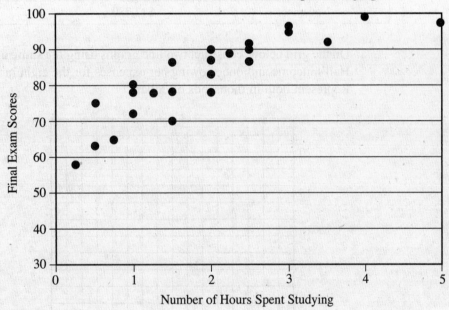

Final Exam Score versus Hours Spent Studying

Number of Hours Spent Studying

Final Exam Scores

Which of the following equations correctly approximates the line of best fit?

   A. $y = -8x + 40$
   B. $y = -8x + 65$
   C. $y = 8x + 40$
   D. $y = 8x + 65$

5. Ms. Hall started her own consulting firm eight months ago. The table below compares her income and expenses for each of the eight months.

Hall's Consulting		
Month	Expenses	Income
April	$10,345	$4,550
May	$11,250	$6,900
June	$12,695	$9,325
July	$13,510	$11,650
August	$14,765	$13,990
September	$15,600	$16,530
October	$16,850	$19,000
November	$17,780	$21,510

a. On the grid below, construct two line graphs using the **same axes**, one showing Ms. Hall's income and one showing her expenses for the eight month period. Represent both in thousands of dollars.

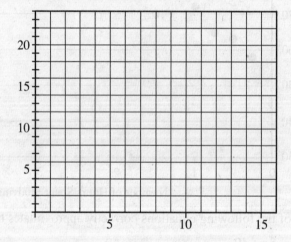

b. Assuming that both her income and expenses continue to grow at their respective current rates, estimate both her income and her expenses for the month of January. Explain or show how you found your estimates.

c. Again assuming that both income and expenses continue to grow at their respective current rates, estimate in which month Ms. Hall's profit (income minus expenses) will for the first time exceed $10,000. Explain or show how you found your estimates.

Use the chart below to answer Question 6.

Nationwide Phone Company			
	Monthly Fee	Number of Free Monthly Minutes	Charge Per Minute (after free minutes are used)
Freedom Plan	$ 14.00	0	$ 0.20
Extended Plan	$ 34.00	250	$ 0.35

6. Ms. Reen needs to select a billing plan for her cellular phone from the chart above. She estimates that she will use her phone less than 250 minutes per month.

   a. If she chooses the Freedom Plan and uses her phone for exactly 250 minutes in one month, what will her monthly bill be?

   b. Write an equation to compute her total bill B for one month if she chooses the Freedom Plan and uses m minutes in that month.

   c. On the grid below, construct a graph that shows the monthly bills for the Freedom Plan, for a monthly use of between 0 and 250 minutes.

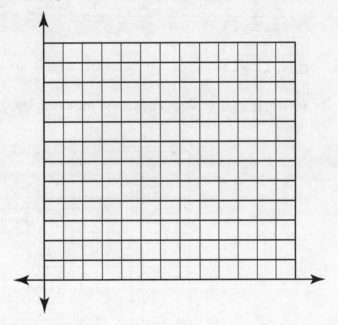

   d. Using your equation or graph, find the number of minutes of cell phone use per month for which the two plans have equal costs. Show or explain how you found your answer.

7. Which of the following equations is best represented by the graph below?

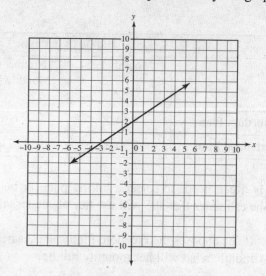

A. $y = \dfrac{3}{2}x - 3$

B. $y = \dfrac{3}{2}x + 2$

C. $y = \dfrac{2}{3}x + 3$

D. $y = \dfrac{2}{3}x + 2$

8. What appears to be the *x*-intercept of the line graphed below?

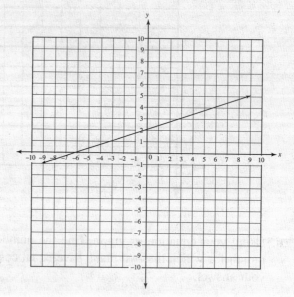

A. (−6, 0)

B. (0, −2)

C. (2, 0)

D. (0, −6)

9. The cost of printing different numbers of brochures for a certain travel company is shown on the graph below.

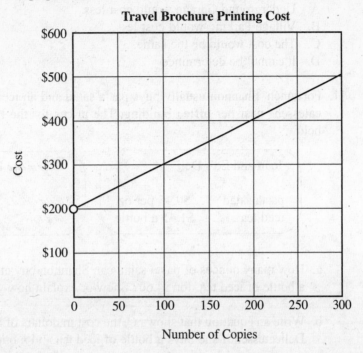

Travel Brochure Printing Cost

Which of the following equations represents the cost, C, of printing n copies of the travel brochure?

A. $C = \dfrac{1}{2}n + 200$

B. $C = 2n + 200$

C. $C = n + 200$

D. $C = 50n + 200$

Use the graphs below to answer Question 10.

Parking Rates

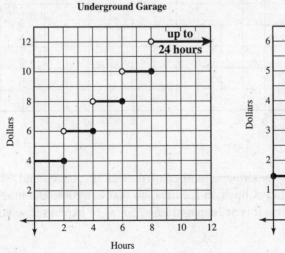

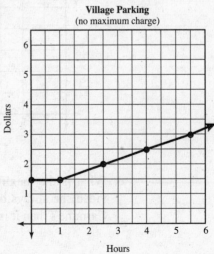

10. Which of the two parking options would give you a better rate if you were to park your car for 24 hours?
    A. Underground Garage would cost less.
    B. Village Parking would cost less.
    C. The cost would be the same.
    D. It cannot be determined.

11. For lunch, Shannon usually buys pasta salad and an iced tea from either of two delicatessens near her office building. The prices for the two different delis are shown below.

    Joan and Ed's Deli

    pasta salad . . . . $0.45 per oz.
    iced tea . . . . . . $1.45 a bottle

    Carmine's Delicatessen

    pasta salad . . . . $0.50 per ounce
    iced tea . . . . $1.00 a bottle

    a. How many ounces of pasta salad can Shannon buy at Joan and Ed's, together with a bottle of iced tea, for $4.60? Show or explain how you found your answer.

    b. Write an equation that shows C, the cost in dollars of Shannon's lunch at Carmine's Delicatessen if she buys a bottle of iced tea and n ounces of pasta salad. Use your equation to determine how much money it would cost Shannon to purchase 8 ounces of pasta salad, along with an iced tea. Show or explain how you found your answer.

    c. Graph the equation you wrote in part b on the grid below, using the horizontal axis for the number of ounces of pasta salad and using the vertical axis for the cost.

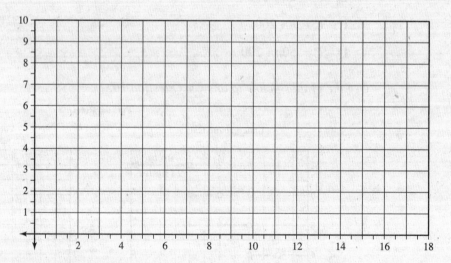

    d. What is the maximum number of ounces of pasta salad Shannon can buy, provided she always buys an iced tea, so that her complete lunch is less expensive at Carmine's than it is at Joan and Ed's? Show or explain how you found your answer.

12. Two linear equations are given below:

$2x + 4y = 9$

$10x - 5y = 16$

Which of the following statements about the equations is true?

A. They represent parallel lines.
B. They represent perpendicular lines.
C. They represent the same line.
D. They represent lines that have no slope.

13. A plumber uses the following formula to determine how much to charge for doing a job. C is the total charge in dollars, and h is the number of hours of work required to complete the job.

$C = 30h + 14$

This formula indicates that for every additional hour the plumber works, the total charge is increased by

A. $14
B. $30
C. $44
D. $420

14. Which of the following points lies on the graph of $3x - y = 6$?
A. (1, 6)
B. (0, 6)
C. (2, 0)
D. (–2, 0)

15. The table below indicates a linear relationship between x and y. Based on the indicated relationship, which of the numbers below belongs in place of the question mark in the table?

x	1	2	3	4	. . .	8
y	6	8	10	12	. . .	?

A. 14
B. 16
C. 18
D. 20

16. Rena has $613 in her bank account now. If she deposits $18 weekly, which of the following formulas will show her balance, B, at the end of n weeks?

A. $B = 613 + \dfrac{18}{n}$

B. $B = 613 \cdot 18n$

C. $B = 613 + 18n$

D. $B = 613 + \dfrac{n}{18}$

17. The conversion formula from degrees Centigrade to degrees Fahrenheit is

$$F = \frac{9}{5}C + 32$$

Convert a temperature of –15° Centigrade to degrees Fahrenheit.

18. What is the y-intercept of the line represented in the equation below?

$6x - 2y = 10$

   A. (0, –5)
   B. (0, –3)
   C. (0, 3)
   D. (0, 5)

19. Which of the following does NOT describe a line on the coordinate plane that is perpendicular to the y-axis?
   A. The slope of the line is equal to 0.
   B. The slope of the line is undefined.
   C. The line is parallel to the x-axis.
   D. The line is a horizontal line.

20. Which of the following is an equation of a line that is not parallel to the line with this equation?

$-x + 5y + 9 = 0$

   A. $y = \frac{1}{5}x + 2$

   B. $y = \frac{1}{5}x - 8$

   C. $-2x + 10y + 19 = 0$

   D. $x + 5y + 7 = 0$

21. What is the equation of the line graphed below?

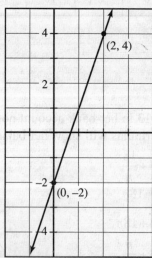

Solutions to Practice: Linear Functions

1. This linear equation is in the form $y = mx + b$. The y-coordinate of the y-intercept is –6.

   Answer: A

2. Try to find the linear equation $y = mx + b$ that relates the numbers in the table. If you can't think of it, compute the slope using any two points (x, y). Try $(3, 7)$ and $(2, 4)$. The slope is $\dfrac{7-4}{3-2} = \dfrac{3}{1}$. You now know that the multiple, or slope, of x is 3. This means that $y = 3x + b$. The table actually gives you the y-intercept. It is the point $(0, –2)$. If you did not notice this, plug one of your points into the formula $y = mx + b$ and solve for b. For example, plugging in the point $(3, 7)$ you get: $3(3) + b = 7$, and b equals –2. Next use the formula $y = 3x - 2$ to find the value of y when $x = -4$. Solving, you get $y = 3(-4) - 2 = -12 - 2 = -14$, so $a = -14$.

   Answer: D

3. **Use your answer choices** and test the equations against the points in the table. If the equation doesn't work for any point, move on to the next equation. If the equation works for one point, make certain that you test a second point before you decide on your answer. Here is the strategy worked out with the point $(1, 2)$:

   ~~A.~~ $y = 5x + 3 \longrightarrow \quad 2 \neq 5(1) + 3, \qquad$ *so answer choice A is incorrect.*
   B. $y = 5x - 3 \longrightarrow \quad 2 = 5(1) - 3, 3 \qquad$ *test the point (1, 2)*
   $\qquad\qquad\qquad\qquad\quad 12 = 5(3) - 3, 3 \qquad$ *test the point (3, 12)*
   $\qquad\qquad\qquad\qquad\quad 22 = 5(5) - 3, 3 \qquad$ *test the point (5, 22)*

   so answer choice B is correct. There are other methods of solving this problem that are more involved, and may prove useful if this question were open-ended. For example, first find the slope choosing any pair of points. Your choice will not change the value of the slope. Suppose you choose $(1, 2)$ and $(5, 22)$. Your slope would be $m = \dfrac{y_2 - y_1}{x_2 - x_1} = \dfrac{22-2}{5-1} = \dfrac{20}{4} = 5$. You can then use either the point-slope formula for the equation of a line, or the slope-intercept formula. Using point-slope:

   $(y - y_1) = m(x - x_1) \longrightarrow (y - 2) = 5(x - 1)$. Solving for y you get: $y = 5x - 3$.

   Using slope–intercept: $y = 5x + b \xrightarrow{\text{plug in a point}} 2 = 5(1) + b \longrightarrow b = -3$. So $y = 5x - 3$.

   Answer: B

4. The *line of best fit* is simply the line that fits the data points the closest. You can **eliminate answer choices** A and B because they show a negative slope and the line has a positive slope, only answer choices C and D are potentially correct. If you imagine drawing a line through the middle of the points, you can see that the *y*-intercept is closer to 65 than it is to 40, so that leaves D as your correct answer.

Answer: D

5 a.

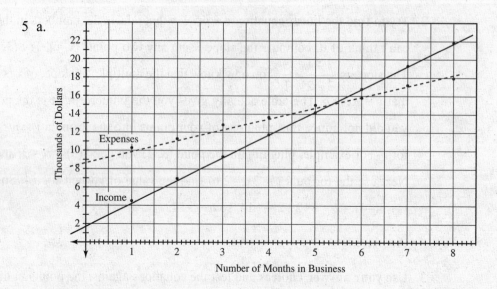

Number of Months in Business

b. Approximate the change in the *y values* between each of the two months. Expenses appear to increase by about $1,000 per month. Income appears to increase by $2,500 per month. You can approximate these values by looking at the slope between any two points. For convenience, consider *y* to be measured in thousands of dollars. Call April the first month in business, May the second, and so on.

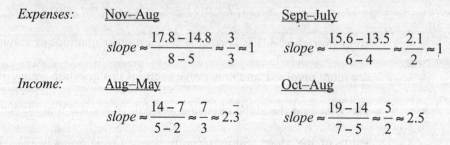

Expenses: Nov–Aug

$$slope \approx \frac{17.8 - 14.8}{8 - 5} \approx \frac{3}{3} \approx 1$$

Sept–July

$$slope \approx \frac{15.6 - 13.5}{6 - 4} \approx \frac{2.1}{2} \approx 1$$

Income: Aug–May

$$slope \approx \frac{14 - 7}{5 - 2} \approx \frac{7}{3} \approx 2.\overline{3}$$

Oct–Aug

$$slope \approx \frac{19 - 14}{7 - 5} \approx \frac{5}{2} \approx 2.5$$

Ms. Hall's expenses in November were approximately 17.8 thousand dollars, so to approximate her income in January you add 17.8 + 2(1). Your answer will be in thousands of dollars. *Expenses in January* ≈ 17.8 + 2(1) = 19.8 thousand dollars = $19,800.

Ms. Hall's income in November was approximately 21.5 thousand dollars, so to approximate her income in January you add 21.5 + 2(2.5). Your answer will be in thousands of dollars. *Income in January* ≈ 21.5 + 2(2.5) = 26.5 thousand dollars = $26,500.

Answer: *Expenses ≈ $19,800*
Income ≈ $26,500

c. *Profit = Income – Expenses*. From the line graphs, you can see that the gap between income and expenses grows after the point of intersection. You can get an equation for profit if you know the equations for income and expenses. Since each is a line, use the formula $y = mx + b$ for the equation of a line. You will have to approximate the y-intercepts from the graph.

> *Expenses Equation:* $y \approx x + 9$ *Income Equation:* $y \approx 2.5x + 2$

Subtract the two equations to get the profit equation.

> *Profit* $\approx$ *Income – Expenses* $= 2.5x + 2 - (x + 9) = 2.5x + 2 - x - 9 = 1.5x - 7$.
> *Profit* $\approx 1.5x - 7$

The profit must exceed \$10,000, so find where the profit is first equal to \$10,000. Remember that y is measured in thousands of dollars, and x is the number of months Ms. Hall has been in business: $10 = 1.5x - 7 \longrightarrow 17 = 1.5x \longrightarrow$ $x \approx 11.3$.

So Ms. Hall would exceed a profit of \$10,000 in roughly the middle of the 11th month of business. Since November is the 8th month, this would make February the 11th month.

Answer: February (Answers may vary)

6. a. The \$14.00 monthly charge is a flat fee and not affected by the number of minutes she uses, so do not multiply this number by 250. Computing her bill, you get *monthly charge* $= 14 + 0.20(250) = \$64$.

Answer: \$64.00

b. Following the formula you used in part a, replace her monthly bill and the number of minutes she used with B and m, respectively: $B = 14 + 0.20(m)$.

Answer: $B = 14 + 0.20(m)$

c. Pick a few points to graph your line. For example, if she used 0 minutes, her bill would be \$14.00. This is the y-intercept. Create a table if you like, where m is the number of minutes she used and B is her monthly bill. Use your formula: $B = 14 + 0.20(m)$.

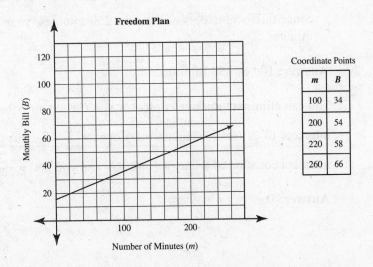

Freedom Plan

Monthly Bill (B) / Number of Minutes (m)

Coordinate Points

m	B
100	34
200	54
220	58
260	66

d. There are two answers. If she used 250 minutes or less on the Extended Plan, her charge would be a flat fee of $34.00. For every minute over 250, she has a charge of $0.35. Graphing the Extended Plan, notice that one of the points of intersection for the two graphs occurs before she exceeds 250 minutes.

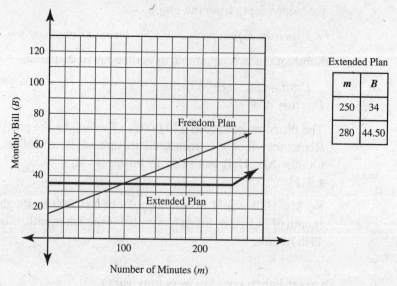

To find this point of intersection, you will need to calculate how many minutes on the Freedom Plan give her a bill of $34.00. Set your equation from part b equal to $34.00 and solve for m:

$$B = 14 + 0.20(m) \rightarrow 34 = 14 + 0.20(m) \rightarrow 20 = 0.20(m) \rightarrow m = 100 \text{ minutes}$$

This is only half of your answer. The cost for using minutes on the Extended Plan is greater than the cost for the Freedom Plan after she has exceeded 250 minutes. The graphs will intersect again. Let x be the number of minutes she has used in excess of 250. For example, if she used 350 minutes, x would be 100. Your equations to compute the bills on each of the plans would be

$$Freedom \ Plan = 64 + 0.2x \qquad Extended \ Plan = 34 + 0.35x$$

Setting these equations equal, you get

$$34 + 0.35x = 64 + 0.2x \rightarrow x = 200 \text{ minutes.}$$

Since this is in excess of the first 250 minutes, your answer is $250 + 200 = 450$ minutes.

Answer: 100 or 450 minutes

7. You can **eliminate answer choices** A and C right away because they do not have a y-intercept of 2. Next, compute the slope: $\dfrac{rise}{run} = \dfrac{2}{3}$. Put these values into the slope-intercept equation of a line, $y = mx + b$, and you get $y = \dfrac{2}{3}x + 2$.

Answer: D

8. The x-intercept is the point where the line crosses the x-axis. The coordinates of that point are $(-6, 0)$, making the x-intercept $= -6$.

    Answer: A

9. The y-coordinate of the y-intercept, b, is 200. Be careful when computing the slope.

    The x- and y- axes are scaled differently so that you cannot count boxes to find your

    slope. Choose any two points and use the formula $m = \dfrac{y_2 - y_1}{x_2 - x_1}$. Using the points

    $(0, 200)$ and $(100, 300)$ you get $m = \dfrac{300 - 200}{100 - 0} = 1$. Plugging into the equation

    $y = mx + b$ you get $C = n + 200$.

    Answer: C

10. The Underground Garage has a constant charge of $12.00 if you park your car for

    between 8 and 24 hours. Village Parking, however, follows a linear function after the first

    hour. First, find the slope of the linear section of the graph by using the formula

    $m = \dfrac{y_2 - y_1}{x_2 - x_1}$. Using the points $(1, 1.5)$ and $(4, 2.5)$, you get $m = \dfrac{2.5 - 1.5}{4 - 1} = \dfrac{1}{3}$. You can

    use this slope to find the dollar cost for parking for 24 hours. Call the dollar cost y and

    the number of hours x. Parking for 24 hours would be the point $(24, y)$. Choose another

    point on the line, such as $(4, 2.5)$. Using the slope formula and setting it equal to $\dfrac{1}{3}$, you

    get $\dfrac{1}{3} = \dfrac{y - 2.5}{24 - 4}$. Solving, you get

    $\dfrac{y - 2.5}{20} = \dfrac{1}{3} \longrightarrow 3(y - 2.5) = 20 \longrightarrow 3y - 7.5 = 20 \longrightarrow 3y = 27.5 \longrightarrow y \approx 9.167.$

    This is approximately $9.17 and is less expensive than the Underground Garage fee.

    Answer: B

11. a. Subtract $1.45 for the iced tea, and Shannon has $4.60 - 1.45 = 3.15$ left for the
        pasta salad. Let n represent the number of ounces of pasta salad: $0.45n = 3.15 \rightarrow$
        $n = 7$.

    Answer: 7 ounces

    b. $C = 1.00 + 0.5n$. Substituting in $n = 8$, you get $C = 1.00 + 0.5(8) = 5.00$.

    Answer: $C = 1.00 + 0.50n = \$5.00$

    c. Plot a few points on the graph and connect them to form a line. If Shannon buys 0
        ounces of pasta salad, her cost will be $1.00 for the iced tea. This is the point

(0, 1) on the graph. If Shannon buys 1 ounce of pasta salad her cost will be 1.00 + 0.50(1) = $1.50. This is the point (1, 1.5). If Shannon buys 2 ounces of pasta salad her cost will be 1.00 + 0.50(2) = $2.00. This is the point (2, 2). If Shannon buys 16 ounces of pasta salad, her cost will be 1.00 + 0.50(16) = $9.00. This is the point (16, 9). These points are enough to get a sketch of the line:

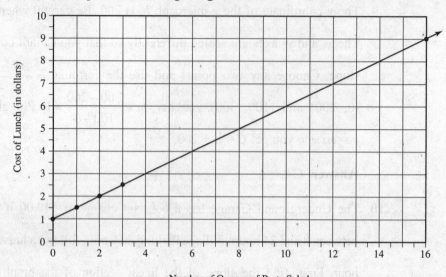

Number of Ounces of Pasta Salad

d. Carmine's < Joan and Ed's → 1.00 + 0.50n < 1.45 + 0.45n → 0.05n < 0.45 → n < 9. Shannon can buy any amount of pasta salad less than 9 ounces.

Answer: less than 9 ounces

12. Solve each equation so that it is in the form $y = mx + b$.

$$2x + 4y = 9 \qquad\qquad 10x - 5y = 16$$
$$4y = -2x + 9 \qquad\qquad -5y = -10x + 16$$
$$y = \frac{-1}{2}x + \frac{9}{4} \qquad\qquad y = 2x - \frac{16}{5}$$

The slope of one of the lines is $-\frac{1}{2}$ and the slope of the other is 2. Because the slopes are opposite reciprocals of each other, they must be perpendicular lines. This makes answer choice B correct. In order for the lines to be parallel, they would have to have the same slope. In order for the equations to represent the same line, they would have to be the same two equations or one of the equations could be multiplied by a constant to arrive at the second equation. Equations of lines that have no slope are of the form $x = some\ constant$ and are vertical lines.

Answer: B

13. The fixed rate in this problem is $14 and for each hour that the plumber works, the charge is increased by $30. You know that $30 is the correct answer because it is the amount that is multiplied by h, the hours worked.

Answer: B

14. Plug in your answer choices.

   ~~A.~~ $3(1) - (6) = 3 - 6 = -3 \neq 6$

   ~~B.~~ $3(0) - (6) = 0 - 6 = -6 \neq 6$

   C. $3(2) - (0) = 6 - 0 = 6$

   ~~D.~~ $3(-2) - (0) = -6 - 0 = -6 \neq 6$

   Answer: C

15. The slope of the line is calculated with the following formula: $\dfrac{change\ in\ y}{change\ in\ x} = \dfrac{y_2 - y_1}{x_2 - x_1}$.

   You can use any two points to calculate the slope. Using (1, 6) and (2, 8), the slope is

   $\dfrac{8-6}{2-1} = 2$. In point slope form, the equation of the line is $y - 6 = 2(x - 1)$.

   To find the y value when $x = 8$, plug 8 into the equation.
   Now, $y - 6 = 2(8 - 1) \rightarrow y - 6 = 2(7) \rightarrow y - 6 = 14 \rightarrow y = 20$.
   Notice that for each 1 unit increase in x, y increases by 2. You could simply complete the table:

x	4	5	6	7	8
y	12	14	16	18	20

   Answer: D

16. Each week. Rena adds $18 to her bank account.
   At the end of 1 week her balance is $B = 613 + 18 \cdot 1 = \$631$.
   At the end of 2 weeks her balance is $B = 613 + 18 \cdot 2 = \$649$.
   At the end of n weeks her balance is $B = 613 + 18 \cdot n = 613 + 18n$.

   Answer: C

17. Plug in $-15°$ into the equation for C:

   $F = \dfrac{9}{5}(-15) + 32 \rightarrow F = 9(-3) + 32 \rightarrow F = -27 + 32 \rightarrow F = 5°$.

   Answer: 5°

18. The y-intercept always has an x-coordinate of 0, so plug 0 for x into your equation:

   $6(0) - 2y = 10 \rightarrow -2y = 10 \rightarrow y = -5$.

   Answer: A

19. The following horizontal line, $y = 3$, is an example of a line that is perpendicular to the y-axis.

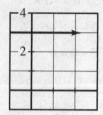

In general, in order for a line to be perpendicular to the y-axis, it must be horizontal. Answer choices A, C, and D are all examples of horizontal lines. Answer choice B has an undefined slope, which means it is a vertical line, not a horizontal.

Answer: B

20. Put $-x + 5y + 9 = 0$ into $y = mx + b$ form. First add x and subtract 9 from both sides of the equation: $5y = x - 9$. Next, divide both sides of the equation by 5: $y = \frac{1}{5}x - \frac{9}{5}$. The slope of the equation is $\frac{1}{5}$, so all lines parallel to it must also have a slope of $\frac{1}{5}$. This means answer choices A and B are parallel to the line. Convert answer choice C to $y = mx + b$ form. $-2x + 10y + 19 = 0 \rightarrow 10y = 2x - 19 \rightarrow y = \frac{1}{5}x - \frac{19}{10}$. Answer choice C also has a slope of $\frac{1}{5}$. Convert answer choice D to $y = mx + b$ form. $x + 5y + 7 = 0 \rightarrow 5y = -x - 7 \rightarrow y = -\frac{1}{5}x - \frac{7}{5}$. Answer choice D has a slope of $-\frac{1}{5}$, which is not equal to $\frac{1}{5}$, so it is not parallel to the given line.

Answer: D

21. Use the equation $y = mx + b$. Find the slope and the y-intercept. The slope of the line is calculated with the following formula: $\frac{change\ in\ y}{change\ in\ x} = \frac{y_2 - y_1}{x_2 - x_1}$.

The slope of this line is $\frac{4 - -2}{2 - 0} = \frac{6}{2} = 3$. You have the y-intercept of $(0, -2)$ so you can put the equation in slope-intercept form: $y = 3x - 2$.

Answer: $y = 3x - 2$

Other Functions

Not all graphs of functions turn out to be lines. There are several other functions that you should be familiar with. In general, you can always pick points to graph a function that you are not familiar with.

Quadratic Functions

- A **quadratic function** is one in which the highest power of the variable is 2. Their graphs are called **parabolas**. Here are a few examples of quadratic functions.

$$y = 3x^2 + 2x + 5 \qquad y = (x-4)^2 \qquad y = 2(x+3)^2 - 1 \qquad y = -x^2 + 7$$

When expanded and simplified, all the equations take on the form: $y = ax^2 + bx + c$. The following are examples of graphs of quadratic functions:

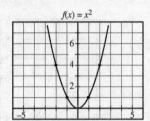
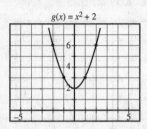
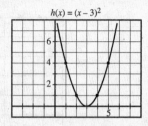

You can plot points to graph a function. Take for example $h(x) = (x-3)^2$. By setting $h(x)$ equal to y, you can generate coordinate points on the curve.

x	y
1	$(1-3)^2 = 4$
2	$(2-3)^2 = 1$
3	$(3-3)^2 = 0$
4	$(4-3)^2 = 1$
5	$(5-3)^2 = 4$

Exponential Functions

- An **exponential function** is one in which the variable is in the exponent. They are of the form $y = a^x$, where a is a constant. Typical problems that use exponential functions involve repeated doubling, tripling, halving, and so on of a certain quantity. When dealing with negative exponents, you may need to use the fact that $a^{-x} = \dfrac{1}{a^x}$. Two exponential functions are plotted and graphed below.

$f(x) = 2^x$ $g(x) = 2^{-x}$

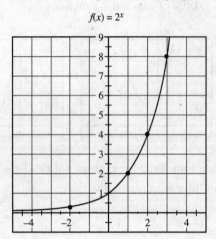 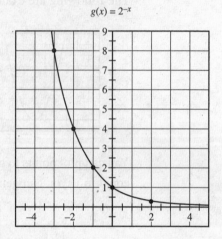

x	$y = 2^x$
3	$2^3 = 8$
2	$2^2 = 4$
1	$2^1 = 2$
-1	$2^{-1} = \dfrac{1}{2^1} = \dfrac{1}{2}$
-2	$2^{-2} = \dfrac{1}{2^2} = \dfrac{1}{4}$

x	$y = 2^{-x} = \dfrac{1}{2^x}$
2	$2^{-2} = \dfrac{1}{2^2} = \dfrac{1}{4}$
1	$2^{-1} = \dfrac{1}{2^1} = \dfrac{1}{2}$
0	$2^0 = 1$
-1	$2^1 = 2$
-2	$2^2 = 4$

> ** Remember: For the exponential functions shown, y values will always be greater than zero.*

Square Root Functions

- The **square root function** is a function of the form $f(x) = \sqrt{x}$. When plotting points, choose x values that are perfect squares. The square root of a negative number is not defined in the real number system. The square root function is plotted and graphed below.

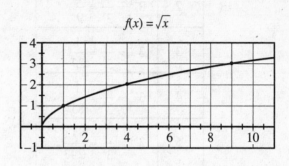

x	$y = \sqrt{x}$
0	$\sqrt{0} = 0$
1	$\sqrt{1} = 1$
4	$\sqrt{4} = 2$
9	$\sqrt{9} = 3$
−1	undefined

Remember: You cannot take the square root of a number that is less than zero.

Examples: Other Functions

Use the equation below to answer Example 1.

$$y = 3^{-x}$$

Example 1. As the value of x increases to a very large positive number, what happens to the value of y?

    A. y becomes negative.
    B. y gets closer to 1.
    C. y gets closer to 0.
    D. y gets infinitely large.

Solution

Remember that $3^{-x} = \dfrac{1}{3^{x}}$. Try plotting some points, and look for the behavior of the graph as x gets larger.

x	$y = 3^{-x} = \dfrac{1}{3^x}$
1	$3^{-1} = \dfrac{1}{3^1} = \dfrac{1}{3}$
2	$3^{-2} = \dfrac{1}{3^x} = \dfrac{1}{9}$
3	$3^{-3} = \dfrac{1}{3^3} = \dfrac{1}{27}$
4	$3^{-4} = \dfrac{1}{3^4} = \dfrac{1}{81}$
5	$3^{-5} = \dfrac{1}{3^5} = \dfrac{1}{243}$

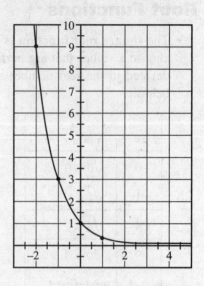

The y value gets smaller and smaller but will never equal zero or become negative.

Answer: C

Practice: Other Functions

1. The area of a circle, A, is found by using the formula:

    $A = \pi r^2$, where r is the radius of the circle.

    Which graph best shows the relationship between the radius and the area of a circle?

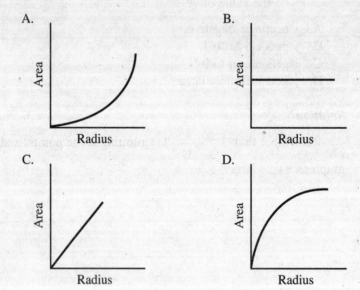

★ 2. The number of bacteria in a sample doubles every three hours. At the end of a 12-hour period, there are 40,000 bacteria present.

a. How many bacteria were initially present at the beginning of the 12-hour period? Show your work.

b. Write a mathematical expression to determine the number of bacteria present at the end of any 3-hour period.

c. During which 3-hour period will 2 million bacteria first be present? Show your work.

3. Which of the following functions will yield the largest value for $x = 25$?
A. $f(x) = 6 + x$
B. $f(x) = 6x$
C. $f(x) = x^6$
D. $f(x) = 6^x$

Use the table below to answer Question 4.

Some triangles with an area of 36 square units

Base (in units)	1	2	3	4	6	9	12	72
Height (in units)	72	36	24	18	12	8	6	1

4. Which graph below represents the relationship between the bases and heights of all triangles with an area of 36 square units?

A.

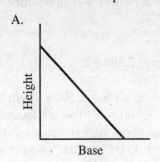

B.

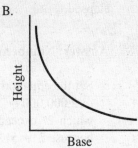

C.

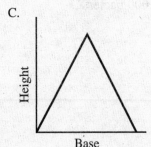

D.

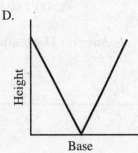

Solutions to Practice: Other Functions

1. The formula $A = \pi r^2$ is a quadratic function because the variable in the problem is squared. The graph looks like half of a parabola, since the radius of a circle can only be positive.

Answer: A

2. a. Let x be the number of bacteria present at the beginning of the 12-hour period. At the end of the first 3-hour period, you would have $2x$, the second $4x$, the third $8x$, and the fourth $16x$. The end of the fourth 3-hour period is also the end of the 12-hour period. Set this equal to 40,000 and solve for x: $16x = 40,000 \rightarrow x = 2,500$.

Answer: $x = 2,500$ bacteria

   b. This is an exponential function. Write out the number of bacteria present at the end of each 3-hour period in terms of 2^n.

Period	Number of Bacteria
initial	$x = 2^0 \cdot x$
first	$2x = 2^1 \cdot x$
second	$4x = 2^2 \cdot x$
third	$8x = 2^3 \cdot x$
fourth	$16x = 2^4 \cdot x$
•	•
•	•
•	•
n th	$2^n \cdot x$

Use your answer from part a and replace x, the initial number of bacteria, with 2,500: *number of bacteria* $= 2,500 \cdot 2^n$, where n is the number of 3-hour periods that have elapsed.

Answer: Number of bacteria $= 2,500 \cdot 2^n$

   c. Set the equation *number of bacteria* $= 2,500 \cdot 2^n$ equal to 2 million, and solve for n: $2,000,000 = 2,500 \cdot 2^n \rightarrow 800 = 2^n$. You are looking for the first value of n for which 2^n exceeds 800. The bacteria first exceed 2 million in the tenth interval, because $2^9 = 512$ and $2^{10} = 1,024$. Checking, you get *number of bacteria* $= 2,500 \cdot 2^{10} = 2500(1,024) = 2,560,000$ bacteria.

Answer: The tenth interval

3. Plugging in 25 for x, it is clear that you can **eliminate answer choices** A and B because they are not the largest. Next compare choices C and D. Consider that choice C can be rewritten as 5^{12} because each factor of 25 is the same as two factors of 5.

~~A.~~ $f(25) = 6 + 25 = 31$

~~B.~~ $f(25) = 6(25) = 150$

C. $f(25) = 25^6 = 25 \cdot 25 \cdot 25 \cdot 25 \cdot 25 \cdot 25 = 5 \cdot 5 \cdot 5 \cdot 5 \cdot 5 \cdot 5 \cdot 5 \cdot 5 \cdot 5 \cdot 5 \cdot 5 \cdot 5$

D. $f(25) = 6^{25} = 6 \cdot 6 \cdot 6 \cdot 6 \cdot 6 \cdot \ldots$

Because 5^{12} is clearly less than 6^{25}, answer choice D is the largest.

Answer: D

4. As the base gets larger, the height gets smaller. This narrows down your answer choices to A and B. The relationship between the base and height is not linear because each unit change in the base does not result in a constant change in the height. This leaves you only with choice B remaining. You may also plot the points to verify your result.

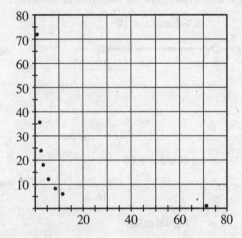

Answer: B

Inequalities and Absolute Value

- An inequality is similar to an equation, except you will see a symbol other than =. Other possible symbols when reading an algebraic sentence from left to right are

<	*less than*	*less than or equal to* (preceded by ≤)
>	*greater than*	*greater than or equal to* (preceded by ≥)

<   *less than*   ≤   *less than or equal to*
>   *greater than*   ≥   *greater than or equal to*

There may be an infinite number of solutions, so you will often need to graph your solution on a number line. The shaded section of the line indicates all the x values that make up the solution. A filled-in circle is used when the number is part of the solution, and an open circle is used when the number is not part of the solution.

Linear Inequalities

- Solve linear inequalities as you would an equation, with the only exception that you will flip the inequality symbol when you multiply or divide the inequality by a negative number.

Flip the sign	*Do not flip the sign*
$-3x > 18$	$3x > -18$
$\dfrac{-3x}{-3} > \dfrac{18}{-3}$	$\dfrac{3x}{3} > \dfrac{-18}{3}$
$x < -6$	$x > -6$

Compound Linear Inequalities

- Two linear inequalities connected by the words *and* or *or* make up a **compound linear inequality**. The word *and* indicates that your solutions will have to satisfy both criteria in order to be part of the solution. The word *or* indicates that your solutions will have to satisfy either criteria to be part of the solution.

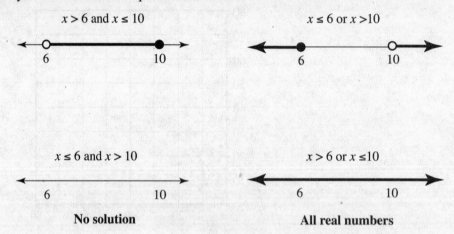

$x > 6$ and $x \leq 10$

$x \leq 6$ or $x > 10$

$x \leq 6$ and $x > 10$

No solution

$x > 6$ or $x \leq 10$

All real numbers

Absolute Value Equations

- The **absolute value** of a number is always positive. For example, there are two numbers whose absolute values are equal to 6. The numbers are 6 and –6. You can write this as $|6| = 6$ and $|-6| = 6$. When solving absolute value equations, you must consider two cases, the positive and the negative.

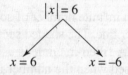

$|x| = 6$

$x = 6$ $x = -6$

> ** Remember: Always isolate the absolute value before breaking it into two separate equations and solving.*

Absolute Value Inequalities

- Solve absolute value inequalities the same way you solve absolute value equations, but flip the inequality sign on the negative side. Your solution will often need to be graphed.

> ** Remember: Use a closed circle on the number line when your symbol includes equality (≥ or ≤); otherwise, use an open circle.*

Examples: Inequalities and Absolute Value

Example 1. Solve for x.

$$3|2x+7| - 5 = 19$$

Solution

$$3|2x+7| - 5 = 19$$
$$3|2x+7| = 24$$
$$|2x+7| = 8 \qquad \textit{Isolate the absolute value.}$$

$2x + 7 = 8$	$2x + 7 = -8$	*Separate into two equations.*
$2x = 1$	$2x = -15$	
$x = \dfrac{1}{2}$	$x = \dfrac{-15}{2}$	

Answer: $x = \dfrac{1}{2}$ and $x = \dfrac{-15}{2}$

Example 2. Solve and graph.

$$2\left|x+6\right|>18$$

Solution

Isolate the absolute value. Don't forget to flip the sign on the negative side when removing the absolute value symbol.

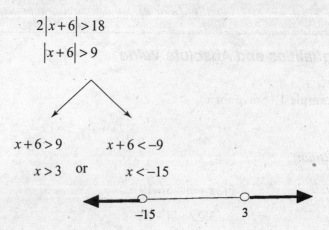

$$2\left|x+6\right|>18$$

$$\left|x+6\right|>9$$

$$x+6>9 \qquad x+6<-9$$

$$x>3 \quad \text{or} \quad x<-15$$

Answer: $x > 3$ or $x < -15$

Practice: Inequalities and Absolute Value

1. Which of the following graphs shows the solution set for the inequality $\left|x-3\right|>5$?

A.

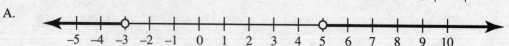

B.

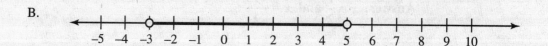

C.

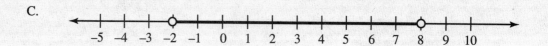

D.

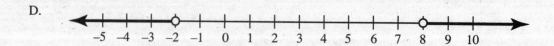

2. Ice cream cones at the Soft Serve Station come in two sizes, small and large. During the summer, ice cream cone sales take in **at least** $2,400 weekly. A small cone costs $2.50 and a large one costs $3.50. If s represents the number of small cones sold in one week, and b represents the number of large cones sold in one week, which algebraic sentence below represents the amount of money received each week from ice cream cone sales?

A. $2.50s + 3.50b = 2,400$
B. $2.50s + 3.50b \geq 2,400$
C. $2.50s + 3.50b > 2,400$
D. $2.50s + 3.50b < 2,400$

3. Which graph below represents the solution set for the inequality $6 - 2x \leq 14$?

A.

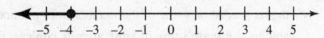

B.

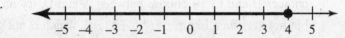

C.

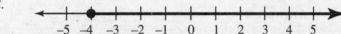

D.

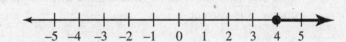

4. Which of the following defines the solution set for the inequality shown below?

$$-4x + 7 \geq 10$$

A. $x \leq -\dfrac{3}{4}$

B. $x \leq \dfrac{3}{4}$

C. $x \geq -\dfrac{3}{4}$

D. $x \geq \dfrac{3}{4}$

5. What are the solutions to the equation below?

$$\left| 9 - 2x \right| = 15$$

A. $x = -3$ and $x = 12$
B. $x = 3$ and $x = 12$
C. $x = -3$ and $x = -12$
D. $x = 3$ and $x = -12$

Solutions to Practice: Inequalities and Absolute Value

1. The absolute value is already isolated, so break into two inequalities, one positive and one negative: $|x-3| > 5$

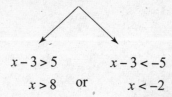

$$x - 3 > 5 \qquad x - 3 < -5$$
$$x > 8 \quad \text{or} \quad x < -2$$

You could also **use your answer choices** to solve this problem. Choose a value for x that is shaded on some of the number lines but not all of them. This way, you will be able to **eliminate some of your answer choices**. For example, try $x = 4$. $|4-3| = 1$, which is not greater than 5. This means it should not be filled in and eliminates answer choices B and C. To choose between A and D, try an x value that is filled in for one but not the other, like $x = 6$. $|6-3| = 3$, which is not greater than 5 and should not be filled in so the correct answer must be D.

Answer: D

2. The statement "at least $2,400" means that the Soft Serve Station is taking in $2,400 or more. This is the same as using the symbol greater than or equal to, $\geq$, so answer choice B is correct.

Answer: B

3. Remember to flip the sign in the step where you divide by a negative number. $6 - 2x \leq 14 \longrightarrow -2x \leq 8 \longrightarrow x \geq -4$. The graph in answer choice C is correct.

Answer: C

4. Subtract 7 on both sides of the inequality: $-4x \geq 3$. Divide both sides by -4 and flip the inequality: $x \leq -\dfrac{3}{4}$.

Answer: A

5. You can solve this by setting up two equations:
$$9 - 2x = 15 \text{ and } 9 - 2x = -15$$
$$-2x = 6 \qquad -2x = -24$$
$$x = -3 \qquad x = 12$$

You can also get this answer by using **your answer choices**. Plug –3 and 12 into the equation to see if they work and if they don't, try another answer choice.

$$\left| 9 - 2(-3) \right| = \left| 9 + 6 \right| = 15$$

$$\left| 9 - 2\left(12\right) \right| = \left| 9 - 24 \right| = \left| -15 \right| = 15$$

Answer: A

Systems of Linear Equations

- A **system of equations** is a combination of two or more equations and two or more variables. In general, it is only possible to solve a system if you have as many equations as you have variables. Solving a system requires you to solve for all the variables present in any of the equations. The values of those variables work in all of the equations. Here is an example of a system.

$$4x - 5y = 37$$
$$2x + y = 1$$

The solution to the system above is $x = 3$ and $y = -5$. You can verify this solution by checking that the values hold true when plugged into both equations.

$$4x - 5y = 37 \xrightarrow[plug\ in\ values]{} 4(3) - 5(-5) = 37$$

$$2x + y = 1 \xrightarrow[plug\ in\ values]{} 2(3) + (-5) = 1$$

For the MCAS, you will only need to know how to solve **linear systems**, which involve only linear equations. Furthermore, you will only be required to solve systems of two equations, and not three or more.

- There are three methods of solving systems of linear equations. They are **graphing, substitution,** and **linear combinations**. Solving systems using linear combinations is often referred to as the **addition method**.

> * *Remember: Check your answers to a system, regardless of which method you choose, by plugging your values into both of the original equations.*

Graphing

- To solve a system by graphing, you must graph both lines on an *x*-*y* coordinate plane, and locate their point of intersection. The coordinates (*x*, *y*) of the point of intersection are the solutions for *x* and *y* in the system.

Substitution Method

- To solve a system of equations using the substitution method, you must first solve for one variable in terms of the other in one of the two equations. You should generally look for any variable that has a coefficient of 1, to avoid the possibility of having to work with fractional expressions.

For example, suppose you were solving the system below with the substitution method.

$$5x - 2y = 7$$
$$6x + y = 22$$

First consider each equation separately. Labeling the equations is always a good idea. You should start by solving for y in equation B to avoid working with fractional expressions.

Equation A: $5x - 2y = 7$ *Equation B:* $6x + y = 22$
$$y = -6x + 22$$

The next step is to replace, or substitute, the expression $-6x + 22$ for y in equation A. It is very important that you substitute into the other equation, or else your variables will disappear, and you will not be able to solve the system.

$$5x - 2(y) = 7 \qquad\qquad y = -6x + 22$$

$$5x - 2(-6x + 22) = 7$$

You are now down to one equation and one unknown. Solving you get

$$5x - 2(-6x + 22) = 7$$
$$5x + 12x - 44 = 7$$
$$17x - 44 = 7$$
$$17x = 51$$
$$x = 3$$

To find the solution for y, all you need to do is take the x value and replace it into any one of the equations above that contains a y variable. It will be easiest to choose the equation that has already been solved for y.

$y = -6x + 22$ **Check answers in original equations:**
$y = -6(3) + 22$ $5x - 2y = 7 \rightarrow 5(3) - 2(4) = 15 - 8 = 7$
$y = -18 + 22$ $6x + y = 22 \rightarrow 6(3) + (4) = 18 + 4 = 22$
$y = 4$

Addition Method or Linear Combinations

- The addition method for solving a system of equations is also known as the process of using Linear Combinations. It comes from two basic algebraic principles. The first is that if $A = B$, then $kA = kB$, where k is any real number. The second principle is that if $A = B$ and $C = D$ then $A + C = B + D$. This can be written as

$$A = B$$
$$\underline{+\ C = D}$$
$$A + C = B + D$$

The idea is to find a multiplier for each equation that needs one, so that when the equations are added together, one variable is eliminated. You can then solve for the variable that remains.

Consider the system made up of equations A and B below. Notice that when equation A is multiplied by –5, the two y terms cancel out when the equations are added, and you can solve for x.

A) $3x + 2y = 26$ → $(-5) \cdot [3x + 2y = 26]$ → $-15x - 10y = -130$
B) $5x + 10y = 30$ $5x + 10y = 30$ $5x + 10y = 30$

$$
\begin{array}{rl}
\text{A)} & -15x - 10y = -130 \\
+ \ \text{B)} & 5x + 10y = 30 \\
\hline
& -10x = -100 \\
& x = 10
\end{array}
$$

After you have solved for x, substitute this value into either original equation, and solve for y.

A) $3x + 2y = 26$
$3(10) + 2y = 26$
$30 + 2y = 26$
$2y = -4$
$y = -2$

Answer: $x = 10$, $y = -2$

Examples: Systems of Linear Equations

Example 1. Solve the system below by graphing.

$y = x + 1$
$y = -2x + 4$

Solution

Graph the two lines using the slope-intercept method.

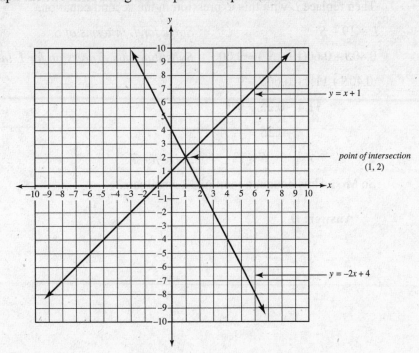

The point of intersection of the two graphs is the solution to the system. Since the point of intersection is (1, 2), the solution is $x = 1$ and $y = 2$. It is always a good idea to check your solution by substituting these values into the original equations, as human error may occur in your process, particularly when you solve using the graphing method.

Check: $y = x + 1 \xrightarrow[\text{plug in values}]{} 2 = 1 + 1$

$\qquad y = -2x + 4 \xrightarrow[\text{plug in values}]{} 2 = -2(1) + 4$

Answer: $x = 1$ and $y = 2$

Example 2. Mrs. Alms purchased 19 glass jars for the tomato sauce she is making, for a total of \$9.00. Each large jar cost \$0.60 and each small jar cost \$0.40. How many small jars did Mrs. Alms purchase?

    A. 6
    B. 7
    C. 10
    D. 12

Solution

There are two unknowns in the problem, the number of small jars and the number of large. Choose a variable for each. For example, let S be the number of small jars and L be the number of large jars that Mrs. Alms bought. Because you have two variables, you will need two equations to solve for them. Here they are:

$$S + L = 19 \qquad\qquad 0.40S + 0.60L = 9.00$$
She bought a total of 19 jars.   *The total cost for the jars was \$9.00.*

Choose a method for solving the system. Substitution works well here, since the coefficient of at least one of the variables is one. Solve for L in terms of S in the first equation. Then replace L with this expression in the second equation.

$L = 19 - S$ *Solve for L in terms of S.*

$0.40S + 0.60(19 - S) = 9.00$ *Substitute this expression for L in the other equation.*

$\quad 0.40S + 11.4 - 0.60S = 9$

$\qquad\qquad 11.4 - 0.2S = 9$

$\qquad\qquad\qquad -0.2S = -2.4$

$\qquad\qquad\qquad\quad S = 12$ *Solve for S.*

So Mrs. Alms bought a total of 12 small jars.

Answer: D

Practice: Systems of Linear Equations

1. If 3 magnets and 2 key rings cost $8.35, and 2 magnets and 5 key rings cost $9.05, what is the cost of one magnet?
   A. $0.95
   B. $1.05
   C. $2.15
   D. $2.45

2. At a high school dance, 120 tickets were sold to juniors and 180 to sophomores. The price per ticket for a sophomore was $5.00 less than the price per ticket for juniors, since the dance was sponsored by the sophomore class. The money raised on ticket sales from each of the two classes was the same. What was the price for a junior ticket?
   A. $10.00
   B. $12.00
   C. $15.00
   D. $25.00

Use the information in the box below to answer Question 3.

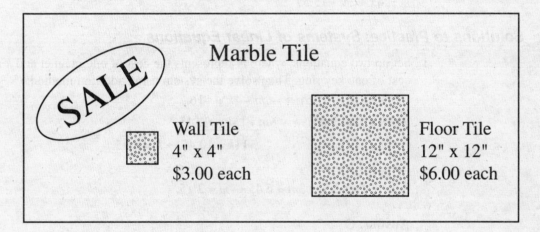

Marble Tile

Wall Tile
4" x 4"
$3.00 each

Floor Tile
12" x 12"
$6.00 each

3. Christina and Christian are tiling their bathroom walls and floor with two different-sized marble tiles. The 4-inch tile is to be used for the walls and the 12-inch tile for the floor. They purchased a total of 120 tiles for a price of $580.00. Which pair of equations could be used to find the number of tiles of each size that they bought?
   A. $3x + 6y = 120$ and $x + y = 580$
   B. $x + y = 120$ and $4x + 12y = 580$
   C. $4x + 12y = 120$ and $3x + 6y = 580$
   D. $x + y = 120$ and $3x + 6y = 580$

4. Helen has 3 times as many quarters as dimes. She has a total of $10.20. How many dimes does she have?
   A. 12
   B. 20
   C. 24
   D. 36

5. Mr. Sanchez purchased 20 theater tickets for a total of $296. The tickets cost $18 for adults and $10 for children under age 14. How many children's tickets did Mr. Sanchez purchase?

6. Meg and Kate bought identically priced bags of potato chips and onion dip that they were each bringing to a party.

- Meg bought 4 bags of chips and 2 containers of onion dip for $9.72.

- Kate bought 5 bags of chips and 4 containers of onion dip for $15.57.

Which of the following systems of equations could be used to find x, the cost of one bag of chips, and y, the cost of one container of onion dip?

A. $x + y = 9.72$
$x + y = 15.57$

B. $9.72x + 15.57y = 15$
$x + y = 15$

C. $4x + 2y = 9.72$
$5x + 4y = 15.57$

D. $5x + 4y = 9.72$
$4x + 2y = 15.57$

Solutions to Practice: Systems of Linear Equations

1. Set up two equations, where m represents the cost of one magnet and k represents the cost of one key ring. Then solve the system using addition method:

$-2(3m + 2k = 8.35) \rightarrow -6m - 4k = -16.7$
$3(2m + 5k = 9.05) \rightarrow \underline{6m + 15k = 27.15}$
$11k = 10.45 \rightarrow k = 0.95$

$3m + 2(.95) = 8.35$
$3m + 1.9 = 8.35 \rightarrow 3m = 6.45 \rightarrow m = 2.15.$

Answer: C

2. Set up two equations. Let j equal the price per ticket for juniors and let s equal the price per ticket for sophomores. Since the money raised for the two classes was the same, $120j = 180s$. Also, sophomores pay $5 less than juniors, $s = j - 5$. Substitute $j - 5$ into the first equation for s and solve for j:

$120j = 180(j - 5) \rightarrow 120j = 180j - 900 \rightarrow j = 15.$

Answer: C

3. Let x and y represent the number of each type of tile that was bought. Since they purchased a total of 120 tiles, the first equation is $x + y = 120$. The cost equation includes the cost per each type of tile: $3x + 6y = 580$.

Answer: D

4. Call the number of dimes, d, and the number of quarters, q. Set up a system:

$q = 3d$

$0.25q + 0.10d = 10.20$

Multiply the second equation by 100 to get rid of the decimals:

$q = 3d$

$25q + 10d = 1020$

Substitute q into the second equation as $3d$.

$25(3d) + 10d = 1020$

$75d + 10d = 1020$

$85d = 1020$

$d = 12$

You can also use your answer choices to solve this problem. If there are 12 dimes, each worth 10 cents, Helen has a total of $1.20 from the dimes. Subtract that from $10.20 and there is $9.00 left. There are 4 quarters in a dollar, so there are 36 quarters in 9 dollars. 36 is 3 times 12, which is how the question began. So answer choice A works!

Answer: A

5. Let x = the number of adult tickets and y = the number of children's tickets. Set up a system:

$x + y = 20$

$18x + 10y = 296$

The question asks for the number of children's tickets purchased, so you should eliminate x, the number of adult tickets, in the two equations. Multiply the first equation by -18.

$-18x - 18y = -360$

$18x + 10y = 296$

Add the two equations together and $-8y = -64 \rightarrow y = 8$.

Answer: 8

6.   A̶. These equations do not take into account the number of bags of chips or containers of onion dip that Meg and Kate bought.

   B̶. These equations are incorrect. The first, multiplies the cost of a bag of chips times Meg's total cost and adds it to the cost of a container of onion dip times Kate's total cost and sets it equal to 15. This does not make sense! Kate's and Meg's expenses shouldn't be in the same equation and the total expense should be the final sum, like in answer choices C and D.

   C. This is the correct system!

   D̶. This is incorrect. It swaps the total amount paid by Meg and Kate.

Answer: C

Patterns

- A **pattern** is a sequence, or list, where terms are generated by some sort of rule. Some patterns are easier to recognize than others. Consider the sequence:

$$2, 5, 8, 11, 14, \ldots$$

The way to start a pattern problem is to look for the difference between terms that are next to each other. Here, you may notice there is a common difference of 3 between each two terms. If you were asked for the eighth term in the pattern, you could arrive at the answer in one of two different ways.

1. You could simply add 3 to each successive term until you've reached the eighth term. When counting, the 2 would be considered the first term.

2. You can also try to come up with the rule that compares the order number, n, of each term in the sequence and the actual term itself, called a_n. For example, for a third term n would be equal to 3, and the term's value would be a_3. In the table below, since the third term is equal to 8, $a_3 = 8$. Generating a table of values may help you figure out the rule.

n	1	2	3	4	5	. . .	n
a_n	2	5	8	11	14	. . .	$3n - 1$

Computing the 8th term is as easy as plugging in the number 8 for n into the rule.

$$\text{rule: } a_n = 3n - 1$$
$$a_8 = 3(8) - 1 = 24 - 1 = 23$$

So why would you ever choose the second method? Consider if you were asked for the 80th term instead of the 8th. It would take you an awfully long time to list all 80 terms by counting, right? But look how easy it would be if you used your formula:

$$a_n = 3n - 1$$
$$a_{80} = 3(80) - 1 = 240 - 1 = 239$$

Arithmetic Sequences

- The sequence you just looked at was an example of an **arithmetic sequence**. An arithmetic sequence is a pattern in which there is a constant difference between each pair of terms. In the last example, this difference was 3. The formula for the nth term will be a linear equation of the form: $a_n = mn + b$. This may remind you of a linear function. In general, you can come up with the formula if you follow the rules:

$$a_n = a_1 + (n - 1)d$$

Here, a_1 is the value of the first term, n is the order number of the term in the sequence (the first term would have the value $n = 1$, etc.), and d is the common difference between the terms in the sequence. The last example would look like

$$a_8 = 2 + (8 - 1)(3) = 2 + 21 = 23$$

Linear Patterns

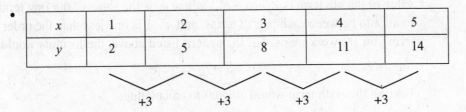

x	1	2	3	4	5
y	2	5	8	11	14

+3   +3   +3   +3

A linear relationship between x and y is shown in the above table. This table is similar to the tables in the Linear Functions section of this chapter. Notice that there is a common difference of 3 between each term in this sequence. When there is a constant difference, the pattern is linear or arithmetic, as shown above.

Quadratic Patterns

- Next consider the sequence: 0, 3, 8, 15, 24, 35, . . .
  There is no common difference between each pair of terms:

$$
\begin{array}{ccccccc}
& +3 & +5 & +7 & +9 & +11 & \\
0, & 3, & 8, & 15, & 24, & 35, \ldots
\end{array}
$$

You may notice the pattern that forms the sequence and be able to generate the next term if you know the previous terms. Here, the number added to each subsequent term increases by 2 each time.

If you need to find a formula for a_n given the order number, n, try looking for a second set of differences. Notice here that they are constantly 2.

$$
\begin{array}{ccccccc}
& +2 & +2 & +2 & +2 & & \\
& +3 & +5 & +7 & +9 & +11 & \\
0, & 3, & 8, & 15, & 24, & 35, \ldots
\end{array}
$$

If the second set of differences is constant, in this case 2, then the pattern can be modeled with a quadratic function. This means that the formula for finding a_n will involve an n^2. The formula for the pattern above is $a_n = n^2 - 1$. The table may help you see this:

n	1	2	3	4	5	. . .	n
a_n	0	3	8	15	24	. . .	$n^2 - 1$

In general, finding a quadratic relationship can be pretty difficult. Most likely, you will only have to compare formulas given to you in the answer choices against values in a table.

Geometric Sequences

- **Geometric sequences** are patterns in which consecutive terms have a common ratio. This means that you could multiply each term by a certain number to get the next term. For example, the common ratio in the following sequence is the number 3.

$$2, 6, 18, 54, 162, \ldots$$

The sixth term in the sequence would be $162 \cdot 3 = 486$. In general, the formula for the value of the nth term is $a_n = a_1 \cdot r^{n-1}$, where a_1 is the value of the first term, r is the common ratio between each pair of terms, and $n - 1$ is one less than the order number of the term you are working on. For the pattern listed above, the formula would be

$$a_n = 2 \cdot 3^{n-1}$$

Finding the sixth term would amount to calculating:

$$a_6 = 2 \cdot 3^{6-1} = 2 \cdot 3^5 = 2 \cdot 243 = 486$$

Miscellaneous Sequences

- Sometimes patterns don't fall into any of the above-mentioned categories. Consider a mathematical favorite, known as the **Fibonacci Sequence**:

$$1, 1, 2, 3, 5, 8, 13, \ldots$$

In this one, the next term is created by adding the two previous terms together. This formula would look like: $a_n = a_{n-1} + a_{n-2}$. Here a_{n-1} is the term immediately before the term a_n. Note that $a_{n-1} \neq a_n - 1$!

- Next, consider the sequence:

$$2, 5, 3, 6, 4, 7, 5, \ldots$$

Notice the back and forth behavior of increasing and decreasing.

$$
\begin{array}{ccccccc}
& +3 & -2 & +3 & -2 & +3 & -2 \\
2, & 5, & 3, & 6, & 4, & 7, & 5, \ldots
\end{array}
$$

The next two terms would be 8 and 6, as $5 + 3 = 8$ and then $8 - 2 = 6$.

- The next pattern may be more difficult to identify.

$$1, 5, 13, 29, 61, \ldots$$

Follow the same process of either trying to see how each term is generated, or finding a relationship between a_n and n.

$$
\begin{array}{ccccc}
+4 & +8 & +16 & +32 \\
1, & 5, & 13, & 29, & 61, \ldots
\end{array}
$$

This pattern is generated by doubling the amount you add to each term, starting with 4. This pattern also follows the rule that each term is formed by doubling the previous term and then adding 3. As a formula, this would look like $a_n = 2a_{n-1} + 3$. You may not always be able to come up with a formula given only n, the number of the term in the sequence. If this is the case, and the MCAS question happens to be multiple choice, all you need to do is test the terms in the sequence against the rule options they give you, to see which rule works for all of the terms.

Examples: Patterns

Example 1. What is the eighth term in the pattern below?

$$3, 4, 6, 9, 13, 18, \ldots$$

A. 23
B. 24
C. 31
D. 43

Solution

This pattern does not have a common difference between the terms, but it appears as though you increase the amount you add by 1 each time. Since the eighth term is only two terms away, do not bother to come up with a formula. Simply add 6 and then 7.

$$
\begin{array}{ccccccc}
+1 & +2 & +3 & +4 & +5 & +6 & +7 \\
\end{array}
$$

$$3, \quad 4, \quad 6, \quad 9, \quad 13, \quad 18, \quad 24, \quad 31$$

The formula happens to be $a_n = \dfrac{1}{2}n^2 - \dfrac{1}{2}n + 3$, but you would not be required to come up with that on your own!

Answer: C

Practice: Patterns

Use the table below to answer Question 1.

n	-1	0	1	2	3	4
a_n	2	1	2	5	10	17

1. If the pattern in the table continues, which of the following expressions represents a_n?
    A. $2n^2$
    B. $2n^2 + 1$
    C. $3n - 1$
    D. $n^2 + 1$

2. Kathy is building a gray brick patio where gray bricks are bordered on two sides with white bricks. The figure below shows how the white bricks border patios with 1×1, 2×2, and 3×3 gray bricks.

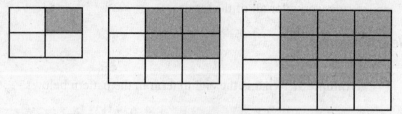

If the pattern continues, which of the expressions below represents the number of white bricks needed to border two sides of a patio made up of $n \times n$ gray bricks?

A. $n + 2$
B. $n^2 + 1$
C. $2n + 1$
D. $2n^2$

★ *Use the pattern below to answer Question 3.*

| 1 | 2 | 5 | 14 | 41 | 122 |

3. The 11th term in this pattern is 29,525. What is the 12th term?
A. 29,528
B. 42,372
C. 68,574
D. 88,574

★ 4. The first four terms in a pattern are shown below.

$$2x^3, 3x^4, 4x^5, 5x^6, \ldots$$

The formula for the pattern is given to be

$$a_n = (n+1)x^{n+2}$$

where n is the order number of the term in the pattern. For example, the term $2x^3$ has a value of $n = 1$ since it is the first term in the pattern. The second term, $3x^4$, has a value of $n = 2$, and so on. When $x = 3$, the first term has a value of $2x^3 = 2(3)^3 = 2(27) = 54$.

a. What is the value of the fifth term in the pattern when $x = 2$. Show your work or explain how you got your answer.

b. Using the formula, find the expression for the sixth term in the pattern. Show your work or explain how you obtained your answer.

c. List the values for the first five terms in the pattern if $x = -1$.

d. Which numbered term in the pattern will have a numerical coefficient of 17? Show your work or explain how you obtained your answer.

5. Joe's Pizzeria charges the following prices for their plain pizzas.

Diameter	Price
8 inch	$6.80
10 inch	$8.00
12 inch	$9.40
14 inch	$11.00

Based on this information, what would you expect a 20-inch pizza to cost?

A. $10.60
B. $11.60
C. $12.80
D. $17.00

6. The first five terms in a geometric sequence are shown below.

$$4, 12, 36, 108, 324, \ldots$$

What is the next term in the sequence?

A. 540
B. 648
C. 972
D. 1,296

7. In the following pattern, the five numbers 1, 9, 2, 4, and 4 keep repeating.

$$1, 9, 2, 4, 4, 1, 9, 2, 4, 4, 1, 9, 2, 4, 4, 1, 9, 2, 4, 4; \ldots$$

Find the 246th number in the pattern.

A. 1
B. 9
C. 2
D. 4

8. The table below shows some powers of 3 and the unit's digit of 3^n.

n	1	2	3	4	5	6	7
3^n	3^1	3^2	3^3	3^4	3^5	3^6	3^7
unit's digit	3	9	7	1	3	9	7

What is the unit's digit of 3^{46}?

A. 3
B. 9
C. 7
D. 1

9. A clown is holding 5 different color balloons and hands them out to people in the following order:

red, purple, green, blue, orange, red, purple, green, blue, orange, red, purple, . . .

According to the pattern above, what color balloon will the 59th person to be handed a balloon receive?

10. What is the next term of the quadratic pattern shown below?

$$-6, -6, -4, 0, 6, 14, 24, \underline{\hspace{2cm}}$$

A. 32
B. 36
C. 40
D. 46

Solutions to Practice: Patterns

1. Test the formulas in the answer choices against the values in the table. As soon as one choice does not work, you can **eliminate the answer choice**.

   A̶. $2(-1)^2 = 2, 2(0)^2 \neq 1$

   B̶. $2(-1)^2 + 1 \neq 2$

   C̶. $3(-1) - 1 \neq 2$

   D. $(-1)^2 + 1 = 2, (0)^2 + 1 = 1, (1)^2 + 1 = 2, (2)^2 + 1 = 5$

   Answer choice D is the only one that works. It is a good idea to test more than one set of values to be sure.

   Answer: D

2. Generate a table that shows the number of gray bricks ($n \times n$) versus the number of white bricks. Then come up with a formula for the number of white bricks, or test the formulas in the table against your values.

n	1	2	3	. . .	n
white bricks	3	5	7	. . .	?

   A̶. $1 + 2 = 3, 2 + 2 \neq 5$

   B̶. $(1)^2 + 1 \neq 3$

   C. $2(1) + 1 = 3, 2(2) + 1 = 5, 2(3) + 1 = 7$ $\checkmark$

   D̶. $2(1)^2 \neq 3$

   Answer choice C is the only one that works.

   Answer: C

3. In this problem, you only have to figure out how to get from one term to the next, since you are given the previous, or 11th, term. It looks like you multiply the previous term by three and then subtract one. The formula, if you were to write it, would look like: $a_n = 3(a_{n-1}) - 1$. Getting from the 11th term to the 12th, you would have $a_{12} = 3(a_{11}) - 1 = 3(29,525) - 1 = 88,574$.

Answer: D

4. a. Using the formula $a_n = (n+1)x^{n+2}$ compute the value of the fifth term, a_5, when $x = 2$. You get: $a_5 = (5+1)2^{(5+2)} = 6 \cdot 2^7 = 768$.

Answer: 768

   b. The sixth term in the pattern would be $a_6 = (6+1)x^{(6+2)} = 7x^8$. You can verify your result by looking at the pattern in the sequence. Both the coefficient and the exponent increase by one for each term generated.

Answer: $7x^8$

   c. Plug in -1 for x in the first five terms of the pattern.

   $$2(-1)^3, \ 3(-1)^4, \ 4(-1)^5, \ 5(-1)^6, 6(-1)^7 = -2, 3, -4, 5, -6$$

Answer: $-2, 3, -4, 5, -6$

   d. Since the coefficient of each term in the pattern $a_n = (n+1)x^{n+2}$ is $(n+1)$, set this equal to 17 and solve for n. $17 = n + 1$, $n = 16$. This means that the 16th term has a coefficient of 17.

Answer: 16th term

5. Complete the table. The diameter of the pizza increases by 2 inches each time. The increase in price goes up by $0.20 each time.

Size	Price	
8	$6.80	+ 1.20
10	$8.00	+ 1.40
12	$9.40	+ 1.60
14	$11.00	+ 1.80
16	$12.80	+ 2.00
18	$14.80	+ 2.20
20	$17.00	

So a 20-inch pizza would cost $17.00 if the pattern continued.

Answer: D

6. Each number in the sequence is 3 times as great as the number before it. To find the next term, multiply 324 by 3.

    Answer: C

7. There are five numbers that keep repeating. Even though the number 4 is used twice in the pattern, you still treat this as a pattern of 5 repeating digits. In other words, ask yourself: When does the pattern begin again? This happens when it hits the number 1, which is after five numbers have been listed. Use the fact that there are five repeating numbers and your knowledge about divisibility by 5 to answer the question. The 245th number must be a 4 because 245 is a multiple of 5. Therefore, the 246th number must be the next number in the pattern, which is a 1.

    Answer: A

8. The unit's digits repeat after 4 digits. The pattern is as follows: 3, 9, 7, 1, 3, 9, 7, 1. . . . The unit's digit of 3^{44} will be 1 because 44 is divisible by 4 and every power divisible by 4 will have a unit's digit of 1. Following the order of the pattern, 3^{45} will have a unit's digit of 3, and 3^{46} will have a unit's digit of 9.

    Answer: B

9. Every fifth person will receive an orange balloon. This means that the 60th person will receive an orange balloon. The 59th person will receive a blue balloon, which is the color before orange.

    Answer: blue

10. Find the difference between each term:

    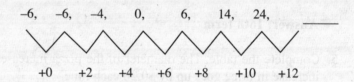

    The next term must be 12 more than the previous so the next term is 24 + 12 = 36.

    Answer: B

Vertex Edge Graphs

• A **vertex edge graph** is a collection of points that are connected by one or more paths that pass through them. The points are called the **vertices**, and the paths connecting them are considered to be the **edges**, even though they need not be straight. To traverse a vertex edge graph on the MCAS, you must usually travel along each edge exactly once, but you may pass through a vertex as many times as you need. When you start and end at the same vertex, but do not use any edge more than once, your path is called a **closed circuit**. Not all vertex edge graphs can be traversed as closed circuits using every edge, and some can only be traveled in this manner if you choose the correct starting point. There are some tricks to help you travel a vertex edge graph at the end of this section.

- Traversing a vertex edge graph as a closed circuit using each and every edge exactly once, is only possible if the graph has at least two edges at each vertex. Here is an example of such as graph:

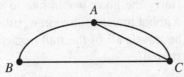

- Point *B* is an **even vertex** because it has an even number of paths feeding into it, namely two. Points *A* and *C* are considered **odd vertices**, because there are three, or an odd number of paths feeding into them. Try starting at point *B* and travelling the graph by passing over each edge exactly once. Notice you get stuck each time. Here is an example of getting stuck at point *C*, unable to cross the path connecting *A* to *B* without using an edge more than once.

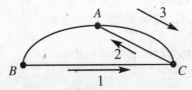

Now try starting at an odd vertex, such as *A*.

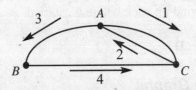

It can be done! This is just one way to traverse the graph using every edge exactly once. You may find a different route, but you must start at an odd vertex.

Tips for Traversing Vertex Edge Graphs

- In general, there are the only two types of vertex edge graphs that can be traversed using every edge exactly once.

1. If *all of the graph's vertices are even*, it can be traversed. You may start at any point, but you will always end up at the same point you started with. This is a closed circuit.
2. If *the graph has two odd vertices*, it can be traversed only if you start with one of the odd vertices, and end with the other.

> * *Remember: If the graph has more than two odd vertices, it is impossible to traverse it using every edge exactly once.*

Examples: Vertex Edge Graphs

Example 1. Harry the hiker would like to walk through all of the trails in a state park without traveling the same path twice. At what point(s) can he begin, so that he travels all of the trails exactly once, and winds up in the same place he started?

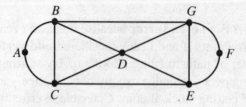

A. A or F
B. B, G, E, or C
C. D
D. Any of the points will work.

Solution

Points A and F both have two edges, while all of the other points have four. Since this vertex edge graph consists of only even vertices, he may start at any point, traverse the network, and wind up back where he started.

Answer: D

Practice: Vertex Edge Graphs

1. Carl the mail carrier delivers mail to his own neighborhood on the final run of his day. If he begins at the post office and ends up at his own home, without taking any of the roads twice, where is his home located?

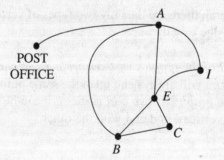

A. At A
B. At B
C. At C
D. At E

2. The figure below shows a map of the exhibits in a museum and the corridors connecting them. If you must start and end at the entrance to the museum and visit each of the seven exhibits exactly once, without retracing any path, list one possible order of exhibits that you could pass through. (You do not have to walk down every corridor).

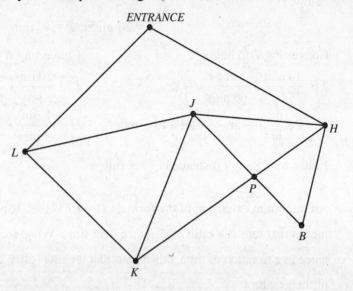

Solutions to Practice: Vertex Edge Graphs

1. Point *B* is the only odd vertex, meaning that he must go to the point, leave it, and go to it again in order to travel along all of the paths. Therefore, this must be his home.

   Answer: B

2. *Entrance, H, B, P, J, K, L, Entrance* and the exact reverse are possibilities.
   Entrance, H, B, P, K, J, L, Entrance and the exact reverse are possibilities.

   Answer: *Entrance, H, B, P, J, K, L, Entrance*
   Entrance, L, K, J, P, B, H, Entrance
   Entrance, H, B, P, K, J, L, Entrance
   Entrance, L, J, K, P, B, H, Entrance

Everyday Problems and Applications

- Algebraic applications may be made to model real-world situations. The MCAS may introduce you to formulas used in physics, economics, geometry, or simply a situation that is made up in the problem. In general, you do not need to have ever seen or even understand the formula that is presented to you in order to use it.

- One formula that you should memorize relates **distance**, **rate**, and **time**.

$$D = RT$$

This says that the *distance*, *D*, an object travels is equal to its *rate*, *R*, multiplied by its *time*, *T*, spent traveling. This is only true if the units of time correspond with the units of the rate. If not, you will have to do a conversion. Take, for example, the following problem.

Sally traveled 20 miles per hour on her bicycle for 40 minutes. How far has she traveled?

You will have to convert either her rate to miles per minute, or the time to hours. See below:

$$R = 20 \text{ mi/hr}, \ T = 40 \text{ min}$$

Converting T to hours:

$$T = \frac{40 \text{ min}}{1} \cdot \frac{1 \text{ hr}}{60 \text{ min}} = \frac{2}{3} \text{ hr}$$

$$D = 20 \frac{\text{mi}}{\text{hr}} \cdot \frac{2}{3} \text{ hr} = \frac{40}{3} \text{ mi} = 13.\overline{3} \text{ miles}$$

Converting R to minutes:

$$R = \frac{20 \text{ mi}}{\text{hr}} \cdot \frac{1 \text{ hr}}{60 \text{ min}} = \frac{1}{3} \frac{\text{mi}}{\text{min}}$$

$$D = \frac{1}{3} \frac{\text{mi}}{\text{min}} \cdot 40 \text{ min} = \frac{40}{3} \text{ mi} = 13.\overline{3} \text{ miles}$$

Either way, Sally's distance is $13.\overline{3}$ miles.

- An important extension of the formula $D = RT$ is that, solved for R, you get $R = \dfrac{D}{T}$. This means that rate is a ratio of distance over time. When looking at a graph that plots distance as a function of time, this means that the rate (often called the velocity) is the slope of the graph.

Examples: Everyday Problems and Applications

Example 1. Peyton rides his bicycle across town according to the distance versus time graph below.

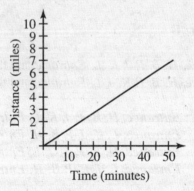

About how fast was Peyton riding?
A. 7.2 mi/hr
B. 8.4 mi/hr
C. 10 mi/hr
D. 12.5 mi/hr

Solution

Peyton's average velocity can be computed using the formula $R = \dfrac{D}{T}$. You can think of this as

$$average \ rate = \frac{total \ distance}{total \ time}$$

He traveled about 7 miles in 50 minutes, but don't forget to convert the units to miles per hour so that the answers match.

$$\text{Rate} = \frac{7 \text{ miles}}{50 \text{ minutes}} \cdot \frac{60 \text{ minutes}}{1 \text{ hr}} = 8.4 \frac{\text{miles}}{\text{hr}}$$

Answer: 8.4 $\dfrac{\text{miles}}{\text{hr}}$

Example 2. The formula used to compute the approximate time t, in seconds, that it takes a pendulum of length l feet to complete one swing back and forth, is represented by the equation:

$$t \approx 6.28 \sqrt{\frac{l}{32}}$$

Which is CLOSEST to the number of seconds it takes a pendulum of 4 feet to complete one full swing back and forth?

A. 2.22 seconds
B. 3.93 seconds
C. 4.62 seconds
D. 4.78 seconds

Solution

Here is an example of a formula that you do not need to be familiar with in order to answer the question. The problem states that l is the length of the pendulum, which is given to be 4 feet. Replace l with the number 4 and compute the value of t.

$$t \approx 6.28 \sqrt{\frac{4}{32}} = 6.28 \sqrt{\frac{1}{8}} = 6.28 \sqrt{.125} \approx 2.22 \text{ seconds}$$

Answer: A

Practice: Everyday Problems and Applications

1. The distance from Providence, Rhode Island, to Hartford, Connecticut, is approximately 87 miles. Find the approximate distance between these two cities in kilometers if 1 mile ≈ 1.609 kilometers.
   A. 54.07 km
   B. 139.98 km
   C. 52.93 km
   D. 145.86 km

2. Suki usually drives the 240 miles from Boston, Massachusetts, to Morristown, New Jersey, in 4 hours. If she increases her speed by 8 miles per hour, approximately how much time will the trip take?
   A. 3 hours and 15 minutes
   B. 3 hours and 30 minutes
   C. 3 hours and 45 minutes
   D. 3 hours and 50 minutes

3. Suppose there is a formula in geometry where $B = \dfrac{A}{H}$ for positive values of A, B, and H. If A remains fixed and H is doubled, then B
   A. stays the same.
   B. gets twice as large.
   C. gets half as large.
   D. gets four times as large.

4. The formula below is often used by bankers to compute the monthly payment, M, on a loan:

$$M = \frac{P(rt+1)}{12t}$$

where P is the principal, r is the annual rate, and t is the total number of years of the loan. Based on this formula, compute to the nearest dollar the monthly payment on a 15-year loan of $40,000 at an annual rate of 8%.

   A. $489
   B. $1,100
   C. $269
   D. $605

Use the graph below to answer Question 5.

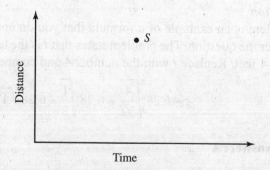

5. Point S on the graph above represents the distance and time that Sammy traveled on his trip. Which of the following represents his average speed?
   A. The x-coordinate of point S
   B. The y-coordinate of point S
   C. The slope of the line through the origin and point S
   D. The distance between point s and the point $(0, 0)$

6. The frequency, or cycles per second, of a block going up and down on the end of a spring is measured by the formula $f = \dfrac{1}{2\pi}\sqrt{\dfrac{k}{m}}$, where k is the spring constant and m is the mass of the block in grams. What is the frequency of a spring-block system if the spring constant is $16\pi^2$ and the mass of the block is 4 grams? (The units of measure for frequency are called Hertz.)
   A. 1 Hertz
   B. 2 Hertz
   C. π Hertz
   D. 2π Hertz

7. A car traveled 10 miles in 12 minutes. What was its average speed for that trip?
   A. 1.2 miles per hour
   B. 50 miles per hour
   C. 80 miles per hour
   D. 120 miles per hour

8. Brian traveled 225 miles in 4 hours and 30 minutes. What was his average speed?
   A. 40 miles per hour
   B. 42.5 miles per hour
   C. 45 miles per hour
   D. 50 miles per hour

Solutions to Practice: Everyday Problems and Applications

1. Multiply to convert from miles to kilometers: $87 \text{ mi} \cdot \dfrac{1.609 \text{ km}}{1 \text{ mi}} \approx 139.98 \text{ km}$.

   Answer: B

2. First, find the speed that she usually travels by rearranging the formula $D = RT$ to $R = \dfrac{D}{T}$. Then plug in the values in the problem: $R = \dfrac{240 \text{ mi}}{4 \text{ hr}} = 60 \text{ mi/hr}$. Next, increase her speed by 8 mi/hr, to 68 mi/hr. Rearrange the distance formula one more time to $T = \dfrac{D}{R}$. Substitute in the new rate, and solve for T. $T = \dfrac{D}{R} = \dfrac{240 \text{ mi}}{68 \text{ mi/hr}} \approx 3.5 \text{ hr}$. Since the answer choices are expressed in hours and minutes, convert 0.5 hours to $0.5 \cdot 60$ min = 30 minutes. Your final answer will be 3 hours and 30 minutes.

   Answer: B

3. H is doubled, so replace H with $2H$ in the original equation.

   $$B_{\text{old}} = \dfrac{A}{H} \xrightarrow{\text{replace with } 2H} B_{\text{new}} = \dfrac{A}{2H} = \dfrac{1}{2}\dfrac{A}{H} = \dfrac{1}{2} \cdot B_{\text{old}}$$

   B will be half as large as the original value.

   Answer: C

4. You do not need to understand the formula here. Simply plug in the values you are given and solve for M. $M = \dfrac{P(rt+1)}{12t} = \dfrac{40,000\big(0.08(15)+1\big)}{12(15)} = \dfrac{88,000}{180} \approx 489$

   The monthly payment is $489.

   Answer: A

5. Rearrange the formula $D = RT$ to $R = \dfrac{D}{T}$. His average speed is his change in distance divided by his change in time. The origin on the graph is the point $(0, 0)$, and represents the beginning of Sammy's trip when both time and distance are zero. His change in distance is the difference in the y-values on the graph, and his change in time is the difference in the x-values on the graph. This makes the rate: $R = \dfrac{\Delta D}{\Delta T} = \dfrac{\Delta y}{\Delta x}$, which is the same as the slope of the line through the origin and point S.

Answer: C

6. Plugging your values into the formula given, you get

$$f = \frac{1}{2\pi}\sqrt{\frac{k}{m}} = \frac{1}{2\pi}\sqrt{\frac{16\pi^2}{4}} = \frac{1}{2\pi}\sqrt{4\pi^2} = \frac{2\pi}{2\pi} = 1 \text{ Hertz}$$

Answer: A

7. There are 60 minutes in an hour, so 12 minutes equals $\dfrac{1}{5}$ of an hour. Since the car traveled 10 minutes in $\dfrac{1}{5}$ of an hour, multiplying 10 by 5, the car traveled 50 miles in one hour.

Answer: B

8. You can use the formula: $distance = rate \cdot time$ or $rate = \dfrac{distance}{time}$.

To find the average speed, or the rate, divide the distance by the time:
$\dfrac{225}{4.5} = 50$ miles per hour

Answer: D

Chapter 6 | Geometry and Measurement

Points, Lines, Segments, Rays, and Planes

- **Points** are used in geometry to indicate a specific location in space. Although they have no size, points are represented by a small dot that is labeled with a capital letter. **Space** is the set of all points.

> •
>
> A This is called point A.

- A **line** is a series of points that extend infinitely in two opposite directions. There are infinitely many points on a line. A line has infinite length but no thickness. To name a line, you may use any two points on the line. You may also use a lowercase letter to name a line. **Collinear** points lie on the same line. **Noncollinear** points do not all lie on the same line.

> Call this line $\overleftrightarrow{FH}$, $\overleftrightarrow{HF}$, $\overleftrightarrow{FG}$, $\overleftrightarrow{GF}$, $\overleftrightarrow{GH}$, or $\overleftrightarrow{HG}$. They are the same line.

> This line does not have specific points labeled on the diagram so just call it line m.

- A **line segment** is that portion of a line contained between two endpoints. Use the two endpoints to name the segment.

> Call this segment $\overline{AB}$ or $\overline{BA}$. They are the same thing.

- A **ray** is a portion of a line with one distinct endpoint that continues infinitely in one direction. The arrow indicates in which direction the ray continues. To name a ray, write the endpoint first and then any other point on the ray.

> $\overrightarrow{CD}$ has endpoint C. You can also name it $\overrightarrow{CE}$.

> $\overrightarrow{GF}$ has endpoint G. $\overrightarrow{GH}$ has endpoint G. The two rays have the same endpoint but opposite directions.

> * Remember: Lines go on forever in both directions.
>
> Rays go on forever in one direction.
>
> Segments end.

- A **midpoint** divides a segment into two congruent segments. Congruent segments have the same length.

C is the midpoint of $\overline{AB}$. The little marks on $\overline{AC}$ and $\overline{CB}$ are called *tick marks*. This means $\overline{AC}$ is congruent to $\overline{CB}$. The symbol for congruent is $\cong$ so we write $\overline{AC} \cong \overline{CB}$.

- A **bisector** divides a segment into two congruent segments.

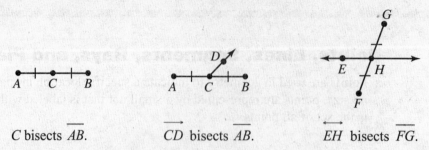

C bisects $\overline{AB}$. $\overrightarrow{CD}$ bisects $\overline{AB}$. $\overleftrightarrow{EH}$ bisects $\overline{FG}$.

- A **plane** is a flat surface that extends in all directions without end. A plane does not have thickness. A plane is often drawn to look like a parallelogram but you should recognize that it actually continues infinitely in all directions. A plane is usually named with a single uppercase letter in one corner, but you can also name it with three noncollinear points.

- Points, lines, segments, rays, and two-dimensional figures that lie in the same plane are **coplanar**. They are **noncoplanar** if they do not lie in the same plane.

Examples: Points, Lines, Segments, Rays, and Planes

Example 1. Five distinct points are shown on the number line below.

How many distinct line segments have two of these points as endpoints?

A. 5
B. 9
C. 10
D. 12

Solution

Use two different points to name a segment. Generate a list in an organized fashion (first start with A, then with B, etc.). $\overline{AB}$ is the same segment as $\overline{BA}$ so don't repeat.

$\overline{AB}$ $\overline{AC}$ $\overline{AD}$ $\overline{AE}$
$\overline{BC}$ $\overline{BD}$ $\overline{BE}$
$\overline{CD}$ $\overline{CE}$
$\overline{DE}$

Answer: C

Practice: Points, Lines, Segments, Rays, and Planes

1. If C is the midpoint of segment $\overline{AE}$, which of the following statements is not necessarily true?

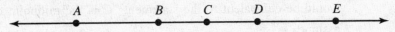

A. $AC = \dfrac{1}{2} AE$

B. $\overline{AC} \cong \overline{CE}$

C. $2CE = AE$

D. $\overline{BC} \cong \overline{CD}$

2. If $AC = BD$ in the figure below, and $AC = 8$ units, $BC = x$ units, and $CD = (2x + 5)$ units, find x.

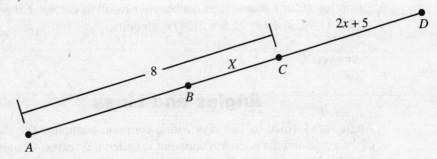

A. $\dfrac{2}{3}$

B. 1

C. $\dfrac{3}{2}$

D. 3

3. If C is the midpoint of $\overline{AB}$, $AC = 10x - 7$ units, $CB = 4x + 11$ units, find the length of AB.

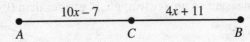

A. 6 units

B. 23 units

C. 46 units

D. 60 units

Solutions to Practice: Points, Lines, Segments, Rays, and Planes

1. By the definition of a midpoint, C divides $\overline{AE}$ into two congruent segments, $\overline{AC}$ and $\overline{CE}$. Go through a process of elimination of the answer choices. Answer choice D would be equivalent to the statement "C is the midpoint of $\overline{BD}$," which we cannot assume.

   Answer: D

2. Set up either of the equations: $AB = CD$: $8 - x = 2x + 5$ **or** $AC = BD$: $8 = 2x + 5 + x$. Solving you get $x = 1$.

   Answer: B

3. C is the midpoint of $\overline{AB}$, so $AC = CB$. Set up the equation: $10x - 7 = 4x + 11$. Solving for x, you get $x = 3$. To find the length of AB, substitute $x = 3$ into either the expression for AC or CB, and then double your result to get AB. $CB = 4x + 11 = 4(3) + 11 = 12 + 11 = 23$. $AB = 2CB = 2(23) = 46$ units.

   Answer: C

Angles and Lines

- **Angles** are formed by two rays with a common endpoint. The rays are called the sides of the angle and the common endpoint is called the vertex. Congruent angles are angles with the same measure. To name an angle, use three points with the vertex in the middle. You can also use a number to name an angle, or, if there is only one angle shown with a certain vertex, you can simply use the vertex point to name the angle.

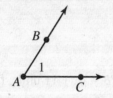

Name the angle $\angle BAC$, $\angle CAB$, $\angle A$, or $\angle 1$.

$\overrightarrow{AB}$ and $\overrightarrow{AC}$ are the sides of $\angle BAC$.
A is the vertex of $\angle BAC$.

- The measure of an **acute** angle is greater than 0° and less than 90°.

> ** Remember: One way to remember this is that acute angles are small and cute!*

- The measure of an **obtuse** angle is greater than 90° and less than 180°.

- The measure of a **right** angle is exactly 90°.

The square mark on ∠B means that the angle is a right angle.

- The measure of a **straight** angle is exactly 180°. A line is a straight angle.

- **Adjacent** angles have the same vertex and share a common side. Also, they have no interior points in common.

∠1 and ∠2 are not adjacent.   ∠BAC and ∠BAD are not adjacent.
They do not share the same vertex.   Point P is an interior point in both angles.

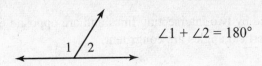

∠BAC and ∠CAD are adjacent. They share vertex A and have the common side $\overrightarrow{AC}$.

- If two angles are adjacent and their noncommon sides are collinear, the angles' sum is 180°.

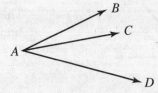

∠1 + ∠2 = 180°

- **Perpendicular** lines form right angles.

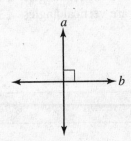

The right angle mark in the diagram indicates that line a is perpendicular to line b. Use the symbol ⊥ to indicate perpendicular, so write $a \perp b$. Since there are four pairs of adjacent angles whose sums are 180°, each angle in this diagram is actually 90°.

- The **perpendicular bisector** of a segment bisects and is perpendicular to that segment.

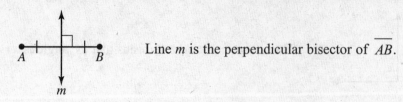

Line *m* is the perpendicular bisector of $\overline{AB}$.

- If two angles are **supplementary**, their sum is 180°.

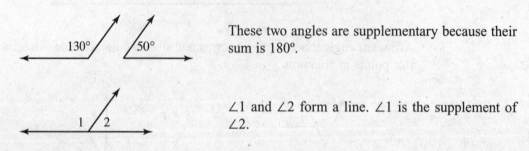

These two angles are supplementary because their sum is 180º.

∠1 and ∠2 form a line. ∠1 is the supplement of ∠2.

- If two angles are **complementary**, their sum is 90º.

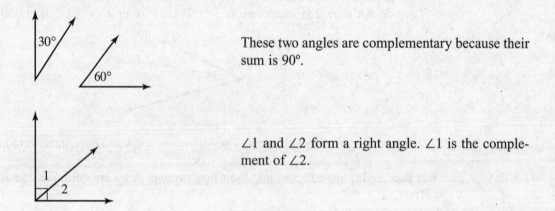

These two angles are complementary because their sum is 90º.

∠1 and ∠2 form a right angle. ∠1 is the complement of ∠2.

- **Vertical** angles are formed by two intersecting lines and are opposite each other. Their sides are opposite rays. Vertical angles are congruent.

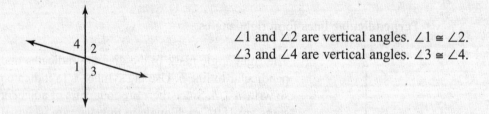

∠1 and ∠2 are vertical angles. ∠1 ≅ ∠2.
∠3 and ∠4 are vertical angles. ∠3 ≅ ∠4.

> ** Memory Tip: Look for a big **X** made out of two lines to find vertical angles.*

- **Parallel** lines are coplanar lines that never intersect. The symbol for parallel is ‖. The arrowheads on the diagram indicate parallel lines. A **transversal** is a line that intersects two or more parallel lines. If a transversal intersects exactly two parallel lines, the transversal forms eight angles that are either **congruent** or **supplementary** to each other.

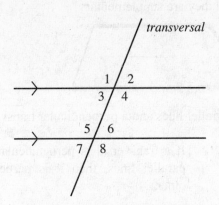

By looking at the diagram, you may notice four **acute** angles, and four **obtuse** angles. You can say that all of the acute angles are **congruent** to each other, and, likewise, so are all of the obtuse. If you have one of each type, that pair is **supplementary**.

While you will only need to know these congruent or supplementary relationships for the MCAS, some angle pairs have names for them. **Corresponding angles**, for example, are angles in the same relative position such as "top right corner" or "bottom left." Corresponding angles are **congruent** to each other. The corresponding angle pairs are

$$\angle 2 \cong \angle 6, \ \angle 4 \cong \angle 8, \ \angle 1 \cong \angle 5, \text{ and } \angle 3 \cong \angle 7$$

Look for the letter **F** when searching for corresponding angles. It can be in any position. Angles 1 and 2 are corresponding in the pictures below, but make sure you have parallel lines before you say they are congruent!

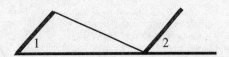

Alternate interior angles are in between the two parallel lines, but on opposite sides of the transversal. Alternate interior angles are **congruent**. The alternate interior pairs are

$$\angle 3 \cong \angle 6 \text{ and } \angle 4 \cong \angle 5$$

Look for the letter **Z** when searching for alternate interior angles. It can be forward or backward. Angles 1 and 2 are alternate interiors in the pictures below, but make sure you have parallel lines before you say they are congruent!

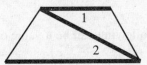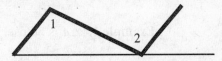

Same side interior angles are in between the two parallel lines, and on the same side of the transversal. Same side interior angles are **supplementary**. Above

$$\angle 4 \text{ is supplementary to } \angle 6 \text{ and } \angle 3 \text{ is supplementary to } \angle 5$$

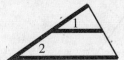

Look for the letter **U** when searching for alternate interior angles. It can be in any position. Angles 1 and 2 are same side interiors in the following picture, but make sure you have parallel lines before you say they are supplementary!

- A couple of theorems apply to parallel lines and a perpendicular transversal.

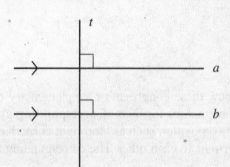

If a transversal is perpendicular to one of two parallel lines, then it is perpendicular to the other.

If a transversal is perpendicular to two lines, then those two lines are parallel.

- Using what you know about parallel lines and straight angles, you can prove a very important fact. Study the diagram below.

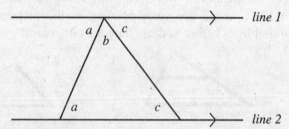

Since *line 1* is straight, the measures $a + b + c = 180°$. Notice that the two angles marked *a* are congruent because they are alternate interiors. Same with the angles marked *c*. Now look inside the triangle. Notice that it is also made up of angles *a*, *b*, and *c*! Therefore, **the sum of the degree measures of the vertices of a triangle is 180°.** This will come up again in the next section of the text.

Examples: Angles and Lines

Example 1. $\angle A$ is obtuse. Which of the following can be a value of *x*?

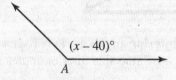

- A. 50
- B. 100
- C. 130
- D. 150

Solution

By the definition of an obtuse angle, $\angle A$ is between 90° and 180°.

Set up the inequality: $90° < \angle A < 180°$. Substituting for $\angle A$: $90° < x - 40 < 180°$.

Add 40 to each side: $130 < x < 220$. You can also **use your answer choices** to solve this problem. Plug in the given values until you find one that is an obtuse angle. For example, $50 - 40 = 10°$, which is an acute angle. However, $150 - 40 = 110°$ which is an obtuse angle.

Answer: D

Example 2. What is the measure of $\angle 3$?

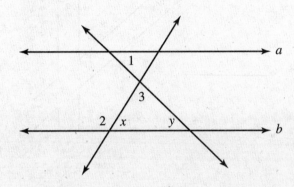

- line a is parallel to line b
- $m \angle 1 = 58°$. (*m* means measure)
- $m \angle 2 = 124°$

A. 56°
B. 58°
C. 66°
D. 68°

Solution

The supplement to $\angle 2$ is x, so $x = 180° - 124° = 56°$. With parallel lines, alternate interior angles are congruent, so $\angle 1 = y = 58°$. The sum of the angles in a triangle equal 180°, so $\angle 3 = 180 - (x + y) = 180 - 114 = 66°$.

Answer: C

Example 3. Given the diagram below, solve for x.

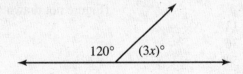

A. 10
B. 20
C. 30
D. 60

Solution

A straight angle contains 180°. $120 + 3x = 180 \rightarrow 3x = 60 \rightarrow x = 20$.

Answer: B

Example 4. Bay Street and Dana Street are perpendicular. Bay Street and Clark Street intersect at the 55° angle shown in the diagram. What is the measure of the ? angle in the diagram?

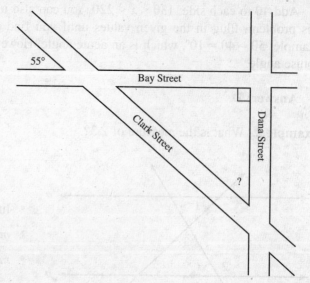

Solution

Call the unknown angle x. Since vertical angles are congruent, the angle opposite the 55° in the diagram is also 55°. The rectangular tick mark indicates a right angle, so that we have the equation $x + 55 + 90 = 180$ or $x = 35°$.

Answer: 35°

Example 5. Angle measures x, y, and z are in a ratio of 3 : 5 : 2, respectively. Find the degree measure of angle z.

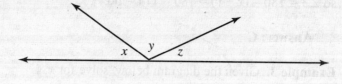

(Figure not drawn to scale)

    A. 18°
    B. 36°
    C. 54°
    D. 110°

Solution

For measurements to be in a ratio, means that there is a constant multiplier, call it n, so that $\angle x = 3n$, $\angle y = 5n$, $\angle z = 2n$. Respectively just means that the order in which the angle measures are stated in the problem is consistent with the order in which the ratio is stated. Set up the equation below which indicates that the sum of the degree measures in a straight angle is 180°, and solve for n. $3n + 5n + 2n = 180$, $10n = 180$, $n = 18$. Solving for $\angle z$, $\angle z = 2n = 36°$.

Answer: B

★ **Example 6.** If $\overrightarrow{BD}$ bisects $\angle ABC$ and the measures $\angle 1$, $\angle 2$, and $\angle ABC$ are given below, which of the following statements is incorrect?

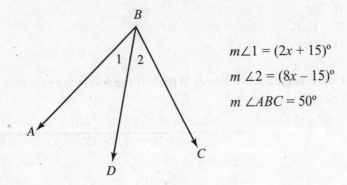

$m\angle 1 = (2x + 15)^\circ$

$m\ \angle 2 = (8x - 15)^\circ$

$m\ \angle ABC = 50^\circ$

A. $2x + 15 = 25$

B. $2(8x - 15) = 50$

C. $50 - 8x - 15 = 2x + 15$

D. $(2x + 15) + (8x - 15) = 50$

Solution

Here is a list of some statements that would be true based on the given information.

$m\angle 1 + m\angle 2 = 50$. This is represented in answer choice D.

$m\angle 1 = m\angle 2 = 25$. This is represented in answer choice A.

$2(m\angle 1) = 2(m\angle 2) = 50$. This is represented in answer choice B.

$50 - (m\angle 1) = m\angle 2$ or $50 - (m\angle 2) = m\angle 1$.

For this to be correctly represented in answer choice C, the statement should read: $50 - (8x - 15) = 2x + 15$ for which you would have to distribute the negative to arrive at the correct statement: $50 - 8x + 15 = 2x + 15$.

Answer: C

Practice: Angles and Lines

1. $\angle B$ is acute. Which of the following cannot be a value of x?

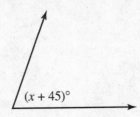

$(x + 45)^\circ$

A. -15

B. 0

C. 40

D. 65

2. $\angle A$ is complementary to $\angle B$, and $\angle B$ is supplementary to $\angle C$. If $m\angle A = 30°$, find $m\angle C$.
   A. 60°
   B. 90°
   C. 120°
   D. 160°

3. Line a is parallel to line b. Which of the following statements is false?

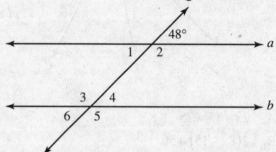

   A. $m\angle 1 = 48°$
   B. $m\angle 3 = 48°$
   C. $m\angle 5 = 132°$
   D. $m\angle 6 = 48°$

4. In the figure below, what is the sum of $x + y$?

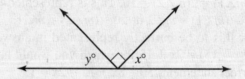

   A. 90
   B. 180
   C. 270
   D. 360

5. In the figure below, $\overline{AB} \perp \overline{BC}$ and the measure of $\angle 1$ is 32°. Find the measure of $\angle EBD$.

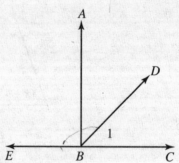

   A. 58°
   B. 90°
   C. 122°
   D. 148°

6. All lines shown below are coplanar. If $l_1 \perp l_2$, $l_1 \perp l_3$, and $l_2 \| l_4$, then which of the following statements is false?

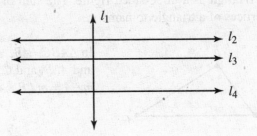

A. $l_2 \| l_3$
B. $l_3 \| l_4$
C. $l_1 \perp l_4$
D. $l_1 \| l_4$

Solutions to Practice: Angles and Lines

1. Since $\angle B$ is acute, set up the inequality $0 < x + 45 < 90$. Subtracting 45 from each side, we get that $-45 < x < 45$, so x cannot equal 65. You can also **use your answer choices** and plug in values until you get an answer that is not an acute angle. $64 + 45 = 110°$, which is not acute.

   Answer: D

2. Since $m\angle A = 30°$, its complement $\angle B = 90° - 30° = 60°$. Since $\angle B$ is supplementary to $\angle C$, $\angle C = 180° - 60° = 120°$.

   Answer: C

3. Vertical angles are congruent, so $\angle 1 = 48°$. With parallel lines, interior angles on the same side of a transversal are supplementary, so $\angle 3 = 180 - 48 = 132°$. Answer choice B is incorrect.

   Answer: B

4. Since you have a straight angle, $x + y + 90 = 180 \rightarrow x + y = 90°$. Notice that you cannot solve for x and y individually.

   Answer: A

5. By the definition of perpendicular segments, $\angle ABC = \angle ABE = 90°$. Therefore, $\angle ABD = 90 - m\angle 1 = 90 - 32 = 58°$ and $\angle EBD = 90 + 58 = 148°$.

   Answer: D

6. In a plane, two lines perpendicular to the same line are parallel, so $l_2 \| l_3$. Since $l_2 \| l_3$ and $l_2 \| l_4$, the transitive property of parallel lines gives us $l_3 \| l_4$. If a line is perpendicular to one of two parallel lines, then it is perpendicular to the other, so $l_1 \perp l_4$. This leaves the visually obvious choice of D as the incorrect statement.

   Answer: D

Angles in Triangles and Circles

- A **triangle** is a three-sided figure. The sum of its interior angles is 180°. Use the three vertices of a triangle to name it.

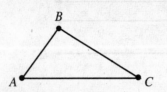

In $\triangle ABC$, $\overline{AB}$, $\overline{BC}$, and $\overline{CA}$ are the sides of the triangle, and A, B, and C are the vertices of the triangle.
$m\angle A + m\angle B + m\angle C = 180°$.

- A **right triangle** is a triangle with exactly one interior right angle. The side opposite the right angle is called the hypotenuse. The other two sides are the legs.

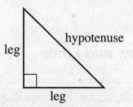

hypotenuse

leg

leg

> *Memory Tip: The word hypotenuse is longer than the word leg and it is also always the longest side.*

- An **acute triangle** is a triangle with all acute interior angles.

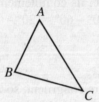

- An **obtuse triangle** is a triangle with exactly one interior obtuse angle.

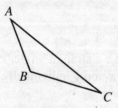

- An **exterior angle** of a triangle is the angle formed by extending a side of a triangle. The exterior angle is supplementary to its adjacent interior angle. The exterior angle is also equal to the sum of the remote interior angles, the other two angles of the triangle that the exterior angle is not adjacent to.

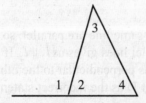

$\angle 1$ is an exterior angle of the triangle.

Get the measure of $\angle 1$ by finding the supplement of $\angle 2$:
$$\angle 1 + \angle 2 = 180°$$
or by finding the sum of $\angle 3 + \angle 4$:
$$\angle 1 = \angle 3 + \angle 4.$$

- A **circle** is the set of all points in a plane that are an equal distance from a center point, also contained in the plane. The distance from the center to any point on the circle is called the **radius**. A **chord** is a segment whose endpoints lie on the circle. The longest chord in a circle passes through the center and is called a **diameter**. The length of the diameter is twice the length of the radius.

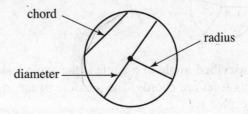

- An **arc** is that portion of a circle bounded by two points on the circle. Arcs are measured in degrees: A **minor arc** measures less than 180°. A **major arc** measures more than 180°. Three letters are used to name a major arc.

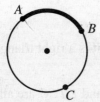

$\overparen{AB}$ is a minor arc. $\overparen{ACB}$ is a major arc.

- A **semicircle** is an arc that is half a circle. Its measure is 180°. Its endpoints are the end-points of a diameter.

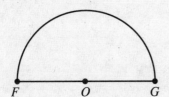

$\overline{FG}$ is the diameter of circle O.

$\overline{FO}$ and $\overline{OG}$ are radii of circle O.

$m\,\overparen{FG} = 180°$.

- A **central angle** of a circle is the angle inside a circle whose vertex is the center of the circle and whose sides are radii. The measure of the central angle is equal to the measure of the intercepted arc.

If A is the center of the circle, $\angle A$ is the central angle, and the intercepted arc is $\overparen{BC}$.

$m\angle A = m\,\overparen{BC}$.

- An entire circle measures 360°. If A is the center of the circle,
$m\angle DAB + m\angle BAC + m\angle CAE + m\angle EAD = 360°$.

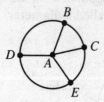

- An **inscribed angle** of a circle is the angle inside a circle whose vertex is on the circle and its sides are chords. The measure of the inscribed angle is half the measure of the intercepted arc.

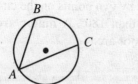

$$m\angle BAC = \frac{1}{2}(m\ \overset{\frown}{BC}).$$

- If a triangle is **inscribed** in a **semicircle**, then it is a right triangle.

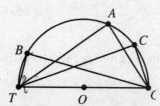

$\angle TAG$, $\angle TBG$, and $\angle TCG$ are all right angles.

You know this because they are all inscribed angles that intercept a semicircle, or 180°.

Examples: Angles in Triangles and Circles

Example 1. Find the measure of the acute angle formed by the hands of the clock at 4:30.

A. 30°
B. 45°
C. 52.5°
D. 60°

Solution

There are 360° in a circle. Since a clock can be divided into 12 angles of equal measure, the angle measure between each number on the face of the clock, in this case the **5** and **6**, is $\frac{360°}{12} = 30°$. The hour hand advances relative to the minute hand, in that the fraction of the total revolution that the minute hand makes around the face of the clock, is equal to the fraction of the turn between the two numbers on the face. For example, since the minute hand is halfway around the clock, the hour hand is halfway between the **4** and the **5**, or 15°. Adding these two measures, we get: 30° + 15° = 45°.

Answer: B

Example 2. The degree measures for $\triangle ABC$ are given below.

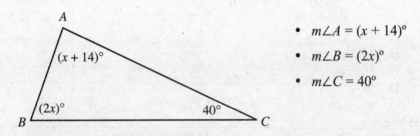

- $m\angle A = (x + 14)°$
- $m\angle B = (2x)°$
- $m\angle C = 40°$

What is the degree measure of $\angle B$?

A. 42°
B. 54°
C. 56°
D. 84°

Solution

The sum of the three vertex angles of a triangle is 180°.

Set up the equation: $x + 14 + 2x + 40 = 180$ and solve for x. We get $x = 42$ and $\angle B = 84°$.

Answer: D

Example 3. In the figure below, $\overline{CB}$ is parallel to $\overline{DA}$. Solve for x.

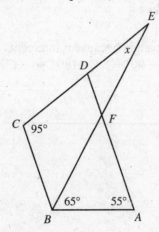

Solution

∠*EDF* = 95º since the corresponding angles formed by parallel lines and a transversal are congruent. Δ*BFA* contains 180º so ∠*BFA* + 65º + 55º = 180º so ∠*BFA* = 60º. Vertical angles are congruent so ∠*EFD* is also 60º. In Δ*EFD*, 95º + 60º + *x* = 180º so *x* = 25º.

Answer: 25º

Example 4. In the figure below $\overline{BA} \perp \overline{CA}$. Find *x*.

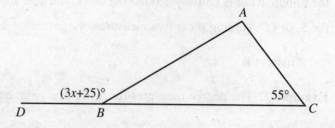

A. 40
B. 42.5
C. 50
D. 55

Solution

By the definition of perpendicular lines, ∠*A* = 90º. Using the exterior angle theorem, ∠*DBA* = ∠*A* + ∠*C*. 3*x* + 25 = 90 + 55 → 3*x* + 25 = 145 → 3*x* = 120 → *x* = 40.

Answer: A

Example 5. • ∠*ABC* is inscribed in semicircle *O*
  • *m*∠*A* = 35º

What is the measure of ∠*C*?

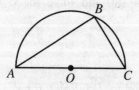

Solution

∠*B* is a right angle because it intercepts a semicircle. Using the triangle sum, we have the equation 35º + 90º + ∠*C* =180º, so ∠*C* = 55º.

Answer: 55º

Example 6. Find the measure of angle C if $\overline{AD} \parallel \overline{BC}$.

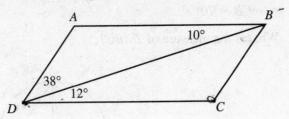

A. 38°

B. 112°

C. 130°

D. 168°

Solution

Look for the angles relating to the given parallel lines. The alternate interiors that are congruent from $\overline{AD} \parallel \overline{BC}$ are $\angle ADB \cong \angle CBD = 38°$. Note that $\overline{AB}$ is NOT parallel to $\overline{DC}$, since their alternate interiors are not congruent ($10° \neq 12°$). Since the sum of the degrees in $\triangle BCD = 180°$, $\angle C = 180 - (12 + 38) = 180 - 50 = 130°$.

Answer: C

Practice: Angles in Triangles and Circles

1. Find the measure of the obtuse angle formed by the hands of the clock at 5:00.

    A. 120°

    B. 135°

    C. 150°

    D. 160°

2. The degree measures of triangle ABC are in a ratio of 2 : 3 : 7. What is the measure of the largest angle in the triangle?

    A. 45°

    B. 55°

    C. 105°

    D. 145°

3. • ∠ABC is inscribed in circle O with diameter $\overline{AC}$.
   • $m\overset{\frown}{CB} = 70°$.

   What is the measure of ∠ABC?

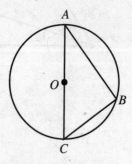

4. In the figure below, what is the sum of $a + b + c + d + e$?

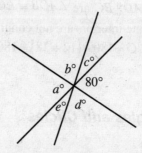

   A. 100
   B. 180
   C. 280
   D. 360

5. △ABC is inscribed in circle O.
   Find m∠B.

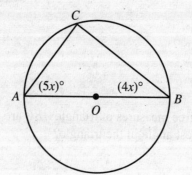

6. $\overline{AC}$ and $\overline{BD}$ are diameters of circle O and $m\angle AOD = 130°$. What is the measure of minor arc $\overset{\frown}{CD}$?

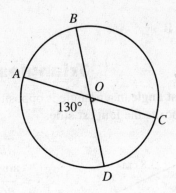

A. 25°
B. 50°
C. 65°
D. 130°

Solutions to Practice: Angles in Triangles and Circles

1. The angle measure between each number on the face of the clock is $\dfrac{360°}{12} = 30°$.
   There are five angle increments between the **12** and the **5**, so $(5)(30°) = 150°$.

   Answer: C

2. Set up an equation where the constant multiplier of the three numbers in the ratio is x.
   Your equation is $2x + 3x + 7x = 180$, and yields $x = 15$. The largest angle in the triangle is $7x = 7(15) = 105°$.

   Answer: C

3. $\angle A$ is the inscribed angle to its intercepted arc $\overset{\frown}{CB}$, so $\angle A = \dfrac{1}{2}\left(70\right) = 35°$. $\angle B = 90°$

   since it intercepts a semicircle, and using the triangle sum, we have $90° + 35° + \angle ACB = 180°$ and $\angle ACB = 55°$.

   Answer: 55°

4. Using the sum of the degrees in a circle, $a + b + c + d + e + 80° = 360°$.
   Subtracting 80° from both sides, you get 280°.

   Answer: C

5. $\angle C$ intercepts a semicircle, so it is a right angle. Set up the equation $90° + 5x + 4x = 180°$, and solve for x. Since $x = 10$, $\angle B = 4x = 4(10) = 40°$.

   Answer: 40°

6. Since the center of the circle is O, minor arc $\overparen{CD}$ is equal to its central angle, $\angle COD$. $\angle COD$ is supplementary to $\angle AOD$, so $\angle COD = 180° - 130° = 50° = m\overparen{CD}$.

Answer: B

Triangles

- The **smallest angle** in a triangle is opposite the **shortest side**. The **largest angle** in a triangle is opposite the **longest side**.

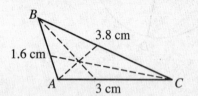

$\overline{AB}$ is the shortest side, so $\angle C$ is the smallest angle.

$\overline{BC}$ is the longest side, so $\angle A$ is the largest angle.

- The **shortest side** in a triangle is opposite the **smallest angle**. The **longest side** in a triangle is opposite the **largest angle**.

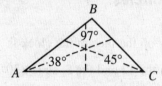

$\angle A$ is the smallest angle, so $\overline{BC}$ is the shortest side.

$\angle B$ is the largest angle, so $\overline{AC}$ is the longest side.

- The sum of the lengths of any two sides of a triangle must be greater than the length of the third side. This is called the *Triangle Inequality Theorem*. This means that the length of each side of a triangle must be between the **difference and the sum** of the lengths of the other two sides.

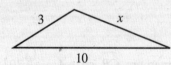

x is greater than 7 and less than 13. You can get this answer with
$(10 - 3) < x < (10 + 3)$
$7 < x < 13$

- In a **scalene** triangle, all the sides are different lengths and all the angles are different measures.

- An **isosceles** triangle has at least two congruent sides. In an isosceles triangle with exactly two congruent sides, the congruent sides are called the legs, and the third side is called the base. The angle opposite the base is called the vertex angle. The angles opposite the legs are called the base angles, and they are congruent.

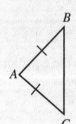

Since $\overline{AC} \cong \overline{AB}$, $\angle C \cong \angle B$.
$\angle A$ is the vertex, and $\overline{BC}$ is the base of $\triangle ABC$.

- A triangle with three congruent sides is **equilateral**. All three angles are congruent, and since the sum of the angles in a triangle is 180°, each angle is 60°.

- In a **right** triangle, the sum of the squares of the lengths of the legs is equal to the square of the length of the hypotenuse. This is called the **Pythagorean Theorem**.

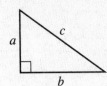

In the triangle, a and b are the legs, and c is the hypotenuse.
Pythagorean Theorem:

$$a^2 + b^2 = c^2$$

- In an **acute** triangle, the sum of the squares of the lengths of the two shorter sides is greater than the square of the length of the longest side.

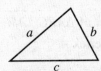

If c is the longest side of the acute triangle, then $a^2 + b^2 > c^2$.

- In an **obtuse** triangle, the sum of the squares of the lengths of the two shorter sides of a triangle is less than the square of the length of the longest side.

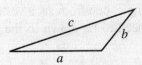

If c is the longest side of the obtuse triangle, then $a^2 + b^2 < c^2$.

- In an **isosceles right triangle (45°-45°-90° triangle)**, the legs of the right triangle are congruent. The angles opposite the legs are each 45°. The length of the hypotenuse in an isosceles right triangle will always be the length of a leg multiplied by $\sqrt{2}$. Likewise, the length of a leg will always be the length of the hypotenuse divided by $\sqrt{2}$. The sides are in a ratio of $1 : 1 : \sqrt{2}$. An alternate way of expressing this ratio is $x : x : x\sqrt{2}$. You do not need to memorize this relationship. It is given on the MCAS formula sheet!

- If each of the angles of a triangle are 30°, 60°, and 90° (**30°-60°-90° triangle**), their sides are in a ratio of $1 : \sqrt{3} : 2$ or $x : x\sqrt{3} : 2x$. This means that the side opposite the 60° angle is $\sqrt{3}$ times the side opposite the 30° angle. The side opposite the 90° angle is twice the side opposite the 30° angle. You do not need to memorize this relationship. It is given on the MCAS formula sheet!

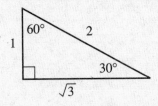 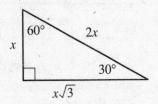

- The **midsegment** of a triangle is a segment whose endpoints are the midpoints of two sides of the triangle. The midsegment is half the length of the third side. It is also parallel to that side.

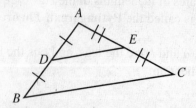

$\overline{DE}$ is a midsegment of $\triangle ABC$.

$$DE = \frac{1}{2} BC.$$

$$\overline{DE} \parallel \overline{BC}.$$

- A **median** of a triangle is a segment whose endpoints are a vertex of the triangle and the midpoint of the opposite side.

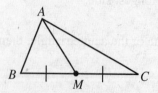

$\overline{AM}$ is a median of $\triangle ABC$. $\overline{AM}$ is the median to side $\overline{BC}$ from vertex A.

- An **altitude** or **height** of a triangle is a segment drawn from a vertex, perpendicular to the opposite side. Its endpoints are the vertex and the point of intersection with the opposite side. There are three altitudes in every triangle, one from each vertex. In the case of an obtuse triangle, two of the altitudes will need to be drawn to the extension of the opposite side in order to form the right angle.

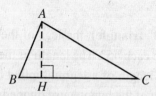

$\overline{AH}$ is an altitude of $\triangle ABC$. $\overline{AH}$ is the altitude to side $\overline{BC}$ from vertex A.

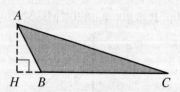

Examples: Triangles

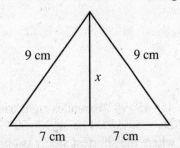

Example 1. What is the measure of the altitude of the triangle below, to the nearest tenth?

9 cm   9 cm

x

7 cm   7 cm

A. 5.7 cm
B. 6.3 cm
C. 7.8 cm
D. 8.0 cm

Solution

Since the altitude forms a right angle with the base, you have two congruent right triangles. Using the Pythagorean Theorem,

$$7^2 + x^2 = 9^2 \rightarrow 49 + x^2 = 81 \rightarrow x^2 = 32 \rightarrow x = \sqrt{32} \approx 5.7.$$

Without your calculator, you should know that the square root of 32 is less than the square root of 36 which equals 6, so that the only choice that is valid is 5.7.

Answer: A

Example 2. If $\overline{AC} \parallel \overline{DE}$, $\angle B = 112°$ and $\angle BED = 23°$, then $\angle A = ?$

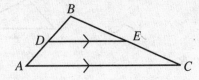

A. 23°
B. 45°
C. 54°
D. 89°

Solution

Since $\overline{AC} \parallel \overline{DE}$, $\angle BDE \cong \angle BAC$ because corresponding angles of parallel lines are congruent. $\angle D = 180° - 112° - 23° = 45° = \angle A$.

Answer: B

Example 3. In the figure below, if $\overline{CB} = 5$, what is the length of $\overline{AD}$?

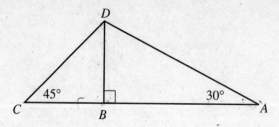

A. 5

B. $5\sqrt{3}$

C. 10

D. $10\sqrt{3}$

Solution

$\triangle BCD$ is a 45°-45°-90°, isosceles right triangle, so its ratio of sides is $x : x : x\sqrt{2}$. Since $CB = BD$, $BD = 5$. $\triangle BDA$ is a 30°-60°-90° special triangle, so its ratio of sides is $x : x\sqrt{3} : 2x$, where the shortest side x is opposite the 30° angle, and the longest side $2x$ is the hypotenuse. $AD = 2(BD) = 2(5) = 10$.

Answer: C

Example 4. If the lengths of two sides of a triangle are 10 and 2 inches, which of the following could be the length of the third side?

A. 10 inches

B. 12 inches

C. 14 inches

D. 16 inches

Solution

Call the third side x. The third side of a triangle must be between the difference and sum of the other two sides. $(10 - 2) < x < (10 + 2) \rightarrow 8 < x < 12$. Only answer choice A falls within this range.

Answer: A

Example 5. The perimeter of an isosceles triangle is 18 inches. Which of the following cannot be the length of the base?

A. 2 inches

B. 4 inches

C. 8 inches

D. 10 inches

Solution

In a triangle, the sum of two sides must be greater than the third. If the base of the triangle were 10 inches, each leg must be 4 inches for the perimeter to equal 18 inches. Since $4 + 4$ is not greater than 10, the base cannot be 10 inches.

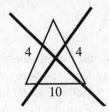

Answer: D

Example 6. $\triangle ABC$ is an obtuse triangle with obtuse $\angle B$. Which of the following is not necessarily true?

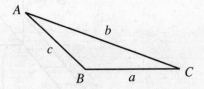

A. $b > a$
B. $c^2 + a^2 < b^2$
C. $\angle C < \angle A$
D. $\angle B > \angle A + \angle C$

Solution

Answer choice A must be true since the longest side in a triangle is opposite the largest angle. Answer choice B is true for an obtuse triangle. D must be true since the sum of the degrees in a triangle is restricted to 180°, and $\angle B$ is greater than 90°. This leaves answer choice C. Unless you know how sides c and a compare, you cannot conclude the relative size of their opposite angles.

Answer: C

Example 7. In the figure below, A, B, and C are collinear. What is the positive difference between the lengths of $\overline{AB}$ and $\overline{BC}$?

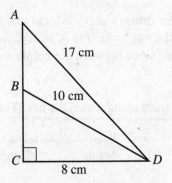

Solution

    $\triangle ACD$ and $\triangle BCD$ are right angles. Use the Pythagorean Theorem to find the lengths of their missing sides: $BC^2 + 8^2 = 10^2$, $BC = 6$. $AC^2 + 8^2 = 17^2$, $AC = 15$. $AB = AC - BC = 15 - 6 = 9$. You want the difference $AB - BC = 9 - 6 = 3$ cm.

Answer: 3 cm

Example 8. Melanie and Susan climb their tree house every afternoon. The ladder sits 10 feet away from the foot of the tree and intersects with the top of the trunk of the tree which is 24 feet high. Melanie says that every day they climb 34 feet because the trunk of the tree is 24 feet high and the ladder is 10 feet away from the bottom of the trunk. Susan says that Melanie's calculations are incorrect and they are actually climbing less than 34 feet. Who is right? Why?

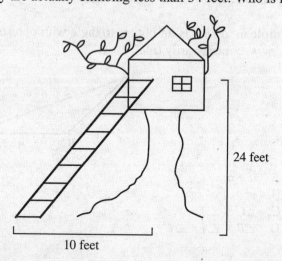

24 feet

10 feet

Solution

    Susan is correct. Counting over the ground and then up is 34 feet, but the shortest distance between any two points (here the base of the ladder to the top) is a straight line.

    You could also think of this problem as the Triangle Inequality Theorem, which states that the sum of two sides (10 feet and 24 feet) is greater than the third (the length of the ladder). A third approach is to calculate the length of the ladder using the Pythagorean Theorem. Calling the ladder's length x, $10^2 + 24^2 = x^2$, $x = 26$ feet.

Answer: Susan

Example 9. In Bruno's backyard, the maple tree, is 20 feet from the magnolia tree, and the magnolia tree is 30 feet from the birch tree. What is the largest possible distance between the maple and the birch? Explain your reasoning.

Solution

    Place the trees along a straight line. The largest possible distance is $20 + 30 = 50$ ft.

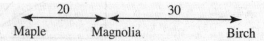

20   30
Maple   Magnolia   Birch

Answer: 50 ft

Example 10. Given circle O with points A, B, C, and D on the circle and diameter $\overline{BD}$, which is not necessarily true?

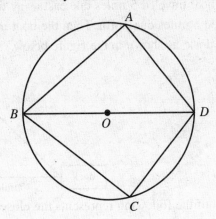

A. $\angle BAD \cong \angle DCB$
B. $\angle ABC \cong \angle ADC$
C. $\angle BAD$ is supplementary to $\angle BCD$
D. $\angle ABC$ is supplementary to $\angle ADC$

Solution

Answer choice A is correct. Since each angle intercepts a semicircle, each must equal 90°. Answer choices C and D are each correct, since the sum of their intercepted arcs is a full circle or 360°, so that the sum of the inscribed angles must be $\frac{1}{2}(360°) = 180°$, making them supplementary. You cannot assume that $\angle ABC \cong \angle ADC$, so answer choice B is not necessarily true.

Answer: B

Example 11. The sides of a triangle are 14, 48, and 50. Is the triangle acute, right, or obtuse? Justify.

Solution

Check which relationship: =, >, or < is true for the expression: $14^2 + 48^2$ [?] 50^2. Always place the largest side by itself in your setup. The quantities on the left and right are equal, so the triangle is right.

Answer: Right triangle

Practice: Triangles

1. A sailboat traveled 5 miles due east away from a dock and then made a 90° turn and traveled 6 miles due north. Then the boat made another turn and sailed directly back to the dock, as shown in the figure below.

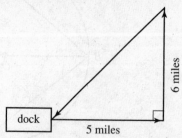

   Which of the following represents the closest total distance the boat traveled, since it left the dock?

   A. 14 miles
   B. 16 miles
   C. 18 miles
   D. 19 miles

2. The angle formed from a point on the ground to the top of a tree is 30°. The point on the ground is 14 feet from the base of the tree. What is the height of the tree to the nearest foot?

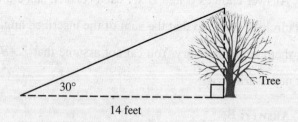

   A. 7 feet
   B. 8 feet
   C. 9 feet
   D. 10 feet

3. Isabella is holding onto a helium balloon attached to a 50 in. ribbon. The wind is blowing the balloon away from her at a 45° angle. What is the approximate height of the balloon?

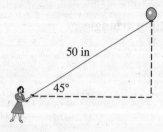

   A. 25 in.
   B. 30 in.
   C. 35 in.
   D. 40 in.

4. What is the measure of ∠A in the figure below?

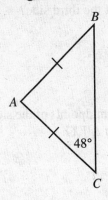

   A. 48°
   B. 84°
   C. 96°
   D. 132°

5. In the figure, if $\overline{CD} = 4$, what is the length of $\overline{AD}$?

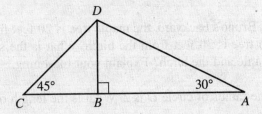

   A. $2\sqrt{2}$
   B. $2\sqrt{3}$
   C. $4\sqrt{2}$
   D. $4\sqrt{3}$

6. Find the length of $\overline{BC}$.

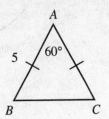

   A. $\dfrac{5}{2}$

   B. $\dfrac{5\sqrt{3}}{2}$

   C. 5
   D. 10

7. Mark is constructing a triangle with sides measuring 4 and 9 inches. Which could not be the length of the third side?
   A. 5 inches
   B. 6 inches
   C. 7 inches
   D. 8 inches

8. W, X, and Y are midpoints of the sides of $\triangle ABC$. The perimeter of $\triangle ABC$ is 23 cm. Find the perimeter of $\triangle WXY$.

   A. $\dfrac{23}{2}$ cm

   B. $\dfrac{25}{2}$ cm

   C. 23 cm

   D. 46 cm

★ 9. How many different isosceles triangles can be made if all the sides are integers and the perimeter is 24? (An isosceles triangle has at least two congruent sides.) Be sure to explain your answer.

10. In Bruno's backyard, the maple tree is 20 feet from the magnolia tree and the magnolia tree is 30 feet from the birch. What is the shortest possible distance between the maple and the birch? Explain your reasoning.

11. The radius of circle O is 2. What is the length of $\overline{AB}$?

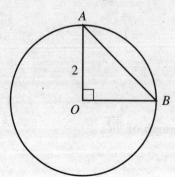

   A. 2
   B. $2\sqrt{2}$
   C. $2\sqrt{3}$
   D. 4

Solutions to Practice: Triangles

1. Set up the Pythagorean Theorem with x as the hypotenuse. $5^2 + 6^2 = x^2$. Solving, you get $x = \sqrt{61} \approx 7.8$ and the total distance traveled to be $5 + 6 + 7.8 \approx 18.8$ miles.

    Answer: D

2. Using special triangles and the diagram, label the ratio of sides in a 30°-60°-90°. Since $14 = x\sqrt{3}$, divide both sides by $\sqrt{3}$ and get $x \approx 8.08$ feet.

    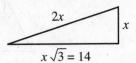

    Answer: B

3. Using special triangles and the diagram, label the ratio of sides in a 45°-45°-90°. Since $50 = x\sqrt{2}$, divide both sides by $\sqrt{2}$ to get $x \approx 35.4$.

    Answer: C

4. In an isosceles triangle, the base angles are congruent so $m\angle B = m\angle C = 48°$. $\angle A = 180 - \angle B + \angle C) = 180 - 2(48) = 84°$.

    Answer: B

5. $\triangle BCD$ is a 45°-45°-90°, isosceles right triangle, so its ratio of sides is $x : x : x\sqrt{2}$. Set up the equation $x\sqrt{2} = 4$. To solve for x, divide by $\sqrt{2}$ and rationalize the denominator: $\dfrac{4}{\sqrt{2}} \cdot \dfrac{\sqrt{2}}{\sqrt{2}} = \dfrac{4\sqrt{2}}{2} = 2\sqrt{2}$. This is the length of $\overline{BD}$. $\triangle BDA$ is a 30°-60°-90° special triangle, so its ratio of sides is $x : x\sqrt{3} : 2x$, where the shortest side x is opposite the 30° angle, and the longest side $2x$ is the hypotenuse. This gives you $AD = 2(BD) = 2(2\sqrt{2}) = 4\sqrt{2}$.

    Answer: C

6. Since the base angles $\angle B$ and $\angle C$ are congruent, you get that each is also 60° and that $\triangle ABC$ is equilateral. This means that the length of each of its sides is 5.

    Answer: C

7. Call the third side x. The third side must be between the difference and sum of the other two sides. $(9-4) < x < (9+4) \rightarrow 5 < x < 13$. Answer choice A does not fall within this range.

Answer: A

8. Using the Midsegment Theorem, the segment formed by joining the midpoints of two of the sides of a triangle is one half the length of the third side.
   Call the sides of $\triangle ABC$ "a, b, c."

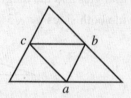

Since each of the three sides of $\triangle WXY$ is one half the length of each side of $\triangle ABC$, the perimeter of $\triangle WXY = \frac{1}{2}a + \frac{1}{2}b + \frac{1}{2}c = \frac{1}{2}(a+b+c) = \frac{1}{2}(23) = \frac{23}{2}$ cm.

Answer: A

9. We have two constraints using the labeled diagram below.

1. The perimeter is 24 so $2x + y = 24$.

2. Using the Triangle Inequality Theorem (the sum of two sides must be greater than the third), $x + x > y$.

Generate a table of possible values:

x	y	Perimeter
7	10	24
8	8	24
9	6	24
10	4	24
11	2	24

There are five possibilities that meet both criteria.

Answer: 5

10. Place the trees along a line as shown below. The shortest possible distance is 10 feet.

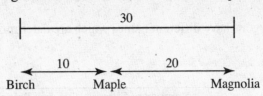

Answer: 10 ft

11. $\triangle AOB$ is an isosceles right, or 45°-45°-90°, triangle, so its ratio of sides is $x:x:x\sqrt{2}$. $AO = x = 2$, so $AB = x\sqrt{2} = 2\sqrt{2}$.

Answer: B

Polygons

• A **polygon** is a closed plane figure with at least three sides. A polygon consists entirely of segments. The consecutive sides of a polygon intersect only at their endpoints. Each vertex must belong to exactly two sides.

• A **convex** polygon is a polygon in which each interior angle is less than 180°.

ABCDE is a convex polygon.

$\overline{AB}$, $\overline{BC}$, $\overline{CD}$, $\overline{DE}$, and $\overline{AE}$ are the sides of the polygon.

A, B, C, D, and E are the vertices of the polygon.

• A **concave** polygon is a polygon in which an interior angle is greater than 180°.

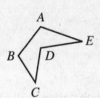

ABCDE is a convex polygon.

$\overline{AB}$, $\overline{BC}$, $\overline{CD}$, $\overline{DE}$, and $\overline{AE}$ are the sides of the polygon.

A, B, C, D, and E are the vertices of the polygon.

> * *Remember: Think of your polygon as being "caved-in"!*

• A **diagonal** of a polygon is any segment that connects two nonconsecutive vertices.

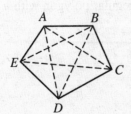

The diagonals of polygon $ABCDE$ are $\overline{AD}$, $\overline{AC}$, $\overline{BE}$, $\overline{BD}$, and $\overline{EC}$.

- The **number of diagonals** in a polygon with n as the number of sides is $\dfrac{n(n-3)}{2}$.

- Polygons have different names which are determined by the number of sides in the polygon.

Number of Sides	Polygon Name
3	triangle
4	quadrilateral
5	pentagon
6	hexagon
7	heptagon or septagon
8	octagon
9	nonagon
10	decagon
12	dodecagon
n	n-gon

- The **sum** of the **interior angles** of a polygon with n sides is $180(n-2)°$.

- The **exterior angles** of a polygon, one at each vertex, are the angles that are formed when the sides of the polygon are extended.

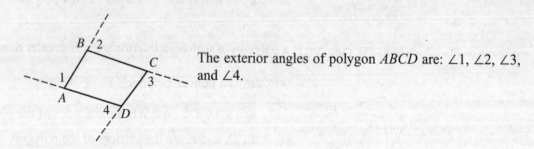

The exterior angles of polygon $ABCD$ are: $\angle 1$, $\angle 2$, $\angle 3$, and $\angle 4$.

- The **sum of the exterior angles** of a polygon, one at each vertex, will always equal 360°.

- A **regular polygon** is a polygon that is **equilateral** (all of the sides are congruent) and **equiangular** (all of the angles are congruent).

- The measure of **one exterior angle** of a **regular polygon** is 360° divided by the number of sides. The formula for an exterior angle of a regular polygon with n sides is $\dfrac{360°}{n}$.

• The measure of **one interior angle** of a **regular polygon** is the sum of the interior angles divided by the number of angles (which is equal to the number of sides). The formula for an interior angle of a regular polygon with n sides is $\dfrac{180(n-2)^\circ}{n}$. An interior angle is also the supplement of an exterior angle, so you can also use the formula $180^\circ - \dfrac{360^\circ}{n}$.

Examples: Polygons

Example 1. What is the sum of the interior angles of a pentagon?

Solution

A pentagon has five sides, so substitute $n = 5$ into the formula:

$$\textit{sum of the interior angles} = 180\,(n-2)^\circ$$

Evaluating, you get $180(5-2) = 180(3) = 540^\circ$.

Answer: 540°

Example 2. What is the measure of each interior angle of a regular octagon?

Solution

There are two ways to do this problem.

<u>Method 1</u>

First find the number of degrees in each exterior angle of the polygon using the formula:

$$E = \frac{360^\circ}{n}$$

where E is the measure of each exterior angle, and n is the number of sides. You get

$$E = 360 \div 8 = 45^\circ$$

Next, take the supplement of the exterior angle by subtracting from 180°. This will leave you with the measure of each interior angle I ! You get each interior, $I = 180 - 45^\circ = 135^\circ$.

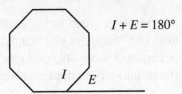

$I + E = 180^\circ$

<u>Method 2</u>

Substitute $n = 8$ into the formula: $I = \dfrac{(n-2)180^\circ}{n} = \dfrac{(8-2)180^\circ}{8} = \dfrac{6 \cdot 180^\circ}{8} = 135^\circ$

Answer: 135°

Example 3. What is the measure of each exterior angle of a regular 15-sided polygon?

Solution

To find the measure of each exterior angle of the polygon, use the formula:

$$E = \frac{360°}{n}$$

where E is the measure of each exterior angle, and n is the number of sides. Substituting $n = 15$, you get $E = \frac{360°}{15} = 24°$.

Answer: 24°

★ **Example 4.** What is the name of a polygon with 27 diagonals?

Solution

The formula for finding the number of diagonals in a polygon is: $d = \frac{n(n-3)}{2}$, where d is the number of diagonals and n is the number of sides.

Using this formula will often be easier than drawing and counting the number of diagonals, particularly for a polygon that has a large number of sides. Substitute $d = 27$ into the equation, and solve for n. You will have a quadratic equation:

$$27 = \frac{n(n-3)}{2} \rightarrow 54 = n(n-3) \rightarrow 54 = n^2 - 3n \rightarrow 0 = n^2 - 3n - 54 \rightarrow 0 = (n-9)(n+6)$$

Solving, you get $n = 9$ or $n = -6$, which is impossible. The polygon must have nine sides.

If you are not comfortable working with quadratic equations, you may be able to guess and check which number works for n. You know it will be an integer, since a polygon cannot have a fractional number of sides!

$$d = \frac{9(9-3)}{2} = \frac{9 \cdot 6}{2} = \frac{54}{2} = 27 \text{ diagonals}$$

A polygon with nine sides is called a nonagon.

Answer: nonagon

Example 5. A concave polygon has at least one interior angle whose measure is greater than 180°. Suppose you wanted to derive a formula for the sum of the interior angles of a concave polygon, such as those shown below, by dividing each figure into a minimum number of triangles.

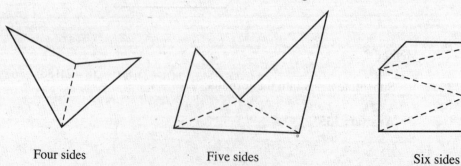

Four sides   Five sides   Six sides

a. Draw a seven-sided concave polygon, and divide it into a minimum number of tri-angles.

b. Fill in the table below with the number of sides *n*, number of triangular sections, and sum of the interior angles in each polygon.

Number of Sides (*n*)	Number of Triangles	Sum of the Interior Angles
4	2	360°
5		
6		
7		

c. Create a formula for *S* in terms of *n*, where *S* is the sum of the interior angles in any concave polygon, and *n* is the number of sides. Show your work or explain how you got your answer.

Solution

a. Draw any seven-sided polygon. *Concave* means that at least one of its interior angles is greater than 180°. Choose any ONE of the seven vertices to draw your diagonals from. Try to choose a vertex such that all the diagonals stay within the polygon. You can connect your diagonals to all but three vertices: the point you are starting from, and those two vertices that are adjacent to the point you are starting from.

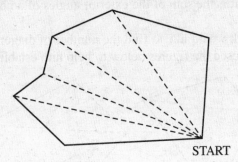

START

b. Completing the table, you get that the sum of the interior angles is the number of triangles in the diagram multiplied by 180°.

Number of Sides (*n*)	Number of Triangles	Sum of the Interior Angles
4	2	360°
5	3	540°
6	4	720°
7	5	900°

c. The number of triangles is always 2 less than the number of vertices, *n*. The sum of the interior angles is the number of triangles in the diagram multiplied by 180°. This makes the formula for *S*, the sum of the interior angles, $S = (n - 2) \cdot 180°$.

Answer: $S = (n - 2) \cdot 180°$

Practice: Polygons

1. What is the measure of each interior angle of a regular octagon?

2. What is the measure of each interior angle of an 18-sided regular polygon?

3. What is the measure of each exterior angle of a regular hexagon?

4. How many diagonals does a decagon have?

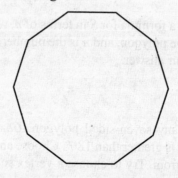

5. What is the sum of the exterior angles of a nonagon?

6. Clark would like to find the number of diagonals in a convex polygon. He used the figures below to help him establish a pattern.

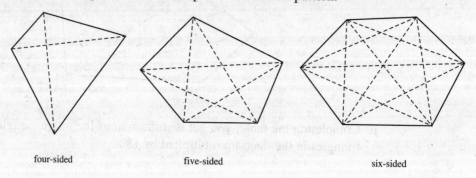

four-sided   five-sided   six-sided

a. Complete the table below with the number of diagonals drawn from a single vertex, and the total number of diagonals in each of the convex polygons listed.

Number of sides	4	5	6	7	8
Number of diagonals drawn from each vertex		2			
Total number of diagonals		5			

b. What is the total number of diagonals in a convex polygon with ten sides? Show your work or explain how you got your answer.

c. Write an expression relating the number of sides of a convex polygon, **n**, and its total number of diagonals, **d**. Show your work or explain how you got your answer.

Solutions to Practice: Polygons

1. An octagon has eight sides, so substitute $n = 8$ into the formula: $I = (n - 2)180°$, where I is the sum of the interior angles. Evaluating, $I = (8 - 2)180° = (6)180° = 1,080°$.

   Answer: 1,080°

2. First find the measure of each exterior angle: $E = \dfrac{360°}{n} = \dfrac{360°}{18} = 20°$. Then take the supplement of this angle to get the measure of each interior angle: $180° - 20° = 160°$.

   Answer: 160°

3. A hexagon has six sides, so substitute $n = 6$ into the formula: $E = \dfrac{360°}{n} = \dfrac{360°}{6} = 60°$.

   Answer: 60°

4. The formula for finding the number of diagonals is: $d = \dfrac{n(n-3)}{2}$, where d is the number of diagonals, and n is the number of sides. A decagon has ten sides, so substitute 10 in for n:

   $$d = \frac{10(10-3)}{2} = \frac{10 \cdot 7}{2} = 35 \text{ diagonals.}$$

   Answer: 35

5. The sum of the measures of the exterior angles of any polygon is 360°.

   Answer: 360°

6. a.

Number of sides	4	5	6	7	8
Number of diagonals drawn from each vertex	1	2	3	4	5
Total number of diagonals	2	5	9	14	20

b. Continuing the pattern, there would be seven diagonals drawn from each vertex of a ten-sided polygon. The number of diagonals is one half the product of the number of vertices times the number of diagonals drawn from each vertex. The number of diagonals in a ten-sided polygon is $\dfrac{10 \cdot 7}{2} = 35$ diagonals.

Answer: 35 diagonals

c. Coming up with a formula, choose a single vertex. Notice that there are $(n - 3)$ vertices to which you can draw a diagonal. (You cannot connect a vertex to itself or to its adjacent vertices.) Since there are n vertices with which to go through this procedure, multiply n times $(n - 3)$. You don't want to count a diagonal twice, (for example, $\overline{AC}$ is the same diagonal as $\overline{CA}$) so divide this product by 2.

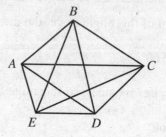

Answer: $d = \dfrac{n(n-3)}{2}$

Quadrilaterals

- A **quadrilateral** is a four-sided polygon.

- A **parallelogram** is a quadrilateral with both pairs of opposite sides parallel. Opposite sides of a parallelogram are congruent. Opposite angles are congruent. Consecutive angles are supplementary. The diagonals bisect each other.

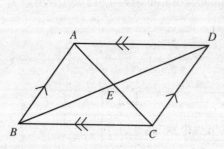

In parallelogram $ABCD$, $\overline{AB} \parallel \overline{DC}$ and $\overline{AD} \parallel \overline{BC}$.

$\overline{AB} \cong \overline{DC}$ and $\overline{AD} \cong \overline{BC}$.

$\angle BAD \cong \angle DCB$ and $\angle ABC \cong \angle ADC$.

$\overline{AE} \cong \overline{EC}$ and $\overline{BE} \cong \overline{ED}$.

$\angle ABC$ is supplementary to $\angle BAD$ and $\angle BCD$.

$\angle ADC$ is supplementary to $\angle BAD$ and $\angle BCD$.

- A **rectangle** is a parallelogram with all right angles. All the properties of a parallelogram apply to a rectangle. The additional characteristics of a rectangle are that all of the vertex angles are right angles and the diagonals of a rectangle are congruent.

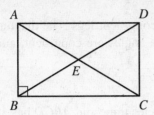

In rectangle *ABCD*, all the properties of a parallelogram apply.

Also, ∠*ABC* ≅ ∠*BCD* ≅ ∠*CDA* ≅ ∠*DAB* = 90°.

$\overline{AC}$ ≅ $\overline{BD}$. $\overline{AE}$ ≅ $\overline{EC}$ ≅ $\overline{BE}$ ≅ $\overline{ED}$.

- A **rhombus** is a parallelogram with all its sides congruent. All of the properties of a parallelogram apply to a rhombus. The additional characteristics of a rhombus are that all the sides are congruent, the diagonals are perpendicular bisectors of each other, and the diagonals bisect the vertex angles of the rhombus.

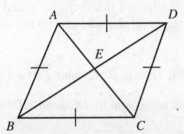

In rhombus *ABCD*, all the properties of a parallelogram apply.

Also, $\overline{AD}$ ≅ $\overline{DC}$ ≅ $\overline{BC}$ ≅ $\overline{AB}$.

∠*AEB* ≅ ∠*AED* ≅ ∠*CED* ≅ ∠*CEB* = 90°.
∠*BAE* ≅ ∠*EAD* ≅ ∠*BCE* ≅ ∠*ECD*.
∠*ADE* ≅ ∠*EDC* ≅ ∠*ABE* ≅ ∠*EBC*.

- A **square** is a parallelogram, rectangle, and a rhombus. Because the vertex angles are 90° and bisected by the diagonals, and the diagonals are perpendicular bisectors of each other, four congruent isosceles right triangles are formed.

∠*BAE* ≅ ∠*EAD* ≅ ∠*ADE* ≅ ∠*EDC* ≅ ∠*DCE* ≅ ∠*ECB* ≅ ∠*EBC* ≅ ∠*ABE* = 45°.

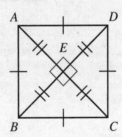

- A **trapezoid** is a quadrilateral with exactly one pair of opposite sides parallel. The parallel sides are called the bases, and the nonparallel sides are called the legs.

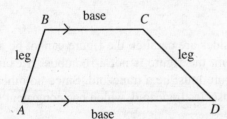

$\overline{BC}$ ‖ $\overline{AD}$.

$\overline{AB}$ is not parallel to $\overline{CD}$.

∠*A* is supplementary to ∠*B*.

∠*C* is supplementary to ∠*D*.

- An **isosceles trapezoid** is a trapezoid with congruent legs. The diagonals of an isosceles trapezoid are congruent. The upper base angles are congruent, and the lower base angles are congruent.

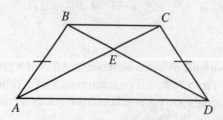

Isosceles trapezoid $ABCD$ has all the properties of a trapezoid.

Also, $\overline{AB} \cong \overline{CD}$, $\overline{AC} \cong \overline{BD}$.

$\angle BAD \cong \angle ADC$ and $\angle ABC \cong \angle BCD$.

- A **kite** is a quadrilateral with two pairs of adjacent sides congruent and no opposite sides congruent. The diagonals of a kite are perpendicular, and exactly one diagonal is the perpendicular bisector of the other.

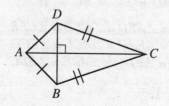

In kite $ABCD$, $\overline{AB} \cong \overline{AD}$ and $\overline{CB} \cong \overline{CD}$.

$\overline{AB}$ is not congruent to $\overline{DC}$, and $\overline{AD}$ is not congruent to $\overline{BC}$.

$\overline{AC}$ is the perpendicular bisector of $\overline{DB}$.

Examples: Quadrilaterals

Example 1. A partial drawing of a quadrilateral is shown below. If $\overline{AB} \parallel \overline{CD}$ and no other sides are congruent or parallel, which best describes the figure?

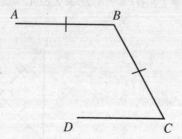

A. Parallelogram
B. Rhombus
C. Trapezoid
D. Isosceles trapezoid

Solution

Since $\overline{AB} \parallel \overline{CD}$ and no other sides are parallel, the figure cannot be a parallelogram. Since a rhombus is a parallelogram, the figure is not a rhombus. If exactly one pair of opposite sides are parallel, the figure must be a trapezoid. Since no other sides are congruent, the figure cannot be an isosceles trapezoid, which has congruent legs. Therefore, the figure is a trapezoid.

Answer: C

Practice: Quadrilaterals

1. Which of the following best describes the quadrilateral below, if the sides and angles are measured as shown?

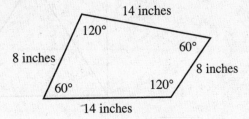

(Not drawn to scale.)

A. Rectangle
B. Parallelogram
C. Trapezoid
D. Kite

2. Joe is building a ladder for his tree house. The rungs of the ladder and the sides of the ladder form parallelograms. If ∠ABC in the diagram measures 130°, what is the measure of ∠EDC?

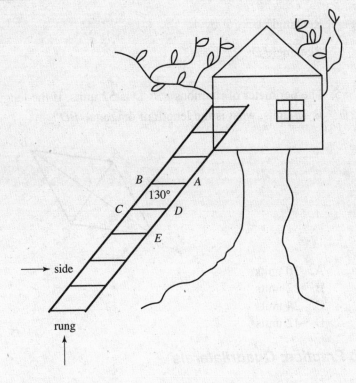

3. In the figure below, $\triangle BED$ is equilateral and $ACDE$ is a rectangle. If the perimeter of $\triangle BED$ is 24 inches, find the length of $\overline{AE}$.

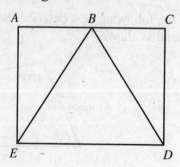

   A. 4 inches
   B. 8 inches
   C. $4\sqrt{2}$ inches
   D. $4\sqrt{3}$ inches

4. List the rectangles below in order, beginning with the one with the shortest diagonal and ending with the rectangle with the longest diagonal.

   Rectangle A: $\sqrt{5}$ by $\sqrt{12}$

   Rectangle B: 4 by $\sqrt{5}$

   Rectangle C: $\sqrt{6}$ by 4

   Rectangle D: $\sqrt{7}$ by $\sqrt{7}$

5. The perimeter of rhombus $ABCD$ is 52 units. If the length of diagonal $\overline{AC}$ is 10 units, what is the length of diagonal $\overline{BD}$?

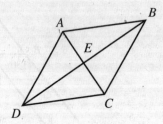

   A. 10 units
   B. 12 units
   C. 24 units
   D. 42 units

Solutions to Practice: Quadrilaterals

1. Since both pairs of opposite sides are congruent, the figure must be a parallelogram. Both pairs of opposite angles congruent is also sufficient information. It cannot be a rectangle because the angles are not right angles.

   Answer: B

2. $\angle ADC = 130°$ because opposite angles of a parallelogram are congruent. $\angle EDC$ is supplementary to $\angle ADC$ so $\angle EDC = 180 - 130 = 50°$.

Answer: 50°

3. $\triangle \underline{BED}$ is equilateral, so each of its sides is 8 inches. The height of $\triangle BED$ is the same as AE, the height of the rectangle. To find the height of $\triangle BED$, use the ratio of sides in a 30°-60°-90° triangle.

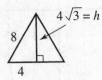

Answer: D

4. Use the Pythagorean Theorem to compute the length of each rectangle's diagonal.

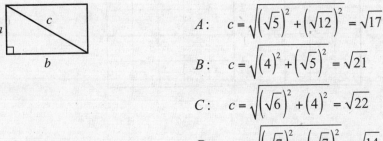

$A: \quad c = \sqrt{\left(\sqrt{5}\right)^2 + \left(\sqrt{12}\right)^2} = \sqrt{17}$

$B: \quad c = \sqrt{\left(4\right)^2 + \left(\sqrt{5}\right)^2} = \sqrt{21}$

$C: \quad c = \sqrt{\left(\sqrt{6}\right)^2 + \left(4\right)^2} = \sqrt{22}$

$D: \quad c = \sqrt{\left(\sqrt{7}\right)^2 + \left(\sqrt{7}\right)^2} = \sqrt{14}$

Answer: D, A, B, C

5. The sides of a rhombus are congruent, so the length of each side is: $52 \div 4 = 13$ inches. The diagonals of a rhombus are perpendicular bisectors of each other. This means they form four congruent right triangles. Use the Pythagorean Theorem to find the value of x:

$$x^2 + 5^2 = 13^2 \longrightarrow x^2 + 25 = 169 \longrightarrow x^2 = 144 \longrightarrow x = 12$$

Double your value of x to get the length of diagonal $\overline{BD}$: $2(12) = 24$.

Answer: C

Coordinate Geometry

- To find the **midpoint** of a segment on a coordinate plane, find the average of the x coordinates of the endpoints and the average of the y coordinates of the endpoints. If the endpoints of a segment are (a, b) and (c, d), the midpoint of the segment is $\left(\dfrac{a+c}{2}, \dfrac{b+d}{2}\right)$.

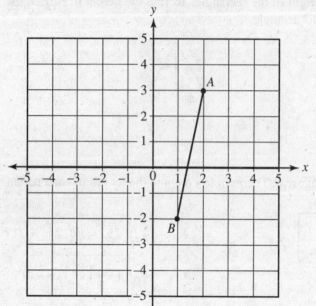

The endpoints of $\overline{AB}$ are $(2, 3)$ and $(1, -2)$.

The midpoint of $\overline{AB}$ is

$$\left(\frac{2+1}{2}, \frac{3+(-2)}{2}\right) = \left(\frac{3}{2}, \frac{1}{2}\right).$$

- To find the **distance between two points** on a coordinate plane, draw in a right triangle. The unknown distance should be the hypotenuse of the right triangle. The length of the horizontal leg is the change in the x-coordinates, and the vertical leg is the change in y-coordinates from one point to the next.

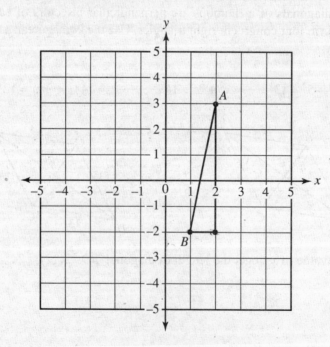

$\overline{AB}$ is the hypotenuse of a right triangle with legs of lengths 1 and 5.

$$1^2 + 5^2 = \left(\overline{AB}\right)^2.$$

$$\left(\overline{AB}\right)^2 = 26.$$

Length of $\overline{AB} = \sqrt{26}$.

- In general, the distance between any two points $A\,(x_1, y_1)$ and $B\,(x_2, y_2)$ can also be found using the **distance formula**:

$$d = \sqrt{\left(x_1 - x_2\right)^2 + \left(y_1 - y_2\right)^2}$$

> * *Memory Tip: This is just the Pythagorean Theorem solved for the hypotenuse!*

Using this formula with the previous example, the distance between $A(2, 3)$ and $B(1, -2)$ is

$$d = \sqrt{\left(2 - 1\right)^2 + \left(3 - (-2)\right)^2} = \sqrt{1^2 + 5^2} = \sqrt{26}$$

- The **slope** of a line is determined by the change in y-values from one point to another divided by the change in x-values.

$$\frac{\Delta y}{\Delta x}, \quad \frac{change\ in\ y}{change\ in\ x}, \quad \frac{y_2 - y_1}{x_2 - x_1}, \quad \frac{vertical\ change}{horizontal\ change}, \quad and \quad \frac{rise}{run}$$

all mean slope. Sometimes the letter m is used to indicate the slope of a line.

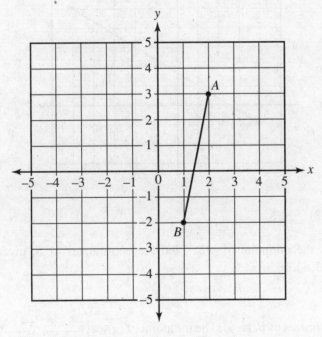

The coordinates of two points on $\overline{AB}$ are $(2, 3)$ and $(1, -2)$.

The slope of

$$\overline{AB} = \frac{3 - (-2)}{2 - 1} = 5.$$

- Points are **collinear** if the slope of every pair of points is the same.

- **Parallel** lines have equal slopes.

- **Perpendicular** lines have opposite reciprocal slopes, and the product of the slopes is -1. The following are examples of some slopes that are opposite reciprocals:

If $m = 5$, then $m_\perp = \dfrac{-1}{5}$.   If $m = \dfrac{2}{3}$, then $m_\perp = \dfrac{-3}{2}$.   If $m = -1$, then $m_\perp = 1$.

- **Horizontal** lines have a slope of 0 because the numerator of the fraction equals 0.

- **Vertical** lines have an undefined slope because you cannot divide by 0.

Examples: Coordinate Geometry

Example 1. What are the coordinates of the midpoint of a line segment with endpoints (−4, −1) and (6, 5)?

Solution

To find the midpoint of a segment, calculate the average of the *x*-coordinates of the endpoints and the average of the *y*-coordinates of the endpoints.

$$\left(\frac{-4+6}{2}, \frac{-1+5}{2}\right) = \left(\frac{2}{2}, \frac{4}{2}\right) = \left(1, 2\right).$$

You may also want to use the grid to help visualize the midpoint.

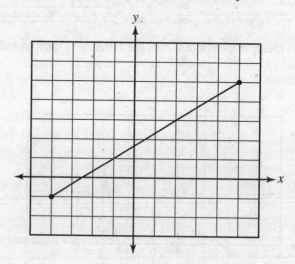

Answer: (1, 2)

Example 2. *M* is the midpoint of $\overline{AB}$. Find the coordinates of *B*, given *A*(−6, −4) and *M*(−3, 1).

Solution

Call the coordinates of *B*, (*x*, *y*). The midpoint of $\overline{AB} = \left(\frac{-6+x}{2}, \frac{-4+y}{2}\right) = M\left(-3, 1\right).$

So, $\frac{-6+x}{2} = -3 \rightarrow -6 + x = -6 \rightarrow x = 0.$ $\frac{-4+y}{2} = 1 \rightarrow -4 + y = 2 \rightarrow y = 6.$ Therefore, *B*(0, 6). Plotting the points on a graph can also help you visualize the answer.

Answer: *B*(0, 6)

Example 3. Which of the following points is not collinear with the others?

$$A(-4, -6) \quad B(8, 3) \quad C(0, -4) \quad D(4, 0)$$

A. Point A
B. Point B
C. Point C
D. Point D

Solution

The slope of $\overline{AB} = \dfrac{-6-3}{-4-8} = \dfrac{3}{4}$. The slope of $\overline{BC} = \dfrac{3+4}{8-0} = \dfrac{7}{8}$. The slope of $\overline{CD} = \dfrac{-4-0}{0-4} = 1$. The slope of $\overline{AD} = \dfrac{-6-0}{-4-4} = \dfrac{3}{4}$. Since the slopes of $\overline{AB}$ and $\overline{AD}$ are the same, the points A, B, and D are collinear. C is not collinear with the others. Plotting may help.

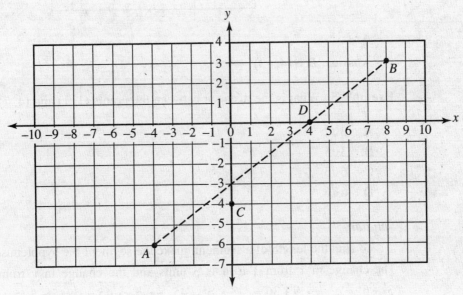

Answer: C

Example 4. Parallelogram $ABCD$ has vertices: $A(0, 0)$, $B(3, 5)$, and $C(7, 2)$. What are the coordinates of point D?

Solution

The slope of $\overline{AB}$ = the slope of $\overline{CD}$. The slope of $\overline{AB} = \dfrac{5-0}{3-0} = \dfrac{5}{3}$. Plot the points on a graph and count down 5 units and to the left 3 units from point C. The coordinates of D = (4, –3).

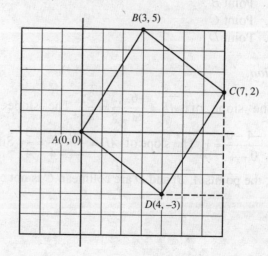

Answer: D = **(4, –3)**

Example 5. What is the distance between the points (1, 1) and (4, 7)?

A. $3\sqrt{2}$
B. $3\sqrt{5}$
C. $6\sqrt{3}$
D. $6\sqrt{6}$

Solution

To find the length of a segment, make the segment the hypotenuse of a right triangle. The change in x from 1 to 4 is 3 units and the change in y from 1 to 7 is 6 units. $3^2 + 6^2 = c^2 \rightarrow 9 + 36 = c^2 \rightarrow c^2 = 45 \rightarrow c = \sqrt{45} = \sqrt{9 \cdot 5} = 3\sqrt{5}$.

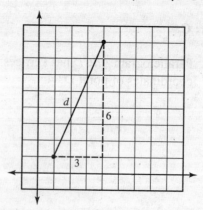

Answer: B

Example 6. Rhombus $ABCD$ has coordinates $A(0, 0)$, $B(3, 4)$, $C(8, 4)$, $D(5, 0)$.

a. What is the slope of diagonal $\overline{AC}$ of the rhombus?

b. What is the slope of diagonal $\overline{BD}$ of the rhombus?

c. What is the equation of the line containing diagonal $\overline{AC}$?

d. What is the relationship between the line containing diagonal $\overline{AC}$ and the line containing diagonal $\overline{BD}$?

Solution

a. The slope of diagonal $\overline{AC} = \dfrac{4-0}{8-0} = \dfrac{4}{8} = \dfrac{1}{2}$.

Answer: $\dfrac{1}{2}$

b. The slope of diagonal $\overline{BD} = \dfrac{4-0}{3-5} = \dfrac{4}{-2} = -2$.

Answer: -2

c. A point on $\overline{AC}$ is $(0, 0)$, and the slope of $\overline{AC}$ is $\dfrac{1}{2}$. The equation of the line is $y = \dfrac{1}{2}x$.

Answer: $y = \dfrac{1}{2}x$

d. The two lines have opposite reciprocal slopes so they are perpendicular.

Answer: $\perp$

Example 7. When a map is placed on a grid, city A is represented by $A(-3, 1)$ and city B is represented by $B(3, 5)$.

a. What is the length of $\overline{AB}$? Show or explain how you got your answer.

b. If each unit on the grid represents 9 actual miles, what is the shortest distance, in miles, from city A to city B? Be sure to include units of measure. Show or explain how you got your answer.

c. On the same map and grid, city C is represented by $C(2, -4)$. What is the least possible number of miles in a complete round trip of the three cities (from A to B to C and back to A)? Be sure to include units of measure. Show or explain how you got your answer.

Solution

a. $\overline{AB} = \sqrt{6^2 + 4^2} = \sqrt{36 + 16} = \sqrt{52} = \sqrt{4 \cdot 13} = 2\sqrt{13}$.

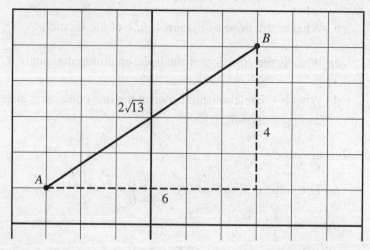

Answer: $2\sqrt{13}$

b. $9 \cdot \overline{AB} = 9 \cdot 2\sqrt{13} = 18\sqrt{13}$ miles. If the question does not ask you to round, leave your answer as an exact answer, $18\sqrt{13}$ miles. If the question asks you to round to the nearest tenth of a mile, use your calculator to determine that $18\sqrt{13} \approx 64.9$ miles.

Answer: 64.9 miles

c. $\overline{AB} = 2\sqrt{13}$. $\overline{BC} = \sqrt{1^2 + 9^2} = \sqrt{1 + 81} = \sqrt{82}$.

$\overline{AC} = \sqrt{5^2 + 5^2} = \sqrt{25 + 25} = \sqrt{50} = \sqrt{25 \cdot 2} = 5\sqrt{2}$.

$\overline{AB} + \overline{BC} + \overline{AC} = 2\sqrt{13} + \sqrt{82} + 5\sqrt{2}$.

$9\left(2\sqrt{13} + \sqrt{82} + 5\sqrt{2}\right) = 18\sqrt{13} + 9\sqrt{82} + 45\sqrt{2}$ miles.

To the nearest tenth of a mile, the answer is 210 miles.

Answer: 210 miles

Example 8. Jose is going to draw $\triangle LMN$ on the grid below so that it is congruent to $\triangle ABC$. He located points $L(-4, 2)$ and $N(-2, -9)$. Which of the following is a possible location for point M?

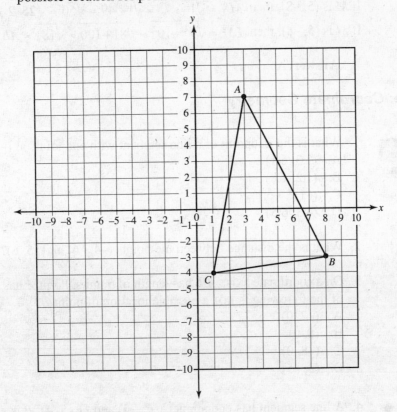

A. $(-9, -8)$
B. $(5, -10)$
C. $(-9, -10)$
D. $(5, -8)$

Solution

Since $\triangle LMN \cong \triangle ABC$, $\overline{LM} \cong \overline{AB}$, $\overline{MN} \cong \overline{BC}$, and $\overline{LN} \cong \overline{AC}$.

$AB = \sqrt{5^2 + 10^2} = \sqrt{25 + 100} = \sqrt{125} = \sqrt{25 \cdot 5} = 5\sqrt{5}$.

$BC = \sqrt{1^2 + 7^2} = \sqrt{1 + 49} = \sqrt{50} = \sqrt{25 \cdot 2} = 5\sqrt{2}$.

$CA = \sqrt{11^2 + 2^2} = \sqrt{121 + 4} = \sqrt{125} = \sqrt{25 \cdot 5} = 5\sqrt{5}$.

If M is $(-9, -8)$, then $MN = \sqrt{1^2 + 7^2} = \sqrt{1 + 49} = \sqrt{50} = \sqrt{25 \cdot 2} = 5\sqrt{2} = BC$.

If M is $(-9, -8)$, then $LM = \sqrt{5^2 + 10^2} = \sqrt{25 + 100} = \sqrt{125} = \sqrt{25 \cdot 5} = 5\sqrt{5} = AB$.

$LN = \sqrt{11^2 + 2^2} = \sqrt{121 + 4} = \sqrt{125} = \sqrt{25 \cdot 5} = 5\sqrt{5} = AC$.

Since all of the corresponding sides are congruent, $(-9, -8)$ is a possible location of point M.

If M is $(5, -10)$, then $MN = \sqrt{1^2 + 7^2} = \sqrt{1 + 49} = \sqrt{50} = \sqrt{25 \cdot 2} = 5\sqrt{2} = BC$.

If M is $(5, -10)$, then $LM = \sqrt{9^2 + 12^2} = \sqrt{81 + 144} = \sqrt{225} = 15 \neq AB$.

If M is $(-9, -10)$, then $MN = \sqrt{1^2 + 7^2} = \sqrt{1 + 49} = \sqrt{50} = \sqrt{25 \cdot 2} = 5\sqrt{2} = BC$.

If M is $(-9, -10)$, then $LM = \sqrt{5^2 + 12^2} = \sqrt{25 + 144} = \sqrt{169} = 13 \neq AB$.

If M is $(5, -8)$, then $MN = \sqrt{1^2 + 7^2} = \sqrt{1 + 49} = \sqrt{50} = \sqrt{25 \cdot 2} = 5\sqrt{2} = BC$.

If M is $(5, -8)$, then $LM = \sqrt{9^2 + 10^2} = \sqrt{81 + 100} = \sqrt{181} \neq AB$.

Answer: A

Practice: Coordinate Geometry

1. What is the midpoint of a line segment with endpoints at $(-6.1, -4.3)$ and $(8.5, 7.9)$?
   A. $(7.3, 6.1)$
   B. $(1.2, 1.8)$
   C. $(-1.2, -6.1)$
   D. $(4.3, 6.5)$

2. What is the distance between the points $(-4, -6)$ and $(5, 6)$?

3. On a coordinate axis, $\overline{AB}$ has length of 5 units. Point A has coordinates $(3, 0)$. Which of the following is NOT a possible location of point B?
   A. $(-2, 0)$
   B. $(8, 0)$
   C. $(-8, 0)$
   D. $(3, -5)$

★ 4. A line segment has endpoints $C(-2, -3)$ and $D(-5, 4)$. P is a point such that $\overline{PC} \perp \overline{CD}$. Find the coordinates of P if P is on the x-axis.

5. If $\angle B$ is a right angle, what is the value of k?

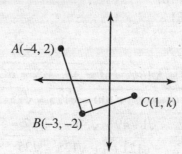

   A. $-\dfrac{1}{2}$
   B. -1
   C. $-\dfrac{3}{2}$
   D. -2

6. Show if the points $(2, 4)$, $(5, 13)$, and $(26, 76)$ are collinear?

7. Quadrilateral *ABDC* is a rectangle. Find the value of *a*.
   A(–2, –1), B(–2, 4), C(–4, a), D(–4, 4)

8. *ABCD* is an isosceles trapezoid with bases $\overline{AD}$ and $\overline{BC}$ and vertices A(3, 0), B(2, 3), and C(–2, 3). Find the coordinates of point *D*.

9. a. Graph the vertices of quadrilateral *ABCD*: A(0, –6), B(–4, 2), C(4, 6), D(8, –2).

   b. Find the slopes of $\overline{AB}$, $\overline{BC}$, $\overline{CD}$, and $\overline{AD}$.

   c. Find the lengths of $\overline{AB}$ and $\overline{BC}$.

   d. What is the most descriptive name for quadrilateral *ABCD*? Explain how you arrived at your answer.

10. a. Graph the vertices of quadrilateral *ABCD*: A(12, 10), B(22, 6), C(19, 0), D(9, 4).

    b. Explain how you know that *ABCD* is a parallelogram.

    c. Explain how you know that *ABCD* is not a rectangle.

11. When the scale drawing of a city grid is placed on a coordinate plane, the intersection of Atwell and Archery Avenues is represented by the point A(3, 2), and the intersection of Baldwin and Bouncer Boulevards is represented by the point B(–4, –1). Graph these points on the grid provided.

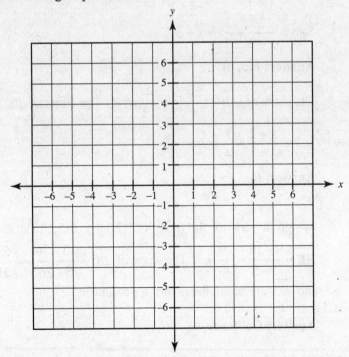

   a. What is the length of the line segment $\overline{AB}$ on the grid? Show or explain how you got your answer.

b. If each unit on the grid represents a quarter of a mile, what is the straight line distance, in miles, between the two intersections? Show or explain how you got your answer.

c. On the same grid, the intersection of Columbus and Canary Courts is represented by the point $C(3, -1)$. Graph point C on the same grid used in part a. What is the least possible number of miles to complete a round trip through all three intersections, assuming that the roads connecting the three intersections are straight line segments? (From A to B to C and back to A). Show or explain your answer.

Solutions to Practice: Coordinate Geometry

1. $\left(\dfrac{-6.1 + 8.5}{2}, \dfrac{-4.3 + 7.9}{2} \right) = (1.2,\ 1.8)$

   Answer: B

2. $\sqrt{9^2 + 12^2} = \sqrt{81 + 144} = \sqrt{225} = 15$

   Answer: 15

3. If $B = (-8, 0)$, then $AB = 11$.

   Answer: C

4. The slope of $\overline{CD} = \dfrac{-3 - 4}{-2 + 5} = \dfrac{-7}{3}$. Let $P = (x, 0)$. The slope of $\overline{PC} = \dfrac{0 + 3}{x + 2} = \dfrac{3}{x + 2}$.

   Solve $\dfrac{3}{x + 2} = \dfrac{3}{7} \rightarrow x = 5$.

   Answer: $P(5, 0)$

5. The slope of $\overline{AB} = \dfrac{2 + 2}{-4 + 3} = \dfrac{4}{-1} = -4$. The slope of $\overline{BC} = \dfrac{k + 2}{1 + 3} = \dfrac{k + 2}{4}$.

   Solve $\dfrac{k + 2}{4} = \dfrac{1}{4} \rightarrow k = -1$.

   Answer: B

6. Assign letters to the points $A(2, 4)$, $B(5, 13)$, and $C(26, 76)$. The slope of $\overline{AB} = \dfrac{4 - 13}{2 - 5} = \dfrac{-9}{-3} = 3$. The slope of $\overline{BC} = \dfrac{13 - 76}{5 - 26} = \dfrac{-63}{-21} = 3$. Since the slopes of $\overline{AB}$ and $\overline{BC}$ are equal, the points are collinear.

   Answer: Collinear

7. $a = -1$. Plot the points on the grid. $\overline{CD}$ must have a length of 5.

   Answer: 5

8. $D = (-3, 0)$. Since the trapezoid is isosceles, $\overline{CD}$ must have the same length as $\overline{AB}$. Plot the points on the grid. To get from point $B(2, 3)$ to point $A(3, 0)$, count one unit to the right and down three units. Similarly, to get from point $C(-3, 0)$ to point D, count one unit to the left and down three units.

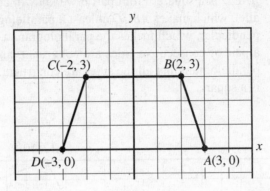

Answer: $(-3, 0)$

9. a.

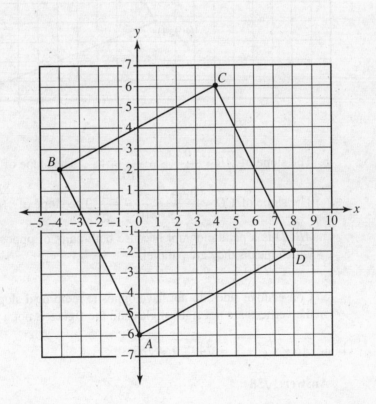

b. The slope of $\overline{AB} = \dfrac{-6-2}{0+4} = \dfrac{-8}{4} = -2$. The slope of $\overline{BC} = \dfrac{2-6}{-4-4} = \dfrac{-4}{-8} = \dfrac{1}{2}$.

The slope of $\overline{CD} = \dfrac{6+2}{4-8} = \dfrac{8}{-4} = -2$. The slope of $\overline{AD} = \dfrac{-6+2}{0-8} = \dfrac{-4}{-8} = \dfrac{1}{2}$.

c. The length of $\overline{AB} = \sqrt{4^2 + 8^2} = \sqrt{16 + 64} = \sqrt{80} = \sqrt{16 \cdot 5} = 4\sqrt{5}.$

The length of $\overline{BC} = \sqrt{4^2 + 8^2} = \sqrt{16 + 64} = \sqrt{80} = \sqrt{16 \cdot 5} = 4\sqrt{5}.$

d. *ABCD* is a square. From part b we know that both pairs of opposite sides are parallel, which makes *ABCD* at least a parallelogram. Also, consecutive sides are perpendicular, which makes the parallelogram a rectangle. From part c, we know that a pair of consecutive sides are congruent, and it follows from the properties of a parallelogram that all the sides are congruent. A rectangle with all congruent sides is a square.

10. a.

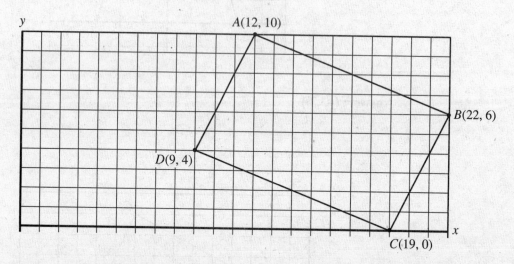

b. The slope of $\overline{AB} = \dfrac{10-6}{12-22} = \dfrac{4}{-10} = -\dfrac{2}{5}.$ The slope of $\overline{BC} = \dfrac{6-0}{22-19} = \dfrac{6}{3} = 2.$

The slope of $\overline{CD} = \dfrac{0-4}{19-9} = \dfrac{-4}{10} = -\dfrac{2}{5}.$ The slope of $\overline{AD} = \dfrac{10-4}{12-9} = \dfrac{6}{3} = 2.$

ABCD is a parallelogram because both pairs of opposite sides have equal slopes, which means they are parallel.

c. Consecutive sides do not have opposite reciprocal slopes (see slopes in part b) so the vertices are not right angles and the figure is not a rectangle.

11. a. $\overline{AB} = \sqrt{7^2 + 3^2} = \sqrt{49 + 9} = \sqrt{58}.$

Answer: $\sqrt{58}$

b. $\dfrac{1}{4}\left(\overline{AB}\right) = \dfrac{1}{4}\sqrt{58}$ miles ≈ 1.9 miles.

Answer: 1.9 miles

c. $\overline{AB} = \sqrt{58}$. $\overline{BC} = 7$. $\overline{AC} = 3$. $\overline{AB} + \overline{BC} + \overline{AC} = \sqrt{58} + 7 + 3 = \sqrt{58} + 10$.

$$\frac{1}{4}\left(\sqrt{58} + 10\right) = \left(\frac{\sqrt{58}}{4} + \frac{5}{2}\right) \text{ miles} \approx 4.4 \text{ miles}.$$

Answer: 4.4 miles

Transformations

- A **transformation** is a process by which a geometric figure is moved. You can achieve this movement by flipping (as in the case of a *reflection*), sliding (called a *translation*), or turning (a *rotation*). The object before its movement is called the **preimage**, and the new figure is the **image**.

- A **reflection** of a figure is the image that is formed when the figure is flipped over a particular line of reflection. The new image is congruent to its preimage.

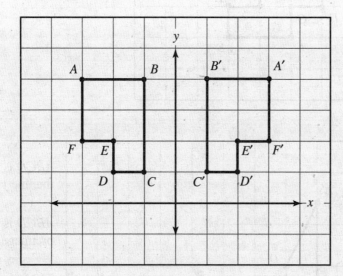

ABCDEF is reflected over the *y*-axis.

ABCDEF is called the preimage.

The new figure is called *A'B'C'D'E'F'*.

ABCDEF ≅ *A'B'C'D'E'F'*.

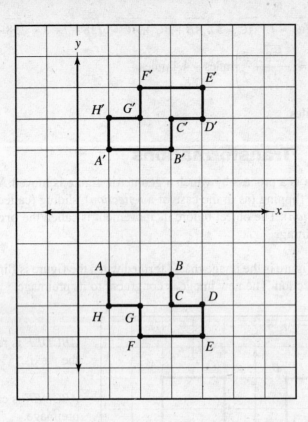

ABCDEFGH is reflected over the *x*-axis.

ABCDEFGH is called the preimage.

The new figure is called *A'B'C'D'E'F'G'H'*.

ABCDEFGH ≅
A'B'C'D'E'F'G'H'.

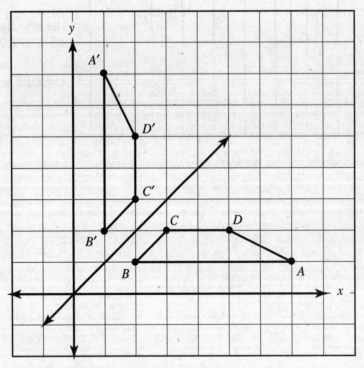

ABCD is reflected over the line *y = x*.

ABCD is called the preimage.

The new figure is called *A'B'C'D'*.

ABCD ≅ *A'B'C'D'*.

- The **line of symmetry** in a figure is the line of reflection that divides the figure into two mirror images of each other. If you flip one of the halves over the line of symmetry, it will lie directly on the other half of the figure. All of the dotted lines below are lines of symmetry.

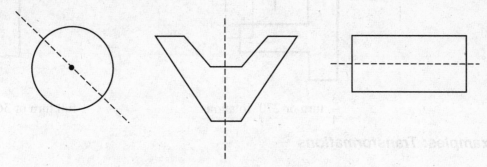

- A **translation** moves a figure by sliding it without turns, flips, or changes to its size. You can translate figures in any direction. Figure *A* is translated 6 units to the right.

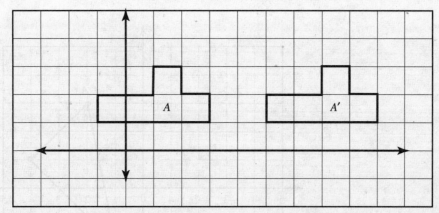

- A **rotation** turns a figure about a particular point. Rotating 90°, means turning the figure $\frac{1}{4}$ of the way around from its original position. Identify the center of rotation with a particular point. Rotate the figure either clockwise or counterclockwise. The figures below are examples of clockwise rotations.

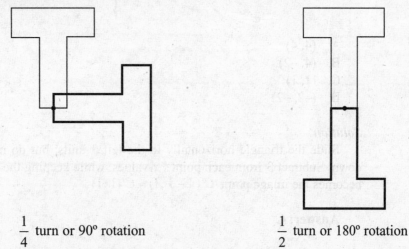

$\frac{1}{4}$ turn or 90° rotation $\frac{1}{2}$ turn or 180° rotation

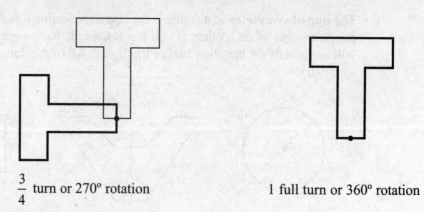

$\dfrac{3}{4}$ turn or 270° rotation   1 full turn or 360° rotation

Examples: Transformations

Example 1. Suppose that $\triangle ABC$ is translated 3 units to the left. What are the coordinates of the image of point C?

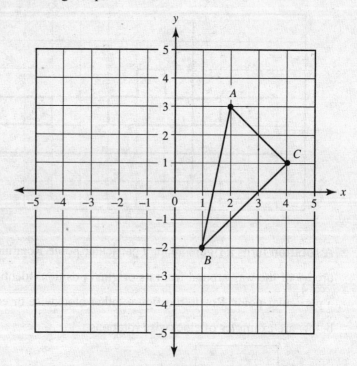

A. (4, 4)
B. (4, –2)
C. (1, 1)
D. (–2, –2)

Solution

Slide the triangle horizontally to the left 3 units, but do not move the figure up or down. Subtract 3 from each point's x-values, while keeping the y-values the same. $C(4,1)$ becomes the image point $C'(4-3,1) = C'(1,1)$.

Answer: C

Example 2. Draw the reflection of $\overline{AB}$ over the *x*-axis and label the new coordinates.

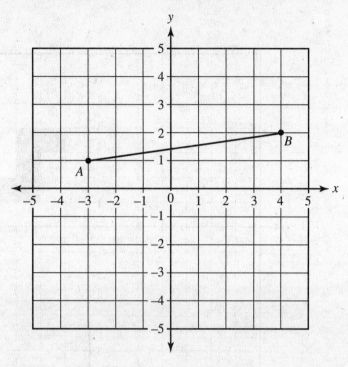

Solution

Use the *x*-axis as your "mirror." A reflection over the *x*-axis transforms the point (x, y) into the point $(x, -y)$. $A(-3, 1)$ becomes $A'(-3, -1)$ and $B(4, 2)$ becomes $B'(4, -2)$.

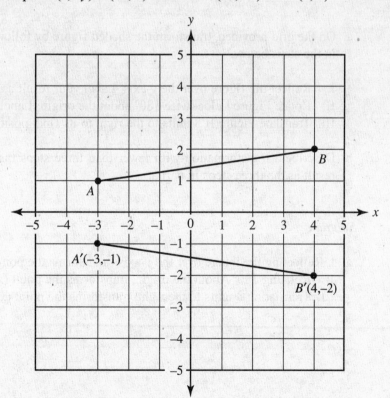

Example 3. *Use the diagram below to answer Example 3.*

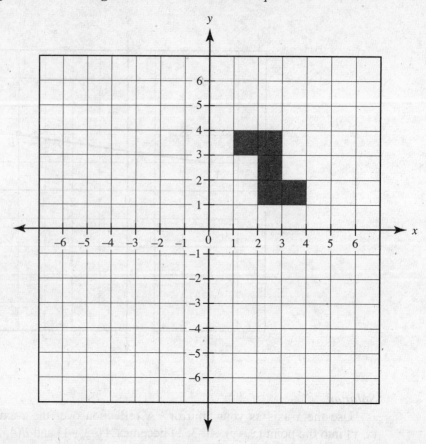

a. On the grid provided, transform the shaded figure by following the sequence outlined in the steps below.

    I.   Reflect the figure over the *y*-axis. Label your result as Figure I.

    II. Rotate Figure I clockwise 180° about the origin. Label your result as Figure II.

    III. Translate Figure II 3 units to the right to its final position. Label as Figure III.

b. Describe a transformation with fewer than three steps that would achieve the same result as the three steps in part a.

Solution

a. I. Reflecting the image over the *y*-axis, transforms the point $(x, y) \rightarrow (-x, y)$.

    II. Rotating 180° About the origin, transforms the point $(x, y) \rightarrow (-x, -y)$.

    III. Translating 3 units to the right, transforms the point $(x, y) \rightarrow (x + 3, y)$.

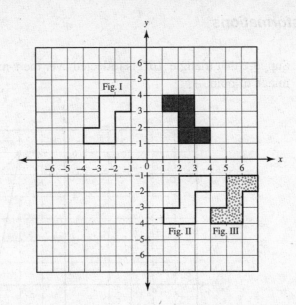

b. To achieve the same result as Figure III, you could reflect the original figure over the x-axis and then translate that image 3 units to the right.

Example 4. The diagram below shows the location of $\overline{AB}$ on the coordinate plane.

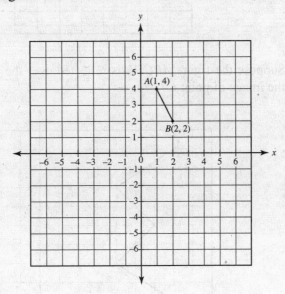

Suppose that $\overline{AB}$ is rotated 180° counterclockwise about the origin. What are the coordinates of the image of point A?

A. (–2, –2)
B. (–1, –4)
C. (–4, –1)
D. (–2, –4)

Solution
Rotating 180° about the origin, transforms the point (x, y) into the image point $(-x, -y)$. This means that the point $A(1, 4)$ becomes $A'(-1, -4)$.

Answer: B

Practice: Transformations

1. Suppose that triangle *ABC* is reflected over the *y*-axis. What are the coordinates of the image of point *A*?

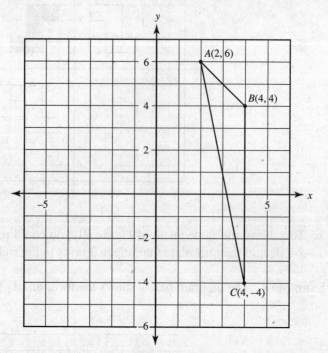

2. Suppose the figure *ABCDE* is reflected over the *y*-axis. What are the coordinates of the image of point *C*?

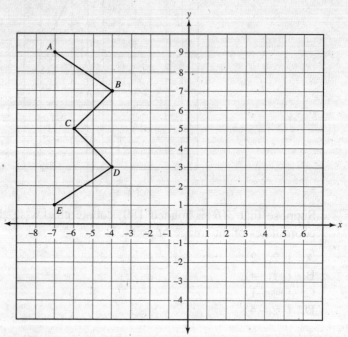

A. (6, 5)
B. (5, 6)
C. (−5, −6)
D. (−6, −5)

3. If trapezoid *ABCD* is translated 3 units up and 4 units to the left, what are the new coordinates of point *B*?

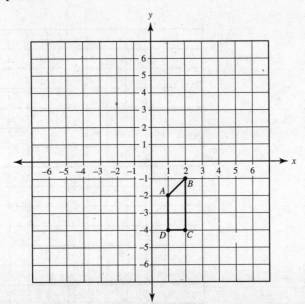

A. (−1, 3)
B. (−2, 1)
C. (−1, 2)
D. (−2, 2)

4. In the graph below, figure *P* was rotated clockwise about the origin to generate figure *S*.

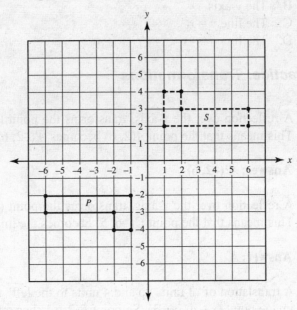

What was the angle of rotation of figure *P* about the origin?

A. 90°
B. 180°
C. 270°
D. 360°

5. *You may wish to use the following coordinate plane to help you answer Question 5.*

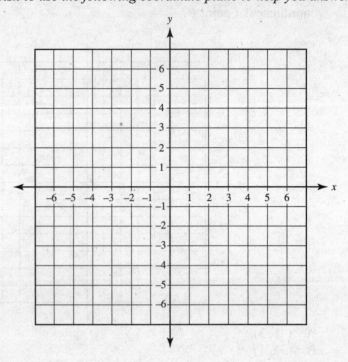

As a result of a certain transformation, the image of point $A(-3, 2)$ is $A'(-2, 3)$. This is an example of a reflection across which of the following?

A. The x-axis
B. The y-axis
C. The line $y = x$
D. The line $y = -x$

Solutions to Practice: Transformations

1. A reflection over the y-axis, transforms the point (x, y) into the image point $(-x, y)$. This means that the point $A(2, 6)$ becomes $A'(-2, 6)$.

   Answer: $A'(-2, 6)$

2. A reflection over the y-axis, transforms the point (x, y) into the image point $(-x, y)$. This means that the point $C(-6, 5)$ becomes the image point $C'(6, 5)$.

   Answer: A

3. A translation of "3 units up and 4 units to the left" transforms the point (x, y) into the image point $(x - 4, y + 3)$. So point $B(2, -1)$ becomes the image point $B'(-2, 2)$.

   Answer: D

4. Choose a point and its image. Notice that if you call the preimage (x, y), the image point would be $(-x, -y)$. The amounts to a 180° rotation about the origin.

   Answer: B

5. Draw in the "mirror" which is the perpendicular bisector of the segment which joins the image to the preimage. Notice that it is the line $y = -x$.

   Answer: D

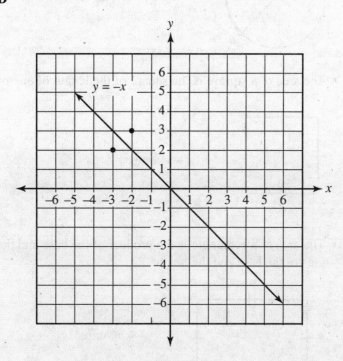

Perimeter and Area

- The **perimeter** of a polygon is the sum of the lengths of its sides. When answering a perimeter question, be sure to include units of measure, such as meters or inches.

- The **area** of a polygon is the number of square units enclosed by the polygon. Area is always measured in square units, such as in.^{2} or cm^2.

- The **perimeter** of a circle is called the **circumference** of the circle. The formula for the circumference of a circle is π multiplied by the diameter or π times twice the radius.

$$C = \pi d = 2\pi r$$

- The **arc length** is a fraction of the circumference of a circle. The arc length is the circumference of the circle multiplied by the fraction $\dfrac{n}{360}$, where n is the measure of the central angle, or the intercepted arc.

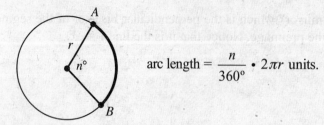

$$\text{arc length} = \dfrac{n}{360°} \cdot 2\pi r \text{ units.}$$

- The area of a **square** is the square of the length of one of its sides.

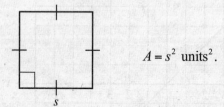

$$A = s^2 \text{ units}^2.$$

- The area of a **rectangle** is the product of the base and the height. The sides of a rectangle are the base and the height.

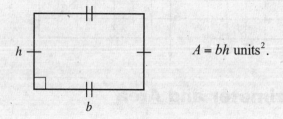

$$A = bh \text{ units}^2.$$

- The area of a **parallelogram** is the product of the base and the height. Any side of a parallelogram may be considered the base. The height is the perpendicular distance between the base and its opposite side.

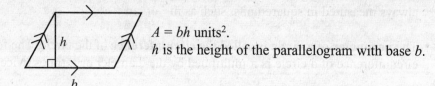

$A = bh \text{ units}^2.$
h is the height of the parallelogram with base b.

- The area of a **triangle** is half the product of the base and the height.

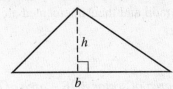

$A = \dfrac{1}{2} bh$ units^2.

h is the height of the triangle if b is the base.

- The area of a **trapezoid** is half the height multiplied by the sum of the bases.

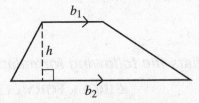

$A = \dfrac{1}{2} h(b_1 + b_2)$ units^2.

> * *Memory Tip: You can think of this formula as the average of the bases times the height:*
>
> $$A = \left(average\ of\ bases\right) \cdot height = \left(\dfrac{b_1 + b_2}{2}\right) \cdot h$$

- The area of a **circle** is the square of the radius multiplied by π.

$A = \pi r^2$ units^2.

- A **sector** of a circle is a figure formed by two radii of a circle and their intercepted arc. The area of the sector is a fraction of the total area of the circle. Its formula is the area of the circle multiplied by the fraction $\dfrac{n}{360}$, where n is the measure of the central angle, or the intercepted arc.

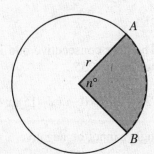

$area\ of\ sector = \dfrac{n}{360°} \cdot \pi r^2$ units^2.

- A **segment** of a circle is the region between a chord and its intercepted arc. Find the area of the segment by subtracting the area of a triangle (formed by two radii and a chord) from the area of a sector (formed by two radii and their intercepted arc).

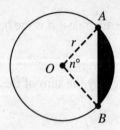

area of segment = area of sector AOB – area of triangle AOB.

The MCAS Mathematics Reference Sheet lists the following formulas:

AREA FORMULAS

triangle . . . . $A = \frac{1}{2}bh$

rectangle . . . . $A = bh$

parallelogram . . . . $A = bh$

square. . . . . $A = s^2$

trapezoid. . . . . $A = \frac{1}{2}h\,(b_1 + b_2)$

CIRCLE FORMULAS

$C = 2\pi r$

$A = \pi r^2$

You do not need to memorize the above formulas because they are on the MCAS Reference Sheet.

Examples: Perimeter and Area

Example 1. A rectangle has sides that are consecutive odd integers. The area is 255 cm². Find the length of the shorter side.

$x + 2$

x | 255 cm²

Solution

Call the smaller side of the rectangle, x. The next consecutive odd integer after x is $x + 2$. If the sides are x and $x + 2$, they must multiply to 255.

$$x(x + 2) = 255 \rightarrow x^2 + 2x = 255 \rightarrow x^2 + 2x - 255 = 0 \rightarrow (x - 15)(x + 17) = 0.$$

$x = 15$ or $x = -17$, but since a side of the rectangle cannot be negative, $x = 15$.

Answer: 15

Example 2. In the figure below, A, C, and D are collinear. The area of $\triangle ABC$ is 30 cm^2, and the area of $\triangle ABD$ is 36 cm^2, what is the length of DC?

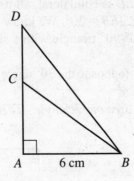

Solution

The legs of a right triangle can be used as the base and height. The area of a triangle is one half the product of the base and the height.

$$\frac{1}{2}(AD \cdot AB) = area\ of\ \triangle DAB \rightarrow \frac{1}{2}(AD \cdot 6) = 36 \rightarrow 3AD = 36 \rightarrow AD = 12 \text{ cm}$$

$$\frac{1}{2}(AC \cdot AB) = area\ of\ \triangle CAB \rightarrow \frac{1}{2}(AC \cdot 6) = 30 \rightarrow 3AC = 30 \rightarrow AC = 10 \text{ cm}$$

$$DC = AD - AC \rightarrow DC = 12 - 10 = 2 \text{ cm}$$

Answer: 2 cm

Example 3. If the radius of a circle is doubled, what is the effect on the circumference of the circle?
A. The circumference stays the same.
B. The circumference is multiplied by 2.
C. The circumference is multiplied by 4.
D. The circumference is squared.

Solution

If the original radius is r, then $C_O = 2\pi r$. If the radius is doubled, the new radius is $2r$. The new circumference is $C_N = 2\pi(2r) = 4\pi r$. $4\pi r$ is twice $2\pi r$.

Answer: B

Example 4. In the figure below, $\triangle BED$ is equilateral, and $ACDE$ is a rectangle. If the perimeter of $\triangle BED$ is 18 inches, find the area of $ACDE$.

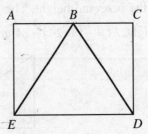

Solution

Since $\triangle BED$ is equilateral, all its sides are congruent. $18 \div 3 = 6$ so each side is 6 inches. Since $\triangle BED$ is equilateral, all its angles measure 60°. The angles of the rectangle are each 90° so $\angle AEB = 30°$. We know that $\angle A = 90°$, so $\angle ABE = 60°$. This means that $\triangle BEA$ is a 30°-60°-90° triangle with a side length of 6 opposite the 90° angle.

$$\frac{1}{2} \cdot 6 = 3 = AB \text{ (opposite the 30° angle)} \rightarrow AE = 3\sqrt{3} \text{ inches (opposite the 60° angle)}.$$

$$area \; of \; rectangle \; AEDC = AE \cdot ED = 3\sqrt{3} \cdot 6 = 18\sqrt{3} \text{ in.}^2$$

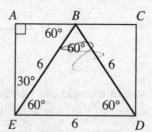

Answer: $18\sqrt{3}$ in.^{2}

Example 5. Katie's bike tires have a radius of 15 inches. If Katie pedals at a constant rate of one revolution per second, how far does she travel in two hours to the nearest foot?

Solution

The distance that 1 revolution travels is $2\pi \cdot 15 = 30\pi$ inches. There are 60 seconds in a minute and 60 minutes in an hour. This means that there are $60 \cdot 60 = 3,600$ seconds in an hour and 7,200 seconds in 2 hours. $7,200 \cdot 30\pi = 216,000\pi$. Katie travels $216,000\pi$ inches. This answer must be divided by 12 to convert to feet. Do not round until the very end of the problem.

$$\frac{216,000\pi}{12} \approx 56,549 \text{ feet}$$

Answer: 56,549 feet

Example 6. The length of the hypotenuse of a right triangle is 25 cm and the length of one leg is 7 cm, what is the area of the triangle?

Solution

Call the unknown leg of the right triangle, x. By the Pythagorean Theorem, $x^2 + 7^2 = 25^2 \rightarrow x^2 + 49 = 625 \rightarrow x^2 = 576 \rightarrow x = \sqrt{576} = 24$. The legs of a right triangle can be used as the base and height. The area of a triangle is one half the product of the base and the height. $A = \frac{1}{2}\left(7 \cdot 24\right) = 84 \text{ cm}^2$.

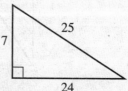

Answer: 84 cm^2

Example 7. Find the area of a circle with a circumference of 18 inches.

A. π in.^{2}

B. $\dfrac{9}{\pi}$ in.^{2}

C. $\dfrac{18}{\pi}$ in.^{2}

D. $\dfrac{81}{\pi}$ in.^{2}

Solution

$$2\pi r = 18 \rightarrow r = \frac{18}{2\pi} \rightarrow r = \frac{9}{\pi}$$

$$A = \pi r^2 \rightarrow A = \pi \cdot \frac{9}{\pi} \cdot \frac{9}{\pi} = \frac{81\pi}{\pi \cdot \pi} = \frac{81}{\pi} \text{ in.}^2$$

Answer: D

Example 8. Find the area of an equilateral triangle with a perimeter of 24 inches.

A. 8 in.^{2}

B. $\dfrac{8}{3}\sqrt{3}$ in.^{2}

C. $8\sqrt{3}$ in.^{2}

D. $16\sqrt{3}$ in.^{2}

Solution

Since the triangle is equilateral, each side is 8 inches. In an equilateral triangle, the height bisects the side of the triangle, dividing it into two congruent 30°-60°-90° triangles that have a side length of 4 opposite the 30° angle and $4\sqrt{3}$ opposite the 60° angle. The *area of the triangle* $= \dfrac{1}{2}bh = \dfrac{1}{2}\left(8 \cdot 4\sqrt{3}\right) = \dfrac{1}{2}\left(32\sqrt{3}\right) = 16\sqrt{3}$ in.^{2}.

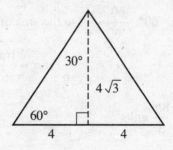

Answer: D

Example 9. The measure of central $\angle AOB$ of circle O is $60°$. The diameter is 8.

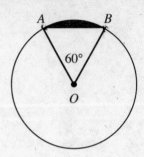

a. What is the length of $\overline{AB}$?

b. What is the area of circle O?

c. What is the area of sector AOB?

d. What is the area of $\triangle AOB$?

e. What is the area of the shaded segment?

Solution

a. $\overline{AO}$ and $\overline{OB}$ are radii of circle O and since all radii of the same circle are congruent, $\overline{AO} \cong \overline{OB} = 4$. If two sides of a triangle are congruent, then their opposite angles are congruent so $\angle OAB \cong \angle ABO$. Since $\angle AOB = 60°$, $\angle OAB + \angle ABO = 180 - 60 = 120°$ so each angle is $60°$. This means that $\triangle AOB$ is equilateral and $\overline{AB} = 4$ units.

Answer: 4 units

b. The radius of the circle is 4 so the area is $\pi \cdot 4^2 = 16\pi$ units^2.

Answer: 16π units^2

c. $\angle AOB = 60°$. $\dfrac{60}{360} = \dfrac{1}{6}$ so the area of sector AOB is $\dfrac{1}{6}$ the area of the entire circle.

$$\frac{1}{6} \cdot 16\pi = \frac{16\pi}{6} = \frac{8\pi}{3} \text{ units}^2.$$

Answer: $\dfrac{8\pi}{3}$ units^2

d. $\triangle AOB$ is equilateral with a side length of 4. Using the 30°-60°-90° triangle, the height of the triangle is $2\sqrt{3}$, and the area of the triangle is $\frac{1}{2} \cdot 4 \cdot 2\sqrt{3} = 4\sqrt{3}$ units².

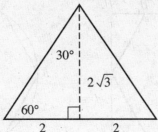

Answer: $4\sqrt{3}$ units²

e. The area of the shaded region is the area of sector AOB – the area of $\triangle AOB$ = $\frac{8\pi}{3} - 4\sqrt{3}$ units².

Answer: $\frac{8\pi}{3} - 4\sqrt{3}$ units²

Example 10. A fly is sitting on the rim of a spoke of a wheel with a radius of x feet. If the wheel makes n complete revolutions, how far has the fly traveled?

   A. $2\pi x$ ft
   B. πx^2 ft
   C. $2\pi x n$ ft
   D. $\pi x n$ ft

Solution

If the radius is x, then one revolution is $C = 2\pi x$. Since there are n revolutions, the circumference must be multiplied by n.

Answer: C

Example 11. In the figures below, regular hexagon *ABCDEF* has a perimeter of 60 inches. The hexagon is encased in rectangle *GHIJ* and is inscribed in circle *O*.

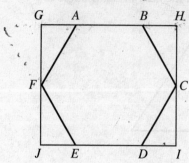
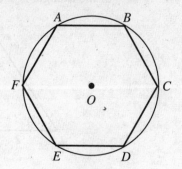

a. What is the area of the hexagon? Be sure to include units of measure in your answer. Show your work or explain how you obtained your answer.

b. What is the area of rectangle *GHIJ*? Be sure to include units of measure in your answer. Show your work or explain how you obtained your answer.

c. What is the area of circle *O*? Be sure to include units of measure in your answer. Show your work or explain how you obtained your answer.

d. Which has a smaller area, rectangle *GHIJ* or circle *O*?

Solution

a. The regular hexagon can be divided into six congruent equilateral triangles with side lengths of 10 inches. Each triangle has a height of $5\sqrt{3}$ inches and an area of $\frac{1}{2}\cdot 10\cdot 5\sqrt{3} = 25\sqrt{3}$ in.^{2}. Since there are six triangles in the hexagon, the area of the hexagon is $6\cdot 25\sqrt{3} = 150\sqrt{3}$ in.^{2}.

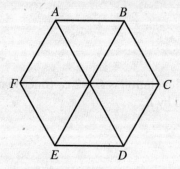
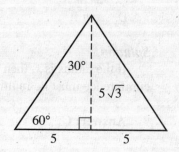

Answer: $150\sqrt{3}$ in.^{2}

b. The measure of one interior angle of a regular polygon is the sum of the interior angles divided by the number of sides. The formula for an interior angle of a regular polygon with number of sides n is $\dfrac{180(n-2)}{n}$. Each interior angle of a regular hexagon is $\dfrac{180(6-2)}{6} = 120°$. Since $\angle FAB = 120°$, $\angle GAF = 60°$ because they are supplementary. $\angle FGA$ is a right angle because $GHIJ$ is a rectangle. This means that $\triangle GAF$ is a 30°-60°-90° triangle with a side length of 10 opposite the 90° angle. From the rules of a 30°-60°-90° triangle, $GA = 5$ and $GF = 5\sqrt{3}$. The same calculations can be applied to $\triangle BHC$, $\triangle CID$, and $\triangle EJF$. $GH = GA + AB + BH = 5 + 10 + 5 = 20$.

$GJ = GF + FJ = 5\sqrt{3} + 5\sqrt{3} = 10\sqrt{3}$. The area of rectangle $GHIJ$ is $GH \cdot GJ = 20 \cdot 10\sqrt{3} = 200\sqrt{3}$ in.^{2}.

Answer: $200\sqrt{3}$ in.^{2}

C. Draw the radius from the center to a vertex of the hexagon. This radius is 10 inches, because it is a side of an equilateral triangle from part a. This makes the area of the circle $\pi \cdot 10^2 = 100\pi$ in.^{2}.

Answer: 100π in.^{2}

D. Estimating the numerical results from parts b and c, or by looking at the diagram, the circle has the smaller area.

Answer: Circle

Example 12. Mr. Smith asked his geometry class to find the area of the concave polygon *KJNML* with their knowledge of finding the areas of triangles, rectangles, and trapezoids.

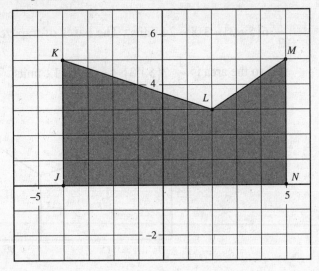

a. Sarah suggested that they divide the polygon into a rectangle and two triangles, and add the three separate areas. Find the total area using Sarah's method. Show or explain how to arrive at her answer.

b. Nabeel suggested partitioning the region into two trapezoids, then adding the areas of both. Find the total area using Nabeel's method. Show or explain how to arrive at his answer.

c. Carrie found the area without dividing the polygon internally into regions, but by subtracting the area of a triangle from a larger rectangle. Show or explain how to arrive at her answer.

Solution

a. Because this diagram is drawn on a grid, you can count boxes for length and you can assume right angles. The area of region I is $\frac{1}{2} \cdot 2 \cdot 6 = 6$ units^2. The area of region II is $\frac{1}{2} \cdot 2 \cdot 3 = 3$ units^2. The area of region III is $9 \cdot 3 = 27$ units^2. The sum of the three regions is $6 + 3 + 27 = 36$ units^2.

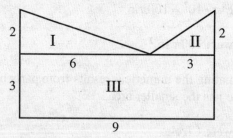

Answer: 36 units^2

b. The bases of trapezoid I are 5 and 3 and the height is 6 so the area is $\frac{1}{2} \cdot 6(5 + 3) = 3 \cdot 8 = 24$ units^2. The bases of trapezoid II are 5 and 3 and the height is 3 so the area is $\frac{1}{2} \cdot 3(5 + 3) = \frac{1}{2} \cdot 3 \cdot 8 = 12$ units^2. The sum of the two regions is $24 + 12 = 36$ units^2.

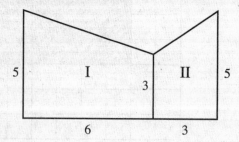

Answer: 36 units^2

c. The rectangle has a width of 5 and a length of 9. The area is $5 \cdot 9 = 45$ units². The triangle has a base of 9 and a height of 2. The area is $\frac{1}{2} \cdot 9 \cdot 2 = 9$ units². The area of the rectangle – the area of the triangle = $45 - 9 = 36$ units².

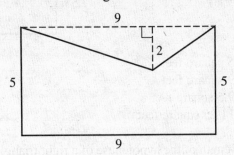

Answer: 36 units²

Example 13. $\triangle ABC$ is similar to $\triangle DEC$. If the length of $\overline{AC}$ is three times the length of $\overline{DC}$, then the area of $\triangle ABC$ is how many times greater than the area of $\triangle DEC$?

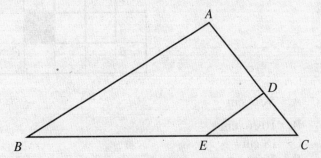

A. 3
B. 4
C. 9
D. 12

Solution

In similar figures, the ratio of the areas is equal to the square of the ratio of the corresponding segments. $\frac{DC}{AC} = \frac{1}{3}$, so $\frac{\triangle ABC}{\triangle DEC} = \left(\frac{1}{3}\right)^2 = \frac{1}{9}$.

Answer: C

Practice: Perimeter and Area

1. A rectangle has a perimeter of 36 inches and an area of 72 square inches. What are the length and width of the rectangle?
   A. 2 inches and 16 inches
   B. 6 inches and 12 inches
   C. 8 inches and 9 inches
   D. 2 inches and 36 inches

2. The rectangle shown below has a width of 2.5 feet and a perimeter of 14 feet. What is the area of the rectangle?

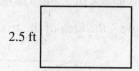

2.5 ft

A. 5 square feet
B. 9 square feet
C. 9.5 square feet
D. 11.25 square feet

3. The length of the hypotenuse of a right triangle is 17 centimeters and the length of one leg is 15 centimeters, what is the area of the triangle?

4. If the area of the shaded square is 6 cm², what is the perimeter of figure *ABCD*?

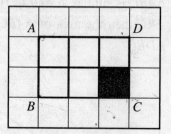

A. $5\sqrt{6}$ cm
B. $10\sqrt{6}$ cm
C. 18 cm
D. 36 cm

5. In the figure shown below, $\triangle BDF$ is formed by joining the midpoints of the sides of equilateral $\triangle ACE$. If the area of $\triangle ACE$ is 24 square inches, what is the area of $\triangle BDF$?

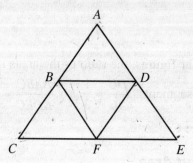

A. 1 square inch
B. 3 square inches
C. 4 square inches
D. 6 square inches

6. In the figure below, A, B, and C are collinear. What is the area of $\triangle ABD$?

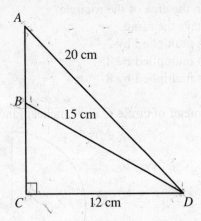

7. A sports arena's field is in the shape of a circle with a diameter of 80 yards. Which of the following is closest to the area of the field?
   A. 126 square yards
   B. 251 square yards
   C. 5,027 square yards
   D. 20,106 square yards

8. The formula, $h = \dfrac{s\sqrt{3}}{2}$, gives the height of an equilateral triangle in terms of s, the length of its side. What is the length of the height of an equilateral triangle with a side length of 16?
   A. $4\sqrt{3}$
   B. $8\sqrt{3}$
   C. $12\sqrt{3}$
   D. $16\sqrt{3}$

9. If the radius of a circle is tripled, what is the effect on the area of the circle?
   A. It stays the same.
   B. It is multiplied by 3.
   C. It is multiplied by 6.
   D. It is multiplied by 9.

10. Charlie's bike's tires are 24 inches in diameter. If he rides his bike so that the front tire makes 25 complete revolutions, how far does Charlie travel to the nearest inch?

11. If the diameter of a circle is doubled, what is the effect on the circumference of the circle?
    A. It stays the same.
    B. It is multiplied by 2.
    C. It is multiplied by 4.
    D. It is multiplied by 8.

12. If the base of a triangle stays the same and the height is multiplied by 4, what is the effect on the area of the triangle?
    A. It stays the same.
    B. It is multiplied by 2.
    C. It is multiplied by 4.
    D. It is multiplied by 8.

13. The diameter of circle O is 10 inches. Find the area of the shaded region.

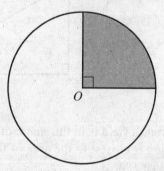

    A. $\dfrac{5}{4}\pi$ in.^{2}

    B. $\dfrac{5}{2}\pi$ in.^{2}

    C. $\dfrac{25}{4}\pi$ in.^{2}

    D. 25π in.^{2}

14. If r is the radius of circle O, which expression represents the area of the shaded region in terms of r?

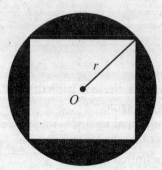

    A. $r^2(2\pi)$
    B. $r^2(\pi+2)$
    C. $r^2(2-\pi)$
    D. $r^2(\pi-2)$

15. The midpoints of the sides of the equilateral triangle in stage 0 are connected to form the shaded triangle in stage 1. The midpoints of the sides of the three unshaded triangles in stage 1 are connected and those new triangles are shaded to form the diagram in stage 2. The pattern continues so that the midpoints of the sides of the unshaded triangles in stage 2 are connected and those new triangles are shaded to create stage 3.

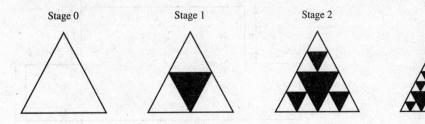

Stage 0   Stage 1   Stage 2   Stage 3

a. If the area of the triangle at stage 0 is 1 in.^{2}, what is the area of the shaded triangle in stage 1?

b. If the perimeter of the triangle at stage 0 is 1 in., what is the perimeter of the triangle that is shaded in stage 1? What is the perimeter of the shaded triangles in stage 2? What is the perimeter of the shaded triangles in stage 3? Fill in the table with the answers.

Stage	0	1	2	3
Perimeter	1 in.			

c. If the perimeter of the triangle at stage 0 is 1 in., what would the perimeter of the shaded triangles be in stage 5? Show or explain how you obtained your answer.

16. The sides of a square are expanded to form a rectangle with side lengths that are 3 inches and 5 inches longer than those of the original square. If the new rectangle's area is 168 in.^{2}, what was the area of the original square?

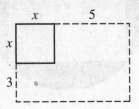

A. 15 in.^{2}
B. 64 in.^{2}
C. 81 in.^{2}
D. 96 in.^{2}

17. Mark is tiling a floor. The diagram below shows the shape of each tile. Mark can combine two tiles side by side to make different shapes. The example of one combination is shown below. Draw the combination of two tiles that would have the smallest perimeter.

One Tile

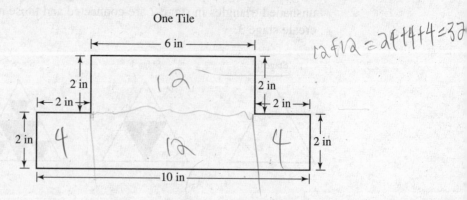

Two Tiles

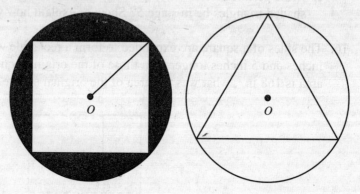

★ 18. An equilateral triangle and a square are each inscribed in circle O, which has a circumference of 8π inches.

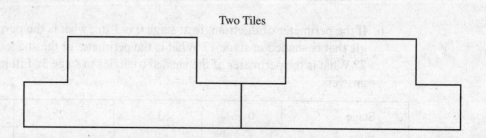

a. Find the area of the square. Be sure to include units of measure in your answer. Show your work or explain how you obtained your answer.

b. Find the area of the equilateral triangle. Be sure to include units of measure in your answer. Show your work or explain how you obtained your answer.

c. What is the ratio of the area of the square to the area of the triangle?

d. What is the area of the shaded region between the circle and the square? Show your work or explain how you obtained your answer.

19. Rectangle *OABC* has coordinates *O*(0, 0), *A*(0, 6), *B*(4, 6), *C*(4, 0). What is the area of rectangle *OABC*?
    A. 12 units²
    B. 20 units²
    C. 22 units²
    D. 24 units²

20. Wooden molding is to be placed around the perimeter of the room shown below. (Assume all of the walls are at right angles to each other.)

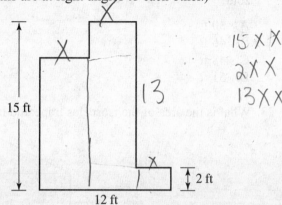

What is the least number of linear feet of molding it will take to go around the room?

    A. 30 feet
    B. 44 feet
    C. 54 feet
    D. 56 feet

21. What is the height of the parallelogram below, if its area is 58 square meters?

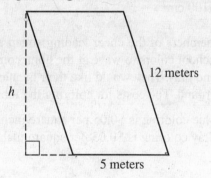

    A. 6.7 meters
    B. 8.4 meters
    C. 11.6 meters
    D. 13.0 meters

22. The trapezoid below has the measurements as shown.

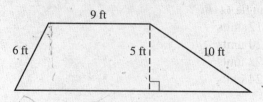

Which of the following integers most closely represents the perimeter of the trapezoid?

A. 30 ft
B. 46 ft
C. 48 ft
D. 51 ft

23. What is the area of the isosceles trapezoid below?

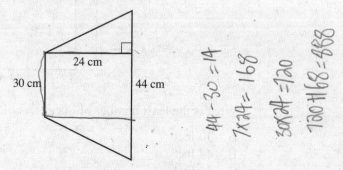

A. 720 cm²
B. 888 cm²
C. 1,056 cm²
D. 1,100 cm²

24. The members of the cheer leading squad at Voorhees High wish to make banners in their school colors to wave at the homecoming football game. Their school colors are blue and gray. They would like their banners to have a giant blue "V" on top of a gray background. The costs for coloring the fabric are as follows:

- Blue coloring is $0.05 per square inch
- Gray coloring is $0.03 per square inch

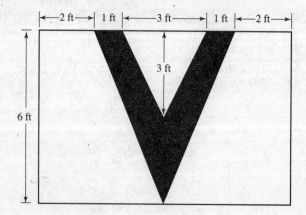

a. What is the area of the blue region? Be sure to include units of measure in your answer. Show or explain how you arrived at your answer.

b. What is the area of the gray region? Be sure to include units of measure in your answer. Show or explain how you arrived at your answer.

c. What is the cost to produce 100 banners? Show or explain how you arrived at your answer.

 25. Sam pedals his bicycle at a constant rate of one revolution per second. The radius of his bicycle wheel is 22 inches. If Sam bicycles for 1 hour, how far will he have traveled to the nearest mile? (5,280 ft = 1 mile)

Solutions to Practice: Perimeter and Area

1. **Use your answer choices** to help you find the answer. You can **eliminate answer choice** C because the perimeter is not 36. Choices A and D do not multiply to an area of 72.

   Answer: B

2. Twice the width is 5 ft, which means that twice the length is

   $14 - 5 = 9$ ft so the length is $\frac{9}{2}$ ft or 4.5 ft. The area of the rectangle is $2.5 \cdot 4.5 = 11.25$ ft^2.

   Answer: D

3. The unknown leg, x, is $x^2 + 15^2 = 17^2 \rightarrow x^2 + 225 = 289 \rightarrow x^2 = 64 \rightarrow x = 8$.
   In a right triangle, the area is half the product of the legs. $A = \frac{1}{2} \cdot 8 \cdot 15 = 60$ cm^2.

   Answer: 60 cm^2

4. Each square has a side length of $\sqrt{6}$ cm. Rectangle $ABCD$ is made up of 10 side lengths of the smaller squares.

   Answer: B

5. Four smaller congruent triangles are formed by joining the midpoints of the sides of an equilateral triangle. Each triangle has an area that is $\frac{1}{4}$ the original area.

   Answer: D

6. Using the Pythagorean Theorem on $\triangle BCD$, $BC = 9$ cm. Using the Pythagorean Theorem on $\triangle ACD$, $AC = 16$ cm. $AB = AC - BC = 16 - 9 = 7$ cm. Using $\overline{AB}$ as the base of $\triangle ABD$, $\overline{CD}$ is the height. The area of $\triangle ABD = \frac{1}{2} \cdot 7 \cdot 12 = 42$ cm^2.

   Answer: 42 cm^2

7. The radius of the circle is 40. The area of a circle with a radius of 40 is $\pi \cdot 40^2 = 1,600\pi$. Because the answer choices are not close in number and this is a noncalculator question, you could round π to 3 and be able to find the answer. $1,600 \cdot 3 = 4,800$. π is a little more than 3 so the answer should be more than 4,800 yards. Don't forget that on a multiple-choice question with the answer choices far apart, **rounding** can be a helpful test-taking strategy.

Answer: C

8. $h = \dfrac{16\sqrt{3}}{2} = 8\sqrt{3}$.

Answer: B

9. If the original radius is r, then the $A_O = \pi r^2$. If the new radius is $3r$, then the $A_N = \pi(3r)^2 = \pi \cdot 9r^2 = 9\pi r^2$. If you are uncomfortable using variables in this problem, you could **choose your own numbers** for the radius. Suppose the original radius is 1, then the area is $\pi(1)^2 = \pi$. Now triple the number 1 and the new radius = 3. The new area is $\pi(3)^2 = 9\pi$. This means that the original area was multiplied by 9.

Answer: D

10. One revolution of the tire is the circumference of the tire. $C = 24\pi$.
$25C = 25 \cdot 24\pi = 600\pi \approx 1,885$ in.

Answer: 1,885 in.

11. If the original diameter is d, then $C_O = \pi d$. If the diameter is doubled, the new diameter is $2d$. The new circumference is $C_N = \pi(2d) = 2\pi d = 2C_O$. If you are uncomfortable using variables in this problem, you could **choose your own numbers**. Suppose $d = 1$, then the circumference = π. Double the diameter, so $d = 2$. Then the new circumference is 2π. This means that the original circumference is doubled.

Answer: B

12. If the original height is h, then $A_O = \dfrac{1}{2}bh$. If the new height is $4h$, the new area is
$A_N = \dfrac{1}{2}b(4h) = 4\left(\dfrac{1}{2}\right)bh = 4A_O$.

Answer: C

13. The radius of the circle is 5 in. The area of the entire circle is 25π in.^{2}. The shaded region is $\dfrac{1}{4}$ the area of the entire circle $= \dfrac{25\pi}{4}$ in.^{2}.

Answer: C

14. The area of the circle is πr^2. Using the rules of 45°-45°-90° triangles, a side length of the square is $r\sqrt{2}$. The area of the square is $\left(r\sqrt{2}\right)^2 = 2r^2$. The area of the shaded region is *area of the circle – area of the square* $= \pi r^2 - 2r^2$. Factor out an r^2, and the area of the shaded region is $r^2(\pi - 2)$.

Answer: D

15. a. $\dfrac{1}{4}$ in.^{2}

    b.

Stage	0	1	2	3
Perimeter	1 in.	$\dfrac{1}{2}$	$\dfrac{1}{2} + 3\left(\dfrac{1}{4}\right) =$ $\dfrac{1}{2} + \dfrac{3}{4} = \dfrac{5}{4}$	$\dfrac{1}{2} + \dfrac{3}{4} + 9\left(\dfrac{1}{8}\right) =$ $\dfrac{1}{2} + \dfrac{3}{4} + \dfrac{9}{8} =$ $\dfrac{19}{8}$

    c. The shaded triangles begin in stage 1. The pattern in part b indicates that the additional fraction being added to the previous stage has a numerator that is 3 times greater than the previous fraction that was added and a denominator that is twice the denominator of the previous fraction that was added.

    Stage 1: $\dfrac{1}{2}$

    Stage 2: $\dfrac{1}{2} + \dfrac{3}{4}$

    Stage 3: $\dfrac{1}{2} + \dfrac{3}{4} + \dfrac{9}{8}$

    Stage 4: $\dfrac{1}{2} + \dfrac{3}{4} + \dfrac{9}{8} + \dfrac{27}{16}$

    Stage 5: $\dfrac{1}{2} + \dfrac{3}{4} + \dfrac{9}{8} + \dfrac{27}{16} + \dfrac{81}{32} = \dfrac{211}{32}$

Answer: $\dfrac{211}{32}$

16. **Use the answer choices** to help you answer this question. If the area of the original square is 81 in.^{2}, then each side of the square is 9 inches. The sides of the rectangle would be 12 and 14, and the area would be $12 \cdot 14 = 168$ in.^{2}.

Answer: C

17. By lining the tiles up back to back along the longest side (10 inches) you are making the perimeter as small as possible because the 10 inches does not count in the perimeter. The perimeter is 36 in.

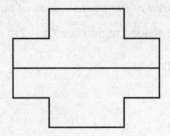

Answer: 36 in.

18. a. The radius of the circle is 4. Using the rules of a 45°-45°-90° triangle, each side of the square has a length of $4\sqrt{2}$ in. The area of the square is $\left(4\sqrt{2}\right)\left(4\sqrt{2}\right) = 16 \cdot 2 = 32$ in.^{2}.

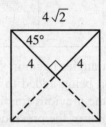

Answer: 32 in.^{2}

b. The radius of the circle is 4. The sides of the 30°-60°-90° triangle drawn in the diagram are 2, $2\sqrt{3}$, and 4. The height of the equilateral triangle is 6 (4 + 2) and the base of the triangle is $2 \cdot 2\sqrt{3} = 4\sqrt{3}$. The area of the equilateral triangle is $\frac{1}{2} \cdot 4\sqrt{3} \cdot 6 = 12\sqrt{3}$ in.^{2}.

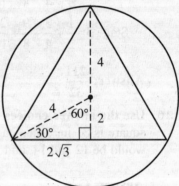

Answer: $12\sqrt{3}$ in.^{2}

c. $\dfrac{32}{12\sqrt{3}} = \dfrac{8}{3\sqrt{3}} \cdot \dfrac{\sqrt{3}}{\sqrt{3}} = \dfrac{8\sqrt{3}}{9}$

Answer: $\dfrac{8\sqrt{3}}{9}$

d. Subtract the area of the square from the area of the circle.

Answer: $(16\pi - 32)$ in.^{2}

19. The sides of the rectangle have lengths 6 and 4. Area $= 6 \cdot 4 = 24$ units^2.

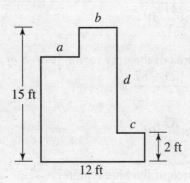

Answer: D

20. $a + b + c = 12$ and $d = 13$.

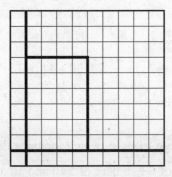

Answer: C

21. If h is the height, then the base is 5. $A = bh \rightarrow 58 = 5h \rightarrow h = \dfrac{58}{5} = 11.6$ meters.

Answer: C

22. Drop a second altitude, which also has a length of 5 ft. Use the Pythagorean Theorem to solve for the missing side of each right triangle. The perimeter is $9 + 10 + \sqrt{75} + 9 + \sqrt{11} + 6 = 34 + \sqrt{11} + \sqrt{75} \approx 46$.

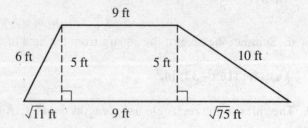

Answer: B

23. $A = \dfrac{1}{2}h(b_1 + b_2) = \dfrac{1}{2} \cdot 24(30 + 44) = 12 \cdot 74 = 888 \text{ cm}^2$.

Answer: B

24. a. The large triangle, which includes the blue area and the small gray triangle, has a height of 6 ft, a base of 5 ft, and an area of 15 square feet. The small triangle has a base of 3 ft, a height of 3 ft, and an area of $\dfrac{9}{2}$ ft^2. The area of the blue region is *area of the large triangle – area of the small triangle* $= 15 - \dfrac{9}{2} = \dfrac{21}{2}$ ft^2.

Answer: $\dfrac{21}{2}$ **ft²**

b. The area of the gray region is *area of the large rectangle – area of the blue region* $= 54 - \dfrac{21}{2} = \dfrac{87}{2}$ ft^2.

Answer: $\dfrac{87}{2}$ **ft²**

c. The area of the blue region is $\dfrac{21}{2}$ ft$^2 = \dfrac{21 \text{ ft}^2}{2} \cdot \dfrac{144 \text{ in.}^2}{1 \text{ ft}^2} = 1512$ in.^{2}.
The cost of the blue region is $0.05 \cdot 1{,}512 = \$75.60$. The area of the gray region is $\dfrac{87}{2}$ ft$^2 = \dfrac{87 \text{ ft}^2}{2} \cdot \dfrac{144 \text{ in.}^2}{1 \text{ ft}^2} = 6264$ in.^{2}. The cost of the gray region is $0.05 \cdot 6{,}264 = \$313.20$. The total cost is $75.60 + 313.20 = \$388.80$.

Answer: $388.80

25. The distance that 1 revolution travels is $2\pi \cdot 22 = 44\pi$ inches. There are 60 seconds in a minute and 60 minutes in an hour. This means that there are $60 \cdot 60 = 3,600$ seconds in an hour. $3,600 \cdot 44\pi = 158,400\pi$. Katie travels $158,400\pi$ inches. This answer must be divided by 12 to convert to feet. $\dfrac{158,400\pi}{12} = 13,200\pi$ feet. This answer must be divided by 5,280 to convert to miles. $\dfrac{13,200\pi}{5,280} \approx 8$ miles.

Answer: 8 miles

Similar and Congruent Polygons

- **Congruent polygons** have all of the corresponding angles congruent and all of the corresponding sides congruent. They are exactly the same shape and size.

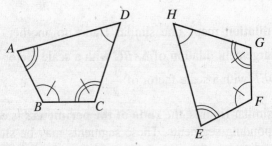

The polygons *ABCD* and *EFGH* are congruent because the measures of all corresponding angles and sides are equal. You can see this from the tick marks. Name the polygons carefully, so that the letters of one figure match the congruent counterpart in the other. Some examples of correct statements are:

$$ABCD \cong EFGH, DCAB \cong HGEF, BCDA \cong FGHE.$$

- **Similar polygons** are figures that have the same shape, but they are not necessarily the same size. The corresponding angles in similar polygons are congruent. The corresponding sides are **proportional**. This means that all pairs of corresponding sides are in the same ratio. The symbol for similar is ~.

- **Similar triangles** can be determined by any of the following three methods:

1. Find at least two pairs of congruent corresponding angles. This method is often called *Angle-Angle* similarity.

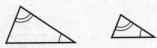

2. Find two pairs of corresponding sides proportional, and the angles in between these two sides (also known as the **included angle**) congruent. This method is often called *Side-Angle-Side* similarity.

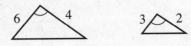

3. Find three pairs of corresponding sides proportional. This method is often called *Side-Side-Side* similarity.

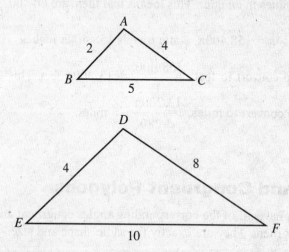

$\triangle ABC \sim \triangle DEF$ because all of the corresponding sides have the same ratio.

$$\frac{\overline{AB}}{\overline{DE}} = \frac{1}{2}, \frac{\overline{AC}}{\overline{DF}} = \frac{1}{2}, \text{ and } \frac{\overline{BC}}{\overline{EF}} = \frac{1}{2}.$$

Since $\triangle ABC \sim \triangle DEF$,
$\angle A \cong \angle D$, $\angle B, \cong \angle E$, and $\angle C \cong \angle F$.

- A **dilation** maps one similar figure to another. In the triangles above, $\triangle DEF$ is an enlargement dilation of $\triangle ABC$ with a scale factor of 2. $\triangle ABC$ is a reduction dilation of $\triangle DEF$ with a scale factor of $\frac{1}{2}$.

- In similar figures, the **ratio of the perimeters** is equal to the ratio of the lengths of corresponding segments. These segments may be sides, altitudes, medians, or any corresponding lengths.

- In similar figures, the **ratio of the areas** is equal to the square of the ratio of the lengths of any corresponding segments.

Figure I is similar to Figure II.

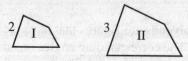

$$\frac{perimeter_I}{perimeter_{II}} = \frac{side_I}{side_{II}} = \frac{2}{3} \qquad \frac{area_I}{area_{II}} = \left(\frac{side_I}{side_{II}}\right)^2 = \frac{4}{9}$$

- In similar solids, the **ratio of the volumes** is equal to the cube of the ratio of the lengths of any corresponding segments.

$$\frac{volume_I}{volume_{II}} = \left(\frac{side_I}{side_{II}}\right)^3$$

Examples: Similar and Congruent Polygons

Example 1. Kaely and Tyrone were on opposite sides of a river. To determine the distance across the river, Kaely placed four stakes in the ground on her side, one directly across from Tyrone, and the other three at straight line positions as shown below, with the stakes at K and B creating right angles.

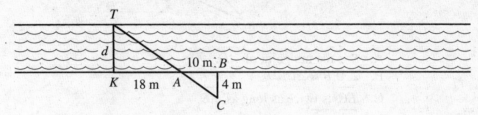

a. In $\triangle ABC$, what is the ratio of side $\overline{AB}$ to side $\overline{BC}$?

b. Are triangles KAT and BAC similar? Explain.

c. Write a proportion that will enable you to find d, the distance across the river.

d. Solve your proportion for d. Be sure to include units of measure in your answer. Show your work or explain how you got your answer.

Solution

a. A ratio is a simplified fraction. The ratio of the sides $\overline{AB}$ to $\overline{BC}$ means the fraction $\dfrac{AB}{BC}$. Simplified, you get $\dfrac{AB}{BC} = \dfrac{10}{4} = \dfrac{5}{2}$.

Answer: $\dfrac{5}{2}$

b. Two triangles are similar if their corresponding angles are congruent and their corresponding sides are proportional. Either one of these criteria is sufficient to show triangles are similar to one another. In our diagram, we have $\angle K \cong \angle B$ since they are both 90°. We also have $\angle T \cong \angle C$, since they are alternate interior angles to parallel lines $\overleftrightarrow{KT}$ and $\overleftrightarrow{BC}$. Finally, we know that $\angle KAT \cong \angle BAC$, since vertical angles are congruent. (Note that finding two pairs of congruent angles would be enough to conclude similar triangles.)

Answer: Yes

c. Since the sides are proportional, set up any of the following proportions to find d. *(A proportion is an equation of equal ratios.)*

$$\frac{d}{18} = \frac{4}{10} \quad \text{or} \quad \frac{d}{4} = \frac{18}{10} \quad \text{or} \quad \frac{4}{d} = \frac{10}{18} \quad \text{or} \quad \frac{18}{d} = \frac{10}{4}$$

d. Cross multiplying, you get $(10)d = (18)(4)$. Solving gives you $d = 7.2$ meters.

Answer: 7.2 meters

Example 2. Which of the following statements provides sufficient information to prove that ΔABE is similar to ΔDCE?

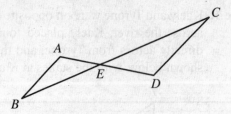

A. E is the midpoint of $\overline{AD}$.
B. $\angle AEB \cong \angle CED$.
C. $\overline{EC}$ is twice as long as $\overline{AE}$.
D. $\overline{AB} \parallel \overline{CD}$.

Solution

Triangles with at least two pairs of congruent angles are similar. With $\overline{AB} \parallel \overline{CD}$, you can conclude $\angle A \cong \angle D$ and $\angle B \cong \angle C$ because alternate interior angles of parallel lines are congruent.

Answer: D

Example 3. If $\overline{CD} \parallel \overline{HE}$ in ΔAHE below, approximately how long is $\overline{CD}$?

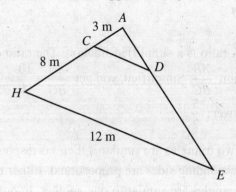

A. 3.3 m
B. 4.0 m
C. 4.5 m
D. 6.9 m

Solution

$\angle ACD \cong \angle AHE$ and $\angle ADC \cong \angle AEH$ since they are corresponding angles to $\overline{CD} \parallel \overline{HE}$.

You have similar triangles, ΔACD ~ ΔAHE, so set up a proportion to solve for $\overline{CD}$, such as $\dfrac{AC}{CD} = \dfrac{AH}{HE}$. Using the values from the diagram, $\dfrac{3}{CD} = \dfrac{11}{12}$. There are several correct proportions that can be set up here, and they all cross multiply to $11 \cdot CD = 3 \cdot 12$. Solving for CD you get $CD = \dfrac{36}{11} \approx 3.3$.

Answer: A

Example 4. In $\triangle ABC$, the lengths of $\overline{BC}$ and $\overline{DE}$ are 2 inches and 8 inches, respectively. If $\overline{AB}$ is 4 inches long, what is the length of $\overline{BD}$?

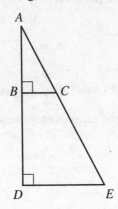

A. 6
B. 10
C. 12
D. 16

Solution

$\angle A$ appears in both triangles, and the two right angles are congruent to each other making $\triangle ABC \sim \triangle ADE$. Set up a proportion to solve for $\overline{AD}$: $\dfrac{AB}{BC} = \dfrac{AD}{DE}$. Using the values in the problem: $\dfrac{4}{2} = \dfrac{AD}{8}$. Cross multiply and solve. $AD = 16$ and $BD = 16 - 4 = 12$ inches.

Answer: C

Example 5. $\overline{AB} \parallel \overline{DE}$, $AB = 2$, and $DE = 5$.

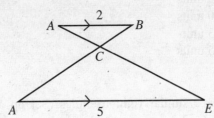

a. Find the ratio of the perimeter of $\triangle ABC$ to the perimeter of $\triangle CDE$.

b. Find the ratio of the area of $\triangle ABC$ to the area of $\triangle CDE$.

Solution

a. Since $\overline{AB} \parallel \overline{DE}$, $\angle BAC \cong \angle CED$ because alternate interior angles of parallel lines are congruent. $\angle ACB \cong \angle DCE$ because vertical angles are congruent. Because two pairs of corresponding angles are congruent, $\triangle ABC \sim \triangle EDC$. The ratio of the sides is $\frac{2}{5}$ and because the ratio of the perimeters is the same as the ratio of the sides, the ratio of the perimeters is $\frac{2}{5}$.

Answer: $\frac{2}{5}$

b. The ratio of the sides is $\frac{2}{5}$ and since the ratio of the areas is the square of the ratio of the sides, the ratio of the areas is $\frac{2}{5} \cdot \frac{2}{5} = \frac{4}{25}$.

Answer: $\frac{4}{25}$

Example 6. A conical paper cup at a water fountain has a height of 9 units and a radius of 5 units, as shown in the figure below. The water in the cup reaches a height of 6 units.

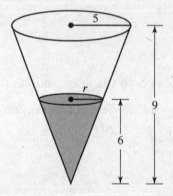

Find r, the radius of the circular surface of the water in the cup, to the nearest tenth.

A. 1.5 units
B. 2.0 units
C. 3.3 units
D. 7.5 units

Solution

You have similar right triangles. Set up a proportion and solve for r: $\frac{5}{r} = \frac{9}{6} \rightarrow 9r = 30 \rightarrow r \approx 3.3$.

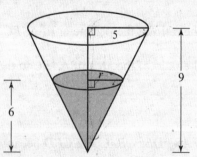

Answer: C

Example 7. $\triangle ABC$ is similar to $\triangle DEC$. If the length of $\overline{AC}$ is three times the length of $\overline{DC}$, then the area of $\triangle ABC$ is how many times greater than the area of $\triangle DEC$?

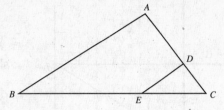

A. 3
B. 4
C. 9
D. 12

Solution

In similar figures, the ratio of the areas is equal to the square of the ratio of the corresponding segments: $\dfrac{DC}{AC} = \dfrac{1}{3}$, so $\dfrac{\triangle ABC}{\triangle DEC} = \left(\dfrac{1}{3}\right)^2 = \dfrac{1}{9}$.

Answer: C

Practice: Similar and Congruent Polygons

1. Which is not necessarily true?

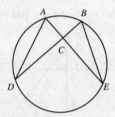

   A. $\triangle ACD \sim \triangle BCE$
   B. $\angle DAC \cong \angle CBE$
   C. $\angle ADB \cong \angle AEB$
   D. $\triangle ACD \cong \triangle BCE$

2. $\triangle H'I'G'$ is a dilation of $\triangle HIG$ by a factor of 2, so the triangles are similar. The measure of $\angle H' = 77°$ and the measure of $\angle I' = 50°$.

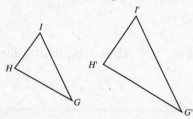

What is the measure of $\angle G$?

   A. 50°
   B. 53°
   C. 77°
   D. 106°

3. To measure the distance across a canal, Jared places rocks on the ground at points *G*, *M*, *K*, and *J* such that *G* and *J* are directly across some point *I* on the other side.

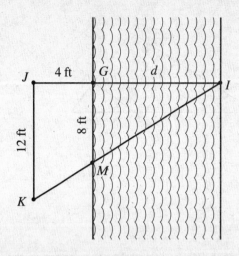

- $\overline{JG}$, $\overline{JK}$, and $\overline{GM}$ have measurements as shown.

- Both $\overline{MG}$ and $\overline{KJ}$ are perpendicular to $\overline{JI}$.

- Point *M* is on $\overline{KI}$.

a. Show or explain how you can conclude that you have similar triangles in the picture using angle measures.

b. Set up a proportion that will enable you to find *d*, the distance across the canal.

c. Solve your equation and find the distance across the canal. Be sure to include units of measure in your answer.

4. If △*ABC* is similar to △*FED*, what is the length of side $\overline{AB}$?

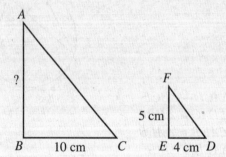

    A.   8 cm
    B.   11 cm
    C.   11.5 cm
    D.   12.5 cm

5. If $\overline{DE} \parallel \overline{BC}$ and $AD = \dfrac{1}{3} AB$, what is the ratio of the areas of △*ADE* to △*ABC*?

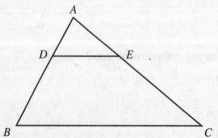

6. Kite *ABCD* is similar to kite *AEFG*. What is the length of side $\overline{AB}$?

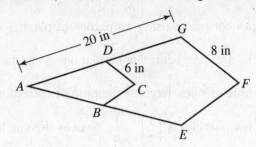

   A. 10 in
   B. 12 in
   C. 15 in
   D. 18 in

Solutions to Practice: Similar and Congruent Polygons

1. $\angle DAC \cong \angle CBE$ because they are both inscribed angles to the intercepted arc $\overset{\frown}{DE}$.

   $\angle ADB \cong \angle AEB$ because they are both inscribed angles to the intercepted arc $\overset{\frown}{AB}$. $\triangle ACD \sim \triangle BCE$ because their corresponding angles are congruent. This leaves answer choice D as not necessarily true. We have no information regarding the lengths of the triangles' sides.

   Answer: D

2. Since the triangles are similar, the three corresponding angle pairs are congruent. This makes $\angle G \cong \angle G'$. $m\angle G' = 180° - 77° - 50° = 53° = m\angle G$.

   Answer: B

3. a. $\triangle IGM \sim \triangle IJK$ because their corresponding angles are congruent. Specifically, $\angle IGM = \angle IJK = 90°$ and $\angle I \cong \angle I$. (It is shared by both triangles.)

   b. Set up either of the following proportions (or the reciprocals of each) to find d. *(A proportion is an equation of equal ratios.)*

   $$\frac{d}{8} = \frac{d+4}{12} \quad or \quad \frac{d}{d+4} = \frac{8}{12}$$

   c. Cross multiply: $12d = 8(d + 4)$. Distribute: $12d = 8d + 32$. Solve: $d = 8$ feet.

   Answer: 8 feet

4. Set up a proportion to solve for $\overline{AB}$: $\frac{AB}{5} = \frac{10}{4}$. Solving you get $AB = \frac{50}{4} = 12.5$ cm.

   Answer: D

5. $\triangle ADE$ is similar to $\triangle ABC$ because we can find at least two pairs of corresponding angles congruent using properties of parallel lines (specifically that corresponding angles are congruent). For similar polygons, the ratio of areas is equal to the square of the ratio of sides. Because the ratio of corresponding sides is $\frac{1}{3}$, the ratio of areas for the two triangles is $\left(\frac{1}{3}\right)^2 = \frac{1}{9}$. Visually this can be demonstrated in the diagram below, in which $\triangle ABC$ is divided into nine triangles congruent to $\triangle ADE$.

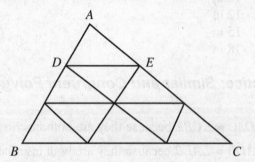

Answer: $\frac{1}{9}$

6. In a kite, two distinct pairs of adjacent sides are congruent. This means that in kite $ABCD$, $AD = AB$. Set up a proportion to solve for $\overline{AD}$: $\frac{AD}{20} = \frac{6}{8}$. Solving you get $AD = \frac{120}{8} = 15$ in. This is the length of $\overline{AB}$.

Answer: C

Surface Area and Volume

• A **prism** is a three-dimensional solid with two parallel faces, called **bases**, that are congruent polygons. The other sides are called **lateral faces**. Each pair of lateral faces has a common **lateral edge**. The lateral edges are parallel segments. The lateral faces of a prism are parallelograms, and in a **right prism** the lateral faces are rectangles. In a right prism, a lateral edge is also an altitude.

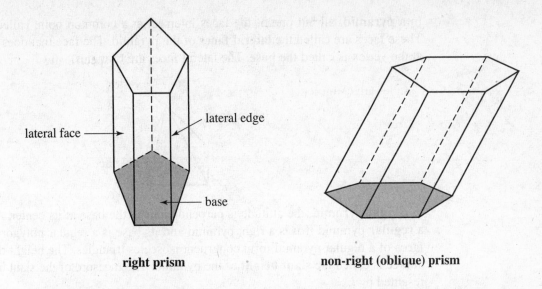

right prism   **non-right (oblique) prism**

Memory Tip: A right prism stands "upright."

- Prisms are classified by the shape of their bases.

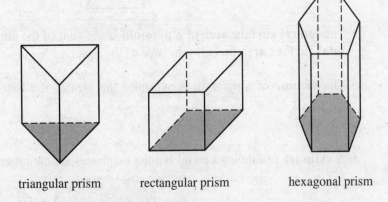

triangular prism   rectangular prism   hexagonal prism

- The **lateral surface area** of a **prism** is the sum of the areas of the lateral faces. The **total surface area** includes the areas of the two bases.

- The **volume** of a **prism** is the area of the base multiplied by the height of the prism or $V = Bh$, where B is the area of the base.

- A **cube** is a regular prism with square sides. The volume of a cube is $V = s^3$, where s is the length of an edge.

- In a **pyramid**, all but one of the faces intersect at a common point called the **vertex**. These faces are called the **lateral faces** of the pyramid. The face that does not intersect at the vertex is called the **base**. The lateral faces are triangles.

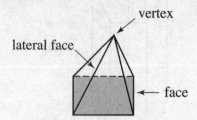

- In a **right pyramid**, the altitude is perpendicular to the base at its center. A pyramid is a **regular** pyramid if it is a right pyramid and its base is a regular polygon. The lateral faces of a regular pyramid form congruent isosceles triangles. The height of each lateral face is called the **slant height** of the pyramid. The measure of the slant height is represented by *l*.

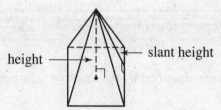

- The **lateral surface area** of a **pyramid** is the sum of the areas of the lateral faces. The **total surface area** includes the area of the base.

- The **volume** of a pyramid is one third the area of the base multiplied by the height:

$$V = \frac{1}{3}Bh.$$

- A **cylinder** resembles a prism but the two bases are congruent circles.

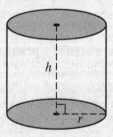

- The **volume** of a **cylinder** is the area of the circular base multiplied by the height:

$$V = \pi r^2 h.$$

- The **lateral surface area** of a **cylinder** is the area of the material used to construct the cylinder not including the circular bases. The lateral surface area of a cylinder is a rectangle whose height is the height of the cylinder and whose width is the circumference of the cylinder. The formula for the lateral surface area is $LA = 2\pi rh$. The **total surface area** of a **cylinder** includes the area of the two circular bases.

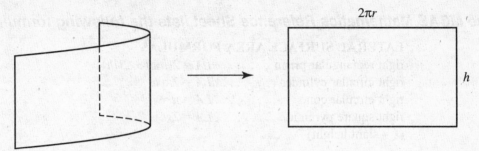

- A **cone** resembles a pyramid but the base is circular. The lateral surface is curved and has a vertex. The slant height is labeled with the letter l.

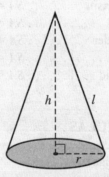

- The **volume** of a **cone** is $V = \dfrac{1}{3}Bh = \dfrac{1}{3}\pi r^2 h.$

- The **lateral surface area** of a **cone** is $LA = \pi rl$. The **total surface area** of a **cone** is the sum of the lateral area and the circular base.

- A **sphere** is the set of all points that are the same distance from a center. A **radius** of a sphere is a segment whose endpoints are the center and a point on the sphere. A **diameter** of a sphere is a segment that joins two points on the sphere and passes through the center.

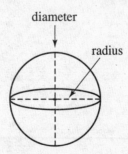

- The **surface area** of a **sphere** is $S = 4\pi r^2.$

- The **volume** of a **sphere** is $V = \dfrac{4}{3}\pi r^3$.

- The **units** of measure for any surface area is square units (units^2).

- The **units** of measure for any volume is cubic units (units^3).

The MCAS Mathematics Reference Sheet lists the following formulas:

LATERAL SURFACE AREA FORMULAS
right rectangular prism . . . . $LA = 2(hw) + 2(lh)$
right circular cylinder . . . . $LA = 2\pi rh$
right circular cone . . . . $LA = \pi r\ell$
right square pyramid . . . . $LA = 2s\ell$
(ℓ = slant height)

TOTAL SURFACE AREA FORMULAS
cube . . . . $SA = 6s^2$
right rectangular prism . . . . $SA = 2(lw) + 2(hw) + 2(lh)$
sphere . . . . $SA = 4\pi r^2$
right circular cylinder . . . . $SA = 2\pi r^2 + 2\pi rh$
right circular cone . . . . $SA = \pi r^2 + \pi r\ell$
right square pyramid . . . . $SA = s^2 + 2s\ell$
(ℓ = slant height)

VOLUME FORMULAS
cube . . . . $V = s^3$
(s = length of an edge)
right rectangular prism . . . . $V = lwh$

OR

(B = area of the base) . . . . $V = Bh$

sphere . . . . $V = \dfrac{4}{3}\pi r^3$

right circular cylinder . . . . $V = \pi r^2 h$

right circular cone . . . . $V = \dfrac{1}{3}\pi r^2 h$

right square pyramid . . . . $V = \dfrac{1}{3}s^2 h$

Examples: Surface Area and Volume

Example 1. A gum ball factory makes one type of gum ball with a radius of 3 cm. The maximum error in measurement is 0.02 cm for the radius. Which of the following is closest to the maximum volume of one of these gum balls?

A. 13.86 cm³
B. 14.42 cm³
C. 110.85 cm³
D. 115.37 cm³

Solution

The formula for the volume of a sphere is $\frac{4}{3}\pi r^3$. If the radius of the ball is 3 cm with a maximum error of 0.02 cm, the largest sphere would have a radius of $r = 3.02$ cm. Plugging into the volume formula, you get a maximum volume of $V = \frac{4}{3}\pi(3.02)^3 \approx 115.37$ cm³.

Answer: D

Example 2. The cone below has a radius of 4 inches and a height of 15 inches. What is the volume of the cone?

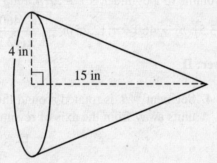

A. 60π cubic inches
B. 80π cubic inches
C. 225π cubic inches
D. 240π cubic inches

Solution

The formula for the volume of a cone is $\frac{1}{3}\pi r^2 h$. Plugging in $r = 4$ for the radius of the cone and $h = 15$ for the height of the cone, you get $V = \frac{1}{3}\pi(4)^2(15) = 80\pi$ cubic inches.

Answer: B

Example 3. The can of peas is a right cylinder with a radius of 3.5 centimeters. The volume of the can is 460 cubic centimeters.

What is the approximate height of the can?

A. 8 cm
B. 9 cm
C. 10 cm
D. 12 cm

Solution

The volume of a cylinder is $V = \pi r^2 h$. Plug in your values of V and r, and solve for h.

$$460 = \pi\left(3.5\right)^2 h \rightarrow 460 = \pi(12.25)h \rightarrow \frac{460}{\pi(12.25)} = h, \text{ which gives you } h \approx 12 \text{ cm.}$$

Answer: D

Example 4. Segment $\overline{AB}$ is rotated around the dotted line. $\overline{AB}$ is 8 units long, and is 3 units away from the axis of revolution.

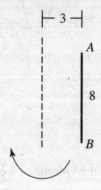

What is the volume of the resulting figure that is formed?

A. 24π units^3
B. 64π units^3
C. 72π units^3
D. 192π units^3

...igure formed is a cylinder with a radius of 3 inches and a height of 8 inches.

Plug into the volume formula for a cylinder:
$V = \pi r^2 h = \pi(3)^2 (8) = 72\pi$ units^3

Answer: C

Example 5. A 9 in. by 9 in. baking pan with a square base is 2 in. high and has slanted sides as shown. Brownie mix is poured into the pan and is leveled at a height of 1 inch. How does the volume of the mix in the pan compare to the total volume of the pan if it were full?

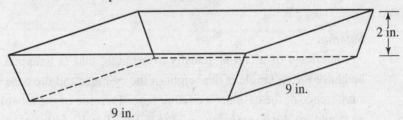

A. It is more than half as much.
B. It is half as much.
C. It is less than half as much.
D. It is twice as much.

Solution

It is true that the height of the mix is one half the height of the pan, but the volume of the mix is not one half that of the pan. Think of the top of the mix as being the base of the empty part of the pan. Notice that this "batter base" is larger than the actual bottom of the pan because the sides are slanted outward. If you were to compute the volume of the mix on the bottom, it would have the same height as the empty part, but with a smaller base. The volume of the mix is therefore smaller than the volume of the empty part, and the pan is therefore less than half full.

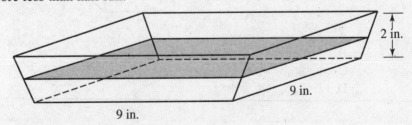

Answer: C

Example 6. American Can Company would like to determine the cost of printing labels for cans with diameter of 14 cm and height of 10 cm. The label for each can will wrap around the side of the can completely, with no overlap. What is the approximate area of one label?

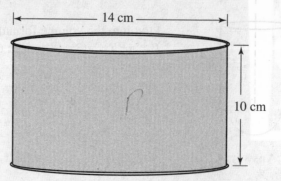

A. 140 cm²
B. 220 cm²
C. 440 cm²
D. 490 cm²

Solution

The label of a can is actually a rectangle that is wrapped around the cylinder. The height of the rectangle is the height of the cylinder and the base of the rectangle is the circumference of the cylinder's circular base. The area of the label is therefore the area of the rectangle or $A = base \cdot height = 2\pi r h = 2\pi(7)(10) \approx 440$ cm². Note that this is the formula for the lateral surface area of a cylinder.

Answer: C

Example 7. Owen keeps a box under his bed to store his summer clothing. The box is in the shape of a rectangular prism as shown in the figure below. Owen's sister, Brooke, made a box that had the same height as Owen's box, but she tripled the length and doubled the width, and it still fit under her bed. What is the ratio of the volume of Owen's box to that of Brooke's?

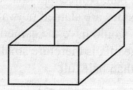

A. 1 : 6
B. 1 : 12
C. 1 : 36
D. 1 : 216

Solution

Let the volume of Owen's box be $V = length \cdot width \cdot height = lwh$. Then the volume of Brooke's box is $V = 3\left(length\right) \cdot 2\left(width\right) \cdot height = 6\left(lwh\right)$. This makes the volume of Brooke's box six times that of Owen's, so the ratio of Owen's to Brooke's is 1 : 6.

Answer: A

Example 8. Beads of glass in the shape of a cube are to be strung together to make a charm for a necklace. The cubes have an edge of 2 cm. A cylindrical hole with diameter of 1 cm is drilled through the bead, so that the string can pass through.

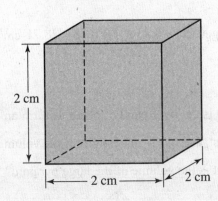 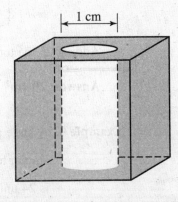

a. What is the total surface area of the cube BEFORE the hole has been drilled? Be sure to include units of measure in your answer. Show your work or explain how you obtained your answer.

b. What is the total surface area of the charm AFTER the hole has been drilled? Round your answer to the nearest whole number. Be sure to include units of measure in your answer. Show your work or explain how you obtained your answer.

Solution

a. The surface area of a cube is the sum of the areas of all six faces, or $SA = 6 \cdot side^2$. The sides of the cube are 2 cm, so the total surface area is $SA = 6 \cdot (2)^2 = $ cm^2.

Answer: 24 cm^2

b. Think of a surface as any part of the charm that would be painted if dumped into a bucket of paint. For our charm, this includes four square sides, two square sides with holes in them, and the lateral area of the cylinder that is now in the middle of the charm.

See how it is broken down below.

$2 \cdot$ ⬜ $= 2(\text{area of square} - \text{area of circle})$

$= 2(4 - \pi r^2) = 2(4 - \pi(0.5)^2) \approx 2(3.2146) \approx 6.43 \text{ cm}^2$

$4 \cdot$ ⬛ $= 4(\text{area of square}) = 4(4) = 16 \text{ cm}^2$

▯ $= 2\pi rh \approx 2\pi(0.5)(2) = 6.28 \text{ cm}^2$

Adding up the total, you get: $SA \approx 6.43 + 16 + 6.28 = 28.71 \text{ cm}^2$

Answer: 29 cm²

Example 9. A large pyramid is cut by a parallel plane to form an upper pyramid that is similar to the first, and has $\frac{1}{2}$ the height. If the volume of the small pyramid is 24 units³, what is the volume of the large pyramid?

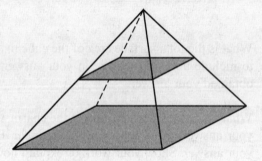

Solution

The ratio of volumes of similar solids is equal to the cube of the ratio of any of its corresponding segments. Since the heights are in a ratio of $\frac{1}{2}$, the volumes are in a ratio of $\left(\frac{1}{2}\right)^3 = \frac{1}{8}$. Set up the proportion $\frac{1}{8} = \frac{24}{x}$, where x is the volume of the large pyramid. Solving we get $x = 192$ units³.

Answer: 192 units³

Practice: Surface Area and Volume

1. A cube has a volume of 227 cm³. Which of the following is closest to the length of an edge of the cube?
   A. 4 cm
   B. 5 cm
   C. 6 cm
   D. 7 cm

2. A right cylindrical can is 5 inches high and the area of its top is 49π square inches. What is the minimum number of square inches of construction paper it would take to cover the lateral surface of the can?
   A. 70 square inches
   B. 70π square inches
   C. 245 square inches
   D. 245π square inches

3. Bud is setting up his new fish tank which is in the shape of a right cylinder with a radius of 15 inches.

   a. First, Bud fills the tank with water until the height of the water is 10 inches. What is the exact volume of the water in the glass? Be sure to include units of measure. Show or explain how you got your answer.

   b. Then, Bud remembers to place the 12 glass marbles of equal size into the tank. The total volume of the contents of the tank increases to 2,700π cubic inches. What is the new height of the water? Be sure to include units of measure. Show or explain how you got your answer.

   c. What is the volume of one of the marbles? Be sure to include units of measure. Show or explain how you got your answer.

   d. What is the radius of one of the marbles to the nearest 100th of an inch? Be sure to include units of measure. Show or explain how you got your answer.

4. A pond is in the shape of a right cylindrical prism that has a diameter of 40 feet.

   a. If the water level in the pond is 1 foot high, find the volume of the water in the pond. Be sure to include units of measure. Show or explain how you got your answer.

   b. During a rainstorm, the water level rises from 1 foot to 1.25 feet. How much water has been added to the pond? Be sure to include units of measure. Show or explain how you got your answer.

   c. If the pond contains 1,200π cubic feet of water, what is the depth of the water in the pond?

5. *Use the cone and the sphere below to answer the following questions.*

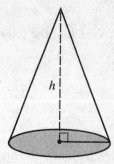
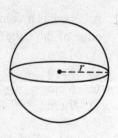

a. If the height of the cone is tripled, the volume of the cone is how many times larger? Show or explain how you got your answer.

b. If the radius of the cone is tripled, the volume of the cone is how many times larger? Show or explain how you got your answer.

c. If the radius of the sphere is tripled, the volume of the sphere is how many times larger? Show or explain how you got your answer.

d. If a cone and a sphere were to have congruent radii and equal volumes, what would be the height of the cone in terms of the radius, r? Show or explain how you got your answer.

6. Segment $\overline{AB}$ is 13 inches long and is to be rotated around the dotted axis of revolution. Point B is located on the axis and point A is 5 inches away from the axis.

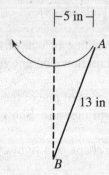

a. What is the geometric name for the shape of the solid that is generated?

b. What is the height of the solid that is formed? Be sure to include units of measure in your answer. Show your work or explain how you obtained your answer.

c. What is the volume of the solid that is formed? Round your answer to the nearest cubic inch. Be sure to include units of measure in your answer. Show your work or explain how you obtained your answer.

d. If 50 cubic inches of water is poured into the solid, how high would the water level rise in the solid? Round your answer to the nearest tenth of an inch. Be sure to include units of measure in your answer. Show your work or explain how you obtained your answer.

7. Mrs. Starks has hired a contractor to build a garage. The garage will be built on an 11 foot by 16 foot slab of cement. The cement is to be poured into the level ground at a depth of 2 feet. If the contractor charges $10.00 per cubic foot of cement, how much will the cement slab cost Mrs. Starks?
   A. $319.00
   B. $352.00
   C. $1,760.00
   D. $3,520.00

8. *Use the figure below to answer the following questions.*

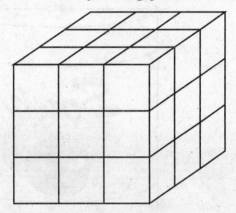

The figure above shows a large cube that is comprised of smaller cubes, each with a volume of 1 cm³.

a. How many smaller cubes make up the large cube?

b. What is the volume of the larger cube? Be sure to include units of measure in your answer. Show your work or explain how you obtained your answer.

c. What is the area of one face of the large cube? Be sure to include units of measure in your answer. Show your work or explain how you obtained your answer.

d. What is the total surface area of the large cube? Be sure to include units of measure in your answer. Show your work or explain how you obtained your answer.

e. If exactly two adjacent faces of the large cube were to be painted red, how many of the smaller cubes would have at least one of their sides painted? Show your work or explain how you obtained your answer.

9. David is making a life-sized model of an igloo for his history project. The igloo is in the shape of a dome (hemisphere) with a diameter 16 feet.

a. What is the lateral surface area of the dome? Be sure to include units of measure. Show or explain how you got your answer.

b. What is the volume of the igloo? Be sure to include units of measure. Show or explain how you got your answer.

c. David plans to paint the outside of the igloo white. He knows that one can of paint will cover 150 square feet. What is the least number of cans of paint David will need to buy to paint the igloo? Be sure to include units of measure. Show or explain how you got your answer.

10. A can shaped like a right circular cylinder holds 20 ounces of soup and has a diameter of 4 inches and a height of $4\frac{1}{4}$ inches.

a. What is the total surface area of the soup can? Be sure to include units of measure in your answer. Show your work or explain how you obtained your answer.

b. What is the volume of the can? Be sure to include units of measure in your answer. Show your work or explain how you obtained your answer.

c. If the label states that the can contains about $2\frac{1}{2}$ servings of soup, how many ounces are considered to be in one serving? Be sure to include units of measure in your answer. Show your work or explain how you obtained your answer.

11. The total surface area of a cube is 84 square inches. Which of the following measures is closest to the length of its edge?
A. 1.5 in.
B. 3.7 in.
C. 4.6 in.
D. 9.1 in.

12. The right circular cylinder and right cone shown below have the same radius and volume. The cylinder has a height of 15 inches.

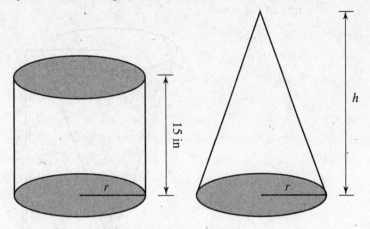

What is h, the height of the cone?

A. 15 in.
B. 20 in.
C. 30 in.
D. 45 in.

13. The right cylinder shown below has a height of 10 inches. The base of the cylinder has a circumference of 8π inches.

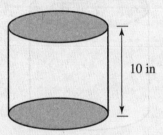

What is the lateral surface area of the cylinder?

A. 80π square inches
B. 112π square inches
C. 160π square inches
D. 640π square inches

14. The volume of the waffle ice cream cone in the diagram below is 16π cubic centimeters. If the height of the ice cream cone is 10 centimeters, what is the radius of the opening of the cone?

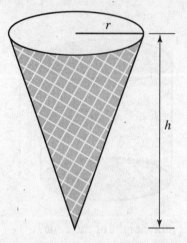

15. The cone and the cylinder below each have a radius of 3 centimeters and equal volume. The cone has a height of 8 centimeters.

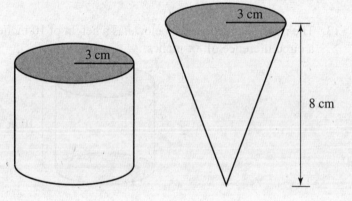

a. What is the volume of the cone? Be sure to include units of measure in your answer. Show your work or explain how you obtained your answer.

b. What is the height of the cylinder? Be sure to include units of measure in your answer. Show your work or explain how you obtained your answer.

c. Which solid has a greater surface area if both shapes are missing their circular top (the gray shaded region)? Show your work or explain how you obtained your answer.

16. A company sells salt in cylindrical shakers of two different sizes, that are similar in shape. Their dimensions are shown below.

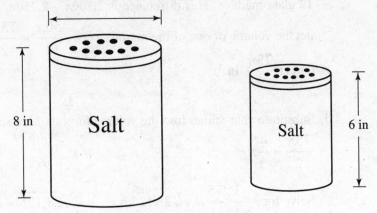

How many cubic inches does the smaller shaker hold?

A. 18π cubic inches

B. $\dfrac{27}{2}\pi$ cubic inches

C. 54π cubic inches

D. $\dfrac{81}{2}\pi$ cubic inches

Solutions to Practice: Surface Area and Volume

1. Cube the length of each edge choice in the answers.
$$4 \times 4 \times 4 = 64 \text{ cm}^3, \ 5 \times 5 \times 5 = 125 \text{ cm}^3, \ 6 \times 6 \times 6 = 216 \text{ cm}^3, \ 7 \times 7 \times 7 = 343 \text{ cm}^3.$$

The closest answer is 6 cm.

Answer: C

2. The lateral area of a cylinder is $LA = 2\pi rh$. We know the height is $h = 5$. Finding the radius, r: $A = \pi r^2$, $49\pi = \pi r^2$, $r = 7$. Plugging into the lateral area formula, $LA = 2\pi(7)(5) = 70\pi$ square inches.

Answer: B

3. a. $V_{\text{cylinder}} = \pi r^2 h$, $V = \pi (15)^2 (10) = 2{,}250\pi$ in.^{3}.

Answer: 2,250π in.^{3}

b. We know the radius and new volume of the tank. Set up the volume equation and substitute 2700π for the volume, 15 for the radius, and solve for the height. $2{,}700\pi = \pi r^2 h$, $2700\pi = \pi (15)^2 h$, $2{,}700\pi = 225\pi h$, $h = 12$ inches.

Answer: 12 in.

c. The difference between the volumes in parts a and b represents the volume of the 12 glass marbles. This difference is $2{,}700\pi - 2{,}250\pi = 450\pi$. Dividing by 12, we get the volume of one of the marbles: $v = \dfrac{450\pi}{12} = \dfrac{75\pi}{2}$ in.^{3}.

Answer: $\dfrac{75\pi}{2}$ in.^{3}

d. Substitute your values into the volume formula for a sphere: $V = \dfrac{4}{3}\pi r^3$. You get $\dfrac{75\pi}{2} = \dfrac{4}{3}\pi r^3$.

Solve for r: $\dfrac{3}{4} \cdot \dfrac{75}{2} = r^3$, $28.125 = r^3$, $r = \sqrt[3]{28.125} = 28.125^{\frac{1}{3}} \approx 3.04$ in.

Answer: 3.04 in.

4. A cylindrical prism looks like

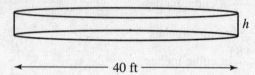

a. the volume formula for a cylinder: $V = \pi r^2 h$. You get $V = \pi(20)^2(1) = 400\pi$ ft^3.

Answer: 400π ft^3

b. If the height increases to 1.25 feet, the new volume is $V = \pi(20)^2(1.25) = 500\pi$ ft^3. The amount (or volume) of water that has been added is $500\pi - 400\pi = 100\pi$ ft^3.

Answer: 100π ft^3

c. We know the volume and radius of the pond. Set up the volume equation and substitute $1{,}200\pi$ for the volume. Then solve for the height, which is the depth of the pond.
$V = 1{,}200\pi = \pi r^2 h$, $1{,}200\pi = \pi(20)^2 h$, $1{,}200\pi = 400\pi h$, $h = 3$ ft.

Answer: 3 ft

5. a. The formula for the volume of a cone is $V = \dfrac{1}{3}\pi r^2 h$. Replacing h with $3h$ to represent a height that has been tripled, you get $\dfrac{1}{3}\pi r^2(3h) = 3\left(\dfrac{1}{3}\pi r^2 h\right) = 3V$.

Answer: 3 times as large

b. The formula for the volume of a cone is $V = \dfrac{1}{3}\pi r^2 h$. Replacing r with $3r$ to represent a radius that has been tripled, you get

$$\frac{1}{3}\pi(3r)^2 h = \frac{1}{3}\pi \cdot 9r^2 h = 9\left(\frac{1}{3}\pi r^2 h\right) = 9V .$$

Answer: 9 times as large

c. The formula for the volume of a sphere is $V = \dfrac{4}{3}\pi r^3$. Replacing r with $3r$ to represent a radius that has been tripled, you get

$$\frac{4}{3}\pi(3r)^3 = \frac{4}{3}\pi \cdot 27r^3 = 27\left(\frac{4}{3}\pi r^3\right) = 27V .$$

Answer: 27 times as large

d. Setting the volume formulas for each solid equal to each other gives us $\dfrac{1}{3}\pi r^2 h = \dfrac{4}{3}\pi r^3$. We want the height of the cone in terms of r, so solve for h. Multiplying by 3 and dividing by πr^2 gives us $h = 4r$.

Answer: $h = 4r$

6. a.   The solid formed by rotating around the axis is a cone.

Answer: cone

b. The height of the cone is the length of the vertical axis of revolution. Because it is perpendicular to the radius, you have a right triangle. Use Pythagorean Theorem: $5^2 + h^2 = 13^2$. Solving for h you get $h = 12$ inches.

Answer: $h = 12$ in.

c. The formula for the volume of a cone is $V = \dfrac{1}{3}\pi r^2 h$. Substituting in our values for r and h, we have: $V = \dfrac{1}{3}\pi(5)^2(12) = 100\pi \approx 314$ cubic inches.

Answer: 314 in.^{3}

d. The water also forms a cone. Its volume is 50 in.^{3} and its ratio of radius to height is $\dfrac{r}{h} = \dfrac{5}{12}$. Solving for r in terms of h, $r = \dfrac{5}{12}h$. Substituting our known values into the volume formula, we get

$$50 = \frac{1}{3}\pi\left(\frac{5}{12}h\right)^2 h \rightarrow 50 = \frac{25}{432}\pi h^3 \rightarrow h^3 = \frac{864}{\pi} \rightarrow h = \sqrt[3]{\frac{864}{\pi}} \approx 6.5 \text{ in.}$$

Answer: 6.5 in.

7. The slab will be a rectangular prism, whose volume is $V = lwh = (11)(16)(2) = 352$ ft³. If each cubic foot costs \$10.00, multiplying by the number of cubic feet we get \$3,520.00.

   Answer: D

8. a. If each of the smaller cubes is 1 unit, then the large cube is made up of $3 \times 3 \times 3$, or $3^3 = 27$ units. (Or just count them up if you wish.)

   Answer: 27

   b. Each smaller block has a volume of 1 cm³ which makes an edge 1 cm. An edge of the large cube would therefore be 3 cm, and its volume would be $3^3 = 27$ cm³.

   Answer: 27 cm³

   c. One face of the large cube is a square, so its area is $3 \times 3 = 9$ cm².

   Answer: 9 cm²

   d. The surface area of a cube is the sum of its six faces, or $6 \times 9 = 54$ cm².

   Answer: 54 cm²

   e. From the diagram below, we see that 12 cubes have paint on one face and 3 cubes have paint on 2 faces. Adding, we get 15 smaller cubes with paint on at least one face.

   Answer: 15

9. a. The lateral area of a hemisphere is one-half that of a sphere, or $\frac{1}{2}\left(4\pi r^2\right) = 2\pi r^2$. Substituting in a radius of 8 ft, you have $LA = 2\pi(8)^2 = 128\pi$ ft².

   Answer: 128π ft².

   b. The volume of a hemisphere is one half that of a sphere, or $\frac{1}{2}\left(\frac{4}{3}\pi r^3\right) = \frac{2}{3}\pi r^3$.

   Substituting in a radius of 8 ft, you have $V = \frac{2}{3}\pi(8)^3 = \frac{1024}{3}\pi$ ft³.

   Answer: $\dfrac{1024}{3}\pi$ ft³

c. From part a, you know that David has a surface area of 128π square feet to cover. Since one can of paint covers 150 square feet, divide the surface area by 150 to get the number of paint cans needed. You get $\dfrac{128\pi}{150} \approx 2.68$ cans, which means that David will have to purchase 3 cans of paint.

Answer: 3 cans

10. a. Add the lateral area of the cylinder to the sum of its two bases.

$$lateral\ area = 2\pi rh = 2\pi(2)\left(\frac{17}{4}\right) = 17\pi \text{ square inches}$$

$$circular\ base = \pi r^2 = \pi(2)^2 = 4\pi \text{ square inches}$$
$$total\ surface\ area = 2(4\pi) + 17\pi = 25\pi \text{ square inches}$$

Answer: 25π in.^{2}

b. Using the volume formula for a cylinder, $V = \pi r^2 h = \pi(2)^2\left(\frac{17}{4}\right) = 17\pi$ in.^{3}.

Answer: 17π in.^{2}

c. If a 20-ounce can is equal to $2\frac{1}{2}$ servings of soup, divide to find the number of servings in each can: $\dfrac{20}{2.5} = 8$ ounces in each serving.

Answer: 8 oz

11. The formula for the surface area of a cube is $SA = 6e^2$ where e is the length of an edge. Substitute 84 for the surface area and solve for e: $84 = 6e^2$, $e = \sqrt{14} \approx 3.7$ in. You can also **use your answer choices** to answer this question. Square each answer and multiply by 6 until you get 84: $(3.7)^2 \cdot 6 \approx 84$.

Answer: B

12. Substituting $h = 15$ for the height of the cylinder and setting the volume formulas for each solid equal to each other gives us: $\pi r^2 (15) = \dfrac{1}{3}\pi r^2 h$. Solving for the height of the cone, we get $h = 45$ inches.

Answer: D

13. The lateral surface area of the cylinder is the circumference of the base times the height.
$LA = 8\pi \times 10 = 80\pi$ square inches.

Answer: A

14. The formula for the volume of a cone is $V = \frac{1}{3}\pi r^2 h$. Substituting in our values for V and h, we have $16\pi = \frac{1}{3}\pi r^2 (10)$. Solving for r, we get $r^2 = \frac{48}{10} = \frac{24}{5}$, which makes

$$r = \sqrt{\frac{24}{5}} = \frac{\sqrt{24}}{\sqrt{5}} \cdot \frac{\sqrt{5}}{\sqrt{5}} = \frac{\sqrt{120}}{5} = \frac{2\sqrt{30}}{5} \text{ centimeters.}$$

Answer: $r = \dfrac{2\sqrt{30}}{5}$ cm

15. a. Substitute into the volume of a cone: $V = \frac{1}{3}\pi r^2 h = \frac{1}{3}\pi (3)^2 (8) = 24\pi$ cm³.

   Answer: 24π cm³

   b. Setting the volume formulas for each solid equal to each other gives us: $\pi r^2 h_{\text{cylinder}} = \frac{1}{3}\pi r^2 h_{\text{cone}}$. Substituting $h = 8$ for the height of the cone and $r = 3$ for the radius of each, our equation becomes: $\pi (3)^2 h = \frac{1}{3}\pi (3)^2 (8)$. Solving for the height of the cylinder, we get $h = \frac{8}{3}$ cm.

   Answer: $h = \dfrac{8}{3}$ cm

   c. The surface area of the topless cylinder is the sum of its lateral area and the area of its circular base. This makes $SA = 2\pi rh + \pi r^2 = 2\pi (3)\left(\frac{8}{3}\right) + \pi (3)^2 = 25\pi \approx 78.5$ cm².

   The surface area of the cone without its top, is just the cone's lateral area $LA = \pi rl$, where l is the cone's slant height. Find this with the Pythagorean Theorem: $3^2 + 8^2 = l^2$ or $l = \sqrt{73}$. This makes $LA = \pi (3)(\sqrt{73}) = 3\pi\sqrt{73} \approx 80.53$ cm². Comparing, we get that the surface area of the cone is greater.

   Answer: cone

16. First find the diameter of the smaller shaker with the proportion: $\frac{4}{8} = \frac{d}{6}$, giving you $d = 3$. Now use the formula for the volume of a cylinder, substituting $h = 6$ and $r = \frac{3}{2}$. $V = \pi \left(\frac{3}{2}\right)^2 (6) = \frac{54}{4}\pi = \frac{27}{2}\pi$ cubic inches.

   Answer: B

Three-Dimensional Figures

- A **net** is a two-dimensional pattern that can be folded to form a three-dimensional figure. To familiarize yourself with nets, you may want to draw nets on a piece of paper and cut them out so that you can fold them into their three-dimensional shapes. The following are some examples of nets:

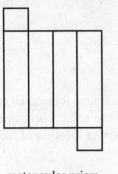

rectangular prism

triangular prism

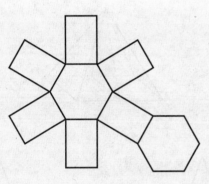

hexagonal prism

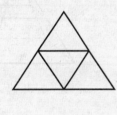

triangular pyramid

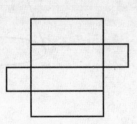

rectangular prism

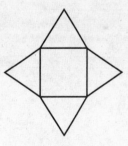

square-based pyramid

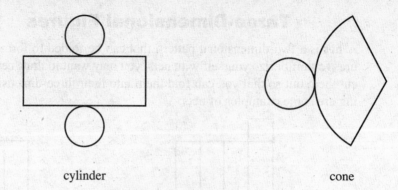

cylinder   cone

- A **cross section** of a solid is a plane figure formed by the intersection of the solid and a plane. The cross section is a slice of the solid. The shape of the cross section depends on the orientation of the plane and the exact location of the intersection. Some examples of cross sections are shown below.

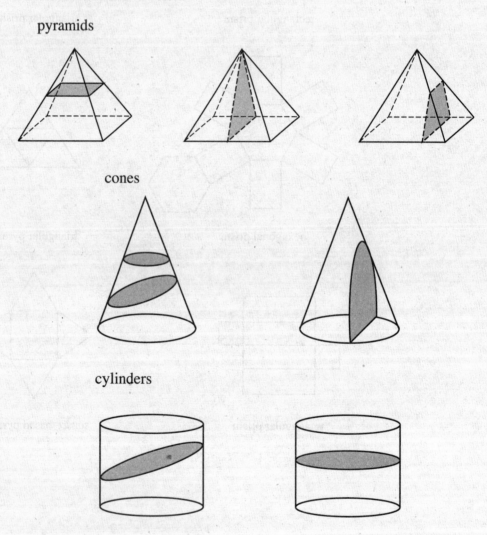

pyramids

cones

cylinders

> *Note: The ovals that you see in the cone and cylinder pictures are called ellipses.*

Examples: Three-Dimensional Figures

Example 1. Two possible cross sections of a right square pyramid and a plane, are a square and an isosceles triangle as shown below.

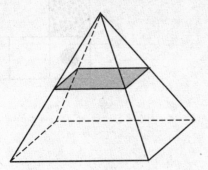 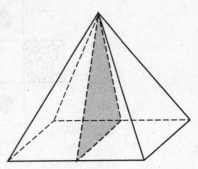

Which of the following is NOT a possible cross section of a plane and a right square pyramid?

A. Point
B. Line
C. Nonsquare rectangle
D. Hexagon

Solution

The diagram below shows that a point, line, and rectangle are all possible cross sections. A hexagon cannot be obtained.

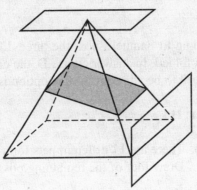

Answer: D

★ **Example 2.** Samuel has a box in the shape of the cube shown below.

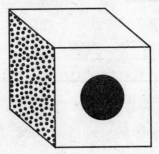

Which of the following patterns would NOT allow Samuel to form the box?

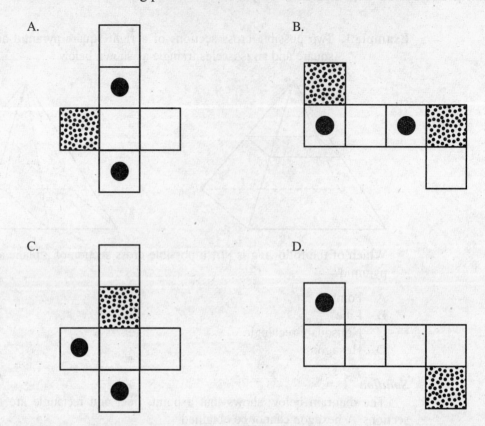

A.

B.

C.

D.

Solution

According to Samuel's box, the three different designs must all be adjacent to each other when folded. In answer choice D, the circle and the tiny dots are on opposing faces and they need to be adjacent, so this option is impossible.

Answer: D

Example 3. There are 11 different nets for a cube. The following are three possible nets. Draw four of the remaining possible 8 nets for a cube.

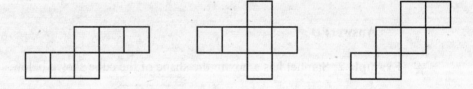

Solution
   The following are the 8 remaining distinct nets that can be drawn that form a cube.

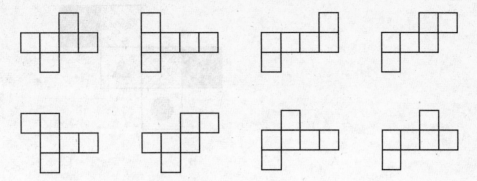

Example 4. Which of the following nets will NOT fold to make a pyramid with a square base?

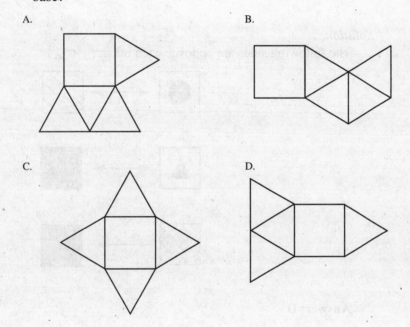

Solution
   When folded, triangles 1 and 2 overlap but no triangle touches the highlighted side of the square base.

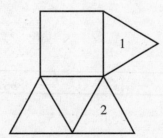

   Answer: A

Example 5. If the following net is folded into a cube, which face will be opposite the face with the circle?

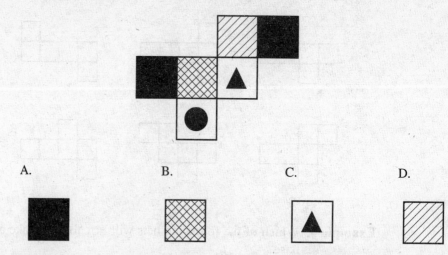

A.   B.   C.   D.

Solution

The following sides are opposite each other:

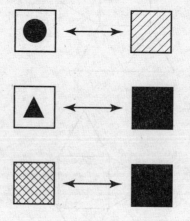

Answer: D

Practice: Three-Dimensional Figures

1. *Use the figure below to answer the following question.*

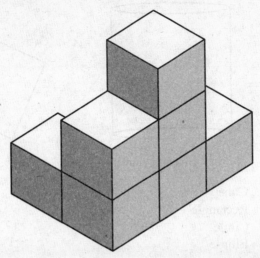

Which diagram could NOT possibly show how the figure looks when it is viewed directly from above?

A.

B.

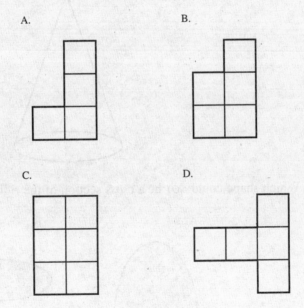

C.

D.

2. Which of the following shapes cannot be formed by the intersection of a right circular cylinder and a plane?

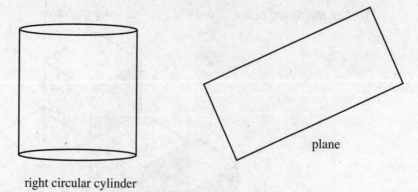

right circular cylinder

plane

A. Cone
B. Rectangle
C. Circle
D. Ellipse

3. A right circular cone is represented by the figure below.

Which shape could NOT be a cross section of the right circular cone above?

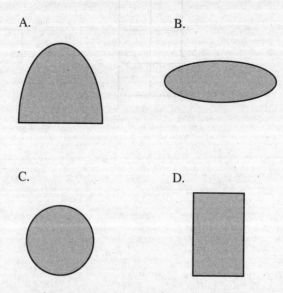

A.

B.

C.

D.

★ 4. *Use the figure below to answer the following question.*

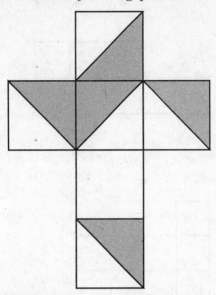

If the above figure is folded into a cube, which of the following figures is NOT a possible view of the solid formed?

A.

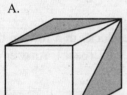

B.

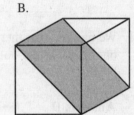

C.

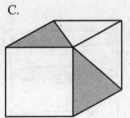

D.

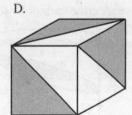

5. Which net will not fold to make a cube?

A.

B.

C.

D.

Solutions to Practice: Three-Dimensional Figures

1. We can see that there are three blocks in a row on the right-hand side, and AT LEAST one block at the bottom of the left (back). Answer choice D does not illustrate this block.

   Answer: D

2. Illustrated below are the cross sections of an ellipse, a circle, and a rectangle. A cone cannot be formed.

 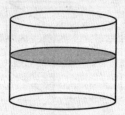 

   Answer: A

3. Answers A, B, and C are illustrated below. You cannot obtain a rectangle from a cone.

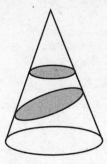 

Answer: D

4. First, let's explore answer choices A and C, with the frontal view of the white face. In the unfolded net, the square on top of the white face, and the square to the right of that one would be adjacent to the white face when folded. Notice that the edges where these three sides touch, connect a solid white edge to another solid white edge, and not to a shaded portion. This renders choice C impossible.

Answer: C

5. If square 3 remains in place and squares 2, 5, and 4 are folded up, square 1 can be folded so that is opposite and parallel to square 3. Square 6, however, would not complete the cube.

		5	6
1	2	3	4

Answer: D

Chapter 7 | Data Analysis, Statistics, and Probability

Statistics

Very often, people make claims about characteristics of a **population**. "*The average length of a pregnancy is _____*"; "*_____% of people under the age of 18 smoke*"; "*The median home price in California is _____.*" Because it is often impossible to ask everyone in the entire population for the data you want, you have to resort to asking just a **sample** from that population. **Statistics** is the science of gathering, organizing, and evaluating data. The word can also be used to mean the actual data itself. The act of gathering data, is referred to as **sampling** or **surveying**. The information you gather from your sample is generally used to understand and evaluate trends or characteristics of the population. To make claims that are representative of the entire population, your **sample size**, or amount of data, should be large, and your sample should be **random** or **unbiased**. Here are some examples of biased and unbiased samples for gathering data about the number of hours American teenagers watch television:

Unbiased	**Biased**
Survey teenagers in all 50 states.	*Survey teenagers only in New Jersey.*
Survey teenagers aged 13 to 18.	*Survey only teenagers that are 14 years old.*
Survey teenagers with different economic backgrounds.	*Survey teenagers only in wealthy communities.*

It may not be obvious to you why your sample size should be large, but consider the statement: "*100% of all teenagers surveyed plan on becoming mathematicians.*" This could very well be true, but perhaps the sample size consisted of just one person!

- **Measures of Central Tendency**
  Mean, median, and mode are three different measures by which to describe the center of data. Depending on the data, one or the other may be more useful in describing the data.
- To calculate the **mean**, or **average** of a group of numbers, use the formula:

$$\text{mean} = \frac{sum\ of\ values}{number\ of\ values}$$

Simply add all the numbers and divide by how many numbers are in the group. For example, the mean of the numbers:

$$24, 14, 19, 20, 20, 18, 11, 19, \text{and } 17$$

is calculated as

$$mean = \frac{24 + 14 + 19 + 20 + 20 + 18 + 11 + 19 + 17}{9} = \frac{162}{9} = 18$$

- The **median** is the number that falls in the middle of data when it is ordered from least to greatest or vice versa. First, order the data. Then cross off the smallest and highest values together, until one number remains in the middle. If two numbers are left in the middle, average these values by adding them and dividing by 2. For an odd number of data entries, such as in this problem, only one number will be left in the middle.

$$\cancel{8}, \cancel{9}, \cancel{9}, \cancel{10}, \cancel{10}, \cancel{10}, \boxed{11}\; \cancel{12}, \cancel{12}, \cancel{12}, \cancel{13}, \cancel{14}, \cancel{16}$$

Suppose the data had been the numbers 2, 4, 8, and 10. The median would be 6 because it the average of the two middle numbers.

If there are a lot of numbers in the data set, finding the middle number can be tricky. To help, use the following formula:

$$middle\; position = \frac{n+1}{2}$$

where n is the total amount of numbers in the data set.

- The **mode** is the number that appears most frequently in the data. If no number is repeated, then there is no mode. It is possible, however, to have more than one mode. The modes of the following numbers are 20 and 19 because they are the most frequently occurring numbers:

11, 14, 17, 18, 19, 19, 20, 20, 24

> *Memory Tip: Mode sounds like the word "most." It's the number that appears the most!*

- The **range** is the difference between the highest number in the data and the lowest number in the data. The range of the list below is 13 because $24 - 11 = 13$.

11, 14, 17, 18, 19, 19, 20, 20, 24

- An **outlier** is a number in the data set that is much higher or lower than the rest of the data. It can be computed mathematically, but the MCAS will not require you to do so. Outliers are often recognizable on scatterplots and line plots because they are separated from the rest of the data. Although both the median and the mean are considered measures of central tendency, the median is preferred when there are outliers, as outliers tend to skew the mean. There is further investigation of this in Example 3 and in the Displaying Data section of this chapter.

Examples: Statistics

Example 1. The mean of ten numbers is 80. When an 11th number is included, the mean changes to 76. What is the 11th number?

A. 36
B. 40
C. 52
D. 76

Solution

If ten numbers have a mean of 80, their sum is 800 because $\dfrac{ten\ numbers}{10} = 80$. Cross multiply and then *ten numbers* = 800. An 11th number, x, is added and the mean changes to 76:

$\dfrac{800 + x}{11} = 76$. Cross multiply and solve for x. $800 + x = 836 \rightarrow x = 36$.

Answer: A

Example 2. Michele monitored her weight gain during her pregnancy. The following table shows her weight at different times during her pregnancy:

Time	Weight in Pounds
End of first month	139
End of second month	141
End of third month	144
End of fourth month	149
End of fifth month	154
End of sixth month	160
End of seventh month	166
End of eighth month	172
End of ninth month	175

Based on the data in the table, what was the mean increase per month of Michele's weight gain?

A. 3.5 pounds
B. 4.5 pounds
C. 5.5 pounds
D. 6.5 pounds

Solution

First calculate Michele's weight gain between each month because the question is asking for the mean of those values: 2, 3, 5, 5, 6, 6, 6, 3. Then add them up and divide by 8 because there are 8 numbers: $\dfrac{2+3+5+5+6+6+6+3}{8} = \dfrac{36}{8} = 4.5$ pounds.

Answer: B

Example 3. Laura is comparing prices and needs to decide between two phone plans. The first plan has a fixed monthly fee and a lesser charge per minute than the second plan. The second plan has no fixed monthly fee but a greater charge per minute than the first plan.

Plan	Fixed Monthly Fee	Charge Per Minute
I	$ 20	$ 0.05
II	$ 0	$ 0.10

a. If Laura uses her phone for a total of 85 minutes for the month, how much will each plan cost? Which is the better deal? Show or explain how you got your answer.

b. If Laura uses her phone for a total of 506 minutes for the month, how much will each plan cost? Which is the better deal? Show or explain how you got your answer.

c. Laura decides to look at her past phone records to see how many minutes she used to predict how many she will need in the future in order to choose a plan. In the past ten months, her total minutes were 234, 345, 268, 356, 434, 210, 330, 323, 1,234, and 346. Find the mean number of minutes that Laura used over the past ten months, and use the mean to determine which phone plan she should choose. Show or explain how you got your answer.

d. In part c, the number 1,234 may be considered an outlier. Calculate the mean of the nine other numbers without 1,234. Does this new mean change which phone plan Laura should choose? Show or explain how you got your answer.

Solution

a. Plan I will cost 20 + (0.05) 85 = $24.25.
Plan II will cost (0.10) 85 = $8.50.
Plan II is the better deal.

Answer: Plan II

b. Plan I will cost 20 + (0.05)506 = $45.30.
Plan II will cost (0.10)506 = $50.60.
Plan I is the better deal.

Answer: Plan I

c. $\dfrac{234 + 345 + 268 + 356 + 434 + 210 + 330 + 323 + 1,234 + 346}{10} = \dfrac{4,080}{10} = 408$. If

Laura really averages 408 minutes a month, then Plan I will cost

20 + (0.05) 408 = $40.40.

Plan II will cost (0.10) 408 = $40.80. By a very small margin of 40 cents, Plan I would be the better deal.

Answer: Plan I

d. Instead of adding the numbers up again without 1,234, just subtract 1,234 from 4,080. $4{,}080 - 1{,}234 = 2{,}846$, and that is your new sum. When you divide this sum by 9, you will get $316.\overline{2}$. Because phone companies will charge for the full minute, we should treat partial minutes in our calculations as full minutes: $\dfrac{2{,}846}{9} \approx 317$. Plan I will cost $20 + (0.05)\,317 = \$35.85$. Plan II will cost $(0.10)\,317 = \$31.70$.

Plan II is the better deal. Yes, it changes which plan should be used. 1,234 appears to be an outlier, and it skews the data.

Answer: Plan II

Example 4. Duncan's relatives and friends all contributed a certain amount of money toward his birthday present for his 15th birthday. They decided to let him then take the total amount of money and buy his own gift. The following table shows the amount of money that Duncan received from the various amounts of people. Calculate the mean amount of money that each person contributed toward Duncan's gift.

Contribution to Duncan's Gift	Number of People
$ 3	3
$ 5	7
$ 8	12
$ 10	4
$ 15	2

A. $ 5.60
B. $ 7.50
C. $ 8.00
D $ 8.20

Solution

Don't fall into the trap of just averaging the values in this question. It is important that you recognize that there are different numbers of people who contributed $3, $5, and so on. If you were to list the data is would look as follows: 3, 3, 3, 5, 5, 5, 5, 5, 5, 5, 8, 8, 8, . . .

Remember that to average the data you are going to find the sum of all these numbers and divide by the total amount of numbers. Rather than listing all of the numbers, you can set up the mean as follows:

$$\frac{(3 \cdot 3) + (5 \cdot 7) + (8 \cdot 12) + (10 \cdot 4) + (15 \cdot 2)}{28} = \frac{9 + 35 + 96 + 40 + 30}{28} = \frac{210}{28} = \$7.50.$$

Answer: B

Example 5. The salaries of the 50 workers in a small law firm are listed in the table below. Find the median salary.

Salaries Per Year	Number of Workers
$ 40,000	4
$ 50,000	6
$ 65,000	9
$ 80,000	13
$ 100,000	18

Solution

Knowing that there are 50 workers, you can calculate the middle worker's position by using the formula $middle\ position = \dfrac{n+1}{2} = \dfrac{50+1}{2} = \dfrac{51}{2} = 25.5$. This is a decimal because there are an even number of data so there are two middle numbers. That the position is 25.5 tells us that we need to average the 25th and 26th worker's salaries. Counting down on the table, the 25th and 26th workers both earn $80,000, so the average of two salaries of $80,000 is still $80,000.

Answer: $80,000

Practice: Statistics

1. When Mr. Juarez goes shopping for CDs to add to his music collection, he finds the prices for eight CDs to be

   $ 9.95 $12.95 $15.75 $17.65
   $13.45 $16.25 $7.95 $17.95

   What is the range of these CD prices?

   A. $10.00
   B. $8.00
   C. $14.00
   D. $17.95

2. The mean salary of the 8 workers at Joey's Hardware is $9.00 per hour. One of the cashiers who had been making $7.00 an hour got a raise of $2.00 per hour. What is the new mean salary of the 8 workers?
   A. $7.00
   B. $9.25
   C. $10.00
   D. $11.00

3. Bobby is on the cross-country team and must run an average of 5 miles per day for the next five days to train for a meet. For the past four days, he ran 4.5, 6, 5.3, and 3.8 miles. How far must he run on the fifth day to average exactly 5 miles per day for the five-day period?

A. 5.4 miles
B. 5.6 miles
C. 5 miles
D. 4.8 miles

4. Mr. Olsen gave the same chemistry test to his two classes and listed their grades by class:

Period 1: 83%, 86%, 92%, 78%, 64%, 58%, 98%, 100%, 85%, 96%
Period 2: 81%, 92%, 65%, 52%, 92%, 80%, 80%, 90%

a. What is the mean grade for period 1? Show your work.

b. What is the mean grade for period 2? Show your work.

c. What is the mean grade for the two classes together? Round your answer to the nearest tenth. Show your work.

d. Is the mean grade for the two classes together closer to the mean grade for period 1 or the mean grade for period 2? Explain your reasoning.

5. The resting heart rate of five runners on a Cross Country Team are shown in the table below.

Team Member	Heart Rate (beats per minute)
Gerry	67
Kate	73
Michael	65
Craig	61
Nora	74

If Nora's resting heart rate decreases from 74 to 68, how will the median of the data be affected?

A. The median will decrease.
B. The median will stay the same.
C. The median will increase.
D. There is not enough information to determine the effect on the median.

6. The following table shows the height in inches of 21 girls in a high school class.

Height in Inches	Number of Students
59	1
60	1
61	1
62	4
63	4
64	0
65	3
66	1
67	4
68	0
69	0
70	0
71	1
72	1

What is the median height of this group of students?

A. 63 inches
B. 65 inches
C. 66 inches
D. 67 inches

7. Melissa went shoe shopping and bought one pair of sandals, and one pair of sneakers. The sandals cost $35.00. The average price for each pair of shoes was $27.50. How much did Melissa's sneakers cost?
A. $27.50
B. $24.00
C. $22.50
D. $20.00

8. The following table shows the maximum distances of the swings for 10 golfers in a tournament.

Golfer's Swing Distance

Player	Distance (yards)
1	203
2	206
3	210
4	227
5	234
6	240
7	240
8	257
9	268
10	273

If an eleventh player with a maximum swing distance of 280 yards were to enter the tournament, which of the following statistical measurements would stay the same?

A. Mean
B. Median
C. Mode
D. Range

9. The mean test score in a class of 20 students is 83. The mean test score in a class of 40 students is 95. What is the mean test score for all 60 students?
   A. 77.5
   B. 89
   C. 91
   D. 94

10. Jovi spends her weekends at the beach over the summer. She recorded the driving time of the trip from her house to the beach for five weekends in a row. Her results are shown in the chart below.

Driving Times to the Beach

Week	Time
1	1 hour, 50 minutes
2	2 hours, 15 minutes
3	2 hours, 5 minutes
4	2 hours, 30 minutes
5	2 hours, 10 minutes

Based on the data in the chart, which is closest to the mean driving time from Jovi's house to the beach?

A. 2 hours, 10 minutes
B. 2 hours, 6 minutes
C. 2 hours, 11 minutes
D. 2 hours, 17 minutes

11. In a senior statistics class, Jacob and Kylie wanted to sample 60 sophomores to record the amount of time they spend per week online. Their results are shown in the table below, rounded to the nearest hour.

Hours Spent Online per Week

Number of Hours Spent Online Per Week	Number of Sophomores
1	3
2	8
4	9
6	10
8	12
9	7
10	6
15	3
18	2

a. What number of hours per week spent online should the students report as the mode for the data?

b. Jacob claims that the median number of hours for this sample of students is 7, but Kylie disagreed. He said that the median was 8. With whom do you agree? Justify your answer.

c. Imagine that Jacob and Kylie had polled the entire 330 person sophomore class. Based on the results from their 60 person sample, what number of the total sophomore class would probably have reported spending 10 hours per week online? Show or explain how you obtained your answer.

Solutions to Practice: Statistics

1. To find the range of the CD prices, subtract the lowest price from the highest: $17.95 - 7.95 = \$10.00$.

   Answer: A

2. The sum of the hourly salaries of the 8 workers is $9 \cdot 8 = \$72$. Now, one of the workers has 2 more dollars added to his/her hourly wage so that the sum of the salaries is now 2 dollars more, or $74. The new mean salary is $\frac{74}{8} = \$9.25$.

   Answer: B

3. $\dfrac{sum\ of\ values}{number\ of\ values} = \dfrac{4.5 + 6 + 5.3 + 3.8 + x}{5} = 5 \rightarrow \dfrac{19.6 + x}{5} = 5 \rightarrow 19.6 + x = 25 \rightarrow x = 5.4.$

   Answer: A

4. a. $\dfrac{sum\ of\ values}{number\ of\ values} = \dfrac{83 + 86 + 92 + 78 + 64 + 58 + 98 + 100 + 85 + 96}{10} = \dfrac{840}{10} = 84$

   Answer: 84

   b. $\dfrac{sum\ of\ values}{number\ of\ values} = \dfrac{81 + 92 + 65 + 52 + 92 + 80 + 80 + 90}{8} = \dfrac{632}{8} = 79$

   Answer: 79

   c. $\dfrac{sum\ of\ values}{number\ of\ values} = \dfrac{840 + 632}{10 + 8} = \dfrac{1,472}{18} = 81.8$

   Answer: 81.8

   d. It is closer to the mean grade for period 1. The difference between 84 and 81.8 is 2.2, but the difference between 81.8 and 79 is 2.8.

   Answer: Period 1

5. The median will not change. The data in order is as follows: 61, 65, 67, 73, 74. The median is 67. If Nora's number changes to 68 and the list changes to: 61, 65, 67, 68, 73, the median is still 67 because Nora's rate is still above the median.

   Answer: B

6. Using the formula: *middle position* $= \dfrac{n+1}{2} = \dfrac{21+1}{2} = \dfrac{22}{2} = 11$, the 11th student's height is the median. Since the table is already arranged in order from least to greatest, you just need to count up to the 11th student. That student has a height of 63 inches.

Answer: A

7. $\dfrac{sum\ of\ values}{number\ of\ values} = \dfrac{35+x}{2} = 27.5 \rightarrow 35+x = 55 \rightarrow x = 20.$ You could also **use your answer choices** as a strategy to solve this problem. The numbers are simple enough to quickly add to 35 and divide by 2 and see which answer choice gives you an answer of $27.50.

Answer: D

8. A. False. The mean of the data would change because 280 is a higher number than any of the other player's swings so it would pull the mean slightly higher.
   B. False. The median would change because prior to the 11th player, the median was the average of the 5th and 6th players swings, which was 237. Once an 11th player is introduced, the median is the distance of the 6th player's swing, which is 240.
   C. True. The mode is still 240.
   D. False because the range changes from 70 when there are 10 players to 77 when there are 11 players.

Answer: C

9. $\dfrac{sum\ of\ values}{number\ of\ values} = \dfrac{(20 \cdot 83) + (40 \cdot 95)}{60} = \dfrac{1,660 + 3,800}{60} = \dfrac{5,460}{60} = 91.$

Answer: C

10. First, add up the total time traveled over the 5 week period. If you compute the hours and minutes separately, the sum of the hours is 9 and the sum of the minutes is 110. It is easier to compute the average of one unit, so convert your hours to minutes. The equivalent of 9 hours is $9 \cdot 60 = 540$ minutes. Add that to the 110 minutes and the total travel time was 650 minutes. Compute the average: $\dfrac{650}{5} = 130$. Two hours is the equivalent of 120 minutes so 130 minutes is the same thing as saying 2 hours and 10 minutes.

Answer: A

11. a. The mode is 8 hours spent online per week because 12 students reported spending that much time online. This is the most frequent reporting of hours spent online, or the most common amount of time.

Answer: 8

b. There are 60 students so the median is the mean of the 30th and 31st students' times. These times are 6 hours and 8 hours, so the mean is 7.

Answer: Jacob

c. Set up a proportion: $\dfrac{6}{60} = \dfrac{x}{330} \rightarrow \dfrac{1}{10} = \dfrac{x}{330} \rightarrow 10x = 330 \rightarrow x = 33.$

Answer: 33

Displaying Data

There are many methods of presenting statistical data. It is important that you be able to interpret the data from these displays as well as create them!

- A **box and whisker plot** uses the following five values in its display: **median, minimum, maximum, lower quartile,** and **upper quartile**. The minimum is the lowest value in the data set and the maximum is the highest number in the data set. As defined previously, the median is the middle of the data. Be sure to put the data in order from least to greatest. The lower quartile is the middle of the lower half of the data to the left of the median. It does not include the median. The upper quartile is the middle of the upper half of the data to the right of the median. It does not include the median. The upper and lower quartiles are like the medians of the upper and lower halves of the data.

To make a box and whisker plot start with an evenly spaced number line that displays the range of your data. Put points on the number line for the five values: minimum, lower quartile, median, upper quartile, and maximum.

Consider the following data set: 55, 73, 74, 75, 77, <u>81, 82,</u> 83, 90, 91, 96, 96

The minimum value is **55**. The maximum is **96**. There are an even amount of numbers so to find the median, you must average the two middle numbers, in this case 81 and 82. The median is **81.5**. The lower half of the data is 55, 73, <u>74, 75,</u> 77, 81. The median of the lower half of the data or lower quartile is **74.5**. The upper half of the data is 82, 83, <u>90, 91,</u> 96, 96. The median of the upper half of the data or upper quartile is **90.5**. Now, put the points on the number line but place the points above the number line in preparation for making the box and whisker.

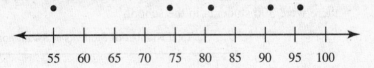

Next, make a box that connects the lower and upper quartiles and make a dividing segment through the median.

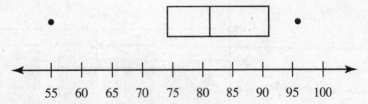

Finally, connect the minimum and maximum values with the lower and upper quartiles in a straight line. These are the whiskers.

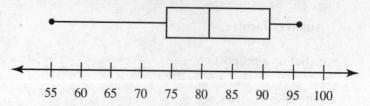

When you are given a box and whisker plot, you can answer questions about the range, median, top quarter of the data, and bottom quarter of the data.

• A **frequency table** contains events next to their frequency of occurrence. Making one of these tables can help you to tally or count up the frequency of an event. The intervals on your table should be of equal size.

• A **frequency histogram** is a bar graph in which data from a frequency table is displayed. The intervals should not overlap, and there should be no gaps between the bars. The frequency table and histogram below both display the same data for the number of people in each age group. The beginning of each interval marks the start of a new frequency.

Frequency Table for Ages 0–49

Interval	Tallies	Frequency
0–9	///	3
10–19	~~////~~	5
20–29	////	4
30–39	~~////~~ /	6
40–49	//	2

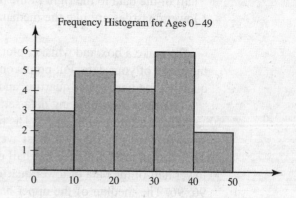

Frequency Histogram for Ages 0–49

• A **bar graph** uses separated bars to compare quantities. The bar graph below displays the student population at Swathmore High over a 5-year period. For example, in 2002 there were 300 students in the school.

Total Number of Students at Swathmore High

- A **line or dot plot** uses dots or x's to mark the quantity of a particular item in the data. The line plot below displays the numbers of each color marble in a bag. It shows that there are 4 reds, 1 green, 2 yellow, 4 purple, 6 orange, 3 blue, and 0 pink marbles.

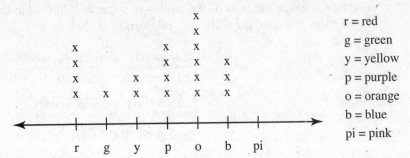

r = red
g = green
y = yellow
p = purple
o = orange
b = blue
pi = pink

Line plots are useful for tallying and providing simple visuals for smaller amounts of data.

- A **stem and leaf plot** separates the units digit from the rest of the number. The stem is the front of the number, and the leaf is the units digit. This way if you have lots of numbers in your data set that all begin the same way, you are only writing the beginning once, and differentiating them only by their endings. The number 23 will be written as follows:

stem   leaf
2 | 3

Now if you have the numbers 23, 23, 25, and 29 in the same data set, they would be displayed as follows:

2 | 3 3 5 9

The 2 is only written once. The 3 must be written twice to show that there are two 23's in the list. The numbers should be written in order from least to greatest. The following is a stem and leaf plot for the numbers: 56, 99, 87, 76, 58, 67, 99, 100, 72, 66, 65, 64, 83, 91, 70, 62, 100.

5	6	8			
6	2	4	5	6	7
7	0	2	6		
8	3	7			
9	1	9	9		
10	0	0			

Stem and leaf plots provide a simple visual for your data and make finding the median fairly simple since the list is ordered.

- A **circle graph or pie chart** displays the different parts of the data as sectors of a circle. All the sectors together make up the entire circle, which represents 100% of the data. The relative sizes of the sectors within a particular circle make it easy to compare data quickly. Since the sum of the angles of a circle is 360° and the entire circle represents 100% of the data, the following proportion is true:

$$\frac{central\ angle}{360} = \frac{percent\ of\ whole}{100}$$

Sam's Favorite TV Shows

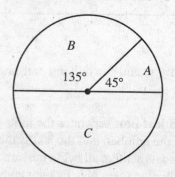

The circle graph above represents the total amount of time that Sam spends watching his favorite television shows.

The percent of the circle represented in sector A is

$$\frac{45}{360} = \frac{percent\ of\ whole}{100} \rightarrow \frac{1}{8} = \frac{x}{100} \rightarrow 8x = 100 \rightarrow x = \frac{100}{8} = 12.5\%$$

This means that 12.5% of Sam's TV watching is spent on television show A.

The percent of the circle represented in sector B is

$$\frac{135}{360} = \frac{percent\ of\ whole}{100} \rightarrow \frac{3}{8} = \frac{x}{100} \rightarrow 8x = 300 \rightarrow x = \frac{300}{8} = 37.5\%$$

Sector C is a semicircle so the central angle is 180°. Set up the proportion:

$$\frac{180}{360} = \frac{percent\ of\ whole}{100} \rightarrow \frac{1}{2} = \frac{x}{100} \rightarrow x = 50\%$$

Notice that 12.5% + 37.5% + 50% = 100%. The entire circle graph represents all of Sam's TV watching, which must be 100% of the data.

- A **scatterplot** displays the relationship between two variables as points on x- and y-axes. When the points are plotted on the scatterplot, the display allows us to see the trend in the data easily. If there is a relationship between the variables, it will stand out.

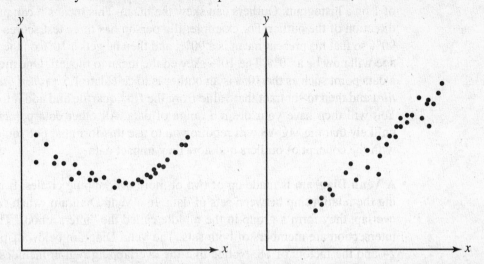

In the scatterplot on the left, the points are clustered in the shape of a parabola. This is useful in predicting information about the data. Suppose you want to know about an x value that is greater than those that are plotted on the graph. You could use your knowledge of quadratic functions and approximate the equation of the parabola and then substitute any value for x that you desire. Alternatively, and perhaps much more easily, you could make a rough sketch of a parabola that is near as many of the points on the scatterplot as possible and then use it to approximate further values of x on that curve.

The MCAS will often ask a question about the line of best fit. This pertains to a scatterplot whose trend is linear. This means that the points are clustered in the form of a line. This will look like the scatterplot on the above right. To answer these questions, sketch a line that is as close to as many points as possible. One useful strategy is to try to get approximately as many points above the line as below the line. Observe the line of best fit in the diagram below.

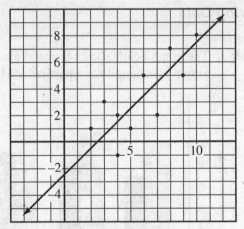

The MCAS questions may come in multiple-choice format asking which equation best represents the line of best first for a particular data set. For these questions, once you have made a sketch, you can use your y intercept and slope to eliminate answer choices.

- An **outlier** is a data point that falls far away from the cluster of values in your data set. You may notice that a point is an outlier because it is far away from the other points on a scatterplot or dot plot. The value may be alone on a stem and leaf plot or have a height of 1 on a histogram. Outliers can skew the mean. This means it can pull the mean in the direction of the outlier. For example, if a person has three test scores of 90%, 90%, and 90% so that his present mean is a 90%, and then he gets a 10% on the next test, his average will now be a 70%. The 10% skewed the mean to the left. One method to verify that a data point such as the 10% is an outlier is to calculate 1.5 • (*third quartile – first quartile*) and then to subtract that value from the first quartile and add it to the third quartile. You will then have your desired range of data. All other data points are outliers. It is unlikely that the MCAS will require you to use this formula, but you should be familiar with the concept of outliers and how they impact data.

- A **Venn Diagram** is made up of two or more overlapping circles. It is helpful in showing the relationship between sets of data. In a Venn Diagram, when two or more circles overlap, they form a group in the middle called the "intersection." The elements in the intersection are members of both sets. The Venn Diagram below displays the factors of 24 and the factors of 18. Notice that the overlapping region includes the numbers that are factors of both numbers.

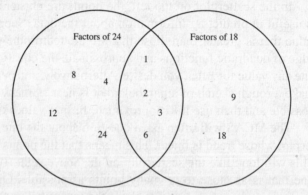

Examples: Displaying Data

Example 1. The graph below shows the total amount of rainfall and snow in inches over a four-year period for a particular Massachusetts town.

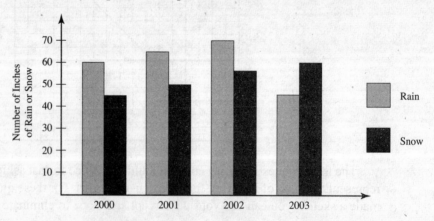

Which of the following is closest the median amount of rainfall over the four-year period?

A. 52 inches
B. 60 inches
C. 63.5 inches
D. 69 inches

Solution

The correct answer is C. The amounts of rainfall in each year are approximately 60, 67, 70, and 44. To find the median, put the numbers in order from least to greatest (44, 60, 67, 70). Because there are an even amount of numbers, you should average the two middle numbers: $\frac{60 + 67}{2} = 63.5$.

Answer: C

Example 2. The box and whisker plot below represents the distribution of scores from a recent English test for Ethan's class.

Test Scores

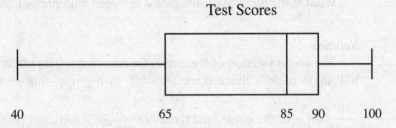

40	65	85	90	100

Ethan's score was in the top 25% of the class, but it was not the highest score. Write a numerical score that could be Ethan's score.

Solution

The box and whisker separates the scores into the lowest 25% (to the left of the box), middle 50% (in the box), and the top 25% (to the right of the box). Any score that is greater than or equal to 90 and less than 100 would be in the top 25%.

Answer: $90 \le x < 100$

Example 3. The box and whisker plot below represents the number of inches of snow that fell across the state of Massachusetts during a particular snow storm.

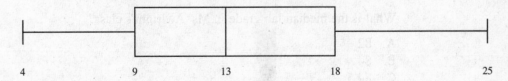

4	9	13	18	25

What is the range of the data?

A. 9 inches
B. 13 inches
C. 16 inches
D. 21 inches

Solution

The range is the difference between the highest and lowest amounts. These are located at the ends of the whiskers, so the range = 25 – 4 = 21 inches.

Answer: D

Example 4. The circle graph below shows the musical preferences of 1,080 Americans.

Musical Preferences

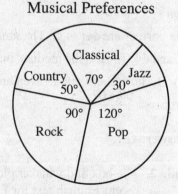

What is the number of Americans sampled who prefer Country music?

Solution

The sector (section of the circle) for Americans who prefer Country music, has a central angle of 50°. Since there are 360° in a circle, this sector represents the fraction $\frac{50°}{360°} = \frac{5}{36}$ of the circle, and therefore $\frac{5}{36}$ of Americans prefer country music. Set up a proportion: $\frac{5}{36} = \frac{x}{1,080} \rightarrow 36x = 5,400 \rightarrow x = 150$ Americans.

Answer: 150

Example 5. The stem and leaf plot below shows the grades on a lab in Ms. Awlright's chemistry class.

9	0 0 3 6 8
8	2 2 4 5 5 6 6 8 9
7	3 4 6 7 9
6	2 7
5	5

What is the median lab grade in Ms. Awlright's class?

A. 82
B. 84
C. 84.5
D. 85

Solution

The median is the score that falls in the middle of the ordered list. Let n be the number of scores. There are $n = 22$ scores. To find the entry in the middle, use the formula

$$middle\ position = \frac{n+1}{2} = \frac{22+1}{2} = 11.5$$

Since there are an even number of scores, the middle falls between two values. The median is therefore the average of the scores in the 11th and 12th positions.

$$median = \frac{84+85}{2} = 84.5$$

Answer: C

Example 6. A recent sleep study tracked the number of hours of sleep of its participants for two weeks. The line plots below show the results for four of its participants.

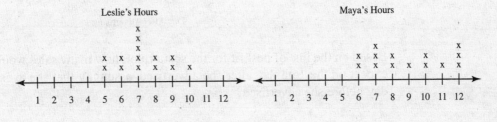

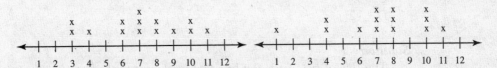

If all of the data were combined onto one line plot, what would be the mode?

A. 6
B. 7
C. 8
D. 9

Solution

The mode is the most frequently appearing number. Count the combined x's on each number and compare. There are 14 x's on the number 7. (The second highest is 9 x's on the number 8.) This makes 7 the mode.

Answer: B

Example 7. The owner of an appliance store recorded the number of daily sales after advertising over the Internet. The following scatterplot shows the results.

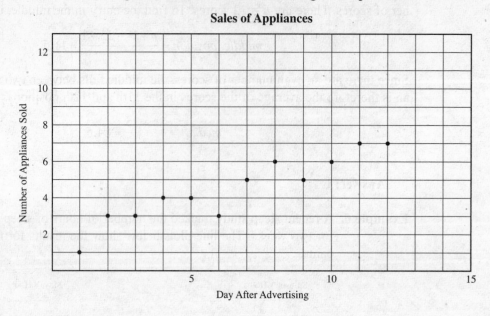

Sales of Appliances

Based on the line of best fit for the scatterplot, how many sales would the store owner expect on the 15th day after she advertised, assuming that she averaged one sale per day before she advertised?

A. 6
B. 7
C. 9
D. 12

Solution

The line of best fit is the line that is closest to the data points. It is the line with the minimum distance between the points and the line itself. If you assume that the store owner averages one sale a day before she advertised, then the y-intercept of your line is the point $(0, 1)$. The graph below shows the line representing 7 sales on the 15th day. Notice that the majority of points fall above the line. This means the estimate is too low. This rules out both answer choices A and B.

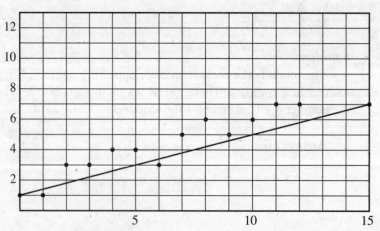

The next line represents 12 sales on the 15th day. Now the majority of points fall below the line. This means the estimate is too high. This rules out answer choice D.

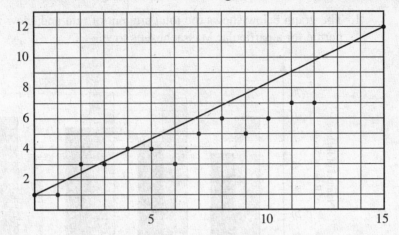

Finally, the line showing 9 sales on the 15th day fits roughly in the middle, and is therefore the best answer choice. Remember, **process of elimination** is a useful test-taking strategy!

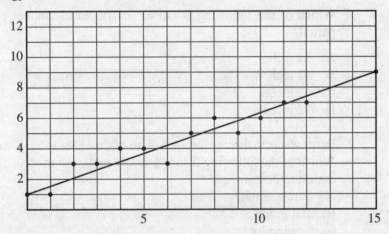

Answer: C

Practice: Displaying Data

1. The graph below shows the total amount of rain and snow in inches over a four-year period for a particular Massachusetts town.

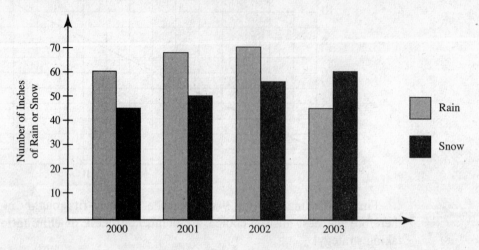

Which of the following is closest to the mean amount of snow over the four-year period?

A. 42 inches
B. 52 inches
C. 62 inches
D. 72 inches

2. Barry wants to display the ages of all of the U.S. Open champions for the past 40 years. Which of the following displays would make the median age of the tennis champions easiest to determine?
A. Circle graph
B. Bar graph
C. Scatterplot
D. Box and whisker plot

3. Antonio's weekly supplemental income varies between the values of $100 and $600. The bar graph below displays the number of weeks in which he earned each of the amounts shown.

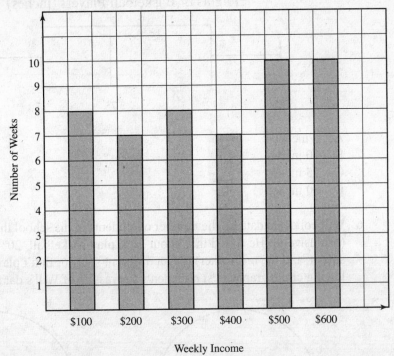

Weekly Income

Based on the bar graph, what is Antonio's median weekly supplemental income?

A. $300
B. $400
C. $500
D. $600

4. The bar graph shows the number of hours per week each of eight teenagers spend watching television.

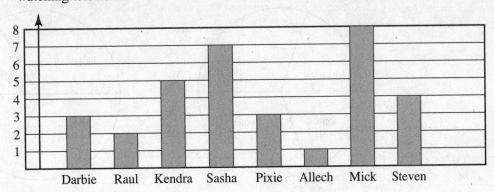

What is the median number of hours per week that these teenagers watch television?

A. 3
B. 3.5
C. 4
D. 4.5

5. The box and whisker plot below shows the heights of basketball players in a certain league. What is the range of the heights?

Heights of Basketball Players (inches)

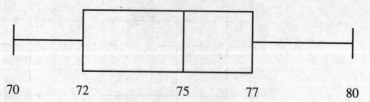

A. 5 inches
B. 10 inches
C. 75 inches
D. 80 inches

6. Will collected data on the number of students in his school that play each type of sport (exclusively). He found that about 20% play basketball, 20% play softball, 30% play soccer, and the rest (other) play a different sport or don't play at all. Which of the following circle graphs best represents the results of Will's data collection?

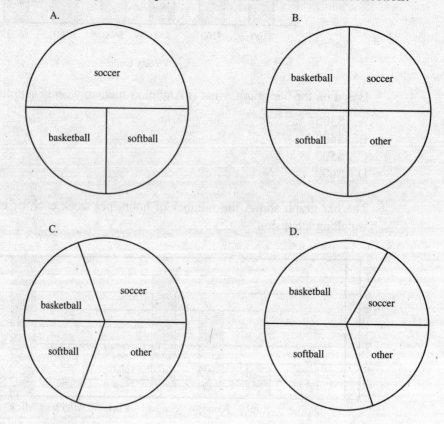

7. The box and whisker plot below shows the starting salaries for employees in a small company.

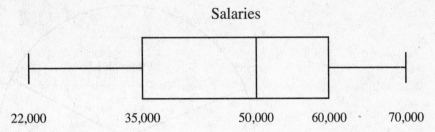

Salaries

22,000   35,000   50,000   60,000   70,000

What is the range of the starting salaries?

A. $ 20,000
B. $ 25,000
C. $ 48,000
D. $ 50,000

8. A class of 20 students is asked to determine approximately how much time the average student spends watching television during a one-week period. Each student is to ask one of his/her friends for the information, making sure that no one student is asked more than once. The reported hours spent watching television per week are as follows:

30, 0, 14, 10, 3, 7, 9, 12, 11, 3, 1, 2, 8, 32, 15, 3, 9, 7, 8, 19

a. Find the mean, median, and mode for these data. Explain or show how you found each answer.

b. Based on this sample, which measure (or measures) that you found in part a best describes the number of hours of TV watched by the typical student? Explain your reasoning.

c. Describe a sampling procedure that would have led to more representative data.

9. The box and whisker plot below shows the number of compact discs owned by a sample of teenagers. What is the median number of compact disks owned by the teenagers in this sample?

Number of Compact Discs

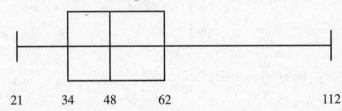

21   34   48   62   112

A. 48
B. 50
C. 55
D. 62

10. The circle graph below represents the ages of the students at Bogota Tennis Club. The degree measures of each sector are given.

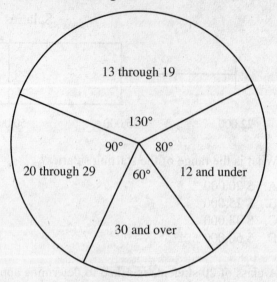

Which of the following is closest to the percent of students whose ages are 30 and over?

A. 17%
B. 20%
C. 30%
D. 60%

11. Mr. Brown displayed the most recent scores for his students in Spanish class using the stem and leaf plot below.

4	6
5	9
6	0 0 1 3 7 7
7	1 2 5 6
8	6 7 8 8 8 9 9
9	0 4
10	0

Note: 8 | 6 = 86

The median student score is

A. 75
B. 75.5
C. 76
D. 81

12. On the varsity soccer team at Columbia High School, there are 1 freshman, 3 sopho-mores, 8 juniors, and 12 seniors. If Kevin made a circle graph for the breakdown of people on the team by class year, what should he make the measure of the central angle for the number of sophomores on the team?
   A. 3°
   B. 8°
   C. 24°
   D. 45°

13. A recent poll asked 2,000 high school students if they prefer to do their homework with music, television, or just quiet in the background. The circle graph shows the results of the poll.

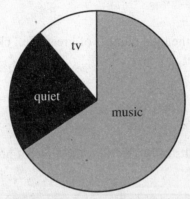

Which of the following is closest to the number of people polled who prefer to have the television on in the background?

   A. 330
   B. 500
   C. 1,000
   D. 1,200

14. A group of students at lunchtime wanted to find out how many potato chips were inside a snack-size bag. The results for the number of chips in each bag are shown below.

10, 9, 12, 14, 8, 12, 11, 12, 10, 9, 13, 16, 10

   a. Determine the range of the data. Show or explain how you got your answer.

   b. Determine the median of the data. Show or explain how you got your answer.

   c. Construct a box and whisker plot that displays the data the students collected. Be sure to label the median, the upper and lower extremes, and the lower (first) and upper (third) quartiles.

   d. Based on the results of the sampling experiment, how many potato chips can some-one expect to get in a bag? Explain your reasoning.

15. The circle graph shows the colors of 720 gum balls in a machine.

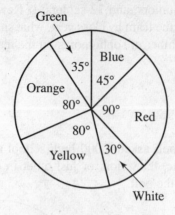

What is the total number of green gum balls?

A. 60
B. 70
C. 80
D. 160

16. The results of Mr. Carter's most recent history test are as follows:

Letter Grade	Number of Students Receiving the Grade
A	5
B	18
C	5
D	7
F	2

Based on the information in the chart, which of the following statements is false?

A. The median score is a B.
B. The median score is a C.
C. Less than 15% of the students got an A.
D. Over 75% scored A, B, or C.

17. The following chart shows the ages of a group taking a bike tour.

22	20	30	45	54	28
44	26	34	31	36	58
31	29	23	48	33	26

Marketers doing research for the touring company constructed a histogram of the tourists' ages. Which of the following histograms best represents the distribution of ages?

A.

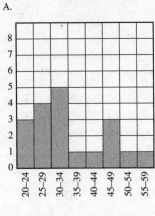

B.

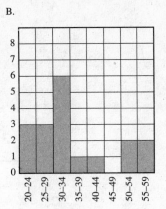

C.

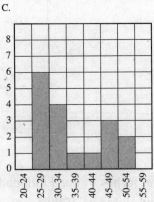

D.

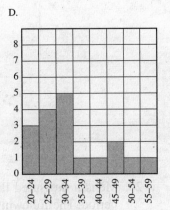

18. A recent sleep study tracked the number of hours of sleep of its participants for two weeks. The line plots show the results for four of its participants.

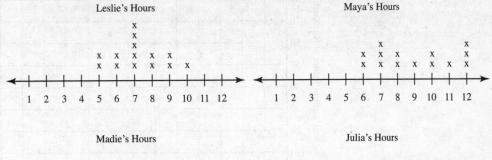

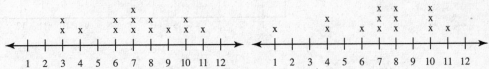

Which person's range of hours of sleep was the greatest?

A. Leslie
B. Maya
C. Madie
D. Julia

19. Which of the following scatterplots below would be best represented by a line of best fit (trend line) with the following equation?

$$y = 3$$

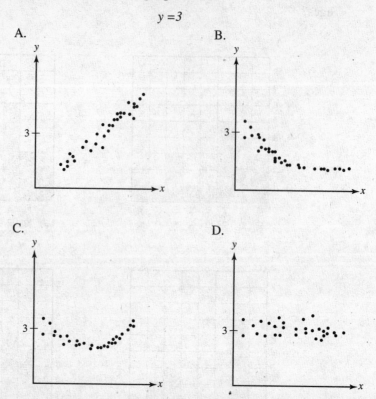

20. Melissa measured the height in inches of her Floribunda rosebush over a ten-week period. The following scatterplot shows the results.

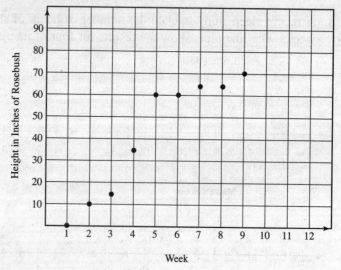

Based on a line of best fit for the scatterplot, approximately how tall can Melissa expect the rosebush to be at week 10?

A. 60 inches
B. 70 inches
C. 90 inches
D. 100 inches

21. The Venn Diagram below represents the relationship between willies, sklimpies, crimpies, and trimpies in Imaginaryland.

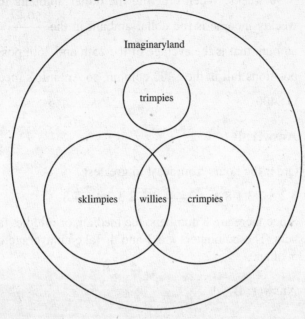

Which of the following statements is incorrect?

A. Every sklimpy is a willy.
B. Every willy is a crimpy.
C. No trimpy is a sklimpy.
D. No crimpy is a trimpy.

Solutions to Practice: Displaying Data

1. The correct answer in B. The amounts of snow in each year are approximately, 44, 50, 55, and 60. To find the mean, or average, of these values, add them up and divide by how many values there are. So, $44 + 50 + 55 + 60 = 209$. In this case, there are four numbers, so $\frac{209}{4} \approx 52$.

   Answer: B

2. The median age is the number in the middle of the data. Because the median is represented and labeled in the middle of a box and whisker plot, it would be easiest to determine the median from this display.

   Answer: D

3. First, count the total number of weeks that Antonio worked: $8 + 7 + 8 + 7 + 10 + 10 = 50$ weeks. When ordering the dollar amounts from least to greatest, the median weekly income is the dollar amount in the $\frac{50+1}{2} = 25.5$ position. This is the dollar amount that is the average of the 25th and 26th positions. Both the 25th and the 26th positions fall in the $400 column, so Antonio's median weekly supplemental income is $400.

Answer: B

4. Order the hours from least to greatest:

3 2 5 7 3 1 8 4 $\xrightarrow{\ ordered\ }$ 1 2 3 3 4 5 7 8

Since there are 8 numbers, the median, or middle, falls between the 4th and 5th numbers. These numbers are 3 and 4. Take an average of 3 and 4 to get 3.5 hours as the median.

Answer: B

5. The range is the difference between the highest and the lowest heights. Computing the range you get $80 - 70 = 10$ inches.

Answer: B

6. Answer choice C is correct. Compare the answer choices to the percents given in the problem. Choice A shows one half or 50% playing soccer, and is wrong. Choice B shows a circle equally divided into four parts, or 25% for each sport and so is wrong. Since students play soccer at a slightly higher percentage than those who play basketball (30% versus 20%), choice D is also incorrect.

Answer: C

7. The range is the difference between the highest and lowest salaries. These are located at the ends of the whiskers, so *range* = $70,000 − $22,000 = $48,000.

Answer: C

8. a. Computing the mean: $\dfrac{sum\ of\ values}{number\ of\ values} = \dfrac{203}{20} \approx 10.15$ hours

Answer: mean = 10.15 hr

The median is the number that falls in the middle of data, when it is ordered from least to greatest or vice versa. First order the data.

0, 1, 2, 3, 3, 3, 7, 7, 8, 8, 9, 9, 10, 11, 12, 14, 15, 19, 30, 32

Then cross off the smallest and highest values together, until one number remains in the middle.

0̸, 1̸, 2̸, 3̸, 3̸, 3̸, 7̸, 7̸, 8̸, (8, 9,) 9̸, 1̸0̸, 1̸1̸, 1̸2̸, 1̸4̸, 1̸5̸, 1̸9̸, 3̸0̸, 3̸2̸

If two numbers are left in the middle, average these values.

$$\text{median} = \frac{8+9}{2} = 8.5$$

Answer: median = 8.5 hr

The mode is the most frequently appearing number. From the ordered list, it is clear that it is the number 3, which appears three times.

Answer: mode = 3 hr

b. The median is preferred when there are extremely low or extremely high data values, called outliers, as outliers tend to skew the mean. The values of 30 and 32 are considerably larger than the rest; they are considered outliers. This makes the median a more representative measure of central tendency and a better indicator of how many hours of TV were watched by a typical student. (Incidentally, the mode of 3 is not representative of the typical student because the vast majority of the teenagers surveyed watched more than 3 hours.)

Answer: Median

c. Large random samples usually make better sampling procedures. Making a sample larger is often not enough. The sample must also be random. The fact that the teenagers asked their friends may have made the sample biased. For example, if all of their friends had similar habits, their sample excludes students with different habits and pastimes. A better sampling procedure would be to ask random students, perhaps of different ages, in different locations throughout the school (students spending free time in the library may have different television watching habits than students spending free time in the cafeteria), teenagers from different schools, with different socioeconomic backgrounds, in different states, etc.

Answers may vary.

9. The median is the number located by the bar inside the box. In this case, that number is 48.

Answer: A

10. The sector (section of the circle) for students 30 and over, has a central angle of 60°. Since there are 360° in a circle, this sector represents the fraction $\frac{60°}{360°} = \frac{1}{6}$ of the circle, and therefore $\frac{1}{6}$ of the students. As a decimal, $1 \div 6 = 0.166 \approx 0.17$ or roughly 17%.

Answer: A

11. The median is the score that falls in the middle of the ordered list. Let n be the number of scores. There are $n = 22$ scores. To find the entry in the middle, use the formula

$$middle\ position = \frac{n+1}{2} = \frac{22+1}{2} = 11.5$$

Since there are an even number of scores, the middle falls between two values. The median is therefore the average of the scores in the 11th and 12th positions.

$$median = \frac{75+76}{2} = 75.5$$

Answer: B

12. First, find the fraction of the team that are sophomores, and then multiply that by the 360° in a circle. The fraction of the team that are sophomores is

$$\frac{number\ of\ sophomores}{total\ number\ of\ players} = \frac{3}{1+3+8+12} = \frac{3}{24} = \frac{1}{8}$$

Multiplying this by 360° to get the central angle, you get: $\frac{1}{8} \cdot 360° = 45°$.

Answer: D

13. You will have to estimate what fraction of the circle is represented by the sector labeled "tv" and multiply that by 2000. You could do this by drawing in sectors of roughly the same size, and estimate the number of them that would complete one circle. This is shown below:

Since there are about 6, estimate that $\frac{1}{6}$ of the students prefer television in the background. Multiplying this fraction by 2,000, you get $\frac{1}{6} \cdot 2000 = 333.\overline{33} \approx 330$.

Answer: A

14. a. The range is the difference between the highest and lowest numbers.

$$range = 16 - 8 = 8\ chips$$

Answer: 8

b. The median is the number that falls in the middle of data, when it is ordered from least to greatest or vice versa. First order the data. Then cross off the smallest and highest values together, until one number remains in the middle. If two numbers are left in the middle, average these values by adding them and dividing by 2. For an odd number of data entries, such as in this problem, only one number will be left in the middle.

$$8, 9, 9, 10, 10, 10, \textcircled{11}, 12, 12, 12, 13, 14, 16$$

Answer: 11

c. Find the five-number summary for the data. Q1, or the first quartile, is the first quarter of the data, or the median of the first half of the data. Q3, or the third quartile, is the third quarter of the data, or the median of the second half of the data.

> Low: 8
> Q1: 9.5
> Median: 11
> Q3: 12.5
> High: 16

Next arrange these numbers on an equally spaced number line, so that you can see the spread.

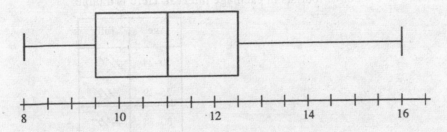

d. Both the median and the mean are considered to be measures of central tendency. The median is preferred when there are extremely low or extremely high data values, called outliers, as outliers tend to skew the mean. Either answer would be sufficient here. Computing the mean, or average, you get

$$mean = \frac{sum\ of\ values}{number\ of\ values} = \frac{146}{13} \approx 11.23$$

Round this number to the nearest whole number to get 11 chips. Both the mean and the median are the same.

Answer: 11

15. The sector (section of the circle) for green gum balls has a central angle of 35°. Since there are 360° in a circle, this sector represents the fraction $\frac{35}{360}$ of the circle, and therefore $\frac{35}{360}$ of the gum balls. Multiplying this fraction by 720, you get $\frac{35}{360} \cdot \frac{720}{1} = 70$ green gum balls.

Answer: B

16. It is impossible for both answer choices A and B to be true! Using **process of elimination,** you can already eliminate answer choices C and D because of the fact that choices A and B cannot both be true. The number of students who took the test is 37, so the middle score is determined using the formula:

$$middle\ position = \frac{n+1}{2} = \frac{37+1}{2} = 19.$$

The first 5 students got A's and the next 18 got B's, which means that the 19th student received a B.

Answer: B

17. You may wish to make either a table or a line plot to help you tally, or count, the number of tourists in each age interval. Here is a table:

Age	Tally
20–24	///
25–29	////
30–34	//////
35–39	/
40–44	/
45–49	//
50–54	/
55–59	/

The bar graph in part D is a match to the data.

Answer: D

18. Julia has the greatest range of hours of sleep. She has the greatest difference between her maximum and minimum number of hours of sleep. Her range is $11 - 1 = 10$ hours.

    Answer: D

19. The line of best fit is the line that goes through the majority of the data points. The line $y = 3$ is the horizontal line shown below.

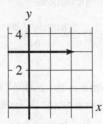

    The scatterplot whose points most closely follow this trend is choice D.

    Answer: D

20. Draw in a line that goes through the middle of the set of data points. You don't necessarily need to go through any points, you just need to minimize, or balance, the gaps between the data and the line.

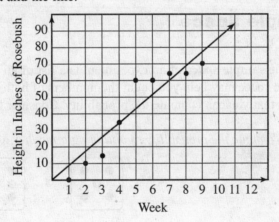

    From this diagram, you can estimate that at week 10, the height of the rosebush will be approximately 90 inches.

    Answer: C

21. Answer choice A is the only incorrect statement, and is therefore the answer to the question. In a Venn Diagram, when two circles overlap, they form a group in the middle called an intersection. The elements in the intersection are members of both sets. In this diagram, willies are members of the sets of both sklimpies and crimpies, so answer choice B is correct. In a Venn Diagram, when two circles do not overlap, they are called mutually exclusive, which means that nobody can be a member of both sets. Since trimpies are separated from everybody else, statements C and D are correct.

    Answer: A

Probability

- **Probability** is a measure of the likelihood of an event occurring. Probabilities may be expressed as either ratios, decimals, or percents. If an event or occurrence is impossible, the probability of it happening is 0. If an event or occurrence must happen, its probability is 1. All other probabilities are ratios or decimals between 0 and 1. The greater the ratio, the greater the probability or likelihood of the occurrence. As a ratio, the probability of event A happening is

$$P(A) = \frac{number\ of\ successful\ or\ favorable\ outcomes}{number\ of\ possible\ outcomes}$$

- A **favorable outcome** is the event or occurrence for which you are finding the probability. For example, if you want to find the probability of picking an orange marble from a bag full of marbles, the number of favorable outcomes would be the number of orange marbles in the bag. The total number of possible outcomes would be the total number of the marbles in the bag.

  It is important to note that the word favorable is used in a different context than you are used to. It is not necessarily something you might want. For example, you can compute the probability of selecting a rotten apple from a barrel. Here, the act of selecting a rotten apple would be considered a favorable outcome!

Listing Sample Space

- The **sample space** of an experiment is a list of all possible outcomes. Listing the sample space may help you count the numbers of both the favorable and possible outcomes so that you can compute the probability. Consider the following question:

  Compute the probability of obtaining a number greater than 4 on one roll of a die.

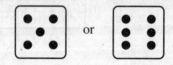

Step 1: List the sample space: 1   2   3   4   5   6

Step 2: Circle the favorable outcomes: 1   2   3   4   ⑤   ⑥

Step 3: Compute the probability:

$$P(greater\ than\ 4) = \frac{number\ of\ favorable\ outcomes}{number\ of\ possible\ outcomes} = \frac{2}{6} = \frac{1}{3}$$

Notice that the fraction is reduced. You could also express the probability as $0.\overline{33}$ or $33.\overline{33}\%$.

It is important that the die in this example is fair, which means that no number is more likely than the others. For the MCAS, you should assume that events are fair, unless there is information in the problem to the contrary.

Adding Probabilities

- In the previous example, notice that the probability of getting either a 5 or a 6 on one toss is equal to the sum of their probabilities. In other words: $P(5 \text{ or } 6) = P(5) + P(6) = \frac{1}{6} + \frac{1}{6} = \frac{2}{6} = \frac{1}{3}$.

In general: $P(A \text{ or } B) = P(A) + P(B)$.

The Sum of Probabilities and Complements

- The sum of the probabilities of all the different outcomes in a single trial or experiment is always equal to 1. For example, consider the different probabilities for selecting a single marble from the bag below:

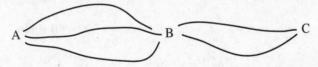

● = gray

● = black

○ = white

$P(\text{gray}) = \frac{4}{9}$

$P(\text{black}) = \frac{3}{9}$

$+ P(\text{white}) = \frac{2}{9}$

$P(\text{gray}) + P(\text{black}) + P(\text{white}) = \frac{9}{9} = 1$

- The **complement** of the probability of an event happening is simply the probability that it won't happen. The sum of a probability and its complement is 1.

In general: $P(A) + P(\text{not } A) = 1$.

Counting Principle

- The **counting principle** states that the total number of ways a multipart event can occur is the product of the number of ways that the individual parts can happen. Consider the next example:

How many ways can you travel from A to C if you must pass through point B?

You could trace each different path and count that there are six possible ways, or you could multiply the number of ways to get from A to B times the number of ways to get from B to C.

Answer: 3 • 2 = 6

The counting principle can help you determine the size of your sample space without listing it all out. You will see this in Example 1 in this section.

Permutations and Combinations

- In determining the size of your sample space, you should determine whether or not order matters. For example, ask yourself if *AB* is the same result as *BA*. When a different order means a different outcome it is called a **permutation**. When a different order does not mean a different outcome, it is called a **combination**. For example, count your sample space for the problems *a* and *b* involving three girls: Amy, Betsey, and Callie.

  a. How many ways can you line two of them up at a door?

  AB   BA   CA
  AC   BC   CB

  (Answer: 6)

  b. How many groups can you form with two of the girls?

  AB   BC
  AC

  (Answer: 3)

  Part *a* is a permutation. The order *Amy* then *Betsey*, is different than *Betsey* then *Amy*. List each.

  Part *b* is a combination. The pair *Amy* and *Betsey* is the same as *Betsey* and *Amy*. List once.

Expected Value

- **Expected value** is the number of times you would expect an event *A* to occur after *n* repeated trials. To calculate the expected value, simply multiply the probability of event *A* by the number of trials, *n*.

  In general: **Expected Value = P(A) • n.**

  For example, to find the number of times you would expect a 4 to land upon 300 tosses of a die, multiply:

  $$\frac{1}{6} \cdot 300 = 50 \text{ times}$$

Compound Probabilities

- The probability of a specific outcome from a combined trial or a multipart event is considered a **compound probability**. This occurs when you want to find the probabilities of more than one thing happening simultaneously, or the probability of getting a desired result after repeated trials. If an event consists of more than one trial and the outcome of the first trial does not affect the probability of the second, you can multiply the probabilities of each event together to get the final probability.

  In general: $P(A \text{ and } B) = P(A) \cdot P(B)$.

> **Remember: You can only multiply the probability of the first event times the second event for the final probability because the outcome of the first does not change the probability of the outcome of the second!*

Independent and Dependent Events

- If the outcome of one event does not effect the outcome of the second, they are called **independent events**. Sometimes in probabilities of repeated trials, the outcome of the first trial does effect the outcome of the second. In this case, they are called **dependent events**.

Tree Diagrams

- With repeated trials, listing the sample space may get tricky. Using a **Tree Diagram** may help. It is a graphic that helps you see all the possible outcomes. List the possible results of each trial in a separate row. Then count the number of "branches" at the end of the tree. This is the size of your sample space, or the number of possible outcomes. Consider the next example:

Compute the probability of getting the number 5 on one toss of a die, and then obtaining a head on one flip of a coin.

$$P(5 \text{ then } H) =$$

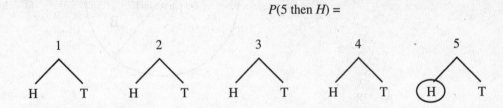

Notice the first row shows all the possible outcomes for the toss of the die. The second row shows the possible outcomes for flipping a coin, underneath each outcome for the die. The final sample space is the last row in the tree, and here includes 12 possible outcomes. There is only one way to get first a 5 and then a head, making $P(5, H) = \dfrac{1}{12}$.

Since this event consists of more than one trial, in this case two trials, one a toss and then a flip, you can multiply the probabilities of each event together to get the final probability.

$$P(5 \text{ and } H) = P(5) \cdot P(H) = \frac{1}{6} \cdot \frac{1}{2} = \frac{1}{12}$$

Remembering this will make probability problems easier because you will not have to list sample spaces or draw tree diagrams.

Examples: Probability

Example 1. How many ways can four out of five people be seated on a four-seat bench?

Solution

Use the counting principle to fill in the blanks. Do not try to list the sample space as it is too large and time consuming. Start by filling in the first blank with the number of ways you can fill the first seat. After that seat is filled, count the number of ways to fill the second seat, and so on. Then, multiply these numbers.

$$\underset{\substack{1^{st} \\ \text{seat}}}{5} \cdot \underset{\substack{2^{nd} \\ \text{seat}}}{4} \cdot \underset{\substack{3^{rd} \\ \text{seat}}}{3} \cdot \underset{\substack{4^{th} \\ \text{seat}}}{2} = 120 \text{ ways}$$

Answer: 120

Example 2. The spinner for a certain board game is shown below. If you spin the arrow 144 times, which of the following is the most likely number of times you would expect to land on the letter C?

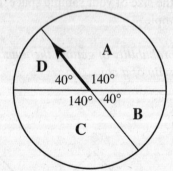

A. 28
B. 56
C. 60
D. 84

Solution

This is an expected value problem. You need to multiply the probability of landing on a C, by the number of times you spin the spinner: Expected Value = $P(C) \cdot 144$. The probability of landing on a section is determined by the measure of the central angle. Compute the probability by expressing the measure of the central angle as a fraction of 360°. Since the central angle for the letter C is 140°, the probability is $\frac{140}{360}$. Multiply this by the number of times you spin the arrow to get the number of times you would expect to land on the letter C: $\frac{140}{360} \cdot 144 = 56$ times.

Answer: B

Example 3. Compute the probability of tossing four dice and obtaining a 5 on each one.

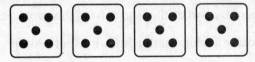

Solution

Using the fact that $P(A \text{ and } B) = P(A) \cdot P(B)$ for any number of repeated trials,

$$P(5, 5, 5, 5) = P(5) \cdot P(5) \cdot P(5) \cdot P(5) = \frac{1}{6} \cdot \frac{1}{6} \cdot \frac{1}{6} \cdot \frac{1}{6} = \left(\frac{1}{6}\right)^4 = \frac{1}{1,296}.$$

Answer: $\dfrac{1}{1,296}$

Example 4. Imagine flipping a coin three times in a row.

a. Find the probability of tossing exactly one head.

b. Find the probability of tossing at least one head.

c. Find the probability of tossing a head on the first toss.

Solution

First list the sample space for flipping a coin three times:

$$\begin{array}{cc} HHH & TTT \\ HHT & TTH \\ HTH & THT \\ HTT & THH \end{array}$$

There are eight possible outcomes. The slightly different questions result in different probabilities. Remember that a favorable outcome is the event for which you are finding a probability. Simply count the number of favorable outcomes for each.

a. There are three ways of getting exactly one head.

Answer: $\dfrac{3}{8}$

b. There are seven ways of getting at least one head.

Answer: $\dfrac{7}{8}$

c. There are four ways of getting a head on the first toss.

Answer: $\dfrac{1}{2}$

Example 5. Find the probability of reaching into the bag below and pulling out a marble that is not white.

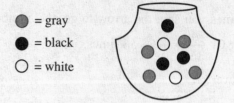

● = gray

● = black

○ = white

Solution

There are two methods to solving this problem. The first is to subtract the probability of choosing a white marble from 1: $P(\text{not white}) = 1 - P(\text{white}) = 1 - \dfrac{2}{9} = \dfrac{7}{9}$. An alternative method is to add the probabilities of choosing a black or gray marble: $P(\text{not white}) = P(\text{black}) + P(\text{gray}) = \dfrac{3}{9} + \dfrac{4}{9} = \dfrac{7}{9}$.

Answer: $\dfrac{7}{9}$

Practice: Probability

1. Robin Hood shoots a bow and arrow blindfolded! What is the probability that if it hits the target, it will land in the UNSHADED portion? Assume these are two concentric circles (circles that share the same center).

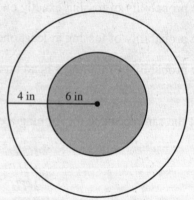

4 in   6 in

A. $\dfrac{4}{25}$

B. $\dfrac{6}{25}$

C. $\dfrac{9}{25}$

D. $\dfrac{16}{25}$

2. A set of 20 cards is numbered with positive integers from 1 to 20. If the cards are shuffled and one is chosen at random, what is the probability that the number on the card is a multiple of both **2** and **3**?

A. $\dfrac{3}{20}$

B. $\dfrac{1}{6}$

C. $\dfrac{1}{2}$

D. $\dfrac{3}{5}$

3. At Dante's Sandwich Shop, there are 2 types of bread (wheat or white), 4 sandwich fillings (cheese, turkey, ham, or peanut butter and jelly), and 3 types of condiments (ketchup, mustard, or mayonnaise). If Eric is choosing a sandwich with one of each category (bread, filling, and condiment), how many different combinations of sandwiches are possible?

A. 4
B. 9
C. 24
D. 48

4. A bag of marbles contains the following:

Color	Number of Marbles
Blue	20
Red	5
White	6
Green	14
Orange	15

If Peter randomly chooses a marble from the bag, what is the probability that the marble will be either white or green?

A. $\dfrac{7}{300}$

B. $\dfrac{3}{50}$

C. $\dfrac{7}{50}$

D. $\dfrac{1}{3}$

5. There are three candidates running for president of student council and two candidates running for vice-president. How many different pairs of candidates can be elected?
   A. 2
   B. 5
   C. 6
   D. 12

6. If the spinner shown below is spun once, what is the closest to the probability it will land on the space labeled 5?

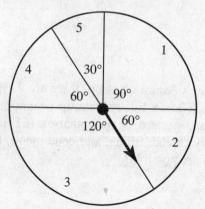

   A. 0.08
   B. 0.16
   C. 0.30
   D. 0.50

7. Eli is playing a game with a standard set of six-sided dice. A standard die has six faces, each with a different integer from one to six.

a. Make a list of all the possible outcomes of rolling two dice.

b. What is the probability that the sum of the outcome of the two dice will be greater than 10?

c. What is the most frequent sum of the two dice? Show or explain how you got your answer.

8. Cherrel had a box that contained some of the letters of the alphabet. It included:

   1 **A**
   4 **H**'s
   2 **I**'s
   1 **M**

Cherrel removed one letter without looking and she wrote the letter down on a piece of paper. She placed the letter back in the box and repeated the procedure one more time and wrote the second letter next to the first, forming a two-digit word. What is the probability that the word is HI, meaning the first letter is an H and the second is an I?

A. $\dfrac{1}{8}$

B. $\dfrac{1}{6}$

C. $\dfrac{1}{4}$

D. $\dfrac{1}{2}$

9. Debbie has two number cubes, each with faces labeled by the numbers –6, –4, –2, 2, 4, and 6. If Debbie rolls the two cubes and multiplies the resulting numbers, what is the probability that the product will be negative?

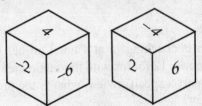

A. $\dfrac{1}{36}$

B. $\dfrac{1}{6}$

C. $\dfrac{1}{2}$

D. $\dfrac{2}{3}$

★ 10. Dena is playing a board game with two spinners with congruent sectors numbered 1 through 8 as shown. If the sum of the numbers you spin is greater than or equal to 10, you win. What is the probability that Dena will win?

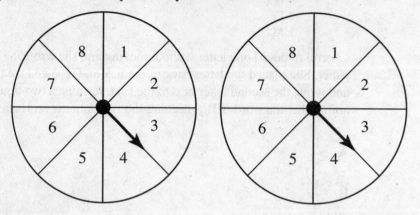

A. $\dfrac{5}{32}$

B. $\dfrac{5}{16}$

C. $\dfrac{7}{16}$

D. $\dfrac{11}{16}$

11. Tabatha is checking in at a hotel on her vacation. There are 8 rooms available with water views, 12 rooms with mountain views, and 16 rooms with city views. If she does not request a specific view, what is the probability that she is assigned a room with a city view?

A. $\dfrac{1}{4}$

B. $\dfrac{1}{3}$

C. $\dfrac{2}{9}$

D. $\dfrac{4}{9}$

12. Lucas noticed that many of the seniors at his school drove cars that had a stick shift. He randomly chose 24 of the seniors who drove and found that 4 drove a car with a stick shift. If Lucas' sample is representative, which of the following is closest to the number of the 420 senior drivers who drive a car with a stick shift?

A. 58

B. 60

C. 70

D. 168

13. Mike is playing a board game with a game piece in the shape of a regular triangular pyramid. The sides of the pyramid are congruent, and each face is of one of four colors: yellow, green, purple, and red.

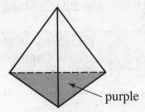
purple

If Mike tosses the game piece 84 times, how many times should he expect purple to be the color facing down?

A. 14
B. 16
C. 21
D. 63

14. A cube with the letters A through F on its faces is tossed. At the same time, an equally spaced spinner with the numbers 1 through 5 is spun. What is the probability that the cube will land with either the letters A or C face up, and the spinner will land on a number less than 4?

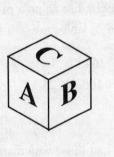 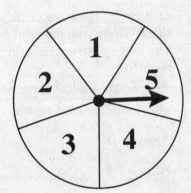

A. $\frac{1}{5}$

B. $\frac{3}{8}$

C. $\frac{4}{15}$

D. $\frac{14}{15}$

15. Two hundred Canada geese in the Jersey Highlands were caught and had a band placed on one leg. Several weeks later, a park ranger caught a number of geese at a random location in the Highlands, recorded the number that were both banded and unbanded, and released them. She did this twice, and the results of her two trials are shown below.

	Total Number of Geese Caught	Number of Banded Geese	Number of Unbanded Geese
Trial #1	35	20	15
Trial #2	55	30	25

Approximately how many geese would you expect to inhabit the Jersey Highlands?

A. 300
B. 360
C. 400
D. 450

Solutions to Practice: Probability

1. The probability is the fraction $\dfrac{\text{area of the unshaded region}}{\text{area of the total region}}$. Compute the area of each circle. The large circle with radius of 10 inches, has an area of 100π in.^{2}. The shaded circle with radius of 6 inches, has an area of 364 in.^{2}.
The *area of the unshaded region* $= 100\pi - 36\pi = 64\pi$ in.^{2}. The final probability is therefore

$$\frac{\text{area of the unshaded region}}{\text{area of the total region}} = \frac{64\pi}{100\pi} = \frac{16}{25}$$

Answer: D

2. There are 20 possible outcomes. List those which are multiples of 2 and 3:

6   12   18

(Notice that to be a multiple of both 2 and 3, the number must be a multiple of 6.)

There are only three favorable outcomes out of 20 possibilities, so the probability is $\dfrac{3}{20}$.

Answer: A

3. The counting principle allows you to multiply the number of options in each sandwich category to find the total number of possible different sandwiches that can be made. There are $2 \cdot 4 \cdot 3 = 24$ possible outcomes.

Answer: C

4. The probability of choosing a white or green marble can be expressed as the following ratio: $\dfrac{\text{total white and green marbles}}{\text{total marbles}} = \dfrac{20}{60} = \dfrac{1}{3}$.

   Answer: D

5. The counting principle allows you to multiply the numbers in each of the candidate's categories to find the total number of possible pairs of candidates that can be elected. There are $3 \cdot 2 = 6$ possible outcomes.

   Answer: C

6. Sector 5 is 30° out of the 360° of the entire circle. The probability of the spinner landing on sector 5 is $\dfrac{30}{360}$. Since this is a noncalculator question, **use your rounding and approximating skills**, and **use your answer choices** to finish off the problem. You know that $\dfrac{30}{300} = 0.10$, so $\dfrac{30}{360}$ must be less than 0.10. The only answer choice that is less than 0.10 is 0.08, answer choice A.

   Answer: A

7. a. There are 6 possible outcomes for the first roll and 6 for the second. The counting principle tells you that there are a total of $6 \cdot 6 = 36$ possible outcomes for rolling two dice. Because there are so many, it may be helpful to make some trees:

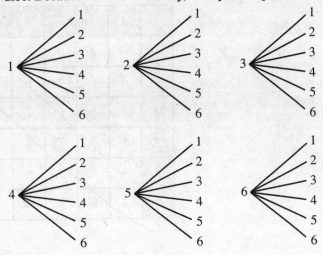

   Here are the possible outcomes, or the sample space is:

1 1	2 1	3 1	4 1	5 1	6 1
1 2	2 2	3 2	4 2	5 2	6 2
1 3	2 3	3 3	4 3	5 3	6 3
1 4	2 4	3 4	4 4	5 4	6 4
1 5	2 5	3 5	4 5	5 5	6 5
1 6	1 6	3 6	4 6	5 6	6 6

b. A common way of listing the possible sums of two dice is through a table. The shaded column and row headers are the numbers on the faces of each of the two dice, and the numbers in the table are the sums of these two faces.

+	1	2	3	4	5	6
1	2	3	4	5	6	7
2	3	4	5	6	7	8
3	4	5	6	7	8	9
4	5	6	7	8	9	10
5	6	7	8	9	10	11
6	7	8	9	10	11	12

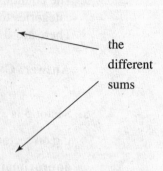

the different sums

There are $6 \times 6 = 36$ possible outcomes. Three of the sums are greater than 10. The probability of obtaining a sum greater than 10 is $P(11 \text{ or } 12) = \dfrac{3}{36} = \dfrac{1}{12}$.

Answer: $\dfrac{1}{12}$

c. Having already listed the outcomes, note that the most commonly occurring sum is 7.

+	1	2	3	4	5	6
1	2	3	4	5	6	7
2	3	4	5	6	7	8
3	4	5	6	7	8	9
4	5	6	7	8	9	10
5	6	7	8	9	10	11
6	7	8	9	10	11	12

Answer: 7

8. The probability of choosing an H for the first drawing of a letter is
$\dfrac{total\ number\ of\ H's}{total\ number\ of\ letters} = \dfrac{4}{8} = \dfrac{1}{2}$. Since the letter is then put back in the box, the total
number of letters does not change for the second drawing. The probability of choos-
ing an I for the second letter is $\dfrac{total\ number\ of\ I's}{total\ number\ of\ letters} = \dfrac{2}{8} = \dfrac{1}{4}$. Using the counting
principle to find the probability of choosing an H and then an I, $\dfrac{1}{2} \cdot \dfrac{1}{4} = \dfrac{1}{8}$.

Answer: A

9. The sample set for the two number cubes is the following:

–6 –6	–4 –6	–2 –6	(2 –6)	(4 –6)	(6 –6)
–6 –4	–4 –4	–2 –4	(2 –4)	(4 –4)	(6 –4)
–6 –2	–4 –2	–2 –2	(2 –2)	(4 –2)	(6 –2)
(–6 2)	(–4 2)	(–2 2)	2 2	4 2	6 2
(–6 4)	(–4 4)	(–2 4)	2 4	4 4	6 4
(–6 6)	(–4 6)	(–2 6)	2 6	4 6	6 6

Each column has 3 pairs of numbers whose product is negative. Therefore the proba-
bility of rolling two numbers whose product is negative is $\dfrac{18}{36} = \dfrac{1}{2}$. You may have real-
ized this without listing all of the possible outcomes.

Answer: C

10. The possible outcomes and their sums are:

+	1	2	3	4	5	6	7	8
1	2	3	4	5	6	7	8	9
2	3	4	5	6	7	8	9	10
3	4	5	6	7	8	9	10	11
4	5	6	7	8	9	10	11	12
5	6	7	8	9	10	11	12	13
6	7	8	9	10	11	12	13	14
7	8	9	10	11	12	13	14	15
8	9	10	11	12	13	14	15	16

The number of winning outcomes increases by 1 per column. If the first spin is a 1, it is impossible for Dena to win, since the highest the second spin could be is 8 and that would be a sum of 9. In the second column however, which shows the outcomes if the first spin is a 2, Dena could win if the second spin is an 8 and the sum is 10. If you see this pattern, you do not have to list all the winning outcomes you could just add $0 + 1 + 2 + 3 + 4 + 5 + 6 + 7 = 28$. There are a total of $8 \cdot 8 = 64$ possible outcomes so the probability of Dena winning is $\dfrac{28}{64} = \dfrac{7}{16}$.

Answer: C

11. Calculate $\dfrac{favorable\ outcomes}{possible\ outcomes}$. In this case, $\dfrac{\#\ rooms\ with\ city\ view}{total\ \#\ of\ rooms} = \dfrac{16}{36} = \dfrac{4}{9}$.

Answer: D

12. The ratio of seniors in the sample that drive stick shift to all the drivers in the sample should be equal to the ratio of all seniors who drive stick out of the total 420 senior drivers. Set up a proportion where x represents the unknown number of seniors who drive stick out of the 420 drivers: $\dfrac{4}{24} = \dfrac{x}{420}$. Reduce $\dfrac{4}{24}$ so that $\dfrac{1}{6} = \dfrac{x}{420}$ and cross multiply. Solving $6x = 420$, you get $x = 70$.

Answer: C

13. Each one of the four faces is equally likely to land facing down when the game piece is tossed. This means that the probability that each color will be rolled is $\dfrac{1}{4}$. If the piece is tossed 84 times, then it should land on each face approximately $\dfrac{1}{4}$ of the time. The piece should land on purple facing down approximately $84 \div 4 = 21$ times.

Answer: C

14. The probability of rolling an A or a C is $P(\text{A or C}) = \dfrac{2}{6} = \dfrac{1}{3}$. The probability of spinning a number less than 4 is $P(1\ or\ 2\ or\ 3) = \dfrac{3}{5}$. Multiplying these probabilities together, you get $\dfrac{1}{\cancel{3}} \cdot \dfrac{\cancel{3}}{5} = \dfrac{1}{5}$.

Answer: A

15. Create a ratio for the number of geese banded to the total number of geese caught for each trial. This becomes the probability of a goose being banded. Then use the concept of **expected value**. Average your two answers.

Let x be the total number of geese in the Highlands. Then $200 = \dfrac{20}{35} \cdot x$ for the first trial, or set up the proportion:

Trial #1: $\dfrac{20}{35} = \dfrac{200}{x} \longrightarrow 20x = 7{,}000 \longrightarrow 350$ geese total

And for the second trial, $200 = \dfrac{30}{55} \cdot x$, or set up the proportion:

Trial #2: $\dfrac{30}{55} = \dfrac{200}{x} \longrightarrow 30x = 11{,}000 \longrightarrow 366.\overline{6}$ geese total

The average of the two values for x is $\dfrac{350 + 367}{2} \approx 359$ geese. Answer choice B is the closest.

Answer: B

Chapter 8 | **MCAS Practice Tests**

Directions for Practice Test 1, Session A

This session contains fourteen multiple-choice questions (1–14), four short-answer questions (15–18), and three open-response questions (19–21).

1. You may not use a calculator during this test.
2. You may use the MCAS Reference Sheet to access formulas.
3. The recommended time is 60 minutes, but your school will give you more time if you need it.

Practice Test 1, Session A
Answer Sheet
Fill in the bubble completely. Erase carefully if an answer is changed.

1. A B C D
2. A B C D
3. A B C D
4. A B C D
5. A B C D
6. A B C D
7. A B C D
8. A B C D
9. A B C D
10. A B C D
11. A B C D
12. A B C D
13. A B C D
14. A B C D

Cut along dotted line.

Massachusetts Comprehensive Assessment System
Grade 10 Mathematics Reference Sheet

AREA FORMULAS

triangle . . . . $A = \dfrac{1}{2}bh$

rectangle . . . . $A = bh$

parallelogram . . . . $A = bh$

square . . . . $A = s^2$

trapezoid . . . . $A = \dfrac{1}{2}h\,(b_1 + b_2)$

CIRCLE FORMULAS

$C = 2\pi r$

$A = \pi r^2$

LATERAL SURFACE AREA FORMULAS

right rectangular prism . . . . $LA = 2(hw) + 2(lh)$
right circular cylinder . . . . $LA = 2\pi rh$
right circular cone . . . . $LA = \pi r\ell$
right square pyramid . . . . $LA = 2s\ell$
(ℓ = slant height)

TOTAL SURFACE AREA FORMULAS

cube . . . . $SA = 6s^2$
right rectangular prism . . . . $SA = 2(lw) + 2(hw) + 2(lh)$
sphere . . . . $SA = 4\pi r^2$
right circular cylinder . . . . $SA = 2\pi r^2 + 2\pi rh$
right circular cone . . . . $SA = \pi r^2 + \pi r\ell$
right square pyramid . . . . $SA = s^2 + 2s\ell$
(ℓ = slant height)

VOLUME FORMULAS

cube . . . . $V = s^3$

(s = length of an edge)
right rectangular prism . . . . $V = lwh$

OR

(B = area of the base) . . . . . $V = Bh$

sphere . . . . $V = \dfrac{4}{3}\pi r^3$

right circular cylinder . . . . . $V = \pi r^2 h$

right circular cone . . . . $V = \dfrac{1}{3}\pi r^2 h$

right square pyramid . . . . . . $V = \dfrac{1}{3}s^2 h$

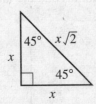

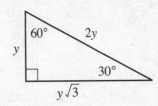

Practice Test 1, Session A

Multiple-Choice Questions

1. Which of the following is the value of $2a - 3b^2$ for $a = 12$ and $b = -3$?

   A. 3
   B. −3
   C. 51
   D. 6

   $24 - 3 \times 9$
   $24 - 27 = -3$

2. If $5 + 2(8x - 9) = 17$, then $8x - 9$ equals

   A. 6
   B. 8
   C. 9
   D. 12

   $5 + 16x - 18 = 17 + 18 = 35 - 5 = 30$
   $+18$
   $16x = 30 \div 16$

3. Darol buys a new couch on an installment plan. He pays $40 a month until the couch is paid off. Which of the following graphs matches the relationship between months and the unpaid balance?

   A.
   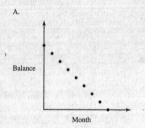

   B.
   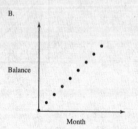

   C.
   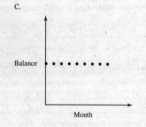

   D.
   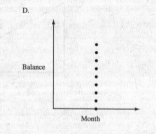

4. In the figure below, if $\overline{CD} = 6$, what is the length of $\overline{AD}$?

   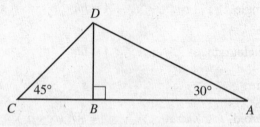

   A. $3\sqrt{2}$
   B. $2\sqrt{3}$
   C. $6\sqrt{2}$
   D. $6\sqrt{3}$

5. The diameter of circle O is 14 inches. Find the area of the shaded region.

   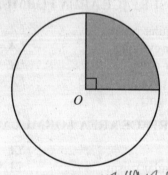

   $7 \times 7 = 49 \times 3.14$

   A. $\dfrac{7}{4}\pi$ in.^{2}
   B. $\dfrac{49}{2}\pi$ in.^{2}
   C. $\dfrac{49}{4}\pi$ in.^{2}
   D. 49π in.^{2}

   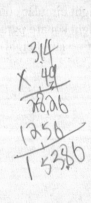

6. The exam scores for 7 out of 9 students in an Advanced Biology class are listed below. If the median score for the entire class is 80, which of the following could have been the scores of the remaining two students?

Exam Scores for Advanced Biology Class	
Student 1	76%
Student 2	80%
Student 3	93%
Student 4	73%
Student 5	93%
Student 6	79%
Student 7	91%

A. 80% and 97%
B. 78% and 79%
C. 91% and 93%
D. 91% and 91%

7. The identity element for the operation of multiplication is 1 since $1 \cdot x = x$ and $x \cdot 1 = x$ for any real number x. The operation $\boxed{\bullet}$ is defined by the following table.

$\boxed{\bullet}$	a	b	c	d
a	b	a	d	c
b	a	b	c	d
c	d	c	b	a
d	c	d	a	b

What is the identity element for the operation $\boxed{\bullet}$?

A. a
B. b
C. c
D. d

8. A company has 126 employees. It plans to increase its work force by 6 employees each month until it triples in size. Which of the following equations will help you to determine the number of months, m, for the company to triple in size?

A. $126 + 6 = 3m$
B. $3(126) = 6m$
C. $(126 + 6)3 = m$
D. $126 + 6m = 3(126)$

9. Which of these pieces of posterboard CANNOT be folded along the dotted lines to make a closed rectangular prism?

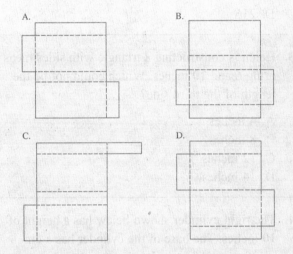

Use the table below to answer Question 10.

x	0	1	2	3	4
y	−2	4	10	16	22

10. Which equation shows the relationship between x and y in the table above?

A. $y = 6x + 2$
B. $y = 6x - 2$
C. $y = -6x + 2$
D. $y = -6x - 2$

11. Let a, b, and x represent real numbers with $a > b$ and $x < 0$. Which of the following statements is **not** true?

A. $ax > bx$

B. $x + a > x + b$

C. $a - x > b - x$

D. $bx > ax$

12. What is the value of the expression below?

$$\left(-1\right)^5 \left(2 \cdot 3^3\right)$$

A. -216

B. -54

C. 54

D. 216

13. Helen is constructing a triangle with sides measuring 6 and 10 inches. Which could not be the length of the third side?

A. 4 inches

B. 8 inches

C. 12 inches

D. 14 inches

14. The right cylinder shown below has a height of 10 inches. The base of the cylinder has a circumference of 6π inches.

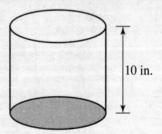

10 in.

What is the lateral surface area of the cylinder?

A. 60π square inches

B. 120π square inches

C. 360π square inches

D. 600π square inches

Short Answer Questions

15. Simplify the following expression:

$$\left(-2x^3 y^7\right)\left(5xy^8\right)$$

16. Square $ABCD$ has coordinates $A(0, 0)$, $B(0, n)$, $C(n, n)$, $D(n, 0)$. What is the area, in terms on n, of square $ABCD$?

17. *You may wish to use the following coordinate plane to help you answer Question 17.*

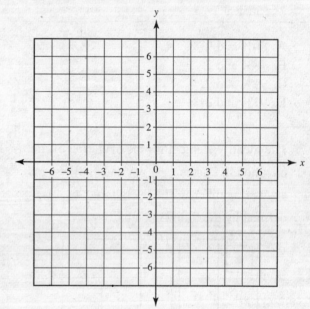

What is the distance between the points $(-5, -4)$ and $(1, 4)$?

18. The stem and leaf plot below shows the most recent test results in Ms. Blakes's math class:

6	0 0 1
7	1 2 5 6
8	6 7 8 8 8 9 9
9	0 4 8 9
10	0

Note: 8 | 6 = 86

What is the median test score?

Open Response Questions

19. Mr. Roberts is selling theater tickets for a community play which will run two performances, one Saturday evening and one Sunday matinee. There are 100 seats in the theater. The Saturday evening tickets will cost $10.00 each, and the Sunday matinee, $6.00 each. Mr. Robert's total expenses for producing the play are $1,200.00.

a. Suppose Mr. Roberts sold 90 tickets on Saturday evening, and 80 tickets for the Sunday matinee. Based on this information, did he make enough money to cover his expenses for producing the play? Show your work or explain how you obtained your answer.

b. Write an equation that represents the amount of money Mr. Roberts needs to collect from the sale of e Saturday evening tickets and m Sunday matinee tickets to pay for his total expenses.

c. What is the MINIMUM number of Saturday evening tickets that he could sell and still break even by the end of the day on Sunday? Show your work or explain how you obtained your answer.

20. In the diagram below, $\triangle ABC \cong \triangle EFG$.

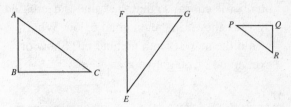

a. If the measure of $\angle C = 36°$, what is the measure, in degrees, of $\angle G$? Show or explain how you got your answer.

b. If the length of $\overline{AC}$ is $(5x + 8)$ centimeters, and the length of $\overline{EG}$ is 23 centimeters, what is the value of x? Show or explain how you got your answer.

c. What is the ratio of the perimeter of $\triangle ABC$ to the perimeter of $\triangle EFG$? Show or explain how you got your answer.

d. $\triangle EFG$ is similar to $\triangle PQR$. The length of $\overline{EG}$ is 23 centimeters, while the length of $\overline{PR}$ is $11\frac{1}{2}$ centimeters. If the area of $\triangle PQR$ is 50 square centimeters, what is the area, in square centimeters, of $\triangle EFG$? Show or explain how you got your answer.

21. The first four square numbers are shown below.

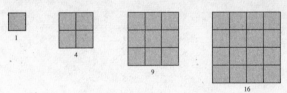

a. What is the seventh square number? Show or explain how you got your answer.

b. Write an formula that represents the numeric value of the nth square number, for any value of n.

c. Suppose the top right corner of each square number is cut off so that the value is decreased by 1, as shown in the diagram below. What would the new seventh number be? Show or explain how you got your answer.

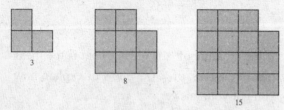

3   8   15

d. Write a formula that represents the numeric value for the nth term in the sequence in part c.

Solutions: Practice Test 1, Session A

1. **B** Substituting $a = 12$ and $b = -3$ into $2a - 3b^2$ you get

$$2(12) - 3(-3)^2 = 24 - 3(9) = 24 - 27 = -3$$

2. **A** Without solving this problem for x, you can find this answer. The question is asking: 5 plus 2 times the amount, $8x - 9$, equals 17. **Use your answer choices.** It makes sense that the correct answer is 6 because $5 + 2 \cdot 6 = 5 + 12 = 17$. To solve this without the answer choices, you would subtract 5 from 17 and then divide by 2.

3. **A** The unpaid balance starts high and continually decreases at a constant rate of $40 a month. The graph should show it decreasing until the balance is 0. The is represented by graph A. Do not be tempted by answer choice B, which actually starts with a balance of 0!

4. **C** ΔBCD is a 45°-45°-90°, isosceles right triangle, so its ratio of sides is $x : x : x\sqrt{2}$. Set up the equation $x\sqrt{2} = 6$. To solve for x, divide by $\sqrt{2}$ and rationalize the denominator: $\dfrac{6}{\sqrt{2}} \cdot \dfrac{\sqrt{2}}{\sqrt{2}} = \dfrac{6\sqrt{2}}{2} = 3\sqrt{2}$. This is the length of $\overline{BD}$. ΔBDA is a 30°-60°-90° special triangle, so its ratio of sides is $x : x\sqrt{3} : 2x$, where the shortest side x is opposite the 30° angle, and the longest side $2x$ is the hypotenuse. This gives you $AD =$

$$2(BD) = 2(3\sqrt{2}) = 6\sqrt{2}.$$

5. **C** The radius of the circle is 7 in. The area of the entire circle is 49π in.². The shaded region is $\dfrac{1}{4}$ the area of the entire circle $= \dfrac{49\pi}{4}$ in.².

6. **A** **Use your answer choices** to find the list that has a median of 80%. A. Correct. In order the scores of all 9 students are 73%, 76%, 79%, 80%, 80%, 91%, 93%, 93%, and 97%. The median is 80%.

   ~~B.~~ Incorrect. The first five scores would be 73%, 76%, 78%, 79%, and 79%, making the median 79%.

   ~~C.~~ Incorrect. The top five scores would be 91%, 91%, 93%, 93%, and 93%, making the median 91.

   ~~D.~~ Incorrect. The top five scores would be 91%, 91%, 91%, 93%, and 93% making the median 91.

7. **B** To find the identity element, (here a variable), look for the variable such that
   $$a \cdot identity = a$$
   $$b \cdot identity = b$$
   $$c \cdot identity = c$$
   $$d \cdot identity = d$$
   Looking at the table: $a \cdot b = a$, $b \cdot b = b$, $c \cdot b = c$, $d \cdot b = d$, so b is the identity element.

8. **D** Tripling the size of the company's current work force gives you $3 \cdot 126$ employees, so the equation must equal this number. Using **process of elimination**, only answer choices B and D are now options. Adding 6 employees each month, would mean that in the first month you would have $126 + 6$ employees, the second month you would have $126 + 6(2)$ employees, the third would be $126 + 6(3)$ employees, and so on. Answer choice B is not correct because it does not take into account the original 126 employees in the company. The correct equation is $126 + 6m = 3(126)$.

9. **D** Answer choice D is impossible. Imagine coloring the three different rectangular faces gray, black, and white. When closed, the rectangular prism will look like

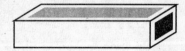

Notice that the same colored faces will never be adjacent to each other. In answer choice D however, both the gray and the white rectangular faces would be adjacent to each other, making this cardboard layout impossible.

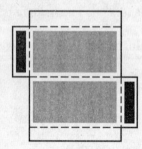

10. **B** You can **use your answer choices** by plugging in the points into the equations to see if they work.

X̸. False because $6 \cdot 0 + 2 = 2$, not -2.

X̸. False because $-6 \cdot 0 + 2 = 2$, not -2.

X̸. False because $-6 \cdot 1 - 2 = -8$, not 4.

B. True because all the points work in the equation. Also, you can take any two points and calculate the slope: $\dfrac{y_2 - y_1}{x_2 - x_1} = \dfrac{4 - (-2)}{1 - (0)} = \dfrac{6}{1} = 6$. You know that the y-intercept is $(0, -2)$, so you can put the equation into slope-intercept form:

$y = 6x - 2$.

11. **A** You are looking for the statement that is **not** true. **Choose your own numbers** that satisfy the given conditions to help you solve this problem. For example, let: $a = 3$, $b = 2$, and $x = -1$. Going through the answer choices:

A. $ax > bx \rightarrow (3)(-1) > (2)(-1) \rightarrow -3 > -2$, which is a false statement. CORRECT.

X̸. $x + a > x + b \rightarrow -1 + 3 > -1 + 2 \rightarrow 2 > 1$, which is a true statement.

X̸. $a - x > b - x \rightarrow 3 - (-1) > 2 - (-1) \rightarrow 4 > 3$, which is a true statement.

X̸. $bx > ax \rightarrow (2)(-1) > (3)(-1) \rightarrow -2 > -3$, which is a true statement.

12. **B** $(-1)^5 (2 \cdot 3^3) = (-1)(2 \cdot 27) = (-1)(54) = -54$.

13. **A** Call the third side x. The third side must be between the difference and sum of the other two sides.

$(10 - 6) < x < (10 + 6) \rightarrow 4 < x < 16$.

Answer choice A does not fall within this range. The side must be greater than 4. It cannot be equal to 4.

14. **A** The lateral surface area of the cylinder is the circumference of the base times the height.
$LA = 6\pi \cdot 10 = 60\pi$ square inches.

15. Rearrange the expression so that constants are in the front, and terms with the same base are next to each other, so that you can simplify exponents.

$(-2x^3 y^7)(5xy^8) = -2 \cdot 5 \cdot x^3 \cdot x^1 \cdot y^7 \cdot y^8$.

Next, multiply the constants together, and multiply variables with the same base by adding their exponents.

$-2 \cdot 5 \cdot x^3 \cdot x^1 \cdot y^7 \cdot y^8 = -10x^4 y^{15}$

Answer: $-10x^4 y^{15}$

16. Each side length has a length of n. The area of the square is n^2.

Answer: n^2

17. Plot the points on the grid, connect them, and make that segment the hypotenuse of a right triangle. The change in x is 6, that is the distance from -5 to 1, and the change in y is 8, that is the distance from -4 to 4. These are the legs of the right triangle.

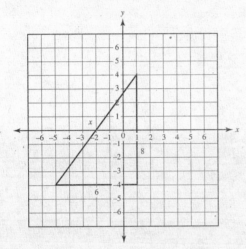

Now use the Pythagorean Theorem to solve for x:

$$6^2 + 8^2 = x^2 \rightarrow 36 + 64 = x^2 \rightarrow 100 = x^2 \rightarrow 10 = x$$

Answer: 10

18. The median is the score that falls in the middle of the ordered list. Let n be the number of scores. There are $n = 19$ scores. You find this by counting the number of leaves in the stem and leaf plot. To find which number is the middle number, use the formula:

$$middle\ position = \frac{n+1}{2} = \frac{19+1}{2} = 10$$

Now count from the beginning or end until you hit the 10th number, which is 88.

Answer: 88

19. a. $10 \cdot 90 + 6 \cdot 80 = 900 + 480 = \$1,380$, which is greater than \$1200 so Mr. Roberts did make enough money to cover his expenses.

Answer: Yes

b. $10e + 6m = 1,200$

c. If all of the tickets are sold on Sunday, Sunday's earnings would be $6 \cdot 100 = \$600$. This leaves $1,200 - 600 = \$600$ that would need to have been earned on Saturday to break even. $10e = 600 \rightarrow e = 60$. If 60 tickets were sold on Saturday and 100 tickets on Sunday, then Mr. Roberts will break even.

Answer: 60

20. a. Since $\triangle ABC \cong \triangle EFG$, all the corresponding angles and sides of the two triangles must be congruent. $\angle C$ and $\angle G$ are corresponding angles (you know this because of the ordering of the statement that $\triangle ABC \cong \triangle EFG$ —the C and G are both the last letters in the statement). $\angle C = 36°$, so $\angle G = 36°$, as well.

Answer: 36°

b. $\overline{AC}$ and $\overline{EG}$ are corresponding sides so they must be congruent. Solve $5x + 8 = 23 \rightarrow 5x = 15 \rightarrow x = 3$.

Answer: $x = 3$

c. Congruent figures are the same size so their perimeters are exactly the same. The ratio of their perimeters must be $1 : 1$.

Answer: 1 : 1

d. $\overline{EG}$ and $\overline{PR}$ are corresponding sides of similar triangles, whose ratio is

$$\frac{PR}{EG} = \frac{11\frac{1}{2}}{23} = \frac{1}{2}.$$

The ratio of the areas of two similar polygons is equal to the square of the ratio of the sides. Set up the following proportion:

$$\left(\frac{1}{2}\right)^2 = \frac{50}{area\ of\ \triangle EFG}.$$

$$\frac{1}{4} = \frac{50}{area\ of\ \triangle EFG} \rightarrow area\ of\ \triangle EFG = 200$$

Answer: 200 cm²

21. a. Square number 1 has a value of $1^2 = 1$.
Square number 2 has a value of $2^2 = 4$.
Square number 3 has a value of $3^2 = 9$.
Square number 4 has a value of $4^2 = 16$.
Each term is being squared to find the value of the term. The seventh square number will have a numeric value of $7^2 = 49$.

Answer: 49

b. The nth square number will have a numeric value of n^2.

Answer: n^2

c. The new seventh number would have a value that is one less than the old square number. The value would be $49 - 1 = 48$.

Answer: 48

d. The shapes in the new sequence each have a numeric value that is one less than the values of the square numbers in part a. The nth term would have a numeric value of $n^2 - 1$.

Answer: $n^2 - 1$

Directions for Practice Test 1, Session B

This session contains eighteen multiple-choice questions (1–18) and three open-response questions (19–21).

1. You may use a calculator during this test.
2. You may use the MCAS Reference Sheet to access formulas.
3. The recommended time is 60 minutes, but your school will give you more time if you need it.

Practice Test 1, Session B
Answer Sheet
Fill in the bubble completely. Erase carefully if an answer is changed.

Cut along dotted line.

1. Ⓐ Ⓑ Ⓒ Ⓓ
    A B C D

2. Ⓐ Ⓑ Ⓒ Ⓓ
    A B C D

3. Ⓐ Ⓑ Ⓒ Ⓓ
    A B C D

4. Ⓐ Ⓑ Ⓒ Ⓓ
    A B C D

5. Ⓐ Ⓑ Ⓒ Ⓓ
    A B C D

6. Ⓐ Ⓑ Ⓒ Ⓓ
    A B C D

7. Ⓐ Ⓑ Ⓒ Ⓓ
    A B C D

8. Ⓐ Ⓑ Ⓒ Ⓓ
    A B C D

9. Ⓐ Ⓑ Ⓒ Ⓓ
    A B C D

10. Ⓐ Ⓑ Ⓒ Ⓓ
    A B C D

11. Ⓐ Ⓑ Ⓒ Ⓓ
    A B C D

12. Ⓐ Ⓑ Ⓒ Ⓓ
    A B C D

13. Ⓐ Ⓑ Ⓒ Ⓓ
    A B C D

14. Ⓐ Ⓑ Ⓒ Ⓓ
    A B C D

15. Ⓐ Ⓑ Ⓒ Ⓓ
    A B C D

16. Ⓐ Ⓑ Ⓒ Ⓓ
    A B C D

17. Ⓐ Ⓑ Ⓒ Ⓓ
    A B C D

18. Ⓐ Ⓑ Ⓒ Ⓓ
    A B C D

Massachusetts Comprehensive Assessment System
Grade 10 Mathematics Reference Sheet

AREA FORMULAS

triangle . . . . $A = \frac{1}{2}bh$

rectangle . . . . $A = bh$

parallelogram . . . . $A = bh$

square . . . . $A = s^2$

trapezoid . . . . $A = \frac{1}{2}h\,(b_1 + b_2)$

CIRCLE FORMULAS

$C = 2\pi r$

$A = \pi r^2$

LATERAL SURFACE AREA FORMULAS

right rectangular prism . . . . $LA = 2(hw) + 2(lh)$
right circular cylinder . . . . $LA = 2\pi rh$
right circular cone . . . . $LA = \pi r\ell$
right square pyramid . . . . $LA = 2s\ell$
(ℓ = slant height)

TOTAL SURFACE AREA FORMULAS

cube . . . . $SA = 6s^2$
right rectangular prism . . . . $SA = 2(lw) + 2(hw) + 2(lh)$
sphere . . . . $SA = 4\pi r^2$
right circular cylinder . . . . $SA = 2\pi r^2 + 2\pi rh$
right circular cone . . . . $SA = \pi r^2 + \pi r\ell$
right square pyramid . . . . $SA = s^2 + 2s\ell$
(ℓ = slant height)

VOLUME FORMULAS

cube . . . . $V = s^3$

(s = length of an edge)
right rectangular prism . . . . $V = lwh$

OR

(B = area of the base) . . . . . $V = Bh$

sphere . . . . $V = \frac{4}{3}\pi r^3$

right circular cylinder . . . . . $V = \pi r^2 h$

right circular cone . . . . $V = \frac{1}{3}\pi r^2 h$

right square pyramid . . . . . . $V = \frac{1}{3}s^2 h$

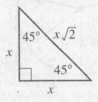

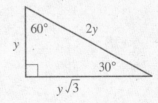

Practice Test 1, Session B

Multiple-Choice Questions

1. How many numbers in the following list of numbers are irrational?

$$\sqrt{36},\ -\frac{8}{2},\ \sqrt{13},\ 1.2,\ 0.\overline{65},\ 5\pi,\ 0,\ 19,\ -\frac{1}{\sqrt{2}}$$

   A. 1
   B. 2
   C. 3
   D. 4

2. The spinner below is separated into 7 equally spaced sectors. If you were to spin the spinner twice, what is the probability of the spinner landing once on an even number and once on an odd, in either order?

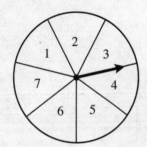

   A. $\dfrac{3}{7}$

   B. $\dfrac{4}{7}$

   C. $\dfrac{12}{49}$

   D. $\dfrac{24}{49}$

3. *Use the inequality below to answer Question 3.*

$$4 - x \le 6$$

   Which graph represents the solution set for the inequality?

   A.
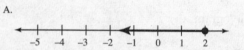

   B.

   C.
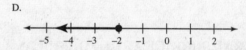

   D.
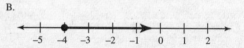

4. If the distributive property is used to simplify the expression below, what is the result?

$$x\left(y + z\right) - p\left(d - q\right)$$

   A. $xy + xz - pd + pq$
   B. $xy + xz - pd - pq$
   C. $xy + z - pd - q$
   D. $xy + z - pd + q$

5. The rectangle shown below has an area of 91.3 square inches and a length of 8.3 inches. What is the perimeter of the rectangle?

   A. 19.3 inches
   B. 38.6 inches
   C. 77.2 inches
   D. 182.6 inches

6. The mean salary of the four florists at Winston's Floral Boutique is $10.50 an hour. If one of the florists who was earning $8.50 per hour gets a raise of $2.00 per hour, what is the new mean salary of the four florists?

A. $ 10.50
B. $ 11.00
C. $ 9.50
D. $ 11.50

7. The expression below represents the amount of money in Donna's saving's account.

$$12,000\left(1+\frac{0.04}{2}\right)^5$$

Which of the following is closest to the amount of money in Donna's saving's account?

A. $13,250
B. $12,390
C. $12,456
D. $13,015

8. Let a, b, and c be real numbers with
$0 < a < b < 1 < c$.
Which of the following is **not** necessarily true?

A. $b^2 > c$
B. $ab < 1$
C. $\dfrac{c}{b} > 1$
D. $c - a > 0$

9. Jeremy wants to fill a community flower bed with potting soil. The bed is in the shape of a rectangular prism, with dimensions as shown below. He is using bags that contain 8 cubic feet of potting soil.

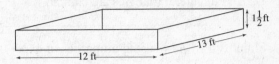

What is the least number of bags Jeremy needs to completely fill the flower bed?

A. 29 bags of potting soil
B. 30 bags of potting soil
C. 32 bags of potting soil
D. 40 bags of potting soil

10. The box and whisker plot shown below represents 420 scores on an exam for a regional math competition.

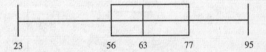

How many students scored between 63 and 77?

A. 14
B. 25
C. 75
D. 105

11. The volume of a rectangular prism is
$\left(-12b^3 - 16b^2 + 8b\right)$. The height of the prism is
$(-4b)$. What is the area of the base of the prism?

A. $\left(3b^2 - 4b - 2\right)$
B. $\left(48b^4 + 64b^3 - 32b^2\right)$
C. $\left(48b^4 - 64b^3 + 32b^2\right)$
D. $\left(3b^2 + 4b - 2\right)$

12. Which of the following statements is always true?

    A. All equilateral triangles are congruent.
    B. All right triangles are similar.
    C. All triangles with equal areas are congruent.
    D. All equilateral triangles are similar.

13. Simplify $\left(9a^4b^{16}\right)^2$ using properties of exponents.

    A. $3a^2b^8$
    B. $3a^2b^4$
    C. $81a^8b^{32}$
    D. $81a^{16}b^{256}$

14. Jenn builds a circular swimming pool with a diameter of 100 feet in her rectangular backyard with dimensions 200 ft by 300 ft. What percentage of her backyard area is the pool?

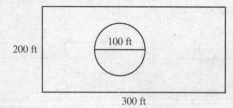

    A. 8%
    B. 13%
    C. 21%
    D. 28%

15. Jaclyn has a bag full of dimes and quarters. She has 72 coins altogether, totaling $11.55. How many quarters does she have in the bag?

    A. 11
    B. 18
    C. 29
    D. 43

16. Physicists use the equation $K = \frac{1}{2}mv^2$ to find the kinetic energy, K, measured in Joules, of an object of mass, m, measured in kilograms, moving at a velocity, v, measured in meters per second. What is the velocity of an object if it has a mass of 12 kilograms and a kinetic energy of 384 Joules?

    A. 64 m/s
    B. 80 m/s
    C. 4 m/s
    D. 8 m/s

17. The back tire of a bicycle is wet and leaves a wet trail on the ground. If the tire's radius is 10 inches and the tire makes 4 complete revolutions, what is the length of the wet trail left by the tire? Find the length to the nearest inch.

    A. 63 inches
    B. 251 inches
    C. 314 inches
    D. 628 inches

18. Which of the following equations is represented by the graph below?

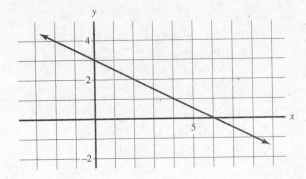

A. $x + y = 3$
B. $2x - y = 3$
C. $x + 2y = 6$
D. $2y - x = 6$

Open Response Questions

19. A local theater did a survey of the ages of the people who bought tickets to a particular teen movie on a certain Saturday night. The results are shown in the table below.

Ages of Movie-Goers on a Saturday Night									
5	6	6	8	8	9	9	9	10	10
10	10	11	11	11	12	12	12	13	13
13	13	13	14	14	14	15	15	15	15
15	16	16	16	16	17	17	17	18	18
19	21	23	26	34	37	38	42	43	45

a. What is the mean of the ages? Show your work or explain how you got your answer.

b. What is the median of the ages? Show your work or explain how you got your answer.

c. What is the mode of the ages? Show your work or explain how you got your answer.

d. Construct a frequency table for the data with age intervals of five years.

e. Using your frequency table in part d, construct a histogram to display the data.

20. The owner of Chocoriffic, Mr. Truffle, buys a new vat to store his fudge. The vat is in the shape of a cylinder that has a diameter of 4 feet and is 5 feet high. Mr. Truffle pours the fudge into a three-gallon jug and then into the vat.

a. Show how to calculate the volume of the cylindrical vat in cubic inches. Round your answer to the nearest cubic inch. Be sure to include units of measure in your answer. Show your work or explain how you obtained your answer.

b. Mr. Truffle fills the three-gallon jug with chocolate and then pours the chocolate from the jug into the vat. How many times will he have to fill the three-gallon jug until he is able to fill the vat? Show your work or explain how you obtained your answer. (Note: 1 gal = 231 cubic inches.)

c. If it takes Mr. Truffle 20 seconds to fill the three-gallon jug and pour it into the vat and he works at a constant rate, how long will it take Mr. Truffle to fill the vat? Round your answer to the nearest minute. Show your work or explain how you obtained your answer.

21. Three out of the four vertices of rhombus $ABCD$ are graphed below.

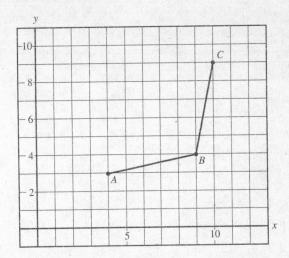

a. If the coordinates of the three vertices of rhombus $ABCD$ are $A(4, 3)$, $B(9, 4)$, and $C(10, 9)$, find the coordinates of point D. Show your work or explain how you got your answer.

b. Find the lengths of sides $\overline{AB}$ and $\overline{BC}$ of rhombus *ABCD*. What can you conclude about the lengths of the sides of a rhombus? Show your work or explain how you got your answer.

c. Find the slopes of the diagonals $\overline{AC}$ and $\overline{BD}$. What can you conclude about the lines containing the diagonals of a rhombus? Show your work or explain how you got your answer.

Solutions: Practice Test 1, Session B

1. C   Irrational numbers cannot be expressed as a ratio of two whole numbers. In general, numbers are rational if they are integers (whether positive or negative), fractions (positive or negative), terminating decimals (decimals that eventually end), and repeating decimals. Numbers are irrational if they are square roots of numbers that are not perfect squares and terms that include π. In this list, three numbers are irrational. Going through the list:

$\sqrt{36} = 6$ is rational. It is an integer.

$-\dfrac{8}{2} = -4$ is rational. It is an integer.

$\sqrt{13}$ is **irrational**. 13 is not a perfect square. If you changed it into a decimal, it would be nonterminating and nonrepeating.

1.2 is rational. It is a terminating decimal.

$0.\overline{65}$ is rational. It is a repeating decimal.

5π is **irrational**. As a decimal, π is approximately $3.141592654\ldots$ and is nonterminating and nonrepeating. 5π is 5 times that amount and is still nonterminating and nonrepeating. 5π cannot be written as a quotient of two integers.

0 and 19 are rational. They are both integers.

$-\dfrac{1}{\sqrt{2}}$ is **irrational**. 2 is not a perfect square. The decimal $-\dfrac{1}{\sqrt{2}}$ is approximately -0.707106781 $\ldots$ and does not terminate or repeat.

2. D   There are 4 odd numbers and 3 even numbers on the spinner. The probability of spinning odd then even is $\dfrac{4}{7} \cdot \dfrac{3}{7} = \dfrac{12}{49}$. The probability of even then odd is $\dfrac{3}{7} \cdot \dfrac{4}{7} = \dfrac{12}{49}$. Since either one of these outcomes is considered favorable, adding them together gets you a total probability of $\dfrac{12}{49} + \dfrac{12}{49} = \dfrac{24}{49}$.

3. C   Subtract 4 from each side and divide by negative 1. Remember to flip the inequality symbol when multiplying or dividing by a negative number.

$$4 - x \le 6 \longrightarrow -x \le 2 \longrightarrow x \ge -2$$

Answer choice C shows the number line shaded for values greater than or equal to -2.

4. A   The distributive property says that each term in the first parentheses should be multiplied by x and each term in the second parentheses should be multiplied by $-p$. Be careful to pay attention to the signs of the variables that you are multiplying. Negative times negative = positive!

$$x\left(y + z\right) - p\left(d - q\right) = xy + xz - pd + pq$$

5. B   The width of the rectangle is $\dfrac{91.3}{8.3} = 11$ in. The perimeter is

$$2(11) + 2(8.3) = 22 + 16.6 = 38.6 \text{ in.}$$

6. B Use the formula:

$$mean = \frac{sum\ of\ salaries}{number\ of\ salaries}.$$

First, find the sum of the salaries of the four florists: $10.50 =

$$\frac{sum\ of\ salaries}{4} \longrightarrow$$

sum of salaries = $42.00. Raising one of the workers salaries by $2.00 (regardless of what it was to begin with) changes the sum of the salaries to $42.00 + $2.00 = $44.00. Using the formula to compute the new mean, you get

$$mean = \frac{\$44.00}{4} = \$11.00.$$

7. A Be sure to familiarize yourself with the parentheses button on your calculator. **Knowing how to use your calculator** is an important test-taking strategy. If your calculator has parentheses, it will most likely handle the order of operations for you, and you may type the expression in as 12,000(1+.04/2)^5 to get the correct answer of 13,248.97. (Check this now!) If not, you will have to follow the order of operations PEMDAS and do your computations in the following sequence:

Step 1: $0.04 \div 2 = 0.02$

$$\longrightarrow 12,000\left(1+.02\right)^5$$

Step 2: $1 + 0.02 = 1.02$

$$\longrightarrow 12,000\left(1.02\right)^5$$

Step 3: $\left(1.02\right)^5 \approx 1.1040808$

$$\longrightarrow 12,000\left(1.1040808\right)$$

Step 4: $12,000\left(1.1040808\right) = 13,248.97$

This answer is closest to answer choice A.

8. A You are looking for the statement that is **not** true. Go through the answer choices.

A. This is the correct answer. The statement is **not** true. **Choose your own numbers** (either fractions or decimals) to convince yourself. Using fractions, suppose $c = 2$ and $b = \frac{1}{2}$, then $b^2 = \left(\frac{1}{2}\right)^2 = \frac{1}{4}$ and $c^2 = 2^2 = 4$. Since $\frac{1}{4} \not> 4$, this makes the statement $b^2 > c$ untrue.

You can also use decimals. Suppose $c = 2$ and $b = 0.5$, then $b^2 = \left(0.5\right)^2 = 0.25$ and 0.25 is not greater than 4.

B. This is a true statement. Let $a = \frac{1}{10}$ and $b = \frac{1}{2}$. Then $ab = \left(\frac{1}{10}\right)\left(\frac{1}{2}\right) = \frac{1}{20}$, or $ab = \left(0.1\right)\left(0.5\right) = 0.05$. This makes $ab < 1$, so choice B is true.

C. This is a true statement. Let $c = 2$ and $b = \frac{1}{2}$. Then $\dfrac{c}{b} = \dfrac{2}{\frac{1}{2}} = 2 \cdot \dfrac{2}{1} = 4$. This makes $\dfrac{c}{b} > 1$, so choice C is true.

D. This is a true statement. Let $a = \frac{1}{10}$ and $c = 2$. Then $c - a = 2 - \frac{1}{10} = 2 - 0.1 = 1.9$, which is greater than 0. This makes $c - a > 0$ so choice D is true.

9. **B** The volume of the flower bed is

$$V = lwh = (12)(13)\left(\frac{3}{2}\right) = 234 \text{ cubic feet. If}$$

each bag contains 8 cubic feet of potting soil, Jeremy needs 234/8 = 29.25 bags. Since he will have to purchase a whole bag to get that .25 cubic feet, round your answer up to 30 bags.

10. **D** The scores between 63 and 77 lie in the third quartile. They represent 25% of the total scores. Multiplying by the number of total scores, gives you 0.25 • 420 = 105 student scores.

11. **D** The volume of a prism is the product of the area of its base and its height or $V = Bh$ where B is the area of the base. Look for which of the answer choices, when multiplied by $(-4b)$, gives you $\left(-12b^3 - 16b^2 + 8b\right)$. Since $(-4b)$ $\left(3b^2 + 4b - 2\right) = \left(-12b^3 - 16b^2 + 8b\right)$ the answer is D.

12. **D** In equilateral triangles, all of the corresponding angles are congruent because they are each 60°. That is enough to know that the triangles are similar. Also, the ratios of the corresponding sides will be equal.

13. **C** Raise each number factor in the parentheses to the second power. Multiply the exponents if there are any. $\left(9a^4b^{16}\right)^2 = 9^2 \cdot a^{4 \cdot 2} \cdot b^{16 \cdot 2} = 81a^8b^{32}$.

14. **B** The area of the circle is $\pi \cdot 50^2 = 2,500\pi \text{ ft}^2$, and the area of the rectangle is $200 \cdot 300 = 60,000 \text{ ft}^2$. The ratio of the area of the pool to the entire backyard is $\frac{2,500\pi}{60,000} \approx 13\%$.

15. **C** Set up a system of equations where d is the number of dimes and q is the number of quarters.

$d + q = 72$ (There are 72 coins altogether.)

$0.10d + 0.25q = 11.55$ (The value of the coins is $11.55.)

Solving for d in terms of q in the first equation gives you: $d = 72 - q$. Substituting this expression in for d in the second equation and solving for q you get:

$$0.10(72 - q) + 0.25q = 11.55$$
$$7.2 - 0.1q + 0.25q = 11.55$$
$$7.2 + 0.15q = 11.55$$
$$0.15q = 4.35$$
$$q = 29$$

You can also **use your answer choices** to solve this problem without ever setting up a system! Start with a middle number and then you could either work your way up or down accordingly. So, suppose the answer is 18 quarters. This means that Jaclyn has 18 • 0.25 = $4.50 in quarters and 72–18 = 54 dimes, which is $5.40 and adds up to a total of $9.90. This is not enough, so try an answer choice that is higher. If Jaclyn has 29 quarters then she has 29 • 0.25 = $7.25 in quarters and 72–29 = 43 dimes, which is $4.30 and adds up to a total of $11.55. This is the correct total.

16. **D** Plugging the values you are given into the formula $K = \frac{1}{2}mv^2$ and solving, you get $384 =$

$$\frac{1}{2}(12)v^2 \longrightarrow 384 = 6v^2 \longrightarrow 64 = v^2 \longrightarrow$$

$v = 8$ meters per second.

17. **B** One revolution of the tire is the circumference of the tire. $C = 20\pi$.

$$4C = 4 \cdot 20\pi = 80\pi \approx 251 \text{ in.}$$

18. **C** The y-intercept of the line in the graph is 3. The slope of the line is $\frac{-3}{6} = -\frac{1}{2}$. Putting these values into the slope-intercept form for the equation of a line, $y = mx + b$, you get $y = -\frac{1}{2}x + 3$. Multiplying both sides of the equation by 2 and bringing the x term to the left-hand side of the equation, gives you $x + 2y = 6$.

You can also **use your answer choices** to solve this problem. Look for the answer choice that has an x value of 6 when y is 0 and a y value of 3 when x is 0. Only answer choice C works!

19. a. Use the formula:

$$mean = \frac{sum\ of\ ages}{number\ of\ people} = \frac{830}{50} = 16.6$$

Answer: 16.6

b. The median age will be the number in the middle of the ordered list. The data is already ordered. Since there are 50 people, the number in the middle is in the $\frac{n+1}{2} = \frac{51}{2} = 25.5$ position. That is the average of the 25th and 26th positions of the list. These are the ages 14 and 14, so the median age is 14 years.

Answer: 14

c. The mode is the most frequently appearing age. Both the ages 13 and 15 appear five times, and this is more than any other age. This data set is considered **bimodal** (having two modes) and the modes are 13 and 15.

Answer: 13 and 15

d. Either table below has age intervals of five years. Be careful not to overlap an age in more than one interval.

Ages	Frequency		Ages	Frequency
1–5	1		5–9	8
6–10	11		10–14	18
11–15	19		15–19	15
16–20	10		20–24	2
21–25	2		25–29	1
26–30	1		30–34	1
31–35	1		35–39	2
36–40	2		40–44	2
41–45	3		45–49	1

e. Using the frequency table above, the histogram (or connected bar graph) looks like:

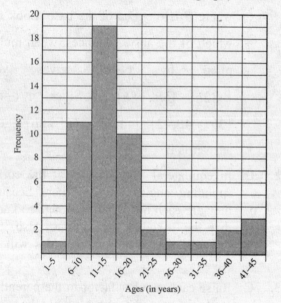

20. a. The height of the vat is 5 feet or $5 \cdot 12 = 60$ inches.
The radius of the vat is 2 feet of $2 \cdot 12 = 24$ inches.
Use the formula for the volume of a cylinder, substituting $h = 60$ and $r = 24$.

$$V = \pi(24)^2(60) = 34560\pi \approx 108,573 \text{ cubic inches.}$$

Answer: 108,573 in.³

b. If 1 gal = 231 cubic inches, then his 3-gallon jug holds $3 \cdot 231 = 693$ cubic inches. Dividing the volume of the vat by the volume of the jug, we get the number of jugs necessary to fill the vat, or $\frac{108,573}{693} = 156.67$ jugs. This means he will have to fill his jug 157 times.

Answer: 157 times

c. If it takes 20 seconds to fill the jug and empty it into the vat, and he has to do this 157 times, it will take Mr. Truffle $20 \cdot 157 = 3,140$ seconds or $\frac{3,140}{60} = 52.33 \approx 52$ minutes.

Answer: 52 minutes

21. a. The opposite sides of a rhombus are parallel to one another, so side $\overline{DA}$ will have the same slope as side $\overline{BC}$. Using the slope formula: $m = \frac{rise}{run} = \frac{y_2 - y_1}{x_2 - x_1}$, you get

$$\overline{BC} = \frac{9-4}{10-9} = \frac{5}{1}$$

To get from point B to point C, you move one unit to the right and 5 units up. Do the same thing to get to point D, only start at point A. You get $D = (4 + 1, 3 + 5) = (5, 8)$.

Answer: $D(5, 8)$

b. To find the length of a side, you can use the distance formula:

$d = \sqrt{\left(x_2 - x_1\right)^2 + \left(y_2 - y_1\right)^2}$, which is really just the Pythagorean Theorem in disguise!

$$AB = \sqrt{\left(9-4\right)^2 + \left(4-3\right)^2} = \sqrt{25+1} = \sqrt{26}$$
$$BC = \sqrt{\left(10-9\right)^2 + \left(9-4\right)^2} = \sqrt{1+25} = \sqrt{26}$$

From these measurements, you can conclude that consecutive (next to each other) sides of a rhombus are congruent to each other. Since a rhombus is a parallelogram, opposite sides are congruent to each other as well, so a rhombus has four congruent sides.

Answer: $AB = BC = \sqrt{26}$
= four congruent sides

c. Using your coordinates for point D and the slope formula, you get

$$m_{\overline{AC}} = \frac{9-3}{10-4} = \frac{6}{6} = 1$$

and $m_{\overline{DB}} = \frac{8-4}{5-9} = \frac{4}{-4} = -1$

These slopes are opposite reciprocals, so the diagonals of the rhombus are perpendicular to each other.

Answer: $m_{\overline{AC}} = 1$ and $m_{\overline{DB}} = -1$
perpendicular diagonals

Directions for Practice Test 2, Session A

This session contains fourteen multiple-choice questions (1–14), four short-answer questions (15–18), and three open-response questions (19–21).

1. You may not use a calculator during this test.
2. You may use the MCAS Reference Sheet to access formulas.
3. The recommended time is 60 minutes, but your school will give you more time if you need it.

Practice Test 2, Session A
Answer Sheet
Fill in the bubble completely. Erase carefully if an answer is changed.

1. ◯ ◯ ◯ ◯
   A B C D

2. ◯ ◯ ◯ ◯
   A B C D

3. ◯ ◯ ◯ ◯
   A B C D

4. ◯ ◯ ◯ ◯
   A B C D

5. ◯ ◯ ◯ ◯
   A B C D

6. ◯ ◯ ◯ ◯
   A B C D

7. ◯ ◯ ◯ ◯
   A B C D

8. ◯ ◯ ◯ ◯
   A B C D

9. ◯ ◯ ◯ ◯
   A B C D

10. ◯ ◯ ◯ ◯
    A B C D

11. ◯ ◯ ◯ ◯
    A B C D

12. ◯ ◯ ◯ ◯
    A B C D

13. ◯ ◯ ◯ ◯
    A B C D

14. ◯ ◯ ◯ ◯
    A B C D

Massachusetts Comprehensive Assessment System
Grade 10 Mathematics Reference Sheet

AREA FORMULAS

triangle . . . . $A = \dfrac{1}{2}bh$

rectangle. . . . . $A = bh$

parallelogram . . . . $A = bh$

square. . . . . $A = s^2$

trapezoid. . . . . $A = \dfrac{1}{2}h\,(b_1 + b_2)$

CIRCLE FORMULAS

$C = 2\pi r$

$A = \pi r^2$

LATERAL SURFACE AREA FORMULAS

right rectangular prism . . . . $LA = 2(hw) + 2(lh)$
right circular cylinder . . . . $LA = 2\pi rh$
right circular cone. . . . . $LA = \pi r\ell$
right square pyramid. . . . . $LA = 2s\ell$
(ℓ = slant height)

TOTAL SURFACE AREA FORMULAS

cube. . . . . $SA = 6s^2$
right rectangular prism . . . . $SA = 2(lw) + 2(hw) + 2(lh)$
sphere . . . . $SA = 4\pi r^2$
right circular cylinder . . . . $SA = 2\pi r^2 + 2\pi rh$
right circular cone. . . . . $SA = \pi r^2 + \pi r\ell$
right square pyramid. . . . . $SA = s^2 + 2s\ell$
(ℓ = slant height)

VOLUME FORMULAS

cube. . . . . $V = s^3$

(s = length of an edge)
right rectangular prism . . . . $V = lwh$

OR

(B = area of the base) . . . . . $V = Bh$

sphere . . . . $V = \dfrac{4}{3}\pi r^3$

right circular cylinder . . . . . $V = \pi r^2 h$

right circular cone. . . . . $V = \dfrac{1}{3}\pi r^2 h$

right square pyramid. . . . . . $V = \dfrac{1}{3}s^2 h$

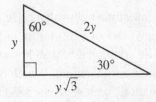

Practice Test 2, Session A

Multiple-Choice Questions

1. What is the value of the expression below?

$$1 - 3\left|2 - 7\right|$$

  A. −14
  B. −10
  C. 10
  D. 14

2. A rational expression is shown below.

$$\frac{x^5 - x^3}{8}$$

What is the value of the expression when $x = 2$?

  A. 1
  B. 3
  C. 8
  D. 9

3. An item is on sale for 20% off of its original price. What percent increase is needed to return the sale item back to its original price?

  A. 20%
  B. 25%
  C. 50%
  D. 100%

4. Karl is an investment consultant. He charges his clients a fixed rate of $200 for an initial consultation and an additional $80 an hour for time spent working for the client. Which of the following equations represents the amount of money, y, paid to Karl by the client, after x number of hours?

  A. $y = 200x + 80$
  B. $y = 200x - 80$
  C. $y = 80x + 200$
  D. $y = 80x - 200$

5. Which of the following demonstrates the distributive property?

  A. $-5xz + 5xz + 3yz = 3yz$
  B. $4xy + (7xy + 5xz) = (4xy + 7xy) + 5xz$
  C. $xz + 6xy + 11xz = xz + 11xz + 6xy$
  D. $8xy - 24xz = 4x(2y - 6z)$

6. What is the value of r?

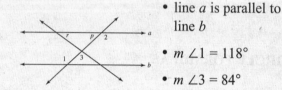

  • line a is parallel to line b
  • $m \angle 1 = 118°$
  • $m \angle 3 = 84°$

  A. 17°
  B. 34°
  C. 42°
  D. 62°

7. Given circle O with points A, B, C, D on the circle and diameter $\overline{BD}$, which is not necessarily true?

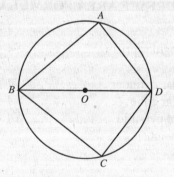

  A. $\angle BAD$ is a right angle
  B. $\angle BAD$ is supplementary to $\angle BCD$
  C. $\overset{\frown}{BC} = 2 \cdot \angle BDC$
  D. $\angle ABD = \angle ADB$

8. The box-and-whisker plot below shows the heights of basketball players in a certain league. What is the median of the heights?

Heights of Basketball Players (inches)

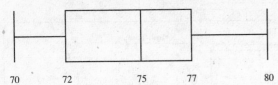

70   72   75   77   80

A. 10 inches
B. 72 inches
C. 75 inches
D. 77 inches

9. Isabella solved a quadratic equation and found the solutions to be -8 and $\dfrac{5}{3}$. Which of the following is equivalent to the quadratic equation that Rebecca solved?

A. $(x + 8)(5x - 3) = 0$
B. $(x + 8)(3x - 5) = 0$
C. $(x - 8)(5x + 3) = 0$
D. $(x - 8)(3x + 5) = 0$

10. Given the diagram below, solve for x.

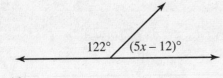

$122°$ $(5x - 12)°$

A. 10
B. 14
C. 27
D. 58

11. What is the y-intercept of the line represented in the equation below?

$$8x - 4y = 32$$

A. $(0, -4)$
B. $(0, -8)$
C. $(0, 4)$
D. $(0, 8)$

12. Find the area of the shaded segment in a circle with radius 5 inches and a central angle of 60°.

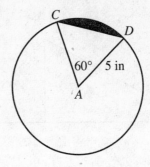

A. $\dfrac{25\sqrt{3}}{4}$ units^2

B. $25\pi - \dfrac{25\sqrt{3}}{4}$ units^2

C. $\dfrac{25\pi}{6} - \dfrac{25\sqrt{3}}{4}$ units^2

D. $\dfrac{25\sqrt{3}}{6}$ units^2

13. Ms. Notari recorded the most recent test scores of her 28 students in the chart below.

Score (percent)	Number of Students
50–59	4
60–69	5
70–79	4
80–89	10
90–100	5

Based on the information in the chart, which interval contains the median score?

A. 60–69
B. 70–79
C. 80–89
D. 90–100

14. In the figure below, if $\overline{CD} = 4\sqrt{2}$ what is the length of $\overline{AD}$?

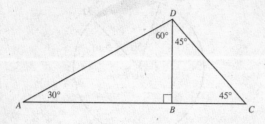

A. $8\sqrt{2}$
B. 16
C. 8
D. $4\sqrt{3}$

Short Answer Questions

15. The table below indicates a linear relationship between x and y.

x	y
2	5
4	11
6	17
8	23
10	29

Write an equation for y in terms of x.

_____

16. Mr. Rabb purchased 20 theater tickets for a total of $288. The tickets cost $16 for adults and $12 for children under age 14. How many children's tickets did Mr. Rabb purchase?

_____

17. If an equilateral triangle has a height of $4\sqrt{3}$ inches, find the length of each side of the triangle.

_____

18. Meredith's test average after taking three math tests is an 80%. What does Meredith need to get on her fourth test in order to raise her average to an 85%?

Open Response Questions

Use the figure below to answer question 19.

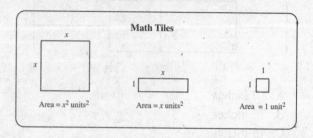

19. Math tiles can be used to build rectangular arrays which represent quadratic expressions. Two different representations are illustrated below.

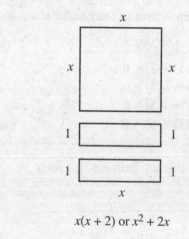

$x(x + 2)$ or $x^2 + 2x$

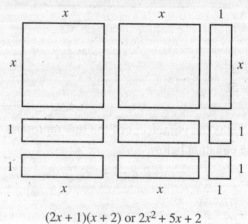

$(2x + 1)(x + 2)$ or $2x^2 + 5x + 2$

a. Build a rectangular array, if possible, for each of the following expressions using the three different math tiles.

$$3x^2 + 3x$$

$$3x^2 + 7x + 2$$

$$4x^2 + 4x + 1$$

b. How can you determine if a rectangular array can be built for an expression using the math tiles?

---

20. In the diagram below, the coordinates of point A are $(-4, 3)$ and the coordinates of point C are $(-1, 1)$.

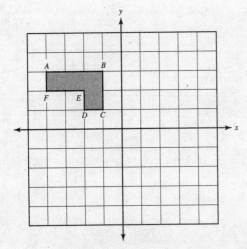

a. If the shaded figure $ABCDEF$ were reflected over the x-axis, what would be the coordinates of the image point A'? Explain or show how you arrived at your answer.

b. Draw the image of the shaded figure reflected over the **y-axis** on the grid provided.

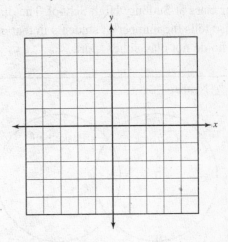

c. If figure $ABCDEF$ were rotated $180°$ clockwise about the origin, draw the resulting figure. Show or explain how you arrived at your answer.

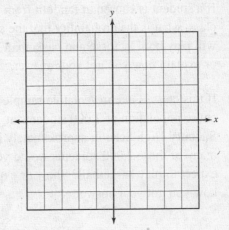

21. The following Venn diagram shows the number of lacrosse and basketball players for a particular class at Sudbury High School. The diagram also tells the number of students in that class who do not play either sport.

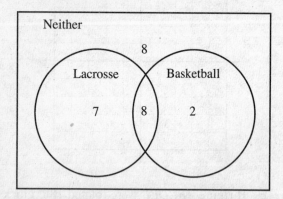

a. How many students are in the class? Show or explain how you got your answer.

b. If a student is chosen at random from the class, what is the probability that the student will play both lacrosse and basketball? Show or explain how you got your answer.

c. If this class is a representative sample of the entire population of 2,000 students at Sudbury High School, approximately how many of those 2,000 students would you expect to play basketball? Show or explain how you got your answer.

Solutions: Practice Test 2, Session A

1. A $1 - 3|2 - 7| = 1 - 3|-5| = 1 - 3 \cdot 5 = 1 - 15 = -14.$

2. B $\dfrac{2^5 - 2^3}{8} = \dfrac{32 - 8}{8} = \dfrac{24}{4} = 3.$

3. B **Choose your own number** to solve this problem. Suppose the item's original cost had been $100. If it is on sale for 20% off, the new price is $80. In order to increase the item to its original price, it will need to increase by $20, which is 25% of the price that it is presently at. The percent increase is 25%.

4. C For every hour that Karl works, he charges the client an additional $80. This means that if he worked 3 hours, the charge would be 3 • 80 = $240, plus an additional $200 for the fixed cost. You can substitute the 3 for x, which can be any number of hours. This is represented by $y = 80x + 200$.

5. D **Eliminate incorrect answer choices.** Looking through the answer choices, answer choice A demonstrates the addition of like terms. Answer B demonstrates the associative property of addition. Answer C demonstrates the commutative property. Only answer D demonstrates the distributive property. $8xy - 24xz = 4x(2y - 6z)$

6. B For parallel lines, alternate interior angles are congruent, so $\angle 1 = \angle 2 = 118°$. The supplement to $\angle 2$ is p, so $p = 180° - 118° = 62°$. Since vertical angles are congruent, the angle above $\angle 3$ is also equal to $84°$. The sum of the angles in a triangle equal to $180°$, so:
$\angle 3 + p + r = 180° \rightarrow 84 + 62 + r = 180$
$\rightarrow 146 + r = 180 \rightarrow r = 34°.$

7. D A is true. $\angle BAD$ intercepts a semicircle. Its degree is half of its intercepted arc. It is $90°$.
B is true. Opposite angles of a quadrilateral inscribed in a semicircle are supplementary.
C is true. The degree of an inscribed angle is half of its intercepted arc.
D is false. You cannot assume that these two angles are congruent.

8. C The median is the dividing line of the box portion of the box-and-whisker plot. In this question, its value is 75.

9. B **Use your answer choices.** Which one would give you Isabella's solutions if you set the parentheses equal to 0 and solved? The correct answer is choice B. Do not confuse this with choice A, which would give you solutions -8 and $\dfrac{3}{5}$.

10. B Two angles that form a straight line add up to $180°$. Your equation and solution will look like: $122 + 5x - 12 = 180 \rightarrow 110 + 5x = 180 \rightarrow 5x = 70 \rightarrow x = 14.$

11. B Plug in 0 for x into the equation to find the y value of the y-intercept. Solve the equation for y: $8 \cdot 0 - 4y = 32 \rightarrow -4y = 32 \rightarrow y = -8.$

12. C The area of the shaded segment is the area of sector *ACD* minus the area of equilateral $\triangle ACD$.

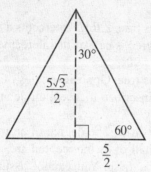

equilateral triangle =

$$\frac{1}{2}bh = \frac{1}{2} \cdot 5 \cdot \frac{5\sqrt{3}}{2} = \frac{25\sqrt{3}}{4} \text{ units}^2$$

$$\text{sector} = \frac{1}{6} \cdot \pi r^2 = \frac{1}{6} \cdot 25\pi = \frac{25\pi}{6} \text{ units}^2$$

$$\text{segment} = \frac{25\pi}{6} - \frac{25\sqrt{3}}{4} \text{ units}^2$$

13. C Knowing that there are 28 students, you can calculate the middle students' position by using the formula

$$\textit{middle position} = \frac{n+1}{2} = \frac{28+1}{2} = \frac{29}{2} = 14.5.$$

This is a decimal because there are an even number of data so there are two middle numbers. That the position is 14.5 tells us that we need to average the 14th and 15th student's scores. Counting down on the table, the 14th and 15th students both fall in the 80–89 interval, so there is no need to average the same interval!

14. C $\triangle BCD$ is a 45°-45°-90°, isosceles right triangle, so its ratio of sides is $x : x : x\sqrt{2}$. Since $CD = x\sqrt{2} = 4\sqrt{2}$, this makes $BD = x = 4$. $\triangle BDA$ is a 30°-60°-90° special triangle, so its ratio of sides is $x : x\sqrt{3} : 2x$, where the shortest side x is opposite the 30° angle, and the longest side $2x$ is the hypotenuse. $AD = 2(BD) = 2(4) = 8$.

15. Take any two points to find the slope of the line: (2, 5) and (4, 11) and calculate $m = \frac{y_2 - y_1}{x_2 - x_1} = \frac{11 - 5}{4 - 2} = \frac{6}{2} = 3$. The difference between each of the *x* values in the table is 2 and the difference in the *y* values is 6. Therefore, for the first *x* value listed, 2 – 2 = 0, and for the *y* value listed 5 – 6 = –1. This means that the *y* intercept is (0, –1) and the equation of the line in *y=mx+b* form is *y=3x–1*.

Answer: *y* = 3*x* – 1

16. Let *x* = the number of adult tickets and *y* = the number of children's tickets.

Set up a system:
$x + y = 20$
$16x + 12y = 288$

The question asks for the number of children's tickets purchased, so you should eliminate *x*, the number of adult tickets, in the two equations. Multiply the first equation by –16.

$-16x = 16y = -320$
$16x + 12y = 288$

Add the two equations together and you get $-4y = -32 \rightarrow y = 8$.

Answer: 8

17. Opposite the 60° angle is the height of $4\sqrt{3}$. This means that opposite the 30° angle is 4 and the entire side is 8 inches.

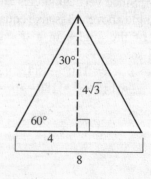

Answer: 8 inches

18. The sum of Meredith's three test scores is 3 • 80 = 240. In order for the average of all four tests to be 85%, the sum would have to be 4 • 85 = 340. The difference between 340 and 240 is 100. Therefore, Meredith would have to get a 100% on her fourth test.

Answer: 100%

19. a. Creating an array with math tiles means arranging the tiles you have into a large rectangle. A single math tile is a rectangle with side of either length x or 1. There are three types of tiles, but only two different dimensions, or lengths of sides. x is the length of the longer side, and 1 is the length of the shorter. Each individual block is named by its area, found by multiplying its base and height together. Here are the three building blocks:

$$x^2 = x \bullet x = \boxed{}\ x \qquad x = x \bullet 1 = \boxed{}\ 1$$

$$1 = 1 \bullet 1 = \square\ 1$$

As an example, if your expression has a $3x^2$ term in it, you must use three of the x^2 tiles. Likewise, $2x$ means that you must use two of x tiles. Creating rectangular arrays that represent the expressions given to you in the problem, you get:

$3x^2 + 3x$ $3x^2 + 7x + 2$

$4x^2 + 4x + 1$

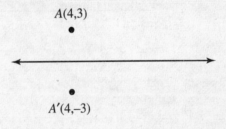

b. Looking at the row and column lengths, you see that the dimensions of the rectangular arrays are the factorizations of the expressions. For example: $3x^2 + 3x = 3x(x + 1)$, $3x^2 + 7x + 2 = (3x + 1)(x + 2)$, $4x^2 + 4x + 1 = (2x + 1)(2x + 1)$
This means that in order to build a rectangular array, the expression must be factorable.

20. a. The reflection of a point over the x-axis transforms the point (x, y) to the point $(x, -y)$. This means that the x-coordinate of the image point remains the same, but the y-coordinate has the opposite sign. The coordinates of $A' = (4, -3)$.

$A(4,3)$

$A'(4,-3)$

b. The reflection of the shaded figure over the y-axis is the unshaded figure $A'B'C'D'E'F'$.

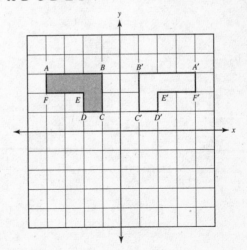

c. A 180° rotation is the same as two 90° rotations. The diagram below shows a rotation of 90° to form the first image figure in white, $A'B'C'D'E'F'$.

The second image figure, in black, is a 90° rotation of the first. This is the final answer.

You could also have approached this problem by finding the coordinates of each point in

$A''B''C''D''E''F''$ using the transformation $(x, y) \xrightarrow{180° \text{rotation}} (-x, -y)$. This gives you coordinates of $C''(1, -1)$, $D''(2, -1)$, $A''(4, -3)$ ... and so on.

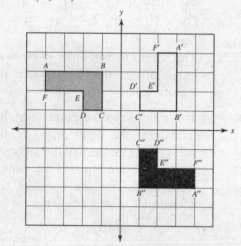

21. a. There are 8 students who are in the neither category, 7 who play lacrosse only, 2 who play basketball only, and 8 who play both basketball and lacrosse. Add these numbers up: $8 + 7 + 2 + 8 = 25$.

Answer: 25 students

b. There are 8 students who play both sports and there are 25 students in the class. The likelihood of choosing one of those students is $\dfrac{8}{25}$.

Answer: $\dfrac{8}{25}$

c. Set up a proportion and solve:

$$\frac{2}{25} = \frac{x}{2000} \rightarrow 25x = 4000 \rightarrow x = 160.$$

Answer: 160 students

Directions for Practice Test 2, Session B

This session contains eighteen multiple-choice questions (1–18) and three open-response questions (19–21).

1. You may use a calculator during this test.
2. You may use the MCAS Reference Sheet to access formulas.
3. The recommended time is 60 minutes, but your school will give you more time if you need it.

Practice Test 2, Session B
Answer Sheet
Fill in the bubble completely. Erase carefully if an answer is changed.

1. ○ ○ ○ ○
   A B C D

2. ○ ○ ○ ○
   A B C D

3. ○ ○ ○ ○
   A B C D

4. ○ ○ ○ ○
   A B C D

5. ○ ○ ○ ○
   A B C D

6. ○ ○ ○ ○
   A B C D

7. ○ ○ ○ ○
   A B C D

8. ○ ○ ○ ○
   A B C D

9. ○ ○ ○ ○
   A B C D

10. ○ ○ ○ ○
    A B C D

11. ○ ○ ○ ○
    A B C D

12. ○ ○ ○ ○
    A B C D

13. ○ ○ ○ ○
    A B C D

14. ○ ○ ○ ○
    A B C D

15. ○ ○ ○ ○
    A B C D

16. ○ ○ ○ ○
    A B C D

17. ○ ○ ○ ○
    A B C D

18. ○ ○ ○ ○
    A B C D

Massachusetts Comprehensive Assessment System
Grade 10 Mathematics Reference Sheet

AREA FORMULAS

triangle . . . . $A = \dfrac{1}{2}bh$

rectangle . . . . $A = bh$

parallelogram . . . . $A = bh$

square . . . . $A = s^2$

trapezoid . . . . $A = \dfrac{1}{2}h\,(b_1 + b_2)$

CIRCLE FORMULAS

$C = 2\pi r$

$A = \pi r^2$

LATERAL SURFACE AREA FORMULAS

right rectangular prism . . . . $LA = 2(hw) + 2(lh)$
right circular cylinder . . . . $LA = 2\pi rh$
right circular cone . . . . $LA = \pi r\ell$
right square pyramid . . . . $LA = 2s\ell$
(ℓ = slant height)

TOTAL SURFACE AREA FORMULAS

cube . . . . $SA = 6s^2$
right rectangular prism . . . . $SA = 2(lw) + 2(hw) + 2(lh)$
sphere . . . . $SA = 4\pi r^2$
right circular cylinder . . . . $SA = 2\pi r^2 + 2\pi rh$
right circular cone . . . . $SA = \pi r^2 + \pi r\ell$
right square pyramid . . . . $SA = s^2 + 2s\ell$
(ℓ = slant height)

VOLUME FORMULAS

cube . . . . $V = s^3$

(s = length of an edge)
right rectangular prism . . . . $V = lwh$

OR

(B = area of the base) . . . . . $V = Bh$

sphere . . . . $V = \dfrac{4}{3}\pi r^3$

right circular cylinder . . . . . $V = \pi r^2 h$

right circular cone . . . . $V = \dfrac{1}{3}\pi r^2 h$

right square pyramid . . . . . . $V = \dfrac{1}{3}s^2 h$

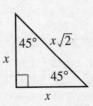

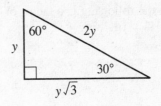

Practice Test 2, Session B

Multiple-Choice Questions

1. Which statement is **not** true?

   A. $\sqrt[3]{8} = 8^{\frac{1}{3}}$

   B. $4^{-2} = \dfrac{1}{16}$

   C. $(-27)^{\frac{1}{3}} = -27^{\frac{1}{3}}$

   D. $-9^2 = (-9)^2$

2. If Danit closes her eyes and picks one of the shapes below, puts it back down and then picks a shape again with her eyes closed, what is the probability that she picks two circles?

   A. $\dfrac{8}{225}$

   B. $\dfrac{1}{2}$

   C. $\dfrac{8}{15}$

   D. $\dfrac{64}{225}$

3. Which of the following is a factor of $5x^4y^2 - x^3y^3 + 10x^2y^2$?

   A. $5xy$

   B. x^2y^2

   C. x^3y^3

   D. $5x^4y^2$

4. In which equation below is the solution equal to the multiplicative inverse of $\dfrac{3}{4}$?

   A. $\dfrac{3}{4} \cdot x = -1$

   B. $\dfrac{3}{4} \cdot x = 0$

   C. $\dfrac{3}{4} \cdot x = 1$

   D. $\dfrac{3}{4} \cdot x = \dfrac{3}{4}$

5. In the figure below, A, B, and C are collinear. What is the positive difference between the lengths of $\overline{AB}$ and $\overline{BC}$ to the nearest tenth of an inch?

   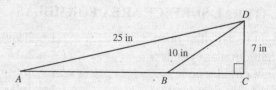

   A. 16.8 in

   B. 7.1 in

   C. 9.7 in

   D. 24.0 in

6. The chart below separates the students majoring in history from students pursuing other majors at a state college.

Students' Majors by Class				
	Freshman	Sophomores	Juniors	Seniors
History Majors	320	120	240	400
Other Majors	1240	1500	1300	1620

What percent of history majors are juniors?

A. 4%
B. 18%
C. 22%
D. 24%

7. Of the people in attendance at a recent symphony performance,

- one-twelfth had balcony seats
- one-eighth had orchestra seats
- the remaining 9,880 people in attendance had other seats.

What was the total number of people in attendance at the symphony?

A. 9,800
B. 10,200
C. 11,935
D. 12,480

8. What is the value of the expression below?

$$3 - 6|2 - 7|$$

A. –27
B. 15
C. 33
D. 90

9. If $\angle A$ is obtuse and $\angle A = (23 - 5x)°$, which of the following can be a value of x?

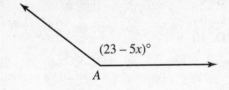

A. 32
B. – 50
C. – 13
D. –17

10. The following table shows the age in years of five people:

Person	Age in Years
Seth	48
Lisa	44
Bouke	34
Mike	37
Shara	27

Which of the following statements is false?

A. The mean age is greater than the median age.
B. The range of the ages is 21.
C. The median age is 34.
D. If Mike were 5 years younger, the median of the data would be different.

11. Angles 1, 2, and 3 are in a ratio of 2: 8: 5. Find the degree measure of $\angle 2$.

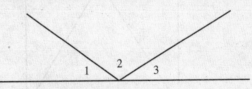

(Figure not drawn to scale.)

A. 12°
B. 60°
C. 96°
D. 102°

12. What value for y will complete the table, given that x and y are in a linear relationship?

x	y
1.2	–2.6
3.7	2.4
6.2	7.4
7.8	

A. 9
B. 10.6
C. 12.4
D. 13.6

13. Which of the answer choices below is the simplified version of the following expression:

$$\left(\frac{-3x^2 y^4 z}{9z}\right)^3$$

A. $\dfrac{-x^6 y^{12}}{9}$

B. $\dfrac{-x^6 y^{12}}{27}$

C. $\dfrac{-x^5 y^7}{27}$

D. $\dfrac{-x^5 y^7}{9}$

---

14. In the figure below, $\triangle BED$ is equilateral and $ACDE$ is a rectangle. If the perimeter of $\triangle BED$ is 27 inches, what is the area of rectangle $ACDE$?

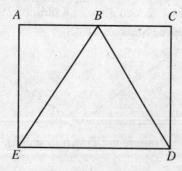

A. $\dfrac{81\sqrt{3}}{4}$ in^2

B. $\dfrac{81\sqrt{3}}{2}$ in^2

C. $81\sqrt{3}$ in^2

D. 81 in^2

15. Jennifer is waiting for a dress to go on sale so that she can afford to buy it. She is ready to buy the dress on the first day that it is on sale for less than $100. She sees a sign in the store window on Sunday which states that on Monday morning, a 6% discount will be applied to all items in the store and each morning that week, an additional 6% discount will be applied to each previous day's discount. If the dress's present cost is $120, on what day should Jennifer buy the dress?

A. Tuesday
B. Wednesday
C. Thursday
D. Friday

---

16. Given $\overline{AE} \parallel \overline{BD}$, $AB = 6$, $AE = 20$, $BD = 8$. Find the length of $\overline{AC}$.

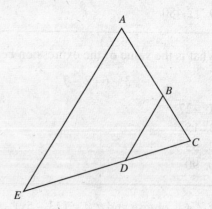

A. 2.4
B. 4
C. 6
D. 10

17. In the figure below, $m\angle LEV = \frac{1}{3}(x+12)$ and $m\angle TEA = \frac{2}{5}x+3$.

What is the value of x?

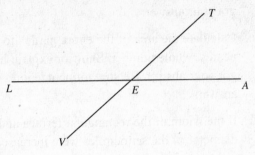

A. 15
B. 30
C. 10
D. 25

18. Which of the following equations is represented by the graph below?

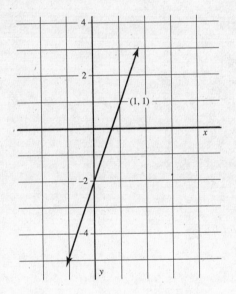

A. $y = -3x - 2$
B. $y = 3x + 2$
C. $y = \frac{1}{3}x - 2$
D. $y = 3x - 2$

Open Response Questions

19. Every student in the ninth grade at Columbia High School must take exactly one of four language classes: French, Spanish, German, or Latin. A student may not take more than one language class. Below is a double bar graph of female and male students in the four different language classes.

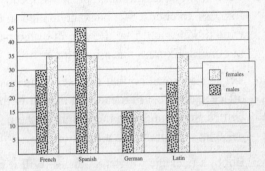

a. What is the total number of students in the ninth grade?

b. What percent of the students in the ninth grade are female? Round your answer to the nearest whole percent. Show or explain how you got your answer.

c. If a student were selected at random from the ninth grade class at Columbia High School, what is the probability that he or she is enrolled in a French class? Show or explain how you got your answer.

d. Draw and label a circle graph that shows the information given in the graph above for the male students in each of the four language classes. The sectors in your sketch do not need to be exact, but should be relatively proportioned. Explain or show how you determined the size of each sector.

20. Bobby is investigating his options for prices for mailing a package within the United States. He is comparing the prices of Speedy Express and his local post office.

- Speedy Express charges 50 cents for every ounce mailed.

- The local post office charges a fixed rate of $1.50 and an additional 20 cents for each ounce.

a. Let f be an equation that represents Speedy Express' total cost of a package mailed in the United States and x be the weight of the package in ounces. Express f as a function of x.

b. Let f be an equation that represents the post office's total cost of a package mailed in the United States and x be the weight of the package in ounces. Express f as a function of x.

c. Bobby's package weighs 8 ounces. Will it be less expensive for Bobby to send the package with Speedy Express or the local post office? Show or explain how you got your answer.

d. How much would a package have to weigh for the price to come out the same from Speedy Express and the post office? Show or explain how you arrived at your answer.

---

21. A public garden is made up of a rectangular terrace with two semicircular flower beds on the ends. The diameter of the semicircles is 40 meters, and the length of the rectangular terrace is 100 meters.

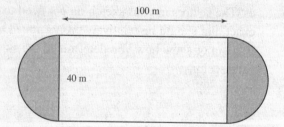

100 m

40 m

a. What is the perimeter of the garden to the nearest meter? Show or explain how you got your answer. Be sure to include units in your answer.

b. If the width of the rectangular terrace and the diameter of the semicircles were increased to 50 meters, but the length remained the same, by what percent would the perimeter of the entire garden be increased? Show or explain how you got your answer.

c. Calculate the area of the entire garden to the nearest whole number. Show or explain how you got your answer. Be sure to include units in your answer.

d. If the width of the rectangular terrace and the diameter of the semicircles were increased to 50 meters, but the length remained the same, by what percent would the area of the entire garden be increased? Show or explain how you got your answer. Be sure to include units in your answer.

Solutions: Practice Test 2, Session B

1. D

A. This is a true statement. The cube root of 8 means the same thing as 8 to the one third power.

B. This is a true statement. To get rid of the negative exponent, rewrite 4^{-2} as $\dfrac{1}{4^2}$. This is $\dfrac{1}{16}$.

C. This is a true statement. The cube root of -27 is -3 because when you multiply $(-3)(-3)(-3)$ the result is -27. Likewise, for $-27^{\frac{1}{3}}$, the rules of PEMDAS say that you first calculate $-27^{\frac{1}{3}}$, which is 3, and then multiply it by -1. So the answer is also -3.

D. This is a false statement. The rules of PEMDAS say that for -9^2 you would first calculate the exponent, $9^2 = 81$, and then multiply that by -1, which is -81. However, $(-9)^2$ is entirely in parentheses, which means $(-9)(-9) = 81$. These are not equal, so the statement is false.

2. D There are 15 items that Danit is picking from the first time and the second time as well.

Each time, she has an $\dfrac{8}{15}$ chance of picking a circle. You multiply these probabilities to find the probability of her picking a circle both times: The probability of picking two circles is: $\dfrac{8}{15} \cdot \dfrac{8}{15} = \dfrac{64}{225}$.

3. B The lowest exponent of x from the three terms is a 2, and the lowest exponent of y from the three terms is also 2. Since the coefficient of the second term is a -1, 5 cannot be a factor. The greatest common factor is x^2y^2. Lower degrees, such as xy and x^2y are also factors, but not the greatest factors.

4. C The multiplicative inverse of $\dfrac{3}{4}$ is $\dfrac{4}{3}$. It is the reciprocal of the number, because the two multiply to 1. Look for the answer choice that when solved, gives you the answer of $x = \dfrac{4}{3}$. All of the answer choices begin with the same left side of the equation: $\dfrac{3}{4} \cdot x$. To isolate the x, multiply both sides of the equation by the multiplicative inverse of $\dfrac{3}{4}$, which is $\dfrac{4}{3}$. Since $1 \cdot \dfrac{4}{3} = \dfrac{4}{3}$, the answer is C.

5. C $\triangle ACD$ and $\triangle BCD$ are right triangles. Use the Pythagorean Theorem to find the lengths of their missing sides. Try not to round your calculations until the last step, if possible. If you must round calculations midway through, be sure to go past the accuracy requested in the problem. $BC^2 + 7^2 = 10^2 \rightarrow BC^2 = 51 \rightarrow BC = \sqrt{51}$. $AC^2 + 7^2 = 25^2 \rightarrow AC = 24$.

$AB = AC - BC \approx 24 - \sqrt{51}$ inches. You want the difference of $AB - BC$ $= \left(24 - \sqrt{51}\right) - \sqrt{51} \approx 9.717$ in.

6. C There are a total of $320 + 120 + 240 + 400 = 1{,}080$ history majors. Out of those, 240 of them are juniors. The percentage of history majors that are juniors is $\dfrac{240}{1080} \approx 22\%$. The number of students who are other majors is irrelevant in this problem.

7. D The fraction of people who sat in the balcony and orchestra seats is $\dfrac{1}{12} + \dfrac{1}{8} = \dfrac{5}{24}$. This means that the remaining people take up $\dfrac{19}{24}$ of the seats. Calling the total number of people x,

$$\dfrac{19}{24}x = 9880 \rightarrow x = 9880 \cdot \dfrac{24}{19} = 12{,}480.$$

8. A $3 - 6|2 - 7| = 3 - 6|-5| = 3 - 6 \cdot 5 = 3 - 30 = -27.$

9. D **Use your answer choices.** An obtuse angle is an angle whose measure is between 90° and 180°. Plug in each value of x.
A. $23 - 5(32) = -137°$
B. $23 - 5(-50) = 273°$
C. $23 - 5(-13) = 88°$
D. $23 - 5(-17) = 108°$
Only answer choice D gives you an obtuse angle measure.

10. C

A. This is a true statement. The mean age is $\dfrac{48 + 44 + 34 + 37 + 27}{5} = 38$ years. The median age is 37 years because when you list the ages in order from least to greatest: 27, 34, 37, 44, 48, the middle number is 37. Since 38 is greater than 37, this statement is true.

B. This is a true statement. The range is the maximum value minus the minimum value, which is 48–27 = 21.

C. This is a false statement. The median age is 37, not 34.

D. This is a true statement. Mike's age, 37, is the median. If Mike's age were different, then the median would be different.

11. C Set up the equation: $2x + 8x + 5x = 180°$. Solve: $15x = 180° \rightarrow x = 12 \rightarrow \angle 2 = 8x = 8(12) = 96°$.

12. B Compute the slope of the line using the formula for slope, m, and any two points.

$$m = \dfrac{y_2 - y_1}{x_2 - x_1} = \dfrac{7.4 - 2.4}{6.2 - 3.7} = \dfrac{5}{2.5} = 2$$

Then choose any point, say (7.4, 6.2) and the point (7.8, y). Substitute back into the slope equation, and solve for y.

$$m = \dfrac{y_2 - y_1}{x_2 - x_1} = \dfrac{7.4 - y}{6.2 - 7.8} = \dfrac{7.4 - y}{-1.6} = 2$$

$$\dfrac{7.4 - y}{-1.6} = 2 \rightarrow 7.4 - y = -3.2 \rightarrow$$

$$7.4 + 3.2 = y \rightarrow y = 10.6$$

13. B First, simplify the inside of the parentheses. The z's cancel and the $\dfrac{3}{9}$ reduces to $\dfrac{1}{3}$ so that $\left(\dfrac{-3x^2 y^4 z}{9z}\right)^3 = \left(\dfrac{-x^2 y^4}{3}\right)^3$. Now cube it. The answer is still negative because $(-1)^3 = -1$. Remember that when you raise an exponent to another exponent, you multiply them. $\left(\dfrac{-x^2 y^4}{3}\right)^3 = \dfrac{-x^6 y^{12}}{27}$.

14. B The perimeter of the triangle is 27 inches, so each side is $27 \div 3 = 9$ inches. Draw the altitude to base $\overline{ED}$ of $\triangle BED$. Using the ratio of sides of a 30°-60°-90° triangle as $x : x\sqrt{3} : 2x$ and setting $2x = 9$, you get that the height of the triangle is $\dfrac{9\sqrt{3}}{2}$, which is also the height of the rectangle.

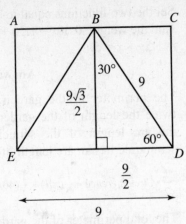

The base of the triangle is also the same as the base of the rectangle, so substituting into the area formula for a rectangle, you get:

$$area = base \cdot height = 9 \cdot \frac{9\sqrt{3}}{2} = \frac{81\sqrt{3}}{2} \ inches^2.$$

15. B On Monday morning the dress will cost $120 \cdot 0.94 = \$112.80$.
On Tuesday morning the dress will cost $112.8 \cdot 0.94 = \$106.03$.
On Wednesday morning the dress will cost $106.03 \cdot 0.94 = \$99.67$.
Jennifer should buy the dress on Wednesday.

16. D Corresponding angles of parallel lines are congruent, so $\angle EAC \cong \angle DBC$ and $\angle AEC \cong \angle BDC$. This means that $\Delta EAC \sim \Delta DBC$. Set up a proportion using similar triangles.

$$\frac{BC}{8} = \frac{BC + 6}{20} \rightarrow 20BC = 8(BC + 6) \rightarrow 20BC$$

$$= 8BC + 48 \rightarrow 12BC = 48 \rightarrow BC = 4.$$

Next, find AC: $AC = 6 + BC = 6 + 4 = 10$.
So the answer is D.

17. A Vertical angles are congruent, so $m\angle LEV = m\angle TEA$. Setting their expressions equal, you get: $\frac{1}{3}(x + 12) = \frac{2}{5}x + 3$. When solving (including multiplying both sides by 15 to eliminate fractions), you get:

$$\frac{1}{3}x + 4 = \frac{2}{5}x + 3 \rightarrow 15 \cdot \left[\frac{1}{3}x + 4 \right] =$$

$$\left[\frac{2}{5}x + 3 \right] \cdot 15 \rightarrow 5x + 60 = 6x + 45 \rightarrow 15 = x.$$

18. D Two points on the line are (1, 1) and (0, –2), so the slope is $\frac{-2 - 1}{0 - 1} = \frac{-3}{-1} = 3$.
The *y*-intercept is (0, –2), so in slope-intercept form, the equation of the line is $y = 3x - 2$.

19. a. Female $= 35 + 35 + 15 + 35 = 120$ students
Male $= 30 + 45 + 15 + 25 = 115$ students
Total number of students $= 120 + 115 = 235$ students

Answer: 235 students

b. Percent of students that are female $=$

$$\frac{number \ of \ female \ students}{total \ number \ of \ students} = \frac{120}{235} \approx 51\%.$$

Answer: 51%

c. Probability of a student in French $=$

$$\frac{number \ of \ students \ in \ French}{total \ number \ of \ students} = \frac{65}{235} = \frac{13}{47} \approx 28\%.$$

Answer: $\frac{13}{47}$ or approximately 28%

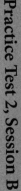

d. Compute the percent of male students in each of the four language classes out of all the male students in the ninth grade.

$$\frac{\text{male students in French}}{\text{total number of male students}} = \frac{30}{115} = 26\%$$

$$\frac{\text{male students in Spanish}}{\text{total number of male students}} = \frac{45}{115} \approx 39\%$$

$$\frac{\text{male students in German}}{\text{total number of male students}} = \frac{15}{115} \approx 13\%$$

$$\frac{\text{male students in Latin}}{\text{total number of male students}} = \frac{25}{115} \approx 22\%$$

Check to make sure that your percents add up to 100%. $26 + 39 + 13 + 22 = 100$

Construct your circle graph using your percents. For example, 26% is slightly more than one quarter of the circle, 39% is slightly more than one third, and so on. Be sure to label each sector.

Percent of Ninth Grade Male Students in Language Class

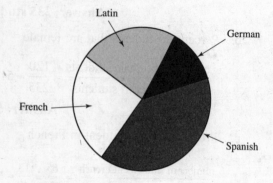

20. a. $f(x) = .50x$

b. $f(x) = 1.50 + 20x$

c. Speedy Express would cost $f(8) = .50(8) = \$4.00$.
The post office would cost $f(8) = 1.50 + .20(8) = \$3.10$.
It is less expensive to send the package with the post office.

Answer: post office

d. Set the two functions equal to each other to find the weight: $0.50x = 1.50 + 0.20x \rightarrow .3x = 1.5 \rightarrow x = 5$.

Answer: 5 ounces

21. a. The perimeter of the garden is equal to twice the length of the garden plus twice the arc length of the semicircles. Each semicircle has an arc length of

$$\frac{1}{2} \cdot Circumference = \frac{1}{2}(\pi d) = \frac{1}{2}(40\pi) = 20\pi \text{ m}$$

The total perimeter of the garden is $2(20\pi) + 2(100) = 40\pi + 200 \approx 326$ m.

Answer: 326 meters

b. If the diameter of the semicircles were increased to 50 meters, the new perimeter of the garden would be:

$$2 \cdot \frac{1}{2}(50\pi) + 200 = 50\pi + 200 \approx 357 \text{ m}.$$

The increase over the original perimeter is approximately 31 meters, which represents an increase of $\frac{31}{326} \approx 0.095$ or about 9.5%.

Answer: about 9.5%

c. The area of the garden is equal to twice the area of the semicircles (which becomes one full circle) plus the area of the rectangle. The area of the circle is $\pi r^2 = \pi(20)^2 = 400\pi$ m^2.
The area of the rectangle is $base \cdot height = 100 \cdot 40 = 4,000$ m^2. The total area of the garden $= 400\pi + 4000 \approx 5257$ m^2.

Answer: 5257 m²

d. If the diameter of the semicircles were increased to 50 meters, the new area of the garden would be:

$$2 \cdot \frac{1}{2}(25^2 \pi) + 50 \cdot 100 = 625\pi + 5000 \approx 6963 \text{ m}^2.$$

The increase over the original area is approximately 1706 square meters, which represents an increase of $\frac{1706}{5257} \approx 0.3245$ or about 32.5%.

Answer: about 32.5%

Index

A

Absolute Value 51, 148–150
  equations 148
  inequalities 149, 150
Angles 180–184
  acute 180
  adjacent 181
  complementary 182
  congruent 180
  corresponding 183
  obtuse 180
  right 181
  straight 181
  supplementary 182
  vertical 182
Area 248, 249
  circle 249
  parallelogram 248
  rectangle 248
  square 248
  trapezoid 249
  triangle 249

B

Bisector 178

C

Circle 191, 192, 247–250
  arc length 248
  central angle 191
  chord 191
  circumference 247
  diameter 191
  inscribed angle 192
  major arc 191
  minor arc 191
  radius 191
  sector 249
  segment 250
  semicircle 191
Coefficient 95
Combinations 358
Counting Principle 357

Cross Multiplying 72
Cross Section 306

D

Decimals 47–49
  repeating 47–49
  terminating 47–49
Degree 96
Displaying Data 329–334
  bar graph 330
  box-and-whisker plot 329
  circle graph 332
  dot plot 331
  frequency histogram 330
  frequency table 330
  lower quartile 329
  maximum 329
  minimum 329
  outlier 318, 334
  scatterplot 333
  stem-and-leaf plot 331
  upper quartile 329
Venn Diagram 334

E

Equations 106–119
  linear 106–115
  quadratic 116–119
  word problems 107
Equations of Lines 120–140
  horizontal 122, 226
  point slope form 122
  slope-intercept form 121
  vertical 122, 226
Estimation 79–88
  approximating with higher powers 79
  approximation of square roots 79
  rounding 79
Exponents 51, 60–62
Expression 95, 96
  cubic 96
  linear 96
  quadratic 96

F

Factors 51, 100–102
  difference of two squares 100, 101
  factoring 100–106
  greatest common factor 100
  trinomials 96–101
Functions 119–147
  exponential 142
  linear 119–139
  parabolas 141
  quadratic 141
  square root 143

I

Identities 52, 53
  additive 52, 53
  multiplicative 52, 53
Inverses 52, 53
  additive 52, 53
  multiplicative 52, 53

L

Line 177, 181–184, 225
  collinear 177
  noncollinear 177
  parallel 182–184, 225
  perpendicular 181, 225
  transversal 182–184
Linear Inequalities 148
  compound 148
Line Segment 177

M

Midpoint 177, 178, 224
Measures of Central Tendency 317, 318
  mean 317
  median 317, 318
  mode 318
Money Problems 89–93
Multiples 51

N

Net 305, 306
Numbers 47–51
  even 50
  integers 47
  irrational 47
  negative 51
  odd 50

perfect squares 47, 59
positive 51
prime 50
rational 47
real 47
whole 47

O

Order of Operations 62, 63

P

Parallel Lines 182–184, 225
  alternate interior angles 183
  same side interior angles 183, 184
Patterns 160–163
  linear 161
  quadratic 161
Percents 72
  fractions 72
Perimeter 247
Permutations 358
Perpendicular Bisector 182
Plane 178
  coplanar 178
  noncoplanar 178
Points 177
  space 177
Polygon 211, 212, 273, 274
  concave 211
  congruent 273
  convex 211
  diagonal 211, 212
  dilation 274
  regular 212
  similar 273
Polynomial 96, 100–102
  binomial 96
  monomial 96
  trinomial 96
Population 317
Probability 356–360
  complement 357
  compound 359
  dependent events 359
  expected value 358
  favorable outcome 356
  independent events 359
  tree diagram 359
Properties of Equality 51–53

associative 52, 53
   commutative 51, 53
   distributive 52, 53
Proportion 72

Q
Quadratic Formula 116
Quadrilateral 218–220
   isosceles trapezoid 220
   kite 220
   parallelogram 218
   rectangle 218
   rhombus 219
   square 219
   trapezoid 219

R
Range 318
Ratio 71, 274
Ray 177
Reciprocal 51
Relation 119
Roots 59, 60
   cube root 60
   square root 59

S
Sample 317
   bias 317
   random 317
   size 317
   unbiased 317
Sequence 160–162
   arithmetic 160, 161
   geometric 162
Slope 121, 225
Squaring Binomials 96
Surface Area 282–285
   bases 282, 283
   cone 285
   cube 291
   cylinder 285
   lateral 282
   prism 282, 283
   pyramid 284
   slant height 284
   sphere 285
Systems of Linear Equations 153–159

   addition 153
   graphing 153
   linear combination 153
   substitution 153

T
Term 95
   constant 95
   like 95
Transformation 237–240
   image 237
   line of symmetry 239
   preimage 237
   reflection 237
   rotation 239, 240
   translation 239
Triangle 190, 198–200, 273, 274
   30°-60°-90° 199
   45°-45°-90° 199
   acute 190, 199
   altitude 200
   equilateral 199
   exterior angle 190
   height 200
   inequality theorem 198
   isosceles 198
   median 200
   midsegment 200
   obtuse 190, 199
   Pythagorean Theorem 199
   right 190, 199
   scalene 198

V
Variable 51, 120
   dependent 120
   independent 120
Vertex Edge Graph 168–171
Volume 283–286
   cone 285
   cube 283
   cylinder 284
   prism 283
   pyramid 284
   sphere 285

NOTES

NOTES

NOTES

THERE'S ONLY ONE PLACE TO TURN FOR TOP SCORES...

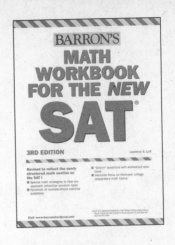
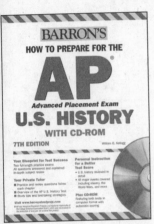
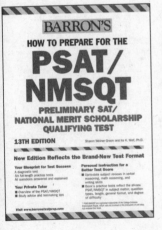
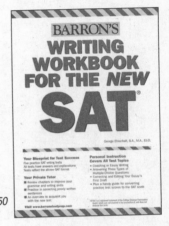
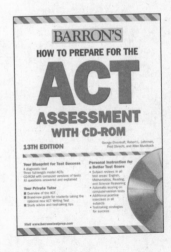

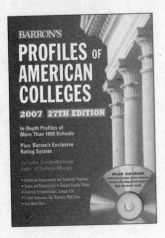

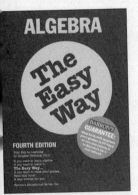